Jean Langlais

Jean Langlais
1907–1991

Jean Langlais

THE MAN AND HIS MUSIC

Ann Labounsky

AMADEUS PRESS
Portland, Oregon

All translations from the French are the author's unless otherwise noted.

Frontispiece: Jean Langlais, publicity photograph for 1952 American tour

Published in 2000 by
Amadeus Press (an imprint of Timber Press, Inc.)
The Haseltine Building
133 S.W. Second Avenue, Suite 450
Portland, Oregon 97204, U.S.A.

ISBN 1-57467-054-9

Printed in Singapore

Library of Congress Cataloging-in-Publication Data

Labounsky, Ann.
    Jean Langlais : the man and his music / Ann Labounsky.
        p.   cm.
    Includes worklist, bibliographical references, and index.
    ISBN 1-57467-054-9
    1. Langlais, Jean, 1907–   . I. Title.
ML410.L2487L33   2000
780'.92—dc21
    [B]   99-42129
                                                              CIP

to Allen Hobbs

Contents

Foreword

One by one, the works and lives of twentieth-century musicians are being thoroughly documented by musicologists—a priceless activity in view of future generations. Let us imagine the understanding we would have if Bach or Beethoven or Liszt (and this is just a sampling) had lived in our age of recordings, computers, interviews, and other seemingly miraculous aids, which record the present for the future! Our machines, however, lack patience, knowledge, experience, and a deep understanding of the particular musician under study. Jean Langlais is the subject of Ann Labounsky's research—a work on a musician whom she understood and respected as a teacher, musician, and friend.

Jean Langlais and I were also friends from 1956 until his death in 1991. He was an excellent teacher for me, although I had told him at the very beginning that I had absolutely no desire to be a concert organist. I wished to be a very good musician and to improvise well; most of his pupils had the desire to have concert careers, but I already knew I would not be up to that, even though I did play a few concerts here and there to make some French organ music better known.

In her preface Ann Labounsky makes an important remark, namely that Jean Langlais was a complex person but denied it. One time Langlais and I were taking a walk, shortly after he had returned from a trip to England. Someone had told him he was not only complex but also "mentally complicated." I could sense that he wanted to discuss this matter with me, thinking that I would agree with him and make quite an issue of the totally insignificant matter.

It so happened that I had recently analyzed Puccini's opera *Tosca*, with more emphasis on the character analysis than on the analysis of the music. Since Jean Langlais wanted my opinion, I told him that I didn't completely agree with either "complex" or "complicated," but that I was certain that he had three very strong facets to his personality, namely, love of music, love of his Roman Catholic faith, and finally, the third facet which I just called "great passion." Furthermore I told him that I thought all three facets worked at the same time, amounting to about ninety percent of his total personality. Tosca had these same three strong points. First, Tosca was a famous opera singer. Next, Act I is entirely set in the church of Sant' Andrea della Valle in Rome. Even before the end of Act II, Tosca has stabbed Scarpia to death, then lights a candle on each side of the corpse, places a crucifix on his chest, dips her handkerchief in water and washes her hands of the whole matter. This was a crime of passion, and I assured Jean Langlais that I did not mean that he was a criminal—just *passionate*.

Langlais was somewhat confused, somewhat irritated by this, but also very interested in discussing my point of view, for Jean Langlais very much liked to be the center of conversation as he wanted to be the center of everything. This was a quality I came to appreciate in him: his independence but also his need for attention. Even if he did not like what was said, he was pleased if he was the center of a conversation. But now, back to the story of *Tosca* . . .

He asked me why and how I felt this way; I told him he should read the libretto of *Tosca*. He said he didn't like Puccini's music, that the stories upon which Puccini's operas were based were too weak. I said to him, "But the opera *Tosca* is based almost one hundred percent on a dramatic work by Sardou." The French dramatic author Victorien Sardou (1831–1908) was one of the best French dramatic writers of his time, and a friend of Widor.

To end this little story, Jean Langlais obtained a braille copy of *Tosca* and studied the leading character. The next week I was his guide to Sainte-Clotilde, where invariably he visited the sacristy to find out the details of the mass of the day. At that time Langlais had taught no other American Catholic organists; whenever I was with Langlais in the sacristy he proudly told everyone "And he is Catholic!!!" But this time he had to explain, adding, "Because of this Catholic, I am now *Monsieur Tosca*!" Since nobody knew what he was talking about, he told the story of *Tosca*, considerably embellished. This is just one of the many memories I have of Jean Langlais.

Professor Ann Labounsky was chosen by Langlais to record his complete organ works, a task for which he forfeited half of his royalties in favor of this seemingly insurmountable recording project. Further, Jean Langlais had his first wife—his beloved Jeannette—request that Labounsky write his biography, for which undertaking she conducted many hours of recorded interviews and assembled documentation of every sort. She also had the very good fortune of taking a sabbatical during which time she lived with Langlais and his second wife. Not long after, Langlais was stricken by an attack that forever altered his ability to communicate.

Ann Labounsky's book, the result of many years of painstaking work, is complete and unbiased in every detail. She gives us an important work of musicology, one that deserves to appear on the shelf of every good library and one that is destined to be used for many generations to come.

Allen Hobbs
Officer of the Legion of Honor

Preface

From 1962 to 1964 I studied with André Marchal under a Fulbright scholarship. Marchal, who was often on tour, suggested that I study with Jean Langlais in his absence. I was also interested in studying improvisation, which Marchal did not teach at that time, and so I began my studies with Langlais at the Schola Cantorum and privately in 1963—the genesis of this book. In 1964 I also served as Langlais's guide on his American tour, and the next year I served as his assistant at Boys Town. In the coming years, Langlais organized series of recitals for me in France and Great Britain; at the conclusion of these performances, he would often improvise. During these summer sojourns of 1973, 1975, 1977, and 1979, for at least a month each time, I continued to study with him. I performed most of his compositions, premiering many in Europe and in the United States.

In the summer of 1973, I learned through his first wife, Jeannette, that Langlais wished me to write his biography. It was his desire that it be translated into French and braille for use by blind students at the Institute for the Blind in Paris, where he himself had studied and taught. Initially he conceived the biography as a doctoral dissertation. He sent me a number of cassette tapes with his recollections, and I in turn would prompt him with lists of broad topics ("Please speak of your early childhood memories"), to which he would respond. He placed great emphasis on expressing himself in these taped interviews; during one of them he said, "Please write a wonderful thesis—it will be a great consolation for me." In 1975, 1977, and 1979, I conducted extensive interviews with him, using a tape recorder, and interviewed family members and friends. Also in

1979 I began to record for the Musical Heritage Society Langlais's complete organ works under his direct supervision—a project which by its completion in 2003 will encompass twenty-four CDs in twelve volumes.

A faculty development grant from Duquesne University in 1984 allowed me to continue my research. Through the generosity of the Langlais family, I was given access to all Langlais's letters, photographs, scores, reviews, and other written matter; I stayed in their apartment in Paris for the month of May while I made copies of these materials, took notes, and conducted more interviews. Langlais often bid his daughter Caroline, who was four years old at the time, to play by herself so that I could keep working.

Jeannette had begun a catalog of her husband's works in 1931, assigning opus numbers to each piece as well as first performances and durations. During the war and as her health declined during the 1970s, the entries were done less systematically, stopping altogether in 1977. His second wife, Marie-Louise, continued Jeannette's catalog; it was the basis for our research in 1984 as together we began filing his scores. Afterward, with his permission, Marie-Louise recataloged all his works, and it is her opus numbers that appear in Appendix C.

My doctoral dissertation for the University of Pittsburgh, completed in 1991, covered Langlais's life and works through 1961. He was, of course, very eager to hear it, and Marie-Louise read him excerpts only two weeks before his death in May 1991. He was angry. Langlais had envisioned a different biography, a kind of eulogy, but this approach seemed less valuable if the book was to be a definitive account of his life and work. Besides needing time to reflect on his life after his passing, I could not ignore such valuable references as Marie-Louise Langlais's dissertation for the University of Paris ("La vie et l'oeuvre de Jean Langlais," 1992) and biography (*Ombre et lumière*, 1995), and Langlais's death obviously changed the ending as well as the focus of this book.

Langlais was a very complex person, although he constantly denied this. He wanted his story told, but in the way he believed it had taken place. He wanted to control its outcome, as he had tried to control his life, and he placed his confidence in me to do this. During the last week of my stay with him in 1984, when I had finished asking him all the questions I could possibly think of, he said jokingly, "Anything that you don't know, just make up." But in the end, truth is stranger than fiction. Nothing in this biography is untrue, damaging, or salacious. Any errors which remain are, of course, my responsibility.

The scope and quantity of Langlais's many instrumental, choral, and vocal compositions place him as one of the most important composers of the French post-Romantic school. In my writing, I have particularly focused on the relationship of Langlais's music to important aspects and inspirations of his life: primarily his Roman Catholicism, his physical handicap, his Breton heritage, his education, and his family and friends, including his relationship with such important twentieth-century musicians as André Marchal, Olivier Messiaen, Paul Dukas, Gaston Litaize, Louis Vierne, and Marcel Dupré. The discussion of Dupré's personality and unique methods of teaching blind students, as well as his methods of teaching repertoire and improvisation, is particularly detailed.

I would like to express my deepest gratitude above all to both Allen Hobbs and Michael Murray, whose unfailing help and wisdom reaches far beyond the mere citing of their names, and to Frances Bertolino Farrell, who prepared the final draft of the manuscript with great sensitivity and uncommon skill. I also wish to acknowledge with gratitude the contributions of the following organizations and people: Duquesne University; the L. J. and Mary C. Skaggs Foundation, for providing a production subsidy; Universal Edition; Fred Bashour, Don Campbell, Jacques Chailley, Pierre Cogen, David Craighead, Paul Engle, Jacqueline Englert-Marchal, Susan Ferré, Michael Fox, Don O. Franklin, Father F. Godard, Eve Goodman, Julia Janeway, Joseph Willcox Jenkins, Claude and Monique Langlais, Flavie Langlais, Jean Langlais, Jeannette Langlais, Marie-Louise Langlais, Gaston Litaize, Robert Sutherland Lord, André Marchal, Marilyn Mason, Robert Noehren, Dora Odarenko, Father Jules Orrière, Antoine Reboulot, Monsignor Francis Schmitt, Paul E. Smith, Rollin Smith, Claire Steele, Lewis M. Steele, Sandy Sterner, Kathleen Thomerson, Ralph Tilden, and many Langlais students and friends, as well as my own students, whose probing questions led me to ponder the deeper meanings in his life and music. Many others, too numerous to mention here, contributed to the rich mosaic of this story.

Preface

I was with Langlais when he composed a number of his works, studied them with him, and performed them. I was eager to bring both them and him to life, and it is my hope that readers who never knew Langlais or his music will feel that they have done so vicariously through this book.

CHAPTER 1

Early Years 1907–1917

I became interested in music because I was blind. Otherwise
I would have been a stonecutter, like my father.

Jean Langlais

Brittany

Rising up in a wheat field near Dol-de-Bretagne, not far from Jean
Langlais's birthplace, stands a chiseled granite menhir, a score of feet
in height. Like its counterparts in Carnac and at Stonehenge, it has
stood time out of mind as a monument to the Celtic people who
erected it. Its purpose shrouded by the mists of antiquity, this menhir may have figured in fertility rites, or pointed to astronomical for-
mations, or commemorated a battle bloodier than usual. Scholarship would endorse the last of these theories since this menhir is
named Mournfulfield, but proof is lacking and the enigma remains.
Perhaps this menhir is a sentinel warning Bretons that they are forever bound by the harsh and unforgiving earth, wind, and sea.

The past thrusts itself on the present in Brittany, defining and
controlling it. When priests outside Brittany speak of the simplicity
and depth of Breton Catholicism, they speak with envious longing.
Isolated for generations, Bretons express their endurance against
the elements through an uncomplicated faith, based on their awe of
God and the sea. Even today life revolves around cycles of feasts,
rituals, sacraments, crosses, and statues of Mary and Saint Anne,
which adorn nearly every home.

Breton legends trace their roots deep into the past, as early as
the first century after Christ. One of them has Joseph of Arimathea
traveling to Brittany by boat, with several drops of Christ's divine

17

blood remaining from the last supper. Mysteriously both the cup and Joseph disappeared without a trace. In the sixth century, King Arthur and his court came to Brittany in search of this Holy Grail. According to a Medieval legend, Tristan was sent to bring Isolde from Ireland to his uncle Mark, the king of the Bretons in Cornouaille, Brittany, but fell in love with her during the sea voyage. Satan supposedly fought a duel with Saint Michael on Mont Dol before taking a giant step to the island where Mont Saint-Michel was founded; Satan's footprint can be detected on the large stone at the top of Mont Dol. This last legend continues to have a following among some Breton priests.

The earliest saints were those who came to Brittany from Great Britain in the fifth century and became the patrons of the first seven religious sites: Saint Malo, Saint Brieuc, Saint Pol-de-Léon, Saint Samson in Dol-de-Bretagne, Saint Tugdual in Tréguier, Saint Corentin in Quimper, and Saint Patern in Vannes. Pilgrimages to each site were popular during the Middle Ages and some continue today. Until the sixteenth century, every Breton was expected to make this pilgrimage once during his life, or as it was understood, after death, traveling the length of his coffin every seven years.[1]

Legend has it there are 7777 local Breton saints, enough to protect the populace from any eventuality. Only five are recognized by Rome, among them Saint Anne and Saint Yves, who is known as the lawyer of the poor. Other saints were specialists: Saint Jacques for sailors, Saint Fiacre for gardeners, Saint Barbe for help in storms, Saint Apolline for toothaches, Saint Mamert for chest pains, Saint Méen for madness, Saint Livertin for headaches, Saint Houarniaule for fear, and Saint Lubin for every conceivable ill. Some saints were important for the well-being of animals, such as Saint Cornély for cattle, Saint Herbot for horses, and Saint Hubert for dogs.

Many saints were Christianized pagan gods. Saint Vénier, for example, derived from Venus, is found in the fourth- or fifth-century Gallo-Roman chapel in Langon. Old Alar in pre-Christian times became Saint Eloi, patron of horses and their riders, and is now also patron of tractors and cars. The pagan symbols for dragons, devils, evil fairies, and Morgane, the Celtic goddess of the water, are often represented in statuary.[2]

Breton folklore imbues other natural elements with religious significance and supernatural powers. Many streams and fountains were believed to have miraculous waters in fountains such as those at Saint Jean-du-Doigt, Barenton, Locarn, said to cure fevers, and Bieuzy, said to cure toothaches. Certain rocks had sacred properties, such as the Druid rock in Lacronan, which was known to bring sterile women fertility. This rock has a rounded indentation, like a chair, where women sit awaiting its graces. Saints were believed to protect the faithful from every affliction and from an untimely death. Ankou, the angel of death, is also found in statuary in churches and cemeteries. Like Charon of the river Styx, he was charged with carrying the souls of the dying to the other side. Belief in the influence of the dead was strong. It was thought that their souls would continue to haunt their descendants. Many people employed a holy person (*l'écouteuse des trépassés*) to listen at the tomb of the deceased for guidance in their present lives. Visitations to the tombs of local saints were thought to cure diseases.[3]

The patron saint of Brittany is Saint Anne, the mother of the Virgin Mary. A fascinating legend concerns her Breton roots: an angel supposedly transported her to Nazareth to save her from an abusive husband. There she gave birth to the Virgin Mary and came back to Brittany to die. The historic Anne de Bretagne is likewise beloved. In 1498 she married Charles VIII while remaining the powerful ruler of Brittany. A year later, after the death of King Charles, she married his successor Louis XII. But above all and in every century, it was the Virgin Mary who inspired the greatest fervor among the Bretons.

Brittany is a peninsula located in the northwestern corner of France, surrounded on two sides by the Atlantic Ocean and to the north by the English Channel. Before falling under Roman rule in the first century B.C., Brittany was inhabited by Armorican tribes. Christianity was established by the fourth century. Celts from Britain, fleeing Anglo-Saxon invaders, settled in Brittany during the fifth and sixth centuries, occupying the entire Armorican peninsula. Brittany was governed as an independent duchy until the sixteenth century and, in its Gallic language and culture, has remained distinctly separate from France. In the last decade of the eighteenth century, a popular uprising, the Chouannarie, pitted the nationalistic Breton nobles against the crown—another bloodbath for Brittany.

In more recent times, two distinct Bretons emerged: the French-speaking Gallo, with a less violent temperament, and the more revengeful and individualistic Gallic-speaking Breton.[4] Both types loved their folklore and were intensely proud of their country. A Breton was first a Breton and only secondly a Frenchman. Because of their poverty and because of the centuries-long suppression of their language and culture by the French, they often lacked self-esteem. They shared their innermost thoughts very slowly and trusted people only after long acquaintance. Centuries of living in poverty also gave them an insular view of the world. Bretons were known to be superstitious, pious, and contentious.

Bretons were also intensely mystical, as may be seen in their veneration of the saints, their fondness of folklore, and their love for intrigue and stories. They were strong in intuition rather than rationality; ambiguity marked their personalities. A joke was often not really a joke, and this tension between comedy and tragedy was a source of great delight, as evidenced by a well-known Breton proverb: "One does not recognize a cat so long as nobody steps on its tail." Their ability to experience life through instinct and imagination was key to their rich nature.[5]

In this poorest region of France, fishing was the economic main-stay. For centuries, unpredictable ocean storms claimed the lives of Breton sailors and fisherman and left the survivors with a fatalistic view of life. When Langlais was a child, his cousin Joseph Marbou drowned off the coast of Newfoundland. Not only poverty but the sea and its cold rainy climate contributed to an attitude of mistrust and discouragement.[6] Such mysteries and characteristics as these informed and shaped Jean Langlais in his personality, his music, and his entire being.

La Fontenelle

La Fontenelle, the small village where Jean Langlais was born, remains much the same as it was in 1900, when its population was approximately seven hundred.[7] It is situated in the department of Ille-et-Vilaine near the border of Brittany and Normandy, about twenty miles due south of Mont Saint-Michel and two miles north-west of Antrain. Bretons lamented that this famous monastery, which lies just north of the mouth of the Couesnon River, narrowly missed being part of Brittany. Small stone houses lined the narrow, winding streets. The Couesnon River flows just east of the town, providing the only source of water for bathing and laundry; drinking water had to be carried from a municipal fountain in Dol-de-Bretagne three miles away. Beyond the village, fruit and nut trees stretched for miles, interrupted only by small farms.

The tough, battered Bretons felt little affinity for their more affluent Norman neighbors. Langlais thought of his Norman colleague Duruflé as someone from another continent, even though their birthplaces were separated by a short distance.

Forebears

According to his parents' recollections, all Langlais's ancestors lived in La Fontenelle and, like so many Bretons, made their living either as stonecutters, farm workers, or fishermen; their wives were seamstresses and domestics. Langlais's maternal grandparents were François Canto, a wheelmaker, and Henriette Charrière, a domestic. His paternal grandparents were Joséphine Lemarchand, a homemaker with eight children, and Jean-Marie Langlais, a stonemason. Langlais's father was the eldest child. Langlais's parents, Jean-Marie Joseph Langlais and Flavie Marie-Joseph Canto, were married on 27 February 1905 in La Fontenelle; Flavie was twenty-two, her husband, twenty-four. The male witnesses to the ceremony, relatives on the Langlais side of the family, were master quarrymen.[8] The quality of granite found near La Fontenelle was famous throughout Brittany, and both Langlais's father and grandfather belonged to a cooperative network of approximately one hundred and forty stonecutters, whose work included mining the stone from the quarry, cutting and sanding it, and fashioning it into curbstones, gravestones, and funeral monuments.[9]

Most families had a small plot of ground for a garden and owned a milk cow and occasionally chickens and rabbits. Langlais's parents were less fortunate; they had only their home, a one-room stone cottage which they rented from a cousin. On the left of the house there was an attic and a much smaller cottage for grandmother Henriette. Although beds (*lits clos*) were built into the walls of many of these small homes, including that of Langlais's father, there were no such beds in their cottage. Neither was there running water or electricity, and food was cooked over an open hearth. Two or three times a week a baker from a neighboring town brought in bread. A sparse vegetable soup containing pieces of bread, a sardine with bread and butter, or bread and jam with nuts constituted a normal meal. Meat was a rarity eaten only on Sundays.[10] In addition to the six-mile trek for drinking water, daily household chores included hauling wood and tending the garden.

Flavie was short and stocky and wore her long dark hair combed straight back in a bun. Her high cheekbones and deep-set eyes gave her a determined look. She owned one of the first sewing machines in La Fontenelle and was an excellent dressmaker and seamstress; after working twelve-hour days in town or on neighboring farms, she often brought sewing home and continued to work at night. Her daughter, also named Flavie, remembered that she sewed very rapidly and used to produce skirts, pants, and other clothes in quick succession. She also sewed for many weddings, making the entire trousseau in addition to quilts and the large decorative drapes (*paradises*) adorned with flowers and wishes for happiness that were used at wedding receptions. Once, long after Jean's childhood, she employed someone to clean their home but found her to be too slow. The life of this dynamic woman was ended by Parkinson's disease; she died in 1947 in the arms of her husband, who followed her, stricken by a heart attack, one year later.[11]

A traditional Breton male, Langlais's father was authoritarian and strict but of a kind disposition. Like many Bretons, Jean-Marie too was short and small-boned but very strong, with penetrating blue eyes, fair skin made ruddy by hard labor, and hands knotted from work. He possessed a high degree of native intelligence, and unlike most Breton laborers, he learned to write. Not only did he write letters for his friends in an elegant hand, but as there was no doctor in La Fontenelle, he also served as a volunteer medic. Both Jean's parents, in fact, served as public health nurses, making the rounds of the villages, administering eyedrops and applying plasters. One evening Jean-Marie was summoned to the bedside of an eerily motionless and obviously already deceased couple; neighbors bore witness that he had not killed them.[12]

His daughter Flavie remembered an amusing incident that revealed her father's methodical nature. When Jean-Marie went to confession, he got dressed in his "Sunday best" suit, with tie and all the accoutrements. On one occasion, having returned and changed back into his plain clothes, he realized that he had forgotten to put on one of the accessories. He then redressed and returned to confess again. Neither parent had musical abilities, although both of them sang at wedding receptions in the granges. Flavie remembered her mother singing a popular piece called "L'Africaine" and both parents singing a duet.[13]

In the prewar years, Jean-Marie tried to improve the economic and social conditions that oppressed him and the rest of the working class in Brittany by serving as a town councillor in La Fontenelle as a member of the Socialist party.[14] Jean-Marie took fierce pride in being a Breton, in speaking the Gallic language, and in being a Socialist. Like all their friends and relatives, the Langlaises were staunchly independent, a trait their firstborn shared.

Birth and Blindness

The composer Jean-Marie-Hyacinthe Langlais was born on the night of 15 February 1907 under the thatched roof of his parents' cottage. Three days later he was baptized, and relatives and family gathered for a meal following the ceremony. After dinner, they sang to him a popular Breton lullaby, "Jean, Jean, mon tout petit Jean, quickly close your eyes. Jean, Jean, mon tout petit Jean, quietly go to sleep." Its augury was lost on the happy party.

During his adult life Langlais gave several different impressions of when his blindness occurred. Jean was told that during his first two years he was able to see, and he did retain a dim memory of having seen red and purple flowers hanging outside the windows of his house.[15] (Red is the last color to be lost with approaching blindness.)

> By the time I was two years old I could not see at all. We never knew exactly what the cause of the blindness was. They told us many things—a stroke of the sun, which could have been gotten as a baby. I never knew the truth and never searched to know the truth.[16]

The cause of his blindness was never ascertained, although infantile glaucoma is suspected. Jean suffered greatly during his first three years from pain, which the light aggravated. They had to keep the red drapes closed, and Jean, fearful, sought comfort in his mother's skirts. Certainly by the age of three all sight was gone and with it the pain.[17]

Jean's mother took him to a number of faith healers, of which there were many in Brittany. For nine consecutive days, she carried him on her back to Pleine-Fougères, a round-trip of about fifteen miles, to kiss the grave of Father Bachelot, who was believed to heal blindness. Through the generosity of his paternal Uncle Jules, a general in the French army, an operation was arranged but was unsuccessful.[18] Flavie and Jean-Marie, determined not to let their son be treated as a handicapped person, were nevertheless hard-pressed to know what he would be able to do. Certainly his blindness would preclude his following the pattern of the firstborn Langlais's becoming a stonemason.

As a very young child Jean was not aware of the extent of his poverty, for he was surrounded by loving parents, his grandmother Henriette, and his cousin Marie, who owned a small shop in the town. An only child until he was eight, he received the undivided attention of four devoted adults. During these years, his mother went to work very early in the morning, while Marie cared for him each afternoon. In later years, Langlais remembered this time as idyllic. Because he had everything he could think of wanting, he had no idea that he was poor and handicapped.

His mother never treated Jean's blindness as a handicap. When he was only four, she helped him take his first steps toward independence by sending him to Marie's store for thread. At first she followed him without his knowing, to make sure that he was all right; once he was able to find his way easily, she let him go alone. By the time he was five years old, he did all the errands and from then on wanted nothing more than to be independent.

When Jean was five, he was enrolled in the local parochial school, and gained a new taste for freedom in being treated like the sighted children. He easily found his place in the classroom without any help. Although he was intelligent and eager to learn, the advantage of attending the regular school was overshadowed by the disadvantage of having a teacher who could not instruct him in braille. Without knowing how to read and write, he could learn very little, and not knowing how to read, especially, pained him terribly.

Rudiments of Faith

In rural Brittany at the turn of the century, the art of storytelling was still one of the chief pleasures, kept alive through Breton story-tellers (*bigoudens*), who traveled from household to household reciting folkloric legends. They could neither read nor write but were masters of the spoken word and kept small groups of people, young and old, spellbound as they wove their long tales. Many of their legends had to do with the ravages of the sea and the heroic lives of local saints. The Langlais family knew these folkloric tales and were themselves gifted storytellers.

Jean thus learned the rudiments of his Catholic faith from his parents and Henriette even before studying his catechism. Henriette explained her faith with the simplest of parables. Years later, Jean remembered her explanation of heaven as "a place where there are carpets everywhere with nothing on top of them, and everyone can walk on them for as long as they like." Jean reflected on this: "Would heaven then be crowded?" "Oh yes, very crowded, because the gracious Lord pardons much." "Would not the carpets then wear out from so many people walking on them?" "Oh, no, these carpets can never, never wear out." But this was illogical to him, and again he asked why. Finally she responded, "They do not become worn for one very simple reason: because the good Lord does not want them to become worn!" Jean stood on the earthen floor and listened to his grandmother's voice.[19]

It seemed to little Jean that God—who was so perfect, so wonderful, so mighty, who had made heaven for man's reward—was also beyond man's understanding. Henriette was as sure her home was in heaven as she was that the tides would rise each day to separate Mont Saint-Michel from the mainland. Years later Jean described her last days: "This brave woman never feared death and very calmly noted, in hearing the tolling of the church bells, that the next time they tolled they would be for her. Her death was two days later, on Tuesday."[20]

Early Musical Experiences

The folk songs of Brittany impressed Jean at a very early age. These songs, like all Breton folklore, expressed the Breton temperament and feelings: they were usually in somber modes, reflecting the hardships of their daily life. Many dealt with the loss of fishermen and the storms at sea. Langlais later recognized their pathos and brooding quality as an important element of his own music.

It was his grandmother Henriette who first encouraged Jean's interest in music. She told him of an uncle who was a priest and also a fine musician, who directed church choirs and bands in a village close to Dol-de-Bretagne, and another uncle who played the cello. Henriette recognized in Jean a similar musical talent. When he was seven or eight, Jean sang in the church choir with the other children. There he gained a large store of his musical experience by singing Gregorian chants. The eight chant modes were to become an integral part of his musical vocabulary.

There was no organ in La Fontenelle, only a small harmonium played by the local blacksmith, who also directed the choir. From time to time, Jean went to mass at a larger church in the neighboring town of Antrain, where the organ had nine stops. "When I heard that for the first time," he was to recall, "I was at mass with my mother. It seemed to me to make a terrific noise and I found it terrifying. I was afraid—terribly afraid."[21] Ironically, it was through the fearsome pipe organ, and his blindness, that he eventually achieved an important musical career; he would later say that he thanked God for this handicap.

Awakening

Hardship did not keep Jean from adventure. One day his cousin Pierre Langlais, who owned a bicycle, offered to teach him to ride it. If Jean felt afraid at first, this emotion was quickly overcome by the desire to be like the other children. It did not take long for him to master riding alone; once secure in his balance, he used to practice riding next to the church, using as guides the twelve wooden posts of the stations of the cross that were spaced in a large semicircle. When he was older, he was able to ride greater distances with his friends or brothers; by having them ride in front of him, he was able to follow the tracks of their wheels. As his parents were too poor to buy him a bicycle, he borrowed Pierre's.

He and his friend Marcel stole into a nearby orchard to feast on hazelnuts. Marcel would climb the trees and pick the nuts. From time to time, he would toss Jean one or two; Jean never asked for more but waited quietly. Eventually, when Marcel was full, he gave Jean some more. Later, when the hazelnuts were ripe, Jean would visit orchards himself, crawling on his hands and knees to gather those that had fallen to the ground and were free for everyone. He carried a large bag and filled it, able at last to take the nuts without having to wait for someone to give them to him. A big bag of hazelnuts was more than a symbol of independence; it was a significant contribution to his family's meager diet. Langlais never lost his fondness for hazelnuts, perhaps considering them a talisman of independence and basic sustenance, and he often carried a few chestnuts in his pocket—to ward off arthritis, as Breton lore had it.

From a very early age, Langlais remembered the sounds of the harmonium in his parish church, and for years wanted to play it. Marcel's father, a shoemaker, was on friendly terms with the pastor, who shared his anti-Socialist bent. The pastor had given Marcel permission to practice on the instrument, but Jean was forbidden to touch it and only permitted to sit in the rectory and listen to Marcel, who had neither talent or training. How his fingers ached to touch the keys! At the end of two hours of listening to Marcel's clumsy attempts, the frustration became too painful. He left, feeling that the pastor had discriminated against him for political reasons. Later he said, "This was Brittany in 1912. Being a Socialist was like being a Communist or anarchist now. Because my father was a Socialist, the priest never let me play the harmonium."[22] Stubborn as he was, his ambition to play redoubled.

This comfortable early childhood, during which Jean was shielded from the psychological pain associated with blindness, was not to last. One day after church, he overheard the parents of some of his friends. "Wouldn't it be better," they mused, "if he had one arm or one leg or was deaf?" He would never forget this moment. "These remarks caused me much pain, for I understood that, for them, my affliction was the most terrible affliction possible—and

Langlais, dressed for his first holy communion, with his mother and sister, Flavie, 1915

that inspired pity, which caused me to have many complexes."[23] It was a cruel awakening that changed him forever. The fear of being dependent, coupled with his native Breton pessimism, would make it impossible for him to ask for help, even in the smallest matters.

Later in life, he would look back on the years before this incident with a feeling of nostalgia: "When I was young, I did not suffer from being blind." He remained grateful to his parents for the way in which they handled his blindness. Like the magic carpet story, his attitude toward it mirrors their own:

> They had a living faith, which they imparted to me. Today they say not to give children complexes. I would have had many reasons to go to psychologists, and I never went and never had reason to confess this to anyone because I had faith and have faith, believing that God would help me. So when humiliating things were said in front of me, I tried to forget them.[24]

Changes

In August 1914, Jean's father was called to enter World War I, and on 20 May 1915, Jean's sister, Flavie, was born. As he would leave La Fontenelle for Paris when she was only two, Jean did not have the opportunity to become close to Flavie while he was young, nor did they become close as adults.

Though Jean's mother recognized in her young chorister both native ability and great love for music, she despaired of finding a way to afford to give him musical training. But his Uncle Jules knew of a school for blind children in Paris and told Jean-Marie about it. Through his military connections, he was able to get Jean a scholarship. Jean would learn how to read and write—and have the opportunity to study music as well. A vast world was now open to him.

CHAPTER 2

National Institute for the Blind
1917–1927

When the human eye is extinguished, the spiritual eye is lighted.

A. G. Sertillanges

History of the Institute

Education for France's blind children came slowly, through a system of instruction first practiced by Valentin Haüy. Haüy was born in 1745 to poor parents in the village of Saint-Just-en-Chaussée. One day in 1771, while he was in Paris completing his studies, he attended a country fair in honor of Saint-Ovide and came upon a group of grotesquely dressed beggars making cacophonous sounds on musical instruments. They wore glasses, pretending to read from small sheets of music placed in front of their sightless eyes. These beggars were the objects of cruel jokes and were teased like circus animals. The spectacle so disgusted Haüy that it became a catalyst which led him to devote the rest of his life to the education of the blind.[1] Haüy first worked with Lesueur, a sixteen-year-old blind youth he found begging at church entrances. Initially they "read" from a book with large raised letters, a practice already in existence but not widely used.

In 1784 Haüy borrowed funds to open the first school for the blind, the Institution Royale des Jeunes Aveugles. The following year the Académie des Sciences approved his teaching methods, and by 1786 Haüy had twenty-four students, both boys and girls. He proudly introduced them to Louis XVI at Versailles, where they impressed the king and his courtiers with their ability to read and write, to perform mathematical calculations, and to sing. Soon Haüy founded an orchestra and choir, which performed at the Chapelle Royale in 1789. Gradually, he gained widespread moral and financial support for his philosophy and his school, which in addition to academic studies included training in such practical trades as chairmaking, printing, weaving, and knitting. Before his death in 1822, Haüy saw the school firmly established and its graduates gainfully employed.

Louis Braille (1809–1852), who had become blind by the age of three, attended the school in 1819 and then taught there from 1828 till his death. Only after his invention of the braille system could blind students be given a full education comparable to that of sighted children.

By 1820 three Parisian churches—Saint-Médard, Saint-Nicolas-des-Champs, and Saint-Étienne-du-Mont—were employing blind organists for one month at a time; and in 1826, the Institute's first organ class for blind students was established. In 1833 fourteen blind organists held positions in Parisian churches; by 1835, twenty others held posts in parishes throughout France. Four of these positions were in cathedrals.[2] In 1822, with the appointment of Gabriel Gauthier (1808–1850), Saint-Étienne-du-Mont began a century-long tradition of employing blind organists.

In 1839 the government granted funds for the present sandstone structure of the National Institute for the Blind under the direction of Parisian architect Pierre-Nicolas-François Philippon (1784–1866). For the inauguration, in 1844, the choir sang a cantata in honor of Haüy with words by Dufau and music by Gauthier.[3] By the 1860s, the school had become a model for the education of the blind, emulated in both North and South America and throughout Europe. In 1886 the Valentin Haüy braille and print lending libraries were opened.[4]

In 1889 Maurice de la Sizeranne (1856–1924) founded the Association Valentin Haüy for the advancement of the blind, comprising both sighted and blind members. Under its aegis a braille printery and a school for massage was established in 1906; in 1910, a lending library with both braille and printed books opened. In 1917 it extended its services to include professional retraining for those blinded during the war. Before Langlais entered the National Institute for the Blind,[5] therefore, it had successively been a private school, a royal school, an imperial school, and a national school, and had occupied seven different locations. When Langlais entered, in 1917, there were more than 230 students.

Today the National Institute for the Blind is situated on the boulevard des Invalides and bordered by the rue Duroc, rue de Sèvres, and rue Maurice de la Sizeranne. A larger-than-life-size statue of Valentin Haüy, bending down to help his first blind student, is the focal point of the large cobblestoned entrance court of honor.

By 1917, in addition to an extensive general collection, the library at the National Institute for the Blind contained for the exclusive use of its students the complete works of Bach, Mozart, Frescobaldi, Couperin, Vierne, and Franck, and the sonatas of Beethoven. It also housed the only copies of certain works by Gauthier and other blind composers and professors of the school. The complex of three-story buildings provided living and instructional facilities for students and faculty. Students were segregated by gender, the girls' quarters to the left and the boys' to the right of the main concert hall and chapel. The ground floor housed a large parlor, classrooms including those with harmoniums and organs, a concert hall and chapel, dining halls, and kitchen. Marble busts of Haüy and Braille dominated the main foyer. The first floor held dormitories and classrooms, and the second was reserved for the infirmary and piano practice rooms. Another part of the building housed the printshop, library, and workshops for handcrafted wares. Outside was a covered playground.

Paris

On 9 November 1917 his mother and aunt took young Jean to Paris to enter the Institute. Fortunately his aunt, the wife of the officer Jules Langlais, had the 270 francs that were unexpectedly required to register him at the school. For Langlais, the first encounter with Paris and the Institute was overwhelming. Now in a place where a myriad of strangers talked rapidly and in a completely different dialect, he was no longer isolated by his blindness alone. Fifty years later its memory would stay fresh.

After always having lived in the country, I was much impressed by the noises of the big city. Someone who sees is easily distracted by what he sees, but those who do not see are very interested by what they hear. When they say that blind people are less distracted than other people, that is not at all true—because in a school of sighted people, for example, the students look at what is happening elsewhere in the hall. But the blind students *listen* to what is happening in the hall, and they are equally distracted. . . . So when I first entered the Institute, I was very interested in the sounds of the tramway. Remember that I was ten years old and had never heard a tramway. Here is a remembrance from my mother. She said that I must not listen to the tramways. It was her only advice to me. And I never forgot that. She meant that she had confidence that I would work. And she was right because I worked very, very hard for thirteen years.[6]

Langlais arrived at the Institute with minimal training in music and none in braille, which put him at an immediate disadvantage. He must have taken Flavie's advice as a form of confidence in him, however, for he soon overcame any deficiencies of background, allowing neither the sounds of the tramway nor the sounds of the hallway to distract him. At first, his motivation was the need to catch up to the level of his classmates; but eventually, singlemindedness of purpose, a competitive spirit, and the ability to screen out distractions were to become the dominant characteristics of his life.

Life at the Institute

In 1917, as now, the National Institute for the Blind was supported by the French government. Most students were admitted on a full scholarship, which even included a limited amount of spending money. Students ate in a common dining room, and the residents shared large dormitories, sleeping thirty to a room. The students were divided by ages: from ten to twelve years, and thirteen to twenty. Resident teachers had their own private rooms apart from the students.

All students followed a rigorous academic schedule. Some concentrated on manual work, such as chairmaking or piano tuning. Others followed a strictly academic course leading at the end of the third year to a brevet élémentaire and entrance to a lycée. For music students, the requirement to fit practicing of their instruments into an already demanding schedule created an extra burden. Each weekday except Thursday followed the same eleven-hour schedule of classes, from 6:30 a.m. to 9:00 p.m. Thursday was a holiday, and the students used the time to study and practice. For Langlais, the first task was to master braille.

The braille system of musical notation is particularly complicated. No attempt is made to synchronize notes on a staff. The time signature is given by two numbers, one above the other, and the key signature follows with the number of sharps and flats. Dynamic markings are written using letter abbreviations, as are tempo indications and slurs. The pitch of the note within the seven-octave range is indicated by a particular combination of six dots, followed by a second notation to indicate the time value of the note of that pitch. The left-hand part is written directly below the right-hand line and, for organ music, the pedal part is directly below that of the left hand. If more than one note is written for each hand on the same beat, each interval is written with a different symbol for unison through the octave. Many abbreviations are used, which aid in the process of memorization. Since sight reading with both hands at a keyboard instrument is impossible, proficiency depends heavily upon the development of memory. Because he was unable to read and write before the age of ten, Langlais relied on his memory more heavily than did a sighted person.

In the upper level classes, students studied history, literature, and mathematics. (Langlais was a poor student in math.) When students reached the age of sixteen, geography, physics, French history, and algebra were added. Music students began their day at 5:30 a.m. and ended at 11:00 p.m. All students were required to sing in the choir for mass and vespers each Sunday.

The trimesters ran from October to Christmas; January to Easter; and Easter to the end of June. Each trimester ended with an exam. Vacations of ten days were granted at Christmas, fifteen days at Easter.

As an adult, Langlais would remember certain things, particularly maps made of wood with raised perforations showing not only foreign countries but also the Paris subway system, and a portable

Langlais, in his Institute uniform, and his sister, Flavie, c. 1918

dollhouse displaying all the parts of a house. There were occasionally unintentional (or intentional) physical encounters and bumps in the hallways.[7] It was a noisy school because the students used their voices to signal their whereabouts. It all made for great camaraderie, and it made Langlais very happy.

And there were lighter moments. When the harmony teacher Albert Mahaut (1867–1943) arrived at eight each morning to meet his class, he inspected the uniforms of all the students to see that their shirts were buttoned correctly. Naturally, most of them were crooked. Each morning, Mahaut began by rebuttoning all the shirts; only then, without saying a word, would he start his class.

Friendships

One student who became a close friend to Langlais was Gaston Litaize (1909–1992), who entered the Institute in February 1919. Litaize was two years younger than Langlais and had already learned braille, piano, and solfège. Although they were together only in the recreation classes and chorus, these two upper level students were sure enough of themselves and eager enough for diversion to indulge in pranks. One occurred when Litaize and Langlais were standing next to one another during a choral rehearsal. The work being rehearsed was a composition by Adolphe Marty, who was also conductor of the chorus. In the Gloria of Marty's mass, there was a canon at the third. Langlais and Litaize changed it to a canon at the second, creating an ear-wrenching dissonance.[8]

At another time, not only Langlais's love for highjinks but also his sense of justice found a fitting target in one Mathieu, the assistant head of the Institute and a mean and petty man. At the end of each semester a concert took place for the students, administrators, and parents. Langlais and Litaize had their revenge on Mathieu by writing a piece for piano and organ that included a play on the administrator's surname; everyone sang the words "Voilà le vieux Mathieu," Langlais played the organ, and Litaize, the piano. Everyone clapped so loudly that they had to repeat the entire number. During the performance, it was not lost on the assistant director, or anyone else in the audience, that Mathieu was being parodied. He was furious; however, without proof, there was little he could do.[9]

Langlais's most lasting friendship was with a piano student from Versailles, André Bourgoin. Years later, when Langlais had become an organist and Bourgoin a piano tuner, they spoke often by telephone and met frequently. Each occasion was a time for hilarious and frequently bawdy bantering, reminiscent of their time together at the school. When at times Langlais would become depressed, only Bourgoin could cheer him up. The two had an intimacy more like ex-soldiers than ex-students, and it continued until Bourgoin's death in 1986.

One reason for the depth of their friendship was the lack of competition between them. Langlais later experienced difficulty in sustaining close friendships with other organists. This was particularly the case with Gaston Litaize, whom Langlais gradually perceived as a rival; Langlais explained the change by saying that it was Litaize who had altered, becoming complicated and proud.

Piano: Maurice Blazy

Langlais's musical training began with piano lessons with Maurice Blazy (1873–1933), organist at the church of Saint-Pierre-de-Montrouge, and like all the Institute faculty, himself blind. Blazy introduced Jean to the piano by showing him the lock where the key was inserted and, under the lock, the two black keys to the left of which was middle C. After he found this key, he was asked to find all the other C keys on the piano. Sometime during his first six months of study, Langlais finished a piece that ended with an F major chord. This sonority seemed especially beautiful to him, and he remarked upon its charm, to which Blazy responded that it sounded as if it were played on the organ.[10]

Solfège: Alexandre Dantot

Langlais studied solfège with Alexandre Dantot, organist at Saint-Étienne-du-Mont, followed by a third year with Albert Mahaut. The braille methods for each level were written by the solfège professors Louis Lebel and Philippe Thomas, although other teachers contributed unsigned exercises. During the first year the exercises were restricted to quarter notes in the key of C, with emphasis on the purity of diatonic intervals. Each class held about fifteen students, and each student had a book of exercises in braille. Normally the students sang in unison, although occasionally there were solos and longer pieces to learn by heart. By the end of the first year, students learned to write down short dictations—in the second year different meters and keys. Little by little students mastered more rapid note values. The teacher would play a theme of about sixteen measures at the harmonium, twice dividing it into sections, which the students would sing. In the third year they sang in compound meters with various rhythms always using movable "do" (or tonic) according to their tessitura. They often practiced two- and three-part choruses outside class, using the solfège syllables.

Classes in ear training (*phrasage*) complemented the training in solfège. The teacher played two measures, and without writing the notes the student first sang them identifying their note values. Then after the teacher played a group of notes, the student sang the names of the notes with solfège syllables.

This type of musical training, in which one- or two-measure segments were repeated, would influence Langlais's compositional style. Such repetition would not only make his pieces easier for him to learn but would also provide an important aural unification.

Harmony: Albert Mahaut

Once the students had completed three years of solfège, they began to study harmony. Langlais's second harmony teacher was Albert Mahaut, a student of Franck, and winner, in 1888, of first prize in organ from the Paris Conservatory. Langlais remembered him as a warm and benevolent man. In his class there was no textbook; Mahaut taught by giving a series of patiently executed explanations, such as that of the most basic major triads, then asking if everyone had understood. Upon request, he explained again, as often as necessary, but after that never repeated the lesson. Without books, the students paid greater attention. Each day there was a harmony assignment to learn by heart and to play without a mistake. Sometimes the assignment was a bass line to which the upper parts were added, at others, a soprano line, which required the addition of lower voices. Gradually the assignments became as long as seventy-five measures in one day, and the students had only one hour alone to prepare. Such training was critical to the development of their memories.

By the end of three years only those who could follow this regimen had developed an advanced technique. The others had to begin the class over. Some of the students spent three years in the first year of harmony. At the beginning of Langlais's first-year class, there were thirty-four students. At the end of the three years, only five were left.

The harmony and solfège classes were held in the large two-hundred-seat Salle de Conférence on the first floor, where the seats were elevated in tiers. Mahaut taught the class from a harmonium in the front of the room. One day Langlais misbehaved, and Mahaut sent him to the last row away from the other students. Langlais recalled that he felt bored there all by himself and pretended not to be able to hear. He called out to his teacher, "I can't hear your explanations because I am too far away." Mahaut answered, "My friend, in the course of history, the mountaineers were always the strongest." He left the restive Breton there.[11]

Mahaut's Influence

Despite the antics in the harmony class, Mahaut was an important influence on Langlais. He admired Mahaut for his legendary musical achievement of being, in 1898, the first person to perform the complete organ works of Franck to critical acclaim. Franck had considered Mahaut one of his best students, and often had him play before French and foreign artists. After his schooling at the Institute and the Conservatory, Mahaut taught music at a school on the isle of Jersey, where he learned English, and shortly thereafter traveled to Germany, where he learned German. He served for many years as organist at Saint-Vincent-de-Paul in Paris.

Mahaut's life was an example of self-sacrifice for the betterment of blind workers. After his appointment as professor of harmony at the National Institute for the Blind in 1890, he developed at the request of Maurice de la Sizeranne an employment service for the graduates. Langlais would emulate Mahaut in spending untold hours helping his students find jobs and recital engagements. This

work led Mahaut to visit both blind and sighted employers throughout France and in Algeria, where he organized concerts, confer-
ences, and visits to schools and churches. His normal correspondence exceeded two thousand typewritten letters a year, an example
Langlais would follow. In addition, Mahaut set up regional branches
of the Association Valentin Haüy for the benefit of the blind in more
than half the departments of France. In a eulogy after his death, in
1943, it was said that he knew how to use each hour to its fullest. A
man of ideas, Mahaut had the gift of singlemindedness of purpose.[12]
Langlais was similarly focused, and even as a student he learned
never to waste time.

During World War I, Mahaut stopped his travels for two years
and wrote *Le Chrétien: l'homme d'action* (The Christian: man of action), published in 1915 and eventually translated into English,
Spanish, Polish, and Italian—and into braille by Mulhouse in 1918.
In 1919 the Académie Française praised it. Father Sertillanges, from
the Institut Catholique de Paris, warned in its foreword that it would
be a mistake for the Catholic leaders to ignore spiritual renewal in
favor of outward gestures: "Apostolic production, if I may dare to
say, depends also on moral values, that is to say, on mystical values."[13] The book was immediately popular as a guide to spiritual life,
almost as a daily missal, and a counter to the prevailing materialistic, demoralized attitude of postwar France. As a young man, Langlais read it often. It became an important spiritual influence in his
life, and musically important as part of the tradition from Franck to
Mahaut. Mahaut's first chapter begins:

> You are twenty years old—a thousand desires, a thousand
> hopes are born in you. You work hard, full of self-confidence in
> your effort, waiting for tomorrow for the possible and the
> impossible; and this yearning for a fruitful future brings a great
> joy to your heart—a high ambition. Yearn, take strength, and
> use these desires. There is nothing of worth, nothing of diffi-
> culty, that you cannot realize.

There are frequent references to the Gospels, particularly Matthew
and John, to the Psalms, and to the third book of the *Imitation of
Christ*. In the prologue, Mahaut defines a Christian as one who looks
for God in all things and attaches himself with love to human real-

ity: "To attain the life of the divine, strive to live fully the life of a reasonable man." For Langlais this divine ideal was to become a cardinal pursuit of his life, and he considered Mahaut a practical as well as a literary example—so much so, indeed, that Langlais remained largely untouched by the secularization brought to France by two cataclysmic wars.

Violin: Rémy Clavers

After several years of piano, solfège, and harmony, Langlais began studying the violin; his teacher was Rémy Clavers (1891–1940), who was principally an organist and had studied for ten years with Alexandre Guilmant. Like Blazy, Clavers taught violin according to the philosophy of the school, which was to train blind pupils to become teachers, not virtuosos; they would be equipped to give lessons in small towns, teaching piano, violin, solfège, harmony, and, occasionally, organ.

Although these students and teachers were versatile on several instruments, it was never the custom to perform on more than one at a time. On Thursday evenings, there were occasional informal concerts. For one of them, Marchal improvised a suite for organ and violin in which, much to the students' delight, he played the organ with his feet and the violin with his hands at the same time.

Langlais continued his violin study until he was twenty, and increasingly Clavers encouraged him to pursue a career as a violinist. One summer when Langlais was visiting a cousin at Antrain, he entered a violin competition without notice by appearing on stage, taking one string from his violin, and playing Jocelyn's *Berceuse* on three strings. The organizer of the competition, who was the only other contestant, was obliged to share the twenty-five-franc prize with him.[14] In 1926, at his penultimate examination, Langlais played the unaccompanied Sonata in G minor by Bach; at the final exam he presented Franck's Violin Sonata, accompanied by Clavers on the piano. He received first prize in violin for his performance; it was a matter of considerable pride to Langlais that Franck's friend Paul Brand and the violinist Robert Dorfer were on the jury.

Nevertheless Langlais decided to abandon the violin, an instrument that seemed to him never complete in itself. As wonderful as

Franck's Sonata was, the difficult accompaniment was as important as the violin part. It was like gathering hazelnuts perhaps: Langlais needed to do it without help. By this time the organ had already become his first love.

Organ: André Marchal

In the fall of 1923, when Langlais was sixteen, he began his organ studies with André Marchal. Marchal, only thirteen years older than Langlais, had attended the Institute from 1903 to 1911, and had studied organ with Adolphe Marty and harmony with Albert Mahaut. In 1913 Marchal obtained the Conservatory's first prize in organ in the class of Eugène Gigout. From 1919 to 1959 he taught organ, improvisation, and composition at the National Institute for the Blind.

At that time there were also two other organ teachers there, Adolphe Marty, the Franck student who had obtained the first prize in organ in 1886, and Joséphine Boulay, another student of Franck, who obtained the same prize in 1889.[15] Mahaut's and Boulay's teaching reflected the traditions of their nineteenth-century models, especially of Franck and Fauré, with a style that emphasized 8' foundation registrations and unrelenting legato playing.

Marchal's appointment as teacher of organ, improvisation, and composition opened the way toward the creation of a new school of organ playing and writing based on a return to the articulation of the seventeenth- and eighteenth-century French Classical school and Bach revival. By 1926 his approach to registration and phrasing was already very different from the familiar nineteenth-century models. His use of the organ in improvisation was also very imaginative and original, and incorporated his innovative types of registration. For Langlais, Marchal's greatest artistic contribution was the assault he led against what was called the "tradition." "Before Marchal all French organists played like Dupré and then, all of a sudden, Marchal came and revolutionized everything by inventing different registrations, changes of manual, and above all, articulation."[16] In 1922, at the age of twenty-eight, Marchal performed in recital, on the organ at the Paris Conservatory, Bach's Toccata, Adagio, and Fugue with a vigorously personal interpretation which, in spite of the delicacy of the choice of stops, made an impressive effect. This brilliant audacity was only the beginning. The total independence continued throughout the long career of "the blind one with fingers of light."[17]

When Langlais began his organ studies, Marchal was inexperienced and had little patience with those who did not follow his explanations quickly. But Langlais, Marchal's first truly gifted pupil, absorbed it all and rapidly put into practice Marchal's innovations, in which each part breathed with its own sense of line. He never lost the sense of elegance and style that he had learned from Marchal. "I owe to him the poetry of the organ. Music without poetry is just mathematics; it is no longer real music."[18]

Perhaps partly because of their nearness in age, Marchal became a close friend to Langlais at a time when Langlais needed a helping hand. Marchal was not only a true mentor but also for many years a confidant, which increased Langlais's importance among the younger students at the school. The relationship remained pivotal for Langlais until Marchal's death in 1980. To Langlais even small details of this friendship seemed significant: he remembered how much both he and Marchal particularly admired Gauthier's Requiem, which they sang frequently at the school. Marchal's wife, Suzanne Greuet, whom Marchal married in 1919, also taught piano and harmony there; Langlais was very fond of her and often accompanied her on the piano.

These two men were polar opposites in temperament, personality, economic background, religious orientation, and attitude toward their handicap. Marchal was born in Paris to an upper-middle-class family, originally from Burgundy. His temperament was easy-going, relaxed, and positive. Langlais was born in Brittany to a very poor family and steeped in Celtic pessimism. Marchal was not without religious conviction but expressed it quite differently from Langlais. Marchal never appeared to suffer from his blindness. If anything, he rather reveled in it—happy to let people wait on him, unlike Langlais, who struggled at all times for independence.

Marchal soon encouraged Langlais to prepare for the entrance examination at the Conservatory. Langlais at first recoiled, thinking that he would never be able to achieve the level of the class taught there by Marcel Dupré, but Marchal was certain he would succeed. So at the age of seventeen, in preparation for his entrance examination into Dupré's class, Langlais began to study fugue with Marchal. (Students not planning to enter the Conservatory did not study fugue.) His examination for Dupré's class at the end of the third year consisted of reading a Gregorian chant, which was then harmonized—a feat accomplished by reading the chant with the right hand and playing the accompaniment with left hand and pedal. Students were trained to read in the original mode and transpose while reading it. Then, a small improvised paraphrase was made on the chant. In addition to this, he improvised an Andante. This was followed by performing a difficult piece; Langlais played Bach's Fugue in G minor (BWV 542).

While he studied organ with Dupré, Langlais also studied composition in Marchal's class at the Institute. A fellow student in the same class, one Renvoisé, was not at all gifted in music. Marchal asked them to write a berceuse for cello and piano. Renvoisé approached Langlais and said that he felt unequal to the task and would only write the melody if Langlais would write a very simple accompaniment that he could memorize easily. Langlais wrote two measures, the first of which he told Renvoisé to repeat twenty times and the second likewise, ending with the first measure again repeated twenty more times. He urged Renvoisé to count very carefully. Predictably, in the performance Renvoisé lost count and they did not end together. Marchal teased Langlais about this, knowing full well that Langlais had written the piece.

Summer Vacations

Every summer Langlais spent several months at home with his family. His father had returned from the war, and economic conditions for the Langlais family gradually improved. Langlais's brother, Louis, was born in 1921; both Jean and Flavie loved him very much and were his godparents. Another brother, Henri, was born four years later. The house was enlarged to include two bedrooms and a storeroom to accommodate the growing family. The family continued to cultivate its vegetable garden but also raised chickens and rabbits.

It happened that his mother's sister had married a train conductor, who brought Jean to Rennes in the engine car; Jean loved touching the controls. Jean would sleep for several days upon his return home, as they were poorly nourished at the Institute. Flavie remembered her brother's visits as an interruption of their normal routine: "My mother would say: 'Be quiet, listen to him. He speaks so well.' And I confess that sometimes I had enough of listening to him. But he was already a personage."[19]

In the summer of 1924, after only one year of organ study, Langlais began to substitute as organist at the church of Notre-Dame in Rennes. At the same time and much to his satisfaction, there was a change of pastor in his home parish. He was at last invited to substitute on the harmonium, which gave him a time of sweet recompense, both financially and psychologically. Although old Jules, the blacksmith and parish organist, did not read music, he could accompany the two masses by DuMont in the second and sixth modes; young Jean amazed him and amused himself by accompanying in F-sharp the mass written in F. Langlais then played for one month at the church in Épinay-sur-Orge. The Sunday mass was at ten o'clock in the morning, the same time that his train arrived. Unfortunately, the pay was less than the cost of the train fare, and he could not continue in that position.[20]

Early Church Jobs

In 1925, at the age of eighteen, Langlais obtained his first church job in Paris, as substitute organist on the beautiful Cavaillé-Coll organ at the church of Saint-Antoine-des-Quinze-Vingts. He considered the monthly salary of 625 francs a gold mine; as a student at the Institute, he received only seven francs spending money every three months. For this position he was indebted to the generous Count Christian de Berthier. Even later as a student at the Conservatory, when he also substituted at Saint-Étienne-du-Mont for Alexandre Dantot, he continued to serve as the count's substitute.

The quality of bravura in his playing had already found a parallel in his relations with people. Despite his diminutive height and late educational start, he was on the surface self-assured, even somewhat cocky. He was not afraid of meeting people, and, unlike many of his colleagues at the Institute, was already at ease around women.

Gregorian Chant

At the Institute chapel, Langlais received the training in Gregorian chant that formed the basis of the majority of his religious and liturgical music. The chapel housed a two-manual Cavaillé-Coll organ.[21] A resident chaplain celebrated high mass each Sunday morning and vespers at 1:30 p.m. The students sang the chants of the propers at the masses and the psalms for vespers—and, occasionally, for compline. Adolphe Marty taught the singing and accompanying of the chant from a braille Solesmes score that contained mistakes. To rectify this, Marty made his own edition without the words, but this presented other difficulties for the student organists. They worked at accompanying the chant one hour each week with between three and five students in each class. Langlais warmly acknowledged his debt to Marty for this training and for his direct knowledge of Franck's style.

During weekends the children were permitted to visit relatives and friends with special permission from the director. Often Langlais's uncle Jules would come to take him to his apartment and for visits around Paris. Toward the end of his studies at the Institute, at the age of nineteen, Jean was momentarily tempted to become a nightclub pianist for its financial rewards.

> I remember one day in Montparnasse, I was with [Uncle Jules], who was a minister's secretary—on Sunday afternoons he wrote a lot of letters. He invited me to come with him to a big bar where some musicians were playing bass, piano, and so forth. One day the manager came to my uncle and said, "The pianist will leave next week. If you wish, your nephew could be our pianist permanently." And the money was fantastic at that time. My uncle said, "No, that is not for him." I was furious because I did not have one penny. I said, "Why did you refuse like that?" And he said, "Because you have something much better to do." He was not a musician, but he was a very intelligent person.[22]

Indeed, he would have much better things to do. In ten years at the Institute, Langlais had overcome his late introduction to braille and acquired both a general and a musical education, in time becoming one of its most outstanding music students. During each of his last three years there, he received the distinction of three gold braids on his uniform for the highest grades in music; seven or eight students had one braid, but Langlais was the only one to have all three.[23] The monastic and spartan environment had both trained him to enormous discipline and shown him the rewards of his own hard work.

In February 1927 Langlais turned twenty. Marchal was planning to present him to Dupré that spring for a preliminary meeting, to determine whether Dupré would consider him ready to enter the Conservatory. There was much to keep him occupied; he had to prepare to improvise a fugue and a thème libre.

CHAPTER 3

The Paris Conservatory 1927–1930

I have the gift of being able to conceal and control my sensitivity about many things.

Ludwig van Beethoven

René Malherbe, the first person Langlais met at the Conservatory, became one of Langlais's closest friends during his three years there. The night before they met, musicologist Paul Landormy had given a lecture on Beethoven at the Institute. His description of Beethoven as being rather ugly had impressed the blind students. So Malherbe's spontaneous reaction to meeting Langlais the next day—"Dis donc, mon vieux, it's amazing how much you look like Beethoven!"—was quite a blow! But Malherbe reassured him, saying that it was only the foreheads that were similar, not the entire body.[1]

This passing jest, however, was in fact quite apt. Like Beethoven, Langlais struggled with a handicap which, rather than suppressing his creativity, enriched it. Both composers struggled for financial and social stability; both shared similar personality traits. Their intense sensitivity made it difficult for them to form and sustain relationships. A contemporary of Beethoven, Xavier Schnyder von Wartensee, described Beethoven as someone who, like Langlais, spoke his mind straightaway, "rough but honest and without pretensions," and like Beethoven, Langlais struggled with disappointment in his youth, which "made him suspicious and grim."[2]

History of the Paris Conservatory

Like the Institute for the Blind, the Paris Conservatory has an involved history grounded in tradition. Bernard Sarrette (1765–1858), who was its first teacher of harmony, founded it in 1795 as the Institut National de Musique. Its original purpose was to train students for musical careers in the military, and as there was no demand for organists in the army and church music was at a low ebb following the French Revolution, there were few organ students in the early years. Nicolas Séjan (1745–1819), organist at Notre-Dame and Saint-Sulpice, was the first organ professor, teaching only from 1799 to 1802. François Benoist (1794–1878) taught from 1819 to 1872. An illustrious group of professors followed: César Franck (1872–1890), Charles-Marie Widor (1890–1896), Alexandre Guilmant (1896–1911), Eugène Gigout (1911–1925), Marcel Dupré (1926–1954), Rolande Falcinelli (1954–1987), and Michel Chapuis (1987–1996).[3]

Like the Institute, the Conservatory was entirely funded and controlled by the French government, and, like many governmental organizations, highly centralized. In order to obtain an important church or teaching position in France, a first prize from the Conservatory was essential. Although by 1927 a number of regional conservatories had sprung up in such cities as Lille, Strasbourg, Amiens, and Lyon, they were not as prestigious as the Conservatory, nor was the level of teaching as high. As a result, the competition to enter the select organ class in Paris was heated.

During Benoist's tenure, the emphasis in organ training was on improvisation; very little Bach and Classical French music literature was studied. Franck's teaching brought the art of improvisation to a new height and had the greatest musical influence (both Dukas and Debussy were auditors in his organ class). Widor developed a strict technique that emphasized exact releases of repeated notes, and he required organ repertoire based on major works of Bach. Guilmant and Gigout continued the tradition.

Their successor, Marcel Dupré (1886–1971), had studied with Vierne, Guilmant, and Widor at the Conservatory and had distinguished himself by winning first prizes there (in piano, organ, and fugue) as well as the Prix de Rome. Forty-one years old and at the height of his career, Dupré had played the complete works of Bach from memory, toured the United States four times, and written some of his best works, including *Trois préludes et fugues* op. 7, *Cortège et litanie*, *Variations sur un vieux noël*, *15 versets sur les vêpres du commun de la Sainte-Vierge*, and *Symphonie-passion*.

Organ Entrance Requirements

In 1927 Dupré had been head of the organ class at the Conservatory for only a year, and he took seriously his responsibility to uphold the traditions of Widor and Guilmant. As part of the entrance requirements, each of his students had to have attained a high level of technical proficiency both in prepared pieces (including Bach and a modern work) and in improvisation. The improvisation requirements included a scholastic fugue complete with a countersubject, three different tonal centers, and strettos; an accompaniment of a Gregorian chant; a prelude based on the chant, in which the chant was heard first in the pedal and then in the treble a fourth higher with florid counterpoint; and a thème libre, a form Langlais would use for one of his earliest pieces.[4]

Although most students stayed in the organ class from two to five years, they could enter at any age and faced no time limit for the completion of their studies. Promising students often attended as auditors, with the expectation that they would be accepted within a year. After admission, they were obliged to pass another preliminary exam in May, which permitted them to take the public exam or competition in June of each scholastic year. Only matriculated students were permitted to take the final exams upon which the prizes were awarded. A panel of outside judges graded each student with written comments, and a majority of votes determined the grade. A student could graduate with several distinctions: deuxième accessit (second place), premier accessit (first honorable mention), and premier prix (first prize). Since there was no limit to the number of first prizes given at one exam, all prizes short of first held little prestige. They only insured graduation.

Audition with Dupré

Langlais's informal audition before Marcel Dupré took place at Marchal's apartment in the spring of 1927. It was unusual for Dupré to come to the home of another organist to hear a prospective student; no doubt Dupré did this as a kindness to his blind colleague and his promising student.

Marchal, only eight years younger than Dupré, was already becoming established in his career; for twelve years he had been titular organist at Saint-Germain-des-Près in Paris and had performed extensively in France and once in Belgium. But since his appointment as teacher of organ, improvisation, and composition at the Institute eight years earlier, he had not produced an organ candidate for the Conservatory. Langlais was the first student to hold such promise. In fact, the Institute had not produced a student who had obtained a premier prix in organ for ten years.[5]

All three men were aware that much rested on this audition. Both Marchal and Dupré were most cordial during the visit and Langlais, while very much in awe of Dupré, did his utmost to remain calm while waiting to receive the themes.

For the audition, Dupré asked Langlais to improvise a fugue and a thème libre. Langlais had a difficult time developing the unexpectedly simple thème libre.[6] Nonetheless his playing must have shown promise, for Dupré admitted him to his organ class as an auditor.

Dupré, thème libre

Marchal, his wife, Suzanne, and their six-year-old daughter Jacqueline lived across the street from the Institute, at 22 rue Duroc, and Langlais frequently went there on Sundays for dinner. The ground-floor apartment had a large dining room, bedroom, and a high-ceilinged salon, which housed Marchal's Gutschenritter, a two-manual mechanical-action organ with eight stops. Langlais already knew this organ well. When anyone played, its sounds could be heard from the street as the two main windows were directly at the level of the sidewalk.

Dupré's Organ Class

The organ class met three afternoons a week from 1:30 to 3:30. On Monday the class studied improvisation of the fugue and the Gregorian paraphrase or prelude. On Wednesday the class studied improvisation of the thème libre. On Friday prepared pieces were performed. As an auditor, Langlais was obliged to attend some of the classes at Dupré's home in Meudon, a suburb about fifteen minutes west of Paris on the train from the Montparnasse station. Langlais resented this burden.

In 1927 Dupré's class included René Malherbe, Olivier Messiaen, Gaston Litaize, Henriette Roget, Joseph Gilles, Henri Cabié, and Noëlie Pierront. In 1928 the class grew to include Odette Gauthier, Denis Joly, Jean Bouvard, and Tommy Desserre, and lost Gilles to premature death. The class changed not at all in 1929, and in 1930 one new student, Rachel Brunschwig, joined.[7] Messiaen, Litaize, Roget, Pierront, and Langlais would all became well known.

Langlais's lifelong friendship with Olivier Messiaen dates from this period. Common religious ideals further yoked their kindred spirits, and the two men were like brothers. Langlais described his friend thus:

> Messiaen, born in 1908, was one year younger than I—and already showing his genius. When he improvised it was splendid. He improvised as well on a Trompette that was abominable and out of tune as if it had been a marvelous Salicional or a Flûte from Sainte-Clotilde. Finally, Messiaen did not hear what he was doing. He was above all natural contingencies: an out-of-tune Trompette was beautiful to him even if it was ugly and out of tune.[8]

Messiaen, a child prodigy, had been admitted to the Conservatory at the age of eleven and had already won prizes in harmony, counterpoint, fugue, and piano accompaniment. Two years later he would have the premier prix in organ. By 1927 Messiaen had already written vocal and piano music, and the following year his organ piece *Le banquet céleste*, would challenge traditional concepts of time and tonality.

While studying at the Conservatory, both Langlais and Litaize continued to live at the Institute. A friend who used to ride with them on the bus remembered these two blind friends dressed in their Institute uniforms and remembered too "their intelligence and sparkling, mischievous wit."[9] After class, all the students would go to a café for hot chocolate and croissants, and Langlais and Litaize were glad for these stops, since they were always hungry. They found all the students in the organ class to be kind and friendly; the group was marked by a remarkable lack of jealousy, something Langlais missed in later years as his success as a performer and composer grew.

Dupré's Discipline

Dupré was partial to students who, like himself, received their early education at the Conservatory; director Henri Rabaud supposedly imposed this point of view on his faculty to uphold the institution's traditions.[10] Langlais, loyal to his teachers at the Institute, especially as they had studied with Franck, felt a conflict between their interpretation of Franck and that of Dupré. "[Dupré] forgot one thing: that we were formed by teachers like Albert Mahaut, who was a student of Franck."[11] One day Langlais brought Franck's *Fantaisie en ut*. In the middle movement just before the recapitulation, the passage in D-flat, Dupré told him to play the right hand part on the Récit. Langlais regarded the change of manuals as incorrect and refused, stating that he had studied the piece with students of Franck at the Institute. A long, painful silence followed. Dupré was noticeably angry. Finally he told Langlais to hold to his interpretation.[12]

Langlais did not realize that Dupré required a new piece be played from memory each week. The first piece he played in class was Bach's Prelude and Fugue in B minor (BWV 544). When he finished, Dupré said, "Good—it's not bad," which led Langlais to believe that it could be improved. So the following week he played the Prelude again. At the end of class Dupré derided him thus:

> When I was in Diémer's piano class, a friend of mine managed to play three études of Chopin during the year: the one in thirds, the one in sixths, and the one in octaves in B minor. If

Langlais wants to play the Prelude in B minor for the whole year, he'll have difficulty because I write down everything that is played.[13]

Crushed by Dupré's sarcasm, Langlais never again played the same piece twice.

Another example of Dupré's severity regarded punctuality. At the close of each session, which lasted from 1:30 to 3:30 p.m., Dupré would shake each student's hand. One day, he varied this ritual and instead announced that he had been informed by the director that he was permitted to exclude any student who came late. From now on, the door would be locked at 1:31 and anyone arriving late would not be admitted. "Amateurs, be advised," he concluded and left abruptly—without shaking hands. This rule of absolute punctuality was an especially severe hardship for several of the married students, who were obliged to support themselves by playing for weddings and funerals. But for Langlais, having come from ten years of regimentation at the Institute, punctuality was a mania.

One day Dupré asked the students how much they practiced each day. One student said five hours, others said four or six. Dupré, furious, told them that at their age he practiced twelve hours daily. No wonder his rare demonstrations showed such phenomenal technique.

Before the exam Dupré worried about Langlais and Litaize being able to learn the themes in time and proposed that they be given twenty minutes for advance preparation. But Langlais would have no more charity hazelnuts, and he and Litaize asked to take the exam under the same conditions as the other students. Dupré, though not happy with their attitude, since he was only trying to be kind, agreed. When he saw that they had done well in the exam, he publicly announced, "In my class there are not two sorts of students, those who are sighted and those who are blind. I have only type of student: musicians!" For Langlais and Litaize it was a sweet moment.

Langlais learned much from Dupré, whose technique was based on a relaxed immobility. He forbade the slightest unnecessary movement, believing it detracted from concentration and musical awareness. Once when Langlais was playing the second section of Bach's Fugue in E-flat, Dupré warned, "Don't move, mon petit, don't move —not the hands, not the head, not the feet!" This was especially helpful advice for blind students, who unknowingly displayed involuntary mannerisms that their blind teachers could not observe. Langlais was grateful to Dupré for this direction; many years later, at Sainte-Clotilde, students told Langlais how disconcerting it was to watch him play a difficult piece—with so little body movement, he made it appear easy.

Dupré's disciplined class was occasionally broken by lighter moments. One day Dupré assigned his students a long, complicated, chromatic theme in B major on which to prepare a thème libre for the following week. Langlais whispered to Malherbe that he would never be able to transpose the theme into F-sharp major the first time. Malherbe, with his oblique sense of humor, offered an easy solution: simply continue to play the theme in B major on a solo Nasard, which stop would sound an octave and a fifth higher than written. Langlais took his advice and prepared it without transposing it. All was going well, and he was proceeding confidently into the bridge when Dupré called out, "Watch out, mon petit, on the Récit you have a Nasard all alone." Langlais answered that it was intended; Dupré said, "Aah!" Langlais continued improvising in the dominant by playing with his hands in B major and the pedal sounding in F-sharp. The students were laughing; even Messiaen was amused. Dupré, however, was far from amused, and again had the perfect reply. "It's too bad that there is no Tierce on this organ. It could be of service to you for themes in minor keys." Dupré always managed to keep even the most obstreperous student in line with just the right cutting remark.

Although he liked playing the naughty boy (Langlais would read Boccaccio's bawdy *Decameron* while Dupré thought he was studying his improvisation notes), Langlais regarded Dupré as a father: "He was a marvelous professor . . . a great man who had played all over the world. He was very paternal, very kind, very gentle; and he found almost everything good—almost, not always everything." His relationship with Dupré deteriorated as Langlais grew as an artist in his own right, but during his six years of study with Dupré—three at the Conservatory and three privately—Langlais idolized him.

Partly for modesty but also for political reasons, Dupré did not encourage his students to study his own works: he would not risk his students making a poor showing in their exams simply because one jury member or another did not like his works. Still, Langlais was permitted to play the prelude and fugue in F minor from Dupré's opus 7 and the first movement of Dupré's *Symphonie-passion*. One day Dupré entered the Salle Berlioz as Langlais was preparing this work and remarked, "When one comes in the door, one hears Langlais playing the *Symphonie-passion* throughout the entire Conservatory," as if this were an embarrassment.

Prélude et fugue

In 1927 Langlais composed his first work for organ, *Prélude et fugue*. The following year it won first prize in composition at the Institute, with the compliments of the jury. Langlais himself performed it, and its technical difficulty testifies to his developed organ technique. Dupré, a member of the jury, recognized Langlais's talent for composition. Langlais had composed this work while studying composition with Marchal, who praised it and later urged Langlais to have it published and dedicated to himself. The style is post-Impressionist and improvisatory, like Fauré's music and Marchal's improvisations, but tightly knit structurally. Based on two contrasting themes, which are combined at the end, the Prelude shows considerable economy of material. The repetition in measures 4 and 5 reflects the years of Institute training in taking dictation in short segments. The Fugue's subject, a variant of the first theme of the Prelude, is set in pulsating

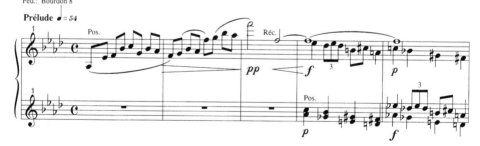

Prélude et fugue, Prelude, mm. 1–5. © 1982 Universal Edition A.G., Wien. All rights reserved. Used by permission of European American Music Distributors Corporation, sole U.S. and Canadian agent for Universal Edition A.G., Wien.

12/8 meter with an unrelenting gigue-like rhythm. The Prelude's second theme appears as a second subject, and in the Fugue, as in the Prelude, the two subjects are combined at the end.

Prélude et fugue, Fugue, mm. 59–61. © 1982 Universal Edition A.G., Wien. All rights reserved. Used by permission of European American Music Distributors Corporation, sole U.S. and Canadian agent for Universal Edition A.G., Wien.

Fugue: Noël Gallon

Although Langlais had made excellent progress in Dupré's organ class, he still had difficulty in improvising a fugue, and at Dupré's suggestion, he attended the class of Noël Gallon, the professor of fugue, as an auditor. Langlais worried that he would find it difficult to prepare for Dupré's class at the same time and wondered how he would come up with the money to pay someone to copy the fugues for him (fortunately, his good friend René Malherbe came to his rescue). In the end, Langlais attended Gallon's class for several months during the 1929–1930 academic year; the weekly discipline was enormously helpful to Langlais, and soon Dupré agreed that it was no longer necessary for him to attend Gallon's class. Langlais admired Gallon as a kind and gentle man, and an excellent professor, and continued to be on good terms with him.[14]

Six fugues that Langlais wrote for Gallon's class are extant, in Malherbe's hand, with a few corrections from Gallon. They demonstrate correct counterpoint and interesting strettos. Each is in a different key and includes opening sections beginning respectively with the bass, alto, and soprano. Fugues beginning in the tenor voice were omitted, possibly because that order of entries was the one normally used for improvised fugues. Surprisingly Langlais never published these fugues nor reworked them into other compositions.

First Compositions

In 1929 Langlais composed *Six préludes*—all except the fourth were unfortunately lost during World War II. He dedicated them to members of his organ class—Messiaen, Litaize, Cabié, Gilles, Roget, and Brunschwig—and premiered them at the Institute the following year. Three preludes were singled out in reviews: "Chant héraldique" must have pleased even Langlais, since he later had it played at his wedding; "Lamentation" is described as a "long crescendo on 8′ foundation stops"; "Image" is "an elusive sketch on the 1′, 2′, and 4′ stops" and specially praised were its "delicate sensitivity, particular predilection for tone color, and use of pure timbre and contrasting colors."[15] "Adoration des bergers," the fourth, is a quiet, meditative prelude in F-sharp major, in the form Langlais would use most frequently in his compositions: A B A. A treble solo for the Hautbois adds a pentatonic flavor over sustained chords in the left hand and lends a calm and simple mood to the short piece, so typical of his early style.

Some of the preludes were more dissonant than "Adoration," at least they appeared so to Louis Vierne (1870–1937), the blind organist-composer at Notre-Dame Cathedral. Vierne visited the Institute frequently and was often present at examinations. He had been both Widor's and Guilmant's assistant and also taught at the Schola Cantorum. Langlais esteemed Vierne and would always remember Vierne's remark to him after hearing him play *Six préludes*, tapping his foot to punctuate the dissonance all the while: "My dear, your music strikes hard, but it doesn't bother me because it is written with sincerity—when youth is too full of things to say, it has to come out."

In late spring 1929, Dupré gave the students as vacation homework themes for composing a thème libre and a prelude based on a Gregorian chant. The opening of Langlais's unpublished thème libre shows stylistic elements that would mark many of his works: a developed chromaticism within a lyrical, improvisational framework. The staccato bridge (on the Quintaton 16, Flûte, and Octavin,

Thème libre, mm. 1–4

marked *plus vif*) contrasts playfully, testifying to Langlais's distinctive and idiomatic sense of humor; the rhythmic and lyrical motifs are developed and build to a climax in the high register. The piece concludes adroitly with two canons at the octave in stretto.

The Gregorian theme was the first-vesper antiphon from the Common of Saints, "Vos amici mei estis." A two-measure ostinato with exact octave doublings in both hands provides an organum-like accompaniment to the chant, heard in augmentation in the pedal at 4′ pitch. The last phrase is treated in canon. The chant-based treatment with the repetitive one- or two-measure phrases would become typical of his style.

At the beginning of his career as a composer, Langlais was a serious student who expressed his own personality without breaking free of the traditions that had shaped his early training. All his early pieces show economy of thematic material, simplicity of harmony, and a quality of youthful innocence. They reflect the style of Fauré and Ravel.

During his term at the Conservatory, from 1927 to 1929, Langlais proudly served as substitute organist at the church of Saint-Étienne-du-Mont, which parish had been served by blind organists for one hundred years. During the same two years, he was assistant organist at Saint-Antoine-des-Quinze-Vingts.

Piano: Lazare-Lévy

Despite the demands of his church positions and Dupré's class, Langlais also studied piano with Lazare-Lévy. Langlais was fond of Lazare-Lévy and grateful to him for charging so little for the lessons, from which he learned much. Once Langlais played on the radio two organ pieces by Lazare-Lévy. Lazare-Lévy told Langlais how pleased he had been to hear the broadcast, as he never heard the works performed. Langlais protested that Vierne had played them for Lazare-Lévy at the Temple de l'Étoile, to which Lazare-Lévy responded, "Yes, but Vierne did not know them."

Final Organ Exam

The culmination of Langlais's study in Dupré's organ class came in June 1930 at the final examination, where he was awarded first prize. Fifty years later the memory of this important event remained fresh in his mind. The jury of eight members included Joseph Bonnet: the Conservatory routinely appointed not only its own faculty members to the juries but always some respected musicians from the community. Joseph Bonnet (1884–1944) was certainly that, a virtuoso pupil of Guilmant and organist since 1906 at Saint-Eustache. He frequently served on organ juries, but he did not like Dupré and always voted against his students. Indeed, the tradition of political intrigue during these final exams has a history as long as the Conservatory itself.

The order of the exam was as follows: a Gregorian chant was given which had to be first read, then harmonized and transposed. As a result of Dupré's training, Langlais could easily do this by playing the chant with the right hand and the bass with the feet while reading the theme with his left hand. After that he improvised a prelude based on the plainsong. Remembering what Messiaen had done at this exam a year earlier, Langlais followed the same form in which a large plenum of four voices combined one part in whole notes, one part in half notes with syncopations, and one part in quarter notes with the final part free. Although this task appeared easy, Langlais required a year to accomplish it because he had to play two parts in the pedal so that his left hand could continue to read the chant. This was followed by a fugue, based on a subject given by Alexandre Cellier (1883–1968), a pupil of Guilmant and Widor at the Conservatory and organist at the Temple de l'Étoile. After the fugue Langlais performed Bach's Toccata in F major. The last part of the exam consisted of a thème libre in A minor, also by Cellier. Langlais mentally transposed it into C major, the relative key, for the second section, but it seemed so ugly to him that he decided to transpose it into E minor instead.

Alexandre Cellier, thème libre

After the exam Dupré came to the bench to lead him off the platform, exclaiming, "Mon enfant, you almost made me die! Did you realize what you did in the thème libre?" "Yes." "Why did you do that? You know very well that it is forbidden!" "I did that because it is more musical than to transpose it into the relative key." "Yes, but while you were doing that, I was looking attentively at all the jury members. They could have refused to award you the prize, but I can tell you that they accepted it and you will surely have your prize." Henceforth Dupré permitted the students to transpose the thème libre into the dominant when it was in a minor key and later included that option in his second volume on improvisation (published in 1937).

The vote of the jury was seven in favor of awarding Langlais the first prize. In one account, Langlais said that Bonnet abstained from voting and in another that he voted against. In any case, Dupré knew the minds of the jury and had prepared Langlais in the best possible way.

Although he won his first prize in 1930, Langlais continued to study privately with Dupré until 1933. The six years of study affected his career in a positive way. Not only had he gained a solid technique, his thorough grounding in the strict forms of improvisation significantly influenced his playing and teaching. Many years later he would continue to improvise strict fugues and Gregorian preludes. Langlais also drew on elements of the thème libre in many of his improvisations and compositions.

Dupré's influence on Langlais was marked by a generally Classical approach to interpretation for all music except Tournemire and French Romantic composers; a nobility of style with emphasis on the larger architecture of the piece; technical precision and economy of motion; and finally an exact adherence to Dupré's rules of legato and metrical release of repeated notes. Regarding Bach, Langlais generally followed Dupré's legato approach rather than Marchal's more articulated touch.

Charles Tournemire (1870–1939), organist of Sainte-Clotilde and professor of chamber music at the Conservatory, had been a member of the jury at Langlais's qualifying examination a month earlier. He had been following Langlais's career with interest and was eager to have him as a pupil, a feeling that turned out to be mutual. On 11 May 1930, Tournemire wrote a brief card. "Dear friend, I will wait for you on Thursday at 6:30. You were excellent at the exam. Faithfully yours, Charles Tournemire."[16]

Normally a student studied organ with only one teacher at a time. Although Langlais continued to study with Dupré, he now began taking lessons in improvisation and repertoire with Tournemire.

CHAPTER 4

Formative Years 1930–1939

It is sometimes good for a genius to belie his own reputation.

Paul Dukas[1]

Appointment to the Institute

In spring 1930 Adolphe Marty died. The following fall, at the age of twenty-three, Langlais was appointed to take his place as an untenured professor at the Institute for the Blind. Within the space of several months, he passed from being a student to being a teacher, and his schoolmates were now his students. From the large common dorm that he had known for the past thirteen years, he moved to faculty quarters where he had, for the first time in his life, a room of his own. Not until 1939, however, did he receive a tenured position, and only after passing several examinations, including, in 1930, the composition of a fugue.

The exam to write a fugue on a given subject occurred on 3 April 1930. All the students knew that he had this important task ahead; the night before, they kept silent in the dormitory room so that he could go to sleep easily and be rested for the next day. He was required to write a fugue on a difficult quasi-modal subject in E-flat minor by Georges Caussade, professor of counterpoint at the Conservatory. At six o'clock in the morning he was placed alone in a room with no instrument. His meals were brought in. By midnight he had finished, never having left the room.[2]

Relationships with Students

The next morning Langlais awakened to a ripping sound. Sitting upright in bed, he asked his classmates what they were doing. They

63

replied that they knew he would soon be moved and therefore wanted a remembrance of him: they were tearing up his student smock. As he entered the refectory for breakfast, the attendant said, "Just because you are a professor doesn't mean that you are permitted to come here without your smock." "But the students ripped it apart this morning," Jean protested—to no avail: he had to go and find another. The next day his classmates pulled apart his pullover sweater. He told the director what had happened and asked him what he thought they would rip apart next. "Probably your pants!" The director moved him to a private room.

The following Sunday afternoon, four or five of his friends entered his new room, closed the window, locked the door, and asked if he had anything to drink. He found a bottle of port wine, and they all settled down to drink it. When the bottle was empty, they lit their pipes, saying they would stay as long as they could breathe. Now Langlais had his own souvenir—his small room smelled of tobacco for a month. But the practical jokes eased his transition from student to professor, and he saw that the students were still his friends. Many years later, Langlais recounted these stories with an air of proud nostalgia, believing that the shredding of his clothes—the only clothes he had—was a rite of passage, a symbol of affection.

Choirmaster

Langlais also assumed Adolphe Marty's position as choirmaster. How did a blind director lead a choir of blind singers who could see neither hand nor baton? As he had learned under Marty, he stood in their midst so that they could hear the quiet snapping of his fingers. This let them stay together at cadences and in rubatos, but no one in the audience could detect it.

The chorus comprised fifty-nine singers, both girls and boys, who sang a broad range of choral literature, from Gregorian chant to Debussy. (The first time he directed, the choir sang two songs by Debussy on texts by Charles d'Orléans, "Dieu! qu'il la fait bon regarder" and "Yver, vous n'estes qu'un villain," both exceedingly difficult.) Every Sunday the chorus sang on the radio from a repertoire that included masses by Palestrina, Dufay, and Victoria, as well as Bach cantatas. Langlais occasionally called extra evening rehearsals to

Langlais in his trademark sunglasses, which his cousin Marie said made him look more professional, c. 1929

which no one objected. "Everyone was content because we loved the music very much."

The choir's fame grew under Langlais's leadership. After World War II, Langlais conducted a performance before the president of the Republic that was used in the film *La nuit est mon royaume*; and on 15 November 1946 Helen Keller heard the choir during her visit to the Institute. While the singers performed a work by Bach for her, with Langlais accompanying at the organ, she passed among them touching their faces. According to one eyewitness, "A profound emotion appeared on Helen Keller's face which she communicated by rapidly touching the lips and hand of her companion who translated her simple words of thanks: 'Each person had the need for an ideal and there is none greater than that of music.'"[3] This homage went straight to the heart of the director and his students, and they applauded the illustrious visitor, who had just received the Legion of Honor, enthusiastically. She then asked Langlais to play for her Bach's Toccata in D minor. As he played, she touched his face feeling the vibrations. She pronounced his performance superb—a moment he never forgot.

Vocational Calling

It was during his transition from student to professor that Langlais played his first organ recital, on 10 August 1930, at the church of Sacré-Coeur in Toulouse. The program, which was shared with the schola of the church, under the direction of Father Jaylès, included Bach's Fugue in D major, Martini's Gavotte, a fugue by Buxtehude, Franck's *Pastorale*, Dupré's *La fileuse*, Vierne's *Berceuse*, and Langlais's "Adoration des bergers" and "Chant héraldique" from *Six préludes*. He ended with an improvisation. A local music critic reviewed the concert.

> A remarkable performer, M. Langlais, is also a talented composer. He showed this in two of his works, "Adoration des bergers" with its primitive *cantilène*, and "Chant héraldique," so harmonious under the Gothic arches. . . . The improvisation finale [showed that] M. Langlais lacks nothing required to be a complete artist. It was a fitting apex of an evening consecrated to the

most beautiful ideals: religious ideals—the harmony of sounds
in the harmony of lines, and also to the most beautiful of works.
Goodness in service to Beauty.[4]

At the recital Father Jaylès, who organized it, gave a lecture on the
relationship of Gothic architecture to sacred music. As the basis for
this esthetic, he referred to Pope Pius X's statement that all religious
services and concerts should lead the faithful to "prayer surrounded
by beauty." Langlais was prepared to be drawn toward this vocation
by Mahaut's *Le Chrétien: l'homme d'action*:

> And this is the marvel of the Catholic religion; this is the great
> initiation: it is a completely mystical order. When you enter into
> a church, have you noticed that something takes hold of you?
> Instinctively you become silent, to listen to a voice that speaks
> without words to your soul. You feel enveloped by the strength
> of infinity. A profound life animates the temple. Something
> great lives here; and in Him who is there, you recognize a friend
> whose invisible presence is perfectly real.

Music, window to the transcendental, would intensify Mahaut's
vision of this mystical experience. This ideal was to become the cor-
nerstone of Langlais's life as a church musician. As Langlais recognized in himself a growing pull toward sacred music, he saw in Charles
Tournemire the best of what a church musician could be. He represented the antithesis of the technical austerity of Widor and Dupré; in
him Langlais found a teacher with a sense of poetry and lyricism that
recalled the qualities of his other Franck-trained teachers at the Institute. He also found himself drawn to Tournemire's unique style of
improvisation and composition based on Gregorian chant.

Improvisation: Charles Tournemire

Tournemire had few private students; he was financially independent and in fact would not accept payment for lessons. Extremely
demanding, he accepted only those students in whom he was gen-
uinely interested. If an initial lesson with a prospective student left
him unimpressed, he would tell him that he was too busy to continue. Tournemire was not concerned with technique but rather

with the poetic elements of improvisation; his students therefore already needed to have the firm grounding in technique that a premier prix in organ from the Conservatory assured. To Langlais, the pressure was extraordinary.[5]

Langlais began to study with Tournemire in the fall of 1930 in preparation for the annual improvisation competition, to be held the following spring, sponsored by Les Amis de l'Orgue. This organization sponsored two such competitions annually, one for composition and the other for improvisation, both noted for their difficulty.[6] Although Langlais's lessons were primarily in improvisation, he also studied Tournemire's compositions including the Advent, Epiphany, and Assumption offices of *L'orgue mystique*.

Tournemire's first lesson in improvising a Gregorian paraphrase was the epitome of generalizations: the theme is to be exposed and then developed while keeping the listener's attention. He asked if Langlais had understood; the answer came in the affirmative, so he told Langlais to begin. Langlais stopped as often as Tournemire requested—about every four measures—at which junctures Tournemire came to the organ to demonstrate. Tournemire kept the nine volumes of Bach's complete works in the Peters edition on the end of the bench, and each time he joined Langlais on the bench, all nine fell to the floor. It happened again and again, with Langlais always carefully replacing the volumes. Tournemire seemed unaware. He was totally absorbed in the music. He believed that in order to impose music on listeners, one had to create an atmosphere—a mood. He advised his pupil thus:

> You must make a large crescendo, and the audience is very much with you—and the audience can no longer breathe. Then play two chords with the full organ. And then the audience feels as if they were dead. And they ask themselves what is going to happen next. What happens then is a moment of silence. And then you play again the two chords—which are terribly dissonant; and then again—a minute of silence. And finally, open the heavens to your audience with a Voix céleste and a Bourdon 8. Don't forget that your audience has earned the heaven you have saved for them. You must play quietly in the beginning and at the end . . . this crescendo is for the middle of the improvisation.[7]

Tournemire followed this plan for the Gregorian paraphrase at every lesson. He had no interest in the fugue, although he taught it and other forms as well. Above all, he insisted on poetic harmonies and sonorities, which teaching method contrasted sharply with that of Dupré: "Modulate to this key," Dupré would say, "add stops, take off stops." Tournemire, by contrast, was "a great poet, but not a technician. Tournemire had a superlative technique himself but did not teach technique."[8]

Improvisation Competition

The improvisation competition was held on 21 June 1931 at the Temple de l'Étoile. Vincent d'Indy presided.[9] Assigned repertoire was heard in the afternoon and improvisation in the evening. Four pieces were required: Bach's Prelude and Fugue in D major and "O Lamm Gottes Unschüldig," a choral by Franck, and a modern French work chosen by the jury from a submitted list of three. The improvisation consisted of four parts: a chorale prelude (*choral figuré*) on a Gregorian chant, a symphonic paraphrase of the same theme (Gregorian paraphrase), a prelude and fugue on a given subject, and a sonata movement on two given themes.

There were only two contestants, Langlais and Gustave Noël, another blind organist. Langlais played the Choral in E by Franck and the Final from Vierne's Fourth Symphony; the chant theme was "Ave maris stella." He won the unanimous vote of the jury—largely on the strength of his improvisations. According to one eyewitness:

From the first measures of the paraphrase of the beautiful liturgical theme "Ave maris stella," M. Jean Langlais displayed the personality of a true musician. A clear, even radiant imagination emanated from him, harmoniously, with a serene gravity that is, to our eyes at least, part of the personality of the organist. He uses the harmonic formulas of our prodigious time ingeniously and liberally, but he avoids excess and artificiality, and he knows how to keep the ear engaged through the bite of the timbres and melodic vivacity. He never loses the attention necessary to follow a logically and orderly musical discourse.[10]

Tournemire's poetic seeds had fallen on fertile ground. His triumph held for Langlais a dual importance. Besides the prestige of winning, the monetary prize was also substantial—a factor of considerable importance to Langlais, who needed the prize money in order to marry.

An Ideal Wife

Jeanne Sartre was a painter whose parents were originally from Escalquens, a small town near Toulouse. She now lived with her family in Maisons-Alfort, a suburb of Paris. When she met Langlais, Jeannette, as she was called, was engaged to Théodore Besset, one of Langlais's students at the Institute, and it was this student who invited Langlais to dinner at the Sartre home one night. Langlais and Jeannette spoke very little during the evening; but several days later he received with delight a beautiful poem by Paul Valéry that Jeannette, who was sighted, had copied for him in braille. He answered her in braille, immediately suspecting that her kind gesture was more than a formality.

Langlais tended to form an almost irreversible first impression of people. It was not surprising that he drew conclusions from so small a gesture as Jeannette's poem. In this case, at least, his suspicions were well founded. The two began a regular correspondence, and perceiving that Jeannette might be in love with him, Langlais had no difficulty starting a courtship.

But his pessimistic nature and fear of failure made it difficult for Langlais to bring the courtship to a happy conclusion. In a self-protective move, he created a little drama out of his proposal. He wrote Jeannette saying that on Good Friday 1931, he would attend the morning office at the church of Saint-Antoine-des-Quinze-Vingts, even though he would not be playing the organ that day. If she wished to marry him, she should appear there at the appointed hour. If she did not wish to marry him, she should not come; he would understand. He stood listening for the sound of her steps and her voice, an unbearable wait. But she came. On that Good Friday, they excitedly declared their love for each other. Then they lunched together, sparingly, because of the Lenten fast.

Jeannette was his first real love, and he could not keep this new and glorious feeling secret. Marchal, his mentor, was one of the first to hear of it, and Langlais proudly invited him to play "Chant héraldique" as the processional at their wedding, which took place on 3 December 1931 in Maisons-Alfort. Messiaen also attended. Shortly after, Langlais composed a theme in G minor based on her name—the first time he used braille musical notation to spell a person's name.

Theme based on the name Jeannette in braille

Jeannette had all the qualities of an ideal wife. Not only did Langlais find her quiet charm and soft melodious voice immediately appealing, but he soon realized that these were the outward expressions of an inward, spiritual peace. Her placid, unruffled disposition complemented Jean's turbulent nature and seemed to soothe the anguish that was a significant part of his psyche. She was small-boned, like him, with blond hair and light blue eyes. She was in her own right an artist and sculptress. Several of her oil paintings were displayed in their apartment—a still life of flowers and fruit and a bust of Jean particularly suggest her talent and craftsmanship. Although not an accomplished musician, she loved poetry, literature, and music. She had studied solfège and later taught it to their children.

It was Jeannette who prepared the scores for Langlais's compositions. The process of composing and transcribing music from braille was painstakingly slow. He would compose at the piano, making sketches in braille. From these he prepared the final braille copy. He then dictated each note to her in the correct order, for example: E, quarter note, first ledger line; G, half note, second line; B, eighth note, third line. Her finished manuscripts were meticulously written in a very small, neat hand.

First Year of Marriage

Since there were no accommodations for married couples at the Institute, Jean and Jeannette had to find their own apartment, not an easy task in Paris. He had never before had to face such mundane questions and was at a loss. Immediately he began to ask friends, and Messiaen's response was prompt, even without a direct request:

> Cher ami, you told my brother that you were looking for information. To find an apartment to rent in Paris you must write to the Régie des Immeubles de la Ville de Paris (place Saint-Thomas-d'Aquin). The prices vary between 35,000 and 65,000 francs [equivalent then to between $700.00 and $1400.00] according to the number of rooms. Very important: *You must go to the office yourself and tell them who you are and your titles.* Affectionate greetings to your wife and to yourself. Ton vieux camarade, Olivier Messiaen[11]

After a short stay in the fifteenth arrondissement, at 160 rue de la Convention, the young couple moved to 22 rue Duroc, to a tiny ground-floor apartment across the hall from the Marchals. In 1936, when a larger but relatively inexpensive fourth-floor apartment became available at 26 rue Duroc on the Place Breteuil, they moved there. Many blind people lived on rue Duroc because of its proximity to the Institute and the Association Valentin Haüy.

In July 1932, misfortune fell upon the young people. Jeannette went into labor, but the midwife was late arriving, and even after a frantic rush to the hospital, their baby was stillborn. Jeannette's recovery was slow and painful. She was hospitalized for several weeks, and it was many months before she fully recovered.

Early Works 1931–1932

Langlais's first published opus, *Deux chansons de Clément Marot* for SATB a cappella chorus, was composed in 1931. Clément Marot (1496–1544) was a court poet known for his use of Medieval forms, such as the rondeau and ballade; Langlais's pieces imitate the musical style of Machaut, who used the same forms. The two love songs, "Je suis aymé de la plus belle" (I am loved by the most beautiful) and "Aux damoiselles paresseuses" (To the lazy young ladies), were a musical offering to Jeannette. The premiere was held on 10 June 1931 at the Association Valentin Haüy, with the composer directing the Institute choir.

Early in 1932, Jeannette transcribed his next published work, *Poèmes évangéliques*, which was conceived as a trilogy depicting the life of Christ: "L'Annonciation," "La Nativité," and "Les rameaux." Langlais probably composed "Les rameaux" first, since he gave its premiere on 22 February 1932, at Saint-Merry, and gave that of the entire work on 29 May 1932, at Saint-Antoine-des-Quinze-Vingts. For the published version in 1933, Langlais dedicated *Poèmes* to Jeannette's doctor, Jean Ravina, in gratitude for having saved Jeannette's life.

"L'Annonciation" displays several traits characteristic of Langlais: the importance of Mary as a source of inspiration for his music, the influence of Tournemire and Messiaen, and the use of Gregorian themes. Based on Luke's account of the appearance of the angel Gabriel to Mary, the ascription by Langlais reads:

> The Angel Gabriel, God's messenger, respectfully greeted the Virgin Mary and spoke to her thus: "Fear not, Mary, for you have found grace with God, and you will conceive a child, and his name shall be called Jesus." Mary's heart was troubled and afraid. Then she answered the angel: "Behold, the handmaiden of the Lord. May it be to me according to your word." And in serene joy, the virgin sang her Magnificat.

Langlais treats this passage reflecting Mary's wonder at the appearance of Gabriel in four meditative sections: "The Angel Gabriel," "Mary," "The Heart of the Virgin," and "The Magnificat." The quiet opening portrays Mary's unsettled recognition of Gabriel's ethereal presence, through a theme with an ambiguous polymodal, quasi-atonal character. The key signature has two sharps but the theme centers around B minor with flatted fifth and seventh scale degrees and several augmented seconds and fourths. This four-measure theme is announced on a solo Bourdon 8; a second accompanying voice still gives no hint of a tonal center even after the theme is transposed down a third and imitated in canon against the third entry in the pedal. The theme of Mary follows without interruption on a solo reed, with even more angular leaps denoting her increasing awareness of the angel and his message.

Her response in the third section, "The Heart of the Virgin" (played on the foundation stops), is marked *légèrement agité*. The first theme of the Angel is developed, intertwined with a descending

73

Poèmes évangéliques, "L'Annonciation," mm. 1–16. © 1933 Editions Combre, Paris. Used by permission.

four-note motif (F, E, D, C-sharp) and passes rapidly through eleven key centers, which lead to a climax in the high tessitura on a dissonant chord. Calm returns. The Magnificat from the first psalm tone is heard as a cantus firmus in half notes in the pedal. (Langlais omits a number of repeated and ornamental neumes while retaining its melodic profile.) The descending four-note motif, which Langlais would later frequently employ, ties this section to the previous section, and the first two themes are united in the coda.

Langlais said of "L'Annonciation," "Unfortunately, and I recognize it well, in this work the influence of Messiaen is very strongly felt." Indeed "L'Annonciation" recalls several early works of Messiaen that Langlais knew well. Messiaen's *Le banquet céleste* (1928) has the identical descending four-note motif, and there are also thematic similarities between it and Messiaen's "Cloches d'angoisse" (from *Huit préludes*), *Les offrandes oubliées*, and *Diptyque*, which organ work Langlais had performed. Still, "L'Annonciation" differs from Messiaen stylistically. Langlais did not use Messiaen's modes of limited transposition in a systematic manner, and Messiaen used neither counterpoint, imitation, nor thematic development in the works just mentioned—devices which Langlais used extensively. Both composers relied heavily on the octatonic scale.

Throughout his life Langlais was obsessed and frustrated by his perceptions of Messiaen's supremacy—a paradox, because Messiaen continually praised Langlais as an original composer. In a letter addressed to Langlais shortly after the premiere, Messiaen was enthusiastic:

> I add a note to tell you how much I appreciated your concert at Saint-Antoine. The playing was impeccable, the registration exquisite—fine balance. The improvisation was formidable, dazzling. I will not tell you again about your recent works: you know how much I appreciate your *Poèmes évangéliques* and your Motet: It is there—true music. I don't think that one can give a greater compliment.[12]

The strongest influence in "L'Annonciation" derives from Langlais's study of improvisation with Tournemire. In the mystical spirit behind the themes, there are more similarities to Tournemire's Final from *L'orgue mystique* op. 55, no. 2, for the Immaculate Conception, than to Messiaen's early works. Tournemire's style of improvisation also runs throughout the work in the thematic development and use of registration.

Langlais called the centerpiece of *Poèmes évangéliques*, "La Nativité," a "very simple piece in four tableaux . . . something very simple, but I find in it a certain poetry." Years later Langlais told his pupil

Allen Hobbs a beautiful story surrounding its creation. Marchal's young daughter, Jacqueline, was given a crèche by her grandparents for Christmas 1927. Langlais had often heard Luke's account of the birth of Christ but could not visualize a nativity scene. Little Jacqueline showed him her new crèche, with its figures of Jesus, Mary, Joseph, and the shepherds. Above the manger hung an angel. Jacqueline led Jean's hand to each of the figures. He was fascinated. At last he understood the relationship of the angel to the manger and saw what the apostle meant. This inspired him to write "La Nativité," whose simplicity and poetic innocence make it one of his most admired and frequently performed works. He titles the four sections "The Manger," "The Angels," "The Shepherds," and "The Holy Family" and again provides a prologue:

> Mary and Joseph await the birth of the Savior Christ in a humble stable on a gentle night. The child is born, and the heavenly host communicates the event in a graceful vision to the shepherds. The shepherds, having come to the manger, offer their most tender melodies to the infant Jesus as a sign of adoration.

The first section evokes the serenity of the manger scene immediately following the birth of Christ. An undulating pentatonic triplet figure forms an accompaniment to the melody, which is played on the Cromorne in the pedal. In the second section, marked *plus animé*, faster groups of ascending eighth-note figures represent the excited flight of the angels, announcing the birth. On an Hautbois, Langlais gives the shepherds a folkloric theme from Brittany. In the third section the undulating triplet figure returns, portraying the Holy Family's peace and serenity.

The concluding piece of *Poèmes évangéliques*, "Les rameaux," is subtitled "The entry of Jesus into Jerusalem": "Jesus in all his majesty enters into Jerusalem where the enthusiastic multitude welcomes him crying: 'Hosanna to the Son of David; Blessed is He who comes in the name of the Lord, the King of Israel; Hosanna in the highest!'" Langlais evokes the pageantry of Palm Sunday with a rapid eighth-note motif based on the Gregorian antiphon "Hosanna filio David," which was sung during the procession of the palms. The opening imitative motif of the introduction then continues above the pedal statement of the entire theme in augmentation. Finally

the Hosanna theme and opening motif build to a joyful climax. Langlais was less confident about the worth of this "very Classical" piece:

> I don't renounce any piece. As Dupré would often say, others
> will do it for me. . . . In "Les rameaux," the manual parts repre-
> sent the enthusiasm of the people who acclaim Christ when he
> arrives on the day of the palms in Jerusalem. The majesty of
> Christ is represented by the pedal. They sing "Hosanna filii." I
> disapprove of using long note values and changing the rhythm
> of the chant as did [Nicolas de] Grigny. Grigny made beautiful
> works but not in the Gregorian [chant style]. I made this same
> mistake . . . in making the simple melody, free rhythm of the
> chant into a chant like a Lutheran chorale. . . . But the work is
> perhaps not a mistake. The proof is that Messiaen plays it all
> the time.

Church Positions

In 1931 Langlais obtained his first regular church position at Notre-
Dame-de-la-Croix, in the northern section of Paris near Ménil-
montant. He loved the large working-class parish of some eighty
thousand parishioners, the beautiful two-manual Cavaillé-Coll
organ, and the generous pastor.

In 1933 his friend René Malherbe helped Langlais obtain his second appointment, as titular organist at Saint-Pierre-de-Montrouge,
where Malherbe was choirmaster. Maurice Blazy, who had been titular organist there, had just died in a way his former student would
always remember:

> My piano teacher, Maurice Blazy, was killed on the street on a
> Thursday. He was to have taken his retirement on Saturday. He
> was hit by a truck. I learned afterward that at the moment he
> died, I was accompanying one of his vocal pieces, "Ave maris
> stella," on the little nine-stop organ in a concert at the Associa-
> tion Valentin Haüy.

Saint-Pierre-de-Montrouge was large and had reverberant
acoustics. Langlais particularly enjoyed the large Cavaillé-Coll organ,
which was one of the first in Paris to have a Barker lever—a device

that greatly reduced the resistance on the main keyboard when the manuals were coupled together. Langlais was to remain at Saint-Pierre for thirteen years.

In addition to the Sunday morning masses, Langlais played for vesper services at Notre-Dame-de-la-Croix, from 1929 to 1935, and at Saint-Pierre-de-Montrouge, from 1933 to 1935. Vesper services were held each Sunday afternoon. An organ procession took place on certain feast days, followed by psalms with antiphons, the Magnificat, and hymns for which the congregation and clergy sang the odd-numbered verses while the organist improvised the even-numbered verses. The organist also played some of the antiphons. The service of benediction often followed vespers, and included such plainchant hymns as "Tantum ergo," "O salutaris hostia," and "Pange lingua." The music for these services was either chant or newer compositions. Choirs were often used, especially on festal Sundays.[13]

Occasionally, from 1935 to 1939, Langlais substituted for Tournemire at Sainte-Clotilde. A June 1935 letter from Tournemire to Langlais gives instructions as to what music was to be played at the services.

> If you would, mass at eleven o'clock (without the screamers), four o'clock vespers, and procession of the feast of the Sacred Heart. Accompany the "Adoramus te," the Credo of "Monsieur" Dumont, the Magnificat of the Suburbs. It is a principle, the screamers always attack everything. The Grand-orgue responds to everything—It is funny . . . and obligatory!! I don't know yet if the mass will be sung at nine o'clock. Since you have a memory of the devil—you will know certainly. Always leave the Amen for the screamers—verses of the Magnificat also short. That is about all.

Tournemire's reference to "screamers" refers to the choir, and "the devil" is choirmaster Jules Meunier.

Tournemire arranged for portions of his *L'orgue mystique* to be performed at Sainte-Clotilde on 25 April 1932, by Daniel-Lesur, Litaize, Langlais, Messiaen, Pierront, Duruflé, and André Fleury. Langlais played the offertory and fantasy from the Epiphany office.

Langlais remained a loyal friend to Messiaen and Litaize. In 1931

Charles Quef, organist at La Trinité, died, and Messiaen submitted his candidature for the post. When Langlais learned that Messiaen was interested in applying for the position at La Trinité, a post in which Langlais was himself interested, he at once reassured his friend that he would withdraw his application. Likewise, when René Malherbe proposed that Langlais accept the position of organist at Notre-Dame-de-la-Croix, where Malherbe was choirmaster, Langlais proposed Litaize's name instead.

Shortly after Langlais's appointment at Saint-Pierre-de-Montrouge, the restoration of the church's organ was undertaken by the firm of Beuchet-Debierre. Langlais asked Vierne to play the dedication of the restored organ, since Vierne had been a friend of Blazy—and also because the pastor wanted Vierne to play. At their next organ lesson, Dupré, who disliked Vierne, tried to get Langlais to change his mind:

> "Your Curé does not care about you—you should inaugurate the organ."
> "Usually it is not the titulaire who inaugurates the organ."
> "Do you believe that if they did the work at Saint-Sulpice, I would ask Joseph Bonnet to play the inauguration?"
> "I don't think so, but between you and Joseph Bonnet there is much less difference than between Vierne and me. I am only a beginner. I am twenty-six years old, and Vierne is a great man, a great artist—it's normal that the Curé ask him."
> "Do you believe that people who can hear Vierne at Notre-Dame, without paying, would pay one hundred sous [five francs] to hear him on your organ?"
> "I hope so."
> "Let him play like a pig, then, if there's nothing you can do."

As Langlais later explained, "Dupré's meanness was like that. But he was wrong, because the church was filled." At the end of the lesson, when Langlais tried to pay Dupré as he always did, Dupré refused and instead invited him to take future lessons without fee, as a friend. But Langlais never went back.

Despite this chill in their relationship, Langlais remained grateful to Dupré, who had written a letter of recommendation to the publisher Hérelle.[14] As a result of that introductory letter, Hérelle published many of Langlais's early works, including in 1933 *Deux chansons de Clément Marot* and *Cinq motets*, in 1935 *Trois paraphrases grégoriennes*, and in 1939 and 1942 *Vingt-quatre pièces*. For several years thereafter, Langlais sent Dupré copies of his music.

Choral and Organ Works 1933–1939

Langlais premiered the first three of his *Cinq motets* at Saint-Antoine-des-Quinze-Vingts on 29 May 1933. These simple pieces for two equal voices with organ accompaniment served a liturgical purpose at vespers. The accompaniments, while fairly simple and quiet, rarely double the voice parts and inject occasional dissonances into the exclusively consonant vocal parts. Of the three, the first, "O salu-taris hostia," treats the vocal line with striking simplicity, giving one note for each syllable; "Ave mundi gloria," the longest, is in A B A form (with the Marian chant, "Sancta Maria, ora pro nobis" from the litany of Loreto). "Tantum ergo," the most tightly structured of the three, is in the form of a binary sentence; the second vocal line adds a short bit of counterpoint in the repeat. The real melody, how-ever, appears in the accompaniment, in a strict two-part canon at the fifth. This economy of material and strict counterpoint so pleased Langlais that, in 1934, he used the accompaniment alone for "Ricer-care" (*Vingt-quatre pièces*).

As an expression of his faith, Langlais again drew from Gregorian chant and his improvisation study with Tournemire for his *Trois par-aphrases grégoriennes*, another trilogy composed in 1933 and 1934. The first piece, "Mors et resurrectio," is dedicated to Henri Cabié, a Conservatory classmate of Langlais who died before graduating. It is one of Langlais's most profound expressions of his Breton assurance of eternal life. The inscription is taken from the first letter of Paul to the Corinthians: "Death, where is thy victory?" As Langlais described it, "'Mors et resurrectio' is based on the [Gregorian] gradual from the Mass for the Dead. For me the theme from the Mass for the Dead represents life—the Resurrection—and it is in minor mode. And then the theme in major in the beginning represents death." Death is symbolized by a two-note ostinato figure, the opening motif from the introit of the Requiem mass, "Requiem aeternum" (Eternal rest grant to them), based on the same text and heard in its entirety on the Trompette. Life hereafter is symbolized by the first section of the gradual, as the full meaning of the words "Requiem aeternam dona eis, Domine" (Eternal rest grant to them, Lord). The two themes are intertwined in a broad tapestry of sound, beginning with the softest sonorities and building to a triumphant conclusion on the full organ.

In the second piece, "Ave Maria, ave, maris stella" (Hail Mary, hail, Star of the Sea), Langlais again develops the mystical intent of the Annunciation, taking the chant antiphon "Ave Maria" from the second vespers of the feast of the Annunciation. This time Langlais treats the chant with a polymodal opening in F-sharp Dorian in the manuals against the pedal in A Dorian. Langlais portrays Gabriel's presence and greeting to Mary ("Ave Maria") with a translucent texture, the pedal Flûte 4 played against soft strings spaced two octaves apart in the hands. A middle section develops the sense of flux and torment with the motif "Sancta Maria" (Holy Mary) of the "Ave Maria" theme on quiet stops, expressing peace and confidence.

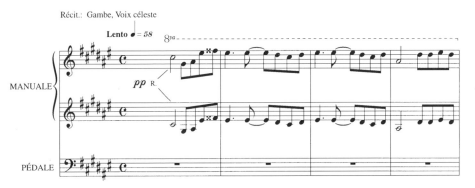

Trois paraphrases grégoriennes, "Ave Maria, ave, maris stella," p. 2, mm. 1–4. © 1934 Editions Combre, Paris. Used by permission.

"Hymne d'action de grâces 'Te Deum'" concludes the work. The "Te Deum" is a chant hymn of thanksgiving sung on festival occasions, and like the text, the musical form is tripartite, starting with the opening chant theme in octaves, followed by dissonant chords with strong, contrasting rhythm. The second section develops the text "In Thee, O Lord, I have trusted: let me never be confounded" with a long crescendo symbolizing this hope. The third section brings this song of triumph to a powerful conclusion on full organ. Stylis-

Trois paraphrases grégoriennes, "Mors et resurrectio," p. 9, mm. 1–10. ©
1934 Editions Combre, Paris. Used by permission.

Trois paraphrases grégoriennes, "Hymne d'action de grâces 'Te Deum,'" p. 19, mm. 5–10. © 1934 Editions Combre, Paris. Used by permission.

tic similarities abound between this work and Tournemire's reconstructed improvisation on the same theme.

Both *Trois paraphrases grégoriennes* and *Poèmes évangéliques* show a growing boldness in the treatment of dissonance and an emerging individual style, for example, in the many dominant and minor seventh and ninth chords in "Mors et resurrectio." Their subjects too are very similar; in *Trois paraphrases grégoriennes*, however, Christ's birth is replaced with the theme of death and resurrection to make the cycle of his life complete.

Striking eleventh chords occur at climaxes near the end of "Hymne d'action de grâces 'Te Deum.'" Bravura flourishes built on arpeggiated chordal inversions (here of an A major chord with a lowered second) are also typical, lending a decidedly improvisational character. This octatonic scale with its permutations is similar to Messiaen's second mode of limited transposition and became a trademark for Langlais's harmonic language. Chords with added nonharmonic tones—second, sixths, and fourths—are common in both works, as well as parallel motion using seventh, ninth, and eleventh chords.

Trois paraphrases grégoriennes was premiered by the composer at the home of Madame Suzanne Flersheim, a wealthy Jewish patroness of the arts. During the early 1930s, few recitals were given in churches or concert halls. House organs were not in great supply, but such affluent music lovers as Madame Flersheim, Madame Schildge-Bianchini, and Count Christian de Berthier held recitals in their homes. Marchal often arranged these concerts by promising young organists.

Vingt-quatre pièces

Between 1933 and 1939 Langlais experimented with compositions in various genres, some of which he later transcribed for other instruments. He wrote only one collection of organ pieces during this period: *Vingt-quatre pièces* "for organ or harmonium," commissioned by Hérelle for *Musique d'Église*, its house journal. This magazine, published from 1922 to 1939, was divided into three sections: text, chant, and pieces for harmonium. As stated in Pope Pius X's *Motu proprio* of 1903, its purpose was to promulgate the use of sacred music in parish churches. In keeping with this idea, the commission stipulated a series of twenty-four short, easy pieces in all major and minor keys. Other composers—Maleingreau, Benoit, Raugel, Potiron, and Fleury—had contributed similar pieces to the journal. Franck in *L'organiste* (1890) and Boëllmann in *Heures mystiques* (1896) provided more pedestrian models, as did Vierne more promisingly in his *Vingt-quatre pièces* (1919). Many of Langlais's pieces were modeled after Vierne's and reflect similar styles, moods, harmonies, and registrations.

Some approximate dates of composition can be surmised based on correspondence; Langlais premiered several of the pieces, and newspaper reviews of these recitals help to date others. While Pierre

Litaize (standing at left, in glasses), mustachioed Marchal (center), and Langlais, chez Madame Flersheim, 1934

Denis was serving in the army in 1939, Langlais sent him a manuscript copy of number fourteen, "Allegro," before it was published. "Fantaisie sur un thème norvégien," number eighteen, is based on a theme which Jo Sandwick, the person to whom the piece is dedicated, sent to Langlais in a letter dated 9 July 1939. From this scattered evidence, it would appear that numbers one through five were composed between 1933 and 1935, numbers nine and thirteen in 1935, and numbers fourteen through twenty-four in 1939.[15] Consequently, Langlais composed most of the first set in 1935 and 1936 and the last set (with the exception of number thirteen) in 1939.

Vingt-quatre pièces was published in two volumes, in 1939 and 1942. The many dedications to schoolmates and students at the Institute and Conservatory are a symbolic mosaic of Langlais's activities and friendships at this time; although he was now a young married teacher, his close circle of friends still centered on persons he had known while a student. Others were dedicated to priests and friends (interestingly enough, many of whom were pharmacists) whom he especially admired, both from Paris and Rodez in southern France. Langlais particularly remembered Julien Bertault, who often accompanied him on Sundays to hear Marchal at Saint-Germain-des-Près and Tournemire at Sainte-Clotilde.

In *Vingt-quatre pièces* Langlais uses such advanced contrapuntal devices as inverted and retrograde canons. Despite the small scale (the average length is two minutes), he likewise uses a variety of forms: variation, fugue, bipartite dance, sonata-allegro, chorale prelude, Gregorian paraphrase, A B A, and arch form. Registrational color is varied and imaginative. The works include elements that remained an integral part of his compositional technique, as shown in the following list.

1. Modality and post-Romantic harmony, typical of Franck and Fauré and demonstrated by many seventh chords, the raised fourth scale degrees, and shifts of tonal centers by thirds:

Vingt-quatre pièces, vol. 1, no. 2, "Hommage," p. 3, mm. 11–16. © 1939 Editions Combre, Paris. Used by permission.

2. Rapid shifts to unrelated keys:

Vingt-quatre pièces, vol. 1, no. 1, "Prélude modal," p. 2, mm. 3–9. © 1939
Editions Combre, Paris. Used by permission.

3. Octave doublings:

Vingt-quatre pièces, vol. 1, no. 10, "Toccata," p. 12, mm. 1–7. © 1939
Editions Combre, Paris. Used by permission.

4. Chromaticism:

Vingt-quatre pièces, vol. 1, no. 9, "Scherzetto," p. 24, mm. 13–16. © 1939 Editions Combre, Paris. Used by permission.

5. Organum-like use of parallel fifths:

Vingt-quatre pièces, vol. 2, no. 15, "Prière," p. 9, mm. 1–6. © 1943 Editions Combre, Paris. Used by permission.

6. Free meter:

Vingt-quatre pièces, vol. 1, no. 12, "Hommage à Fr. Landino," p. 29, mm. 1–7. © 1939 Editions Combre, Paris. Used by permission.

7. Toccata figures with parallel repeated chords in step-wise motion, and toccata figures with sixteenth notes divided between the hands:

Vingt-quatre pièces, vol. 2, no. 21, "Fantaisie," p. 23, mm. 1–6. © 1943 Editions Combre, Paris. Used by permission.

8. Parallel motion using step-wise motion in one or more voices within a sustained chord:

Vingt-quatre pièces, vol. 1, no. 3, "Arabesque," p. 5, mm. 1–8. © 1939 Editions Combre, Paris. Used by permission.

9. Use of modality, especially Lydian with raised fourth degree:

Vingt-quatre pièces, vol. 2, no. 19, "Prélude et fuguette," p. 19, mm. 1–8. © 1943 Editions Combre, Paris. Used by permission.

Composition: Paul Dukas

Confident in his first published pieces for voice and organ, Langlais next set his heart on studying with Paul Dukas, one of the Conservatory's leading teachers of composition, so as to master the techniques of writing for orchestral instruments. Dukas was one of the most demanding and authoritarian teachers in Paris, a teacher who had little use for students who were not sure of themselves. His reputation caused many students, including Litaize and Reboulot, to fear studying with him. Langlais did not wish to be a regular student, burdened with the pressures of examinations; therefore, in the fall of 1933, he requested admittance into Dukas's class at the Conservatory as an auditor.

For the audition, Langlais played from his copy of "Mors et resurrectio," on the piano, with Dukas playing the bass part. Dukas was impressed: "My friend, I have nothing to teach you. You are a born composer. I can teach you only to orchestrate. A prize in composition won't hurt you." Dukas found only one mistake in the piece, and Langlais bravely offered that he would have it corrected for the second edition. "Second edition!" snorted Dukas. "I have never seen a second edition of organ music." Little did he know that the future would bring Langlais many second editions.

But Jean had missed by one day the deadline for taking the entrance exam, so the disappointed Dukas obtained permission from the director of the Conservatory to have Langlais enter the class as a regular student. For the young composer, it was a tremendous compliment to have such a great composer and teacher place immediate confidence in him.

This class posed a greater struggle for Langlais than the class in fugue, since Dukas expected an assignment in orchestration each week. Moreover, Langlais was no longer only a student but had full-time teaching responsibilities at the Institute. Although Langlais brought ten pages of orchestration the next week, his first assignment was wanting: "Dukas read each measure and told what was wrong—everything. First, the clarinet was not good, the flute part was poor, the cello part was too high, the double bass was too low, and the trumpet part was poorly written." Langlais had read the treatises on orchestration by Widor and Berlioz; Dukas used Gevaert's, which he had also studied, but apparently studying text-books on orchestration was very different from writing for orchestra. Langlais lacked technical knowledge of the ranges and quality of each instrument in question. These ten pages, which he would keep among his sketches, were the opening of an original piece and are similar to the opening of *La voix du vent*, a work for orchestra, chorus, and soprano soloist, composed in 1934.

For the first exam, in January 1934, Langlais presented his *Deux chansons de Clément Marot*, with four of his friends singing the parts a cappella. Not knowing the rules, which specified that the exam piece be unpublished, Langlais gave copies to the members of the jury—who were unable to get their own compositions published! They almost refused to judge the work. Dukas, who did not know it had been published, regretted having permitted him to enter it.

Dukas suggested that Langlais orchestrate two of his earlier works, one loud and the other a contrasting, soft piece. More careful now, Langlais brought to the next class only four measures with thirty-one lines for each measure. This time Dukas changed nothing. In June 1934 Langlais received a second prize in composition for these orchestral versions, *Hymne d'action de grâces 'Te Deum'* (*Trois paraphrases grégoriennes*) and *L'essai sur l'évangile de Noël* (*Poèmes évangéliques*, "La Nativité").[16] In 1938 Langlais performed both works in Paris with favorable reviews.[17]

In late 1934 Langlais transcribed two other works from *Vingt-quatre pièces* ("Fuguette" and "Scherzetto") as the concluding move-ments of the four-movement *Suite brève* for flute, violin, and viola. The first movement he called "Prélude blanc"; he said the sonority reminded him of the color white—one of the few instances in which he appeared to have a sense for color, or rather the absence of it, and to find its counterpart in a musical texture. The first movement contrasts the timbres of the three instruments, in exact imitation, at the octave of the five-measure iambic theme. This melody is then embellished a fourth higher with double stops in the viola, which gives an added richness. The second movement, "Guirlandes," is equally contrapuntal; its contrasting short and long phrases are like intertwining garlands that weave short points of dissonance throughout. Early in 1935, Langlais orchestrated two movements from his *Suite bretonne*, originally written for piano four-hands, as

Cloches de deuil; he did so in memory of an aunt who was a nun and with whom he had been close.

Langlais found his fellow students in Dukas's class interesting and stimulating. Among them were Jehan Alain, Tony Aubain, Félicien Wolff, Pierre Maillard-Verger, Pierre Auclair, Joaquín Nin-Cumell, and Jean Hubeau; Elsa Barraine, Messiaen, and Duruflé continued to study composition at the Conservatory although they already held prizes in it.

Paul Dukas (first row, third from the left) and his class, 1934

Langlais's friendship with Messiaen deepened during 1933 and 1934. Every Wednesday from five to nine in the evening he would go by himself, as he was proud to say, to Messiaen's apartment on rue des Plantes, near Saint-Pierre-de-Montrouge. There Messiaen played through quantities of scores for him on the piano, such as Ravel's *Ma mère l'oye* and Dukas's *Sorcerer's Apprentice*. Messiaen would first play the brass parts, then the woodwinds, then the strings, and finally the ensemble—a painstaking process, but one that helped Langlais immeasurably. An undated letter from Messiaen carefully explains how to write for French horns.

> Dear friend, you know that the four horns are always written in F crossing so: with four horns in F playing the chord in C major. I have written from the bass to the treble without accounting for the tessituras which I have given in the musical example. You copy them separately as one writes them in the score, that is to say, first and second, and third and fourth together. (Of course each is copied on a different line.) I think that my explanation is sufficiently clear?

Langlais wanted to give him a present or some other token of gratitude, but Messiaen refused, saying that he would happily repeat the sessions all over again if necessary. (Langlais did take Messiaen's brother Alain as an organ student. Although a fine poet, Alain was a difficult student.) Langlais called Messiaen "the great maker" of his sense for orchestration.

Dukas's influence went far beyond orchestration: he imparted a fresh understanding of music in general and had a special way of explaining what was unique in each composer. In explaining Beethoven's sometimes over-long development sections, for example, Dukas said that Beethoven had forgotten his hat and unfortunately came back to look for it. Dukas's modesty, like Mahaut's, also made a lasting impression on his young disciple. One day the students excitedly told Dukas that they had just heard his *Sorcerer's Apprentice* marvelously performed at the Concerts de Colonne—had he heard it? "Oh no," Dukas replied, "it has been a very long time since I was able to listen to that."

One day in class, Dukas asked how many of the students had already heard their works played by an orchestra. Langlais said that he had, thinking of a recent performance of *La voix du vent* in Rennes, that he himself had conducted. Dukas asked whether Langlais thought it had sounded better or worse than he thought it would and whether he had been at all surprised. Langlais, sure of himself, answered that he had not been at all surprised because it was exactly what he thought it would be, to which Dukas responded, "Then my friend, it is because you know how to orchestrate." Indeed, Langlais was on friendly terms with Dukas. Dukas had a very large library of books and scores, which he offered to lend to Langlais at any time— a privilege he did not extend to the other students. Dukas's praise for his music convinced Langlais that the comment Dukas had made at their first meeting was true: he was a born composer.

Dukas believed a composer should continually change his style and find something new to say, to keep himself fresh and innovative. Forms that had been brought to perfection by earlier composers were to be avoided, for fear of creating a pastiche. This is one reason Langlais wrote few fugues; he believed that Bach had exhausted both the fugue and the passacaglia, and that no one could improve on what Bach had done. Instead, it was better to find new forms and to renovate old forms into fresh ones. This attitude was Dukas's most important legacy to Langlais.

Humilis

On 17 May 1935 Paul Dukas died. Though he was seventy, his death was completely unexpected and came as a shock to Langlais, whose initial response was to type a three-page eulogy, which remained unpublished.

> None of us had the premonition of such a brutal and sudden end, as he had remained young and vivacious; the passing years had not seemed to have had the slightest influence on the unbelievable intellectual lucidity and the powerful moral strength of this great man. His last class, which took place at the Conservatory on 15 May, was as brilliant as his earlier ones. Two days later, after a terrible coughing bout, Paul Dukas left us. His death puts all those for whom music is a way of life in the ranks of the most sad spiritual orphans.[18]

Three days after Dukas's death, Dupré played twelve Bach chorales during the cremation; Langlais kept the program.

In the fall of 1935, Langlais found a more profound response to the death of Dukas in composing and dedicating to his memory *Humilis*, six untitled pieces for treble voice and piano based on a text by the contemporary symbolist poet Pierre-Jean Jouve (1887–1976). He had shared some of these verses with Dukas before his death; Dukas had not understood them and asked Langlais if he had written them. Both Langlais and Jeannette knew Jouve's writings and admired his spirituality (he was a convert to Roman Catholicism), his use of symbolism, and his graphic use of poetic images dealing with loss, despair, death, blindness, and eternity. Langlais chose six verses from Jouve's 1926 collection *Nouvelles noces*. "Humilis" was Jouve's title for them; to Langlais they were "meditations on the search for God in the spirit of humility: God in space, God in love, in Man's imagination, and in voluntary deprivation. . . . We are so small that we cannot even say His name."[19]

Although the pieces are very short, with no development (the total performance time is eight minutes), all six express the pathos of Jouve's texts, with monosyllabic simplicity of vocal line. Images of eternity and grief permeate both text and music. When Jouve heard the work, he told Langlais that the second piece reminded him of a Gregorian chant in two parts; its very slow and sustained single-line accompaniment is built around a tritone ostinato, enhancing the idea of nothingness. The fourth piece, the most personal of the six, refers to Langlais's blindness as well as to the image of blindness as ignorance of God: to know God fully, one must first die.

> I weep, I cannot speak, I am afraid of lying.
> O kill me for this despicable blindness
> This noise of life lodging in my stomach
> Lord, I must die before beholding You.[20]

The accompaniment—deep, dissonant chords and a rhythmic triplet figure and ostinato based on the notes of E, F-sharp, B-flat—is symbolic of grief.

The image of blindness recurs in the sixth piece, which portrays the transition of the body to death. Somber connected chords in the

Humilis, no. 4, mm. 1–6

low register reflect the darkness of this endless night, befitting his grief over Dukas's passing and the pathos of the poem.

> Having renounced vision, and darkest night
> The hand's vain servitudes, the heart's blood
> The mouth's bloody blot of beauty
> And the words neither relic nor eternal
> The Tree saves itself in letting its leaves fall.
> Stripped, alone, the heart is known.

The first public performance of *Humilis* was on 12 January 1936 at the Société Nationale, with Suzanne Greuet-Marchal singing soprano, accompanied by Langlais. Messiaen was in the audience and greeted the work with enthusiasm. (Langlais recalled this vividly, even years later; he had no memory of its first private performance, with soprano Guelfuocci-Auer, on 31 May 1935.)

Humilis, no. 6, mm. 1–8

Summer Vacations

Each July the Langlaises traveled to Brittany to visit Jean's family, relatives, and friends, especially Father Vigour, whom Jean had known earlier at Saint-Vincent's in Rennes. Father Vigour spent each summer in La Richardais on the Rance River, near Saint-Malo, with the Costards, a doctor and his wife, who owned a beautiful villa not far from the beach. This spacious nineteenth-century home, of white stucco with traditional dark green shutters, was typical of Brittany's wealthy residences. In the dining room, with its massive carved Breton furniture, hung several of Jeannette's paintings. The Bigours, a mother and her daughter, Marie, tended the large kitchen. Langlais was particularly taken with Marie and frequently spoke of her: "I know a young girl who was blind, deaf, and paralyzed—she was cured after a visit to the shrine at Lourdes. I have not gone to Lourdes hoping for a cure. I have had such a privilege to be a musician, composer, and teacher, I do not wish to change anything in my life."

Jean and Jeannette loved this part of Brittany so much that they bought a narrow, corner stone row house at 9 rue du Suet, not far from the Costards. (In 1997 this street was renamed rue Jean Langlais.) It had one large room on the main floor with the kitchen at the rear and a front staircase leading to two bedrooms upstairs. An old upright pedal piano stood to the right of the entrance; Jean practiced on it and for a time gave piano lessons to a young girl who lived next door. There was no bath and only one sink for bathing and cooking. They furnished the house with native Breton furniture and planted a small garden. At the back of the property was a small garage, where they later added a bath.

Jean was not much of a holiday maker. One hot summer day, they decided to pack a picnic lunch and spend part of the day at the beach. They loaded the food and gear together and finally got it all unpacked on the beach. Everyone settled down to enjoy the sun and go swimming. But Langlais never learned to swim and did not particularly like the water; soon after they arrived, he suggested that it was time to go home.

Each August they traveled to Escalquens, where Jeannette's relatives owned a farm. The Sartre home was a simple row house in the full sun with many flowers. The church had a Gonzalez organ on which Langlais gave a recital each summer. Jean enjoyed his wife's parents and this sunny region of France, so different from Brittany. He loved its wine and the outgoing, happy spirit of the people. Its unique and difficult language, the Langue d'Oc, fascinated him, and he learned to speak it so that he could converse and tell jokes with

Jeannette's large extended family. He soon became interested in the region's folklore and folk songs, many of which later found their way into his music. What he learned here made it easier for him to relate to students from the south of France.

In the summer of 1935 he composed his first mass, *Messe pour deux voix*, for the parish choir of Escalquens. It was first performed there in September, with Langlais at the harmonium. Perhaps hearing that choir struggle to sing masses was his first inspiration to help small congregations; in any case, Mahaut would have been pleased that, as usual, he had used each moment creatively, even while on vacation. The mass appears to have been written rapidly and with great simplicity of both melodic line and accompaniment. It includes a motif from the bells of the small church, which he later used for an extended work in memory of Jeannette.

Janine Langlais

Since the death of their first child, Jean and Jeannette had tried without success to have another. Not wishing to remain childless, they decided to adopt a baby, and in March 1936, five-month-old Janine came into their lives. As usual in such cases, the child arrived without personal history. And as conscientious Catholic parents, the Langlaises' first concern was that she be baptized. At her baptism the priest had to use a new formula for children whose baptism was in question since, as Langlais ever emphasized, one cannot be baptized twice. A letter from Tournemire dated 28 March 1936 shared the young couple's joy.

> Mon cher ami, bravo. That is worth more than two symphonies *even for the organ*! A child is the most beautiful "symphony" that can be found in the world. I imagine that the family celebration must have been quite happy, especially with a godfather of Litaize's temperament. . . . Mme. Tournemire and I send *our best wishes* to you as well as to Madame.

This adorable little girl with brown hair and brown eyes brought much joy to their home. One day when Langlais came home for lunch from the Institute, she took her first steps walking toward him; both her parents always remembered that day with great pleasure. Langlais presented *Légende de Saint-Nicolas*, first improvised for a 1937 radio broadcast, as a Christmas gift to little Janine that year.

Tenure

As part of his application for tenure at the Institute for the Blind, Langlais was required to write a treatise on teaching blind students (see Appendix B). This short, undated study is not a method but rather a collection of ideas that elucidates his own teaching style. Records from the Institute state that a written exam was administered on 9 February 1939 and that an oral exam was given on 25 February by Valtou, the director of the Institute, Noël Gallon, Marcel Dupré, Rémy Clavers, and Soula, supervisor of the Institute. Langlais was awarded the tenured position of professor of musical teaching on 3 June 1939; unfortunately, despite his recollection to the contrary, the Institute has no record of the treatise as being part of the process.

Orchestral Works 1936–1939

The happiness of Langlais's marriage found its musical expression in *Pièce en forme libre* for string quartet and organ, composed in the fall of 1935. It was the first piece he dedicated to Jeannette, and "Quintette," as he first called it, remained one of his favorite works and, in his estimation, one of his best. When it was published in 1960, by H. W. Gray (now Belwin Mills), Langlais gave it a new title: *Piece in Free Form*. In 1984 Combre republished it as *Pièce en forme libre*. Its first title hints only at the number of instruments involved; the final title points to the form of the piece, suggesting the form of the improvised thème libre. Langlais had a clear mental image of the work before rapidly composing it: "I wrote this piece exactly as I wished it to sound. . . . The music came to me by itself; I did not need to search."

The work is loosely based on one theme with a development and recapitulation. The "free" aspect of the title, however, is more significant: here Langlais puts into action Tournemire's lesson in improvising a Gregorian paraphrase. This dramatic form allows for great contrasts of emotion and color from subito *pianissimo* to long crescendos, from sustained lyrical polyphony at the beginning and end to rapid staccato alternations between the organ and strings. The crescendos are controlled by use of fugal entries and imitation in the organ part.

Langlais arranged *Pièce en forme libre* as the first movement of a longer work, *Pièce symphonique*, in 1937. For the second movement, he made an arrangement for brass and organ of "Toccata" from *Vingt-quatre pièces*. The third movement is a theme and variations over a fifteen-measure ground bass. In 1938 he entered this last movement, "Thème, variations et final," as a separate work for organ, string orchestra, trumpets, and trombones in the composition contest sponsored by Les Amis de l'Orgue. Langlais played an orchestral reduction on the piano with Maurice Béché; André Fleury played the organ part. It was the only work submitted, but he nevertheless was awarded two thousand francs for it.

In 1936 the cellist Maurice Maréchal commissioned Langlais to write a concerto for cello and orchestra. *Suite concertante* was his first full-scale work for full orchestra (duration 25:00), scored for flute, clarinets, bassoon, horns, strings, and percussion. His command of orchestration is evident throughout, and the cello cadenzas show a thorough understanding of the cello's technical possibilities. The first of the four movements, the Adagio sostenuto, is an arrangement of "Prière pour les morts" (*Vingt-quatre pièces*). The same year he arranged the first two movements as *Symphonie concertante* for piano and orchestra, replacing some of the idiomatic cello figures with more extended pianistic flourishes.

Two other works for piano, *Mouvement perpétuel*, written in 1936 and *Suite armoricaine*, written in 1938, both evoke the sea. *Mouvement perpétuel*, a brilliant cascade of incessant scale figurations, was commissioned by the virtuoso pianist Ida Périn, who played the premiere on 27 April 1944 at the Association Valentin Haüy. *Suite armoricaine* is dedicated to his doctor from Brittany, Stanislas de Sèze; its pieces have picturesque titles, like those bestowed by Erik Satie (whom Langlais greatly admired), such as "Épitaphe pour les marins qui n'ont pas eu de tombe" (Epitaph for sailors who have no grave) and "Conciliabule chez les mouettes" (Secret meeting at the seagulls' habitat). Perhaps while bored at a beach picnic, his mind was already turning over themes and contrasting moods for these whimsical pieces. Their original melodies are all modal, like Breton folk songs;

only in the last movement does one find a polytonal play of staccato chords between the white and black keys, like the chatter of excited seagulls. Pleased with the *Suite armoricaine*, he orchestrated the first movement as the *Suite bretonne* for string ensemble, which he premiered on 21 December 1938 at the Institute.

Death of Louis Vierne

On 2 June 1937, Louis Vierne died of a heart attack during a performance at Notre-Dame. His death was a particularly public event. He was playing before a large audience, in a recital sponsored by Les Amis de l'Orgue. He had just finished his *Triptyque* when all at once his left foot hung on to a low pedal E. A dissonant chord echoed through the nave. Langlais remembered an immediate rumbling from the large crowd, which sensed something terrible had happened. Every Parisian organist present feared the worst: this great musician—whom the clergy of the cathedral had forbidden to give further public recitals at Notre-Dame—had died. At last Maurice Duruflé quieted the pandemonium by courageously finishing the recital before a stunned audience.

Langlais felt the loss intensely. He could not bring himself to visit Vierne's grave until 1978, on which occasion he was accompanied by his student Pierre Whalon:

> The pressed concrete gravestone was hard and the writing faded. Jean Langlais talked a lot about Vierne and made out the letters on the tombstone with his fingers. He said, "Ah, it was stupid for me not to have come." He seemed to be talking to Vierne. Then he told the story of when Vierne was laid out in the cathedral, students kept vigil. He spoke of how one could confide in Vierne even though Vierne often exaggerated things. Then he swallowed hard and reproached himself again for not having come to visit his grave sooner.[21]

With Vierne's death, a number of Parisian organists, including Langlais, applied for the position at Notre-Dame. Les Amis de l'Orgue tried to convince the clergy that Vierne's successor should be an artist worthy of his tradition and that the decision should be made only after a competition. In 1900 Vierne himself had been appointed as a result of a competition, and he had requested that his successor be chosen in this same way. A petition was signed by the leading Parisian organists and other musicians. Unfortunately, the clergy appointed Vierne's assistant, Léonce de Saint-Martin.

The Sainte-Clotilde Promise

In June 1939 Tournemire fell ill following a prostate operation. On 14 June he called Langlais and Jeannette to his apartment. Langlais told him that it would be very difficult, for they would have to find someone to care for three-year-old Janine at the last minute. Tournemire was adamant, and so the couple arrived at his apartment, not knowing what to expect. Tournemire then announced that he wished Langlais to be his successor and that he intended to put this stipulation in his will: "I have just been operated on. I have seen death very near, and I have realized that one thing is very close to my heart before my death—my succession at Sainte-Clotilde." Langlais was shocked. "But I do not feel capable of succeeding Charles Tournemire!" Tournemire answered with annoyance, "So, I don't know anything!" Langlais finally babbled something that resembled an acceptance, and Tournemire declared, "What I have just said to you must remain secret until my death; then you will find this wish expressed in writing."[22]

Tournemire died the following November, but it would be six years before his wish would be fulfilled and Langlais gained the coveted post. In the interim all France would be changed by the menace of Nazi Germany.

CHAPTER 5

War Years 1940–1945

Victory at all costs, victory in spite of terror, victory however long and hard the road may be; for without victory there is no survival.

Winston Churchill

Tournemire died in November 1939, four months after his meeting with Langlais. The mystery surrounding his death—ostensibly the result of drowning in the Arcachon Bay near his country home near Bordeaux—remains unsolved. On 1 November he had gone for a walk, but his body was not found until 3 November. He was buried in Arcachon on 5 November without a funeral, the same day the death certificate and burial permit were issued.[1] Alice Espir Tournemire, his second wife, claimed that no funeral took place because the war necessitated her hasty return to Paris, and that, had the church not been closed, she would have arranged a fitting ceremony at Sainte-Clotilde.[2] Suicide? Simple drowning? Rumors circulated long after his death but nothing was ever confirmed, adding to Langlais's sense of tragedy. Not only was his world turned upside down by this unexplained death, but with it came the fear of the advancing Nazi armies, who had already invaded Poland.

Ten years later Langlais wrote:

On 4 November 1939, the news of Charles Tournemire's death struck the musical world. It was then, the day of his feast, that this great master, whose message was so in advance of our conception of art, left us. But thanks to his work, he lives. . . . He erected a monument, a religious and artistic summation, in his *L'orgue mystique*, which makes him one of the greatest servants of Christian art and even of art in general. Such an anniversary

105

must deeply grieve all who are attached to Sainte-Clotilde, which he served with passion, and with a feeling so common to many great men, that of not being understood except by a small number of devotees.[3]

The Promise Withheld

Much to Langlais's consternation, Madame Tournemire, who had been present at the meeting with her husband and the Langlaises, refused to acknowledge Tournemire's verbal codicil. Langlais never knew whether Tournemire actually put this request in his will, as he had promised; Madame Tournemire insisted that he left no mention of it. The moody Tournemire could easily have changed his mind or could equally have added a note, which was either set aside intentionally or lost by mistake.

It thus became a question of Langlais's word against that of Madame Tournemire, whom Langlais found to be deceitful and manipulative. Although her husband's lengthy correspondence with Langlais showed a close bond, she reported to mutual friends that Tournemire scarcely knew Langlais. That she should be in a place to prevent Langlais from succeeding to the position he had worked for and been promised seemed to him a terrible injustice, and it rankled long after the event. She, in turn, was put off by his rough manners, such as his speaking to her while smoking.[4]

A competition was scheduled shortly after Tournemire's death. Marchal, Reboulot, Duruflé, and several others wanted the position, but under the circumstances, withdrew their applications, leaving Langlais as the sole candidate. Then Norbert Dufourcq and Marchal, who were on close terms with the pastor, Canon Verdier, convinced him to cancel the competition on the premise that it was unfair to have it with only one candidate.

Losing Sainte-Clotilde was far more than a professional disappointment; it was a personal injustice that separated Langlais from old colleagues and tested his faith in the hierarchy of the Church. He did not take the defeat quietly, but spoke openly about it to everyone he knew. Langlais was infuriated that both Marchal and Dufourcq, as well as Madame Tournemire, had placed themselves against him; his sense of betrayal was intense, and his bitterness toward Marchal over the incident marked the end of their mentor-pupil relationship.

Tournemire had favored organists who consistently played chant-based music, which he equated with sacred music, rather than symphonic or programmatic secular music. He considered Marchal a secular organist and therefore unchristian; other fine organists, such as Vierne and Widor, also fell short of Tournemire's narrow ideal of an organist, whom he saw embodied in Langlais. "To my great joy, you are attracted by religious music, *the only music*. . . . All music, as beautiful as it may be, if it does not praise God, is totally useless."[5] At another time he repeated these convictions to Langlais. "All music that does not have as its basis the glorification of God is useless." "But Debussy, Ravel, or Bartók?" was Langlais's rejoinder. "Useless."[6]

In the fall of 1940, without a competition, Canon Verdier appointed Joseph Ermend-Bonnal (1880–1944) organist of Sainte-Clotilde. A student of both Tournemire and Vierne, Ermend-Bonnal had been director of the École de Musique and organist of Saint-André in Bayonne. He was, like Charles Tournemire, a native of Bordeaux. Obviously he no more fit Tournemire's idea of a religious organist than Widor or Vierne. His organ compositions are generally secular; one exception was his *Symphonie d'après media vita*, which won the 1932 composition competition of Les Amis de l'Orgue.

Marchal denied having anything to do with Ermend-Bonnal's appointment and years later expressed surprise at Langlais's hurt:

> I have never understood why Langlais has never wanted to tell the truth, [which] is very simple. We all know it. At the death of Tournemire (he says it is the fault of Madame Tournemire), they named Ermend-Bonnal, and Ermend-Bonnal was organist at Sainte-Clotilde until his death in 1944. He was a good musician. He was not partial. On the contrary, he said one day, "I saw Langlais. I don't know why Langlais pretends to take the direct succession of Tournemire." There you have it. . . . [Ermend-Bonnal] was appointed as Langlais was afterward.[7]

Despite his official appointment, Ermend-Bonnal rarely played for services at Sainte-Clotilde. While the Germans occupied Paris, from 1940 to 1945, the organ was not used because the sanctuary was unheated. At the end of the war, another competition was announced, and again Langlais was the only candidate. This time, however, he was appointed without a competition by the archbishop of Paris and the pastor of Sainte-Clotilde.

German Invasion and Occupation

The French were weary of war, still reeling from the heavy casualties suffered in the Franco-Prussian War and World War I. Yet by August 1939 five million men had been called up—practically every man from the ages of twenty to forty-nine. Langlais and his family extended their vacation stay at the home of Jeannette's family, in Escalquens, until the Institute reopened at 5 rue Duroc, a neighboring building that housed the Association Valentin Haüy, in December 1939.

In April and May 1940, Germany invaded Denmark, Norway, the Netherlands, and Luxembourg, and the French saw they did not have long to wait. Messiaen, who was among those drafted, wrote to Langlais from Verdun, near the German border, that he had at last been assigned to the music and theater center there.

> Take note of my new address. This address—which is permanent—(after two changes of corps) shows you that my troubles are over, at least in part. For even if I am making music, I am still separated from my wife and my little Pascal, separated from my composing and all that makes my rainbow. Thank you for all that you have done for me, thank you! . . . I find myself *to be better* here; in spite of the inconveniences of military life.[8]

Three months later Messiaen was captured and sent to a concentration camp in Görlitz, Silesia, where he was held until 1942.

On 5 June 1940 the Germans attacked along a hundred-mile front northwest of Paris from Laon to the English Channel and, by avoiding fortifications to the east, quickly overcame the French forces. From there they marched toward Paris. When they arrived on 14 June, however, there was little to occupy—the city was almost deserted. Most Parisians had fled to the unoccupied south. By 16 June, the French cabinet had voted for an armistice, which was signed 22 June. Within less than a month, German troops occupied more than half of the country, including much of the north and the entire Atlantic coast. Parts of the south and Brittany still remained free.

A heavy toll was exacted on the French population physically and morally. The ordeal of the German Occupation, the Resistance movements, the settling of accounts at the time of the Liberation, and the birth of the Fourth Republic—all these events added up to one tremendous, traumatic experience, one that has had deep and pervasive impact on today's France.[9]

Writers and musicians found themselves at the cultural center of the nation, representing the people's voice. Whether in armies, concentration camps, Resistance movements, or more comfortably in exile, it was the artist that assumed the position of moral authority. The old order was finished, and new writers such as Sartre and Camus and poets such as Cayrol, Prévert, and Péguy held the imagination of the French. Langlais experienced intense frustration, partly because his handicap forced him to play a passive role rather than to serve in the military like his friends. But he gradually found his own ways to fight.

Langlais recalled the day "when the Germans came to Paris."[10] He was alone, having sent Jeannette and Janine to La Richardais, and had just arrived to teach his class at the Institute. The director informed him that the school was closed, and the Germans were gaining control of Paris—he was to get out as fast as possible. Fortunately the last train to Brittany was about to leave, and he rushed to the station just in time. Thirty hours later he arrived in Rennes; he then took a bus to Dinard and a taxi thence to La Richardais. Upon arriving at his home, his fears mounted—no one answered his call. He hastened to the Costards where, at last, he found Jeannette and Janine unharmed. They returned to their summer home at 9 rue du Suet.

German officers had already occupied the house next door, separated from theirs only by a common wall, and Langlais could hear the frightening sounds of officers screaming at soldiers—sounds that seemed almost to come from the same room. He did not understand the words, but he long remembered his fear.

The reunited family decided to flee to the south, which German troops had not yet occupied. But their train was blockaded nine miles from Rennes. "This turned out to be our good fortune because there was a bombing in Rennes which caused seven thousand deaths. We could not reach the south. So we went to my parents. Afterward we went back to Paris where we stayed during the entire war."

The Langlaises home on rue du Suet was used by the Germans for the four years of the Occupation. The house was almost destroyed, and the garage was reduced to ashes. The beautiful church was demolished, and the village itself was nearly leveled. But Saint-Malo, Saint-Lô, and many other towns in France fared even worse.

Back in Paris Langlais was among those who stayed briefly at the Institute in order to keep the Germans from taking it over. There were very few students. Many parents were fearful of having their children in Paris during the war, but there were some whose families were still living there, and despite everything, classes as well as liturgies continued at the Institute. One Palm Sunday, Langlais directed the choir while Marchal provided the accompaniment; there were not enough students both to sing and to accompany.

Langlais continued to compose amid the fear and chaos. While students remained at the Institute, in 1940, he wrote a short "Tantum ergo" for eight mixed voices and organ, which the choir sang on 25 June 1942, with Langlais conducting and Litaize accompanying. The accompaniment primarily doubles the voice parts, providing a rich texture for the mildly dissonant modal harmony. This was Langlais's only attempt at eight-part vocal writing. In 1941 and 1942, respectively, he completed the last two of his *Cinq motets*, "O bone Jesu" and "Chant litanique" (on the text "Stella maris, O Maria").

And Langlais continued to perform. In 1941 he performed in Boulogne, Toulouse, Albi, Rodez, Lyon, Nancy, Angers, Nantes, and Bayeux. His friendship with Father Vigour, choirmaster of Saint-Germain in Rennes, permitted him to play a recital there on 15 May 1941. It received a favorable review the same day:

> Jean Langlais, a blind man from La Fontenelle, has become one of the great masters of sacred music. He tells us, "An artist should be an apostle; at least I have always wanted to consider a 'career' as an apostolate; for me it is an honor and a joy to put music to the service of good. There is hardly a greater work than to give a pauper a piece of bread." A blind man said these simple and beautiful words to me during an interview. Behind the

dark glasses, I imagined a deep look which scrutinized me, and suddenly the idea came to me that Providence is always just and good, that in closing the eyes of little Jean Langlais from La Fontenelle, he gave to him the sensitivity of a very great artist. . . . "There will always be artichokes in your music," the Baron of Montrichard said jokingly to Langlais—meaning, "Your music carries a Breton character, and inspiration is always found in it."[11]

In June 1943 Langlais was asked to give a concert at the Palais de Chaillot as part of a recital series that featured his colleagues Duruflé, Fleury, Marchal, and Litaize. Defiantly, he scheduled the *Carillon de Westminster* by Vierne, but the Germans refused to let him play it because of its British connotation. So he put in its place Vierne's *Sur le Rhin*, a long dramatic depiction of the majestic Rhine River—and played the *Carillon de Westminster* as an encore, dangerous as it was to do.

Première symphonie

At the same concert, Langlais also gave the first performance of his *Première symphonie* for organ, composed during 1941 and 1942—a work he later described as "a cruel piece—it is the war itself." In it he found a musical vehicle in which to express the anger, fear, and deprivation that the Parisians experienced during the Occupation. He uses a new and more piercingly dissonant harmonic language than ever before. Together the four movements (Allegro, Eglogue, Choral, and Final) last more than thirty minutes; only *Cinq méditations sur l'apocalypse* (1973) is longer. An unrelenting rhythmic force marks the opening and closing movements, poignantly embodying his sense of outrage. Dufourcq gave the work a mixed review, which greatly displeased Langlais and intensified his animosity. What began as praise—"The logical symmetry of the form in which the two themes, treated in the spirit of Beethoven, maintain a unity of form and savage color"—ended negatively:

> All this is firm, well-considered, and cerebral. But should not music address itself as much to feelings as to the intellect? And if the composer writes a work of pure music for organ, should

111

he forget to move us and to ignore the possibilities that pipes offer him in this domain?[12]

Was it only by chance that in the next paragraph Dufourcq praised Ermend-Bonnal's organ symphony (along with Langlais's *Trois paraphrases grégoriennes* and *Poèmes évangéliques*) as program music which successfully united "the most objective realism to colors, modes, and even plainsong"?

Première symphonie is among Langlais's most innovative and ambitious compositions—innovative in its bolder uses of dissonance, demanding intense concentration of both listener and performer, and ambitious in that the very title implies that more symphonies would follow (in fact only two, and those less important, were to come).

In the Allegro, thirteenth chords with both sharp and natural thirteenths are common, such as the one based on C-sharp with both A-natural and A-sharp. Dissonance is also exploited through polytonality, using an E-flat triad against an E-natural. In the Eglogue, Langlais borrows the second theme from the first movement and transforms it into a quiet pastoral poem. He captures the freedom of the shepherd's melody with an unmetered time signature and a short scherzo, which concludes the movement. The Choral is also innovative: five different sonorities are employed simultaneously, using four manuals and pedal. Langlais was particularly proud of this feat; his fingerings are meticulously written in each part. For the Final, Langlais again borrows from the Allegro; this time it is the first theme that is transformed.

Robert Bernard, who reviewed Langlais's premiere of the work, described the work as "powerful, concentrated, strong, and perfected by the hand of a master. . . . One discovers here a personality, a true poetical nature which is served by a penetrating technique and learned craftsmanship."[13] Once again, significant events in Langlais's life found their expression through his music. "I wrote this work in a complicated style and language because I felt myself in a complicated and tormented world. Attacked from all sides by the war, by injustice, my only manner of fighting was to create a work that represented the sum of everything that I knew in music."[14]

The war years were terrifying. Sometimes the Germans herded a hundred people into the street and killed them. Said Langlais,

"With the Germans, we never knew if we were going to live the next day. With the Germans, one *never* knew what would happen." Langlais's outrage at the injustice of the Occupation showed itself on several occasions. One day on leaving Saint-Pierre-de-Montrouge, someone asked him if he had heard the Berlin Philharmonic the evening before, to which he answered that he had not. When asked why, he responded that he was waiting for the war to be over. He later learned that his indiscretion could have landed him before a firing squad.

Neuf pièces

Langlais's response to the war continued with his *Neuf pièces*, composed in 1942 and 1943. One of them, "Chant héroïque," described the loss of Jehan Alain, who was "killed heroically for France when defending Saumur, in 1940," according to the inscription in the printed score. His death was a blow to Langlais; Alain had come to visit Langlais shortly beforehand and told him that he was not afraid of his motorcycle assignment and was sure he would soon be back in Paris. In "Chant héroïque" Langlais suggests anger and tragedy by means of a pounding triplet figure interrupted, in minor mode, by abbreviated strains of the "Marseillaise." Three other pieces from the collection also reflect the pathos of the war and Langlais's sense of loss: Paul Dukas is commemorated in "Chant de peine," François Vidal in "De profundis," and Charles Tournemire in "Rhapsodie grégorienne." Langlais contrasts the anguish in these pieces with the joy ("Chant de joie") and peace ("Chant de paix") of others.

The Parisian publisher Bornemann commissioned the work, asking Langlais to include pieces based on Lutheran chorales and Gregorian chants. Chorales (Langlais's first use of them) are treated in "Dans une douce joie" ("In dulci jubilo"), "De profundis" ("Aus tiefer Not"), and "Mon âme cherche" ("Herzlich tut mich verlangen"). Chants are treated in "Prélude sur une antienne" ("Vos amici mei estis") and "Rhapsodie grégorienne" ("Sacris solemniis," "Verbum supernum," "Lauda Sion"). This last, which Langlais composed in a single evening, shows a hasty preparation and would haunt him for years for its lesser quality. He would later revise it, but with only questionable success.

Mystère du Vendredi-Saint

In 1943, during the darkest period of the war, Langlais composed *Mystère du Vendredi-Saint*, two short pieces for chorus, strings, and organ. The first, "O crux ave" (Hail, blessed cross), is based on the liturgical text for Good Friday. It begins with a soft, sustained prelude for strings and ends with a *pianissimo* entrance of the chorus. The strings abruptly shatter the sustained low G-sharp minor chord of the choir with piercing, dissonant chords in syncopated rhythms— a more common stylistic device in his later works. The dynamic musical shock here was like the bombardments that marked daily life in Paris during the latter months of the Occupation. The second piece, "Miserere mei, Deus" (subtitled "Déploration") uses the first line of Psalm 50; it had no string parts and so was performed on Good Friday 1943 at Saint-Pierre-de-Montrouge with Gustave Helbig conducting the parish choir and Antoine Reboulot playing the organ accompaniment. Langlais would later borrow his setting of the second phrase of the text ("secundum magnum misericordiam tuam") for *Psaume solennel no. 2*.

Deux offertoires

In 1943 Langlais wrote *Deux offertoires*, a commissioned work for organ; the first piece is in memory of Abel Decaux, organ professor at the Schola Cantorum, the second in memory of Albert Mahaut. Both are based exclusively on ordinary chants from the mass. The first piece is a paraphrase of the chants of the Kyrie, Sanctus, and Agnus Dei from Mass 13, "Stelliferi conditor orbis." The Kyrie chant is combined with both the Sanctus and Agnus Dei chants in a style reminiscent of Jehan Alain. The second piece is a paraphrase of the Kyrie, Sanctus, and Agnus Dei from Mass 5, "Magnae Deus potentiae." Here the Sanctus and Agnus Dei are quoted in their entirety.

During the same year, Langlais composed two vocal works with instrumental and organ accompaniment: "Pie Jesu" and *Trois motets*. In each, the solo voice and choir alternate in singing each phrase of the entire text. Both are expressive, lyrical, and chant-like, their sustained accompaniments in a Romantic vein. They were composed for weddings and other church services for which instrumentalists were likely to be hired. Langlais also composed a short "Ave Maria" for voice, organ, violin, and cello. The work's similarity to "Pie Jesu" suggests it was composed at about the same time. The undated manuscript is not written in the same hand as the "Pie Jesu," and it appears to have been well worn from use. Marked *andante religioso*, both the melody and accompaniment have an artful simplicity typical of Langlais's liturgical style.

Claude Langlais

In 1943 the Langlaises were gladdened as well as concerned by the news of Jeannette's pregnancy. Because of Jeannette's previous difficulty with labor, the doctor decided on a caesarean birth and gave them the option of birth dates between 10 and 17 December. Langlais, who had a penchant for number symbolism, chose 16 December, the birth date of Beethoven, with whom he felt a special musical as well as physical kinship. The delivery of their baby boy, named Claude, went well, and the doctor foresaw no difficulties. And yet what followed was a nightmare of postpartum complications, made worse by wartime privations. For fifty-six days with baby Claude, Jeannette lay immobilized in a hospital near the Gare de l'Est, far from home and often in great pain from the phlebitis she had endured since the death of their first child more than ten years earlier. Every day during this fearful period, Langlais visited her in the hospital. The train he took was stopped without warning and its passengers detained for several hours on more than one occasion.

Langlais was all alone at Christmas that year; a friend had taken eight-year-old Janine. It was terribly cold, and he had neither food nor wood for the fire. Two of his students from the Institute visited on Christmas Eve, around ten-thirty in the evening, bringing along a large log and a bottle of wine. Langlais was embarrassed by their generosity. He decided to take the bottle of wine to Jeannette, knowing she was much worse off than he, and placed it in his briefcase. The next day he found it had been broken by the extreme cold. Despite the hardships, Langlais and Jeannette had a son who would be to them a lasting source of comfort.

Suite concertante

In the midst of the war, Langlais was commissioned to write a duo for violin and cello; he composed it in August and September 1943. The bravura character of the writing, giving the effect of a string orchestra pitted against subito *piano* passages, explains the title, *Suite concertante*. It is a tightly knit, twelve-minute piece in four movements. "Danse rustique" displays a strong passepied character in a dance-like triple meter. "Cantilène," based on an original tune played by the cello, has a simple, folk-like quality, with the violin providing the accompaniment. "Chasse et danse" intersperses a fast 6/8 meter with a slower, syncopated dance in 5/4 meter. The cello begins the last movement slowly, in the low register, with a passacaglia theme that gradually grows in speed, reaching a brilliant arpeggiated end.

The premiere of the work was given by Maurice Maréchal, cello, and François Pollain, violin, at the Salle Rossini in 1943, in a concert sponsored by Le Triptyque, a chamber music society. During the performance, the Allies were bombing Villeneuve-Saint-Georges, where many train lines converge. The performance continued through the deafening explosions. The terror Langlais experienced during the frequent bombings never left him; he was dependent on sleeping pills for the rest of his life.

Parisian musicians were divided over performing for the enemy. Some of them, such as Dupré and Cortot, agreed to play on the German-controlled radio. Those who refused included Langlais, Litaize, and Lazare-Lévy; loyalty to the Resistance won Langlais many commissions to compose orchestral music for radio dramas and invitations to perform on the radio after the war. Those who had collaborated with the Germans during the war were not permitted to play on the radio for several years.

During the last two years of the Occupation, Langlais composed little; his creative forces seem to have been spent, and no doubt sheer exhaustion kept him from producing more. In 1944 he wrote *Trois danses*, for woodwinds, piano, and percussion, and reworked pieces from his *Vingt-quatre pièces* for *Suite pour clavecin*. But the end drew near: the Allies landed on the beaches of Normandy in June 1944 and finally liberated Paris on 25 August.

The Liberation

That so much bombing took place in Brittany intensified Langlais's remembrances. If the details of this one story seemed exaggerated, so did Langlais's memory of them.

> During the fighting in Brittany and Normandy after the Allied invasion on 6 June 1944, in Saint-Malo, a German plane shot down an American plane, killing its American pilot. A Breton nurse was caring for him before he was placed in a coffin in the cemetery. When she had finished preparing his body for burial, she embraced him in the presence of a German general, who asked her why she had done this. She responded that she was doing that in place of his mother, who was in America. The German general then asked her if she would have done the same things if the pilot had been German. But she answered by saying, "No!" The Germans decided to bury the American at five a.m. in hopes that few people would be there, but ten thousand people came, with quantities of flowers. The Germans were so furious that they condemned the men of Saint-Malo to stay at the cemetery next to the grave of the American pilot until all the flowers had died.

This tale grew to epic proportions, like the ancient Breton legends. In the decades that followed, Langlais often repeated it to Americans in order to dispel the notion that the French were anti-American.

Langlais recalled the final weeks before the Liberation, and the day itself, 25 August 1944, vividly. Seeing the world by the church calendar, even in wartime, he found it significant that the Liberation of Paris occurred on the feast of Saint Louis, patron saint of Paris.

> Naturally at that time, life in Paris was terrible. There was no milk for the children. And Claude, who was born in 1943—and this was August 1944—went without milk for eight months. We had no gas, no electricity—nothing to eat. But still we were not dead. I don't know why. . . . [The day of the Liberation] was one of the happiest days of our lives. I went to sit down on a bench on the boulevard des Invalides next to the Duroc metro station, by the Institute. The Germans in their jeeps and tanks passed by almost touching us, and I could have received a gun

shot from a German solider. But I did not think about that even for a minute. I stayed there for perhaps three hours, laughing in front of the Germans about their defeat, showing how happy we were that they were leaving, since they had made us suffer so much. . . . There were other people armed with guns on the rooftops. One man fell from the roof and was killed. Apparently there were French members of the Resistance and some Japanese with them. We never knew exactly who they were. . . .

In any case, after this shameful retreat, de Gaulle said that there would be a "Te Deum" at Notre-Dame Cathedral. I went to Notre-Dame with two friends—two women, since my wife could not go with me because she was taking care of Claude. We had to go by foot since there was no transportation. Arriving at Notre-Dame early, we had a bizarre impression: first, there were no bells, and one side of the cathedral was still occupied by those who had come to sing. The organist, Léonce de Saint-Martin, had not been authorized to go up to the organ. And as soon as de Gaulle entered, actually before he entered, he was fired upon while still outside. While we were entering the cathedral and were in the cathedral, we were also fired upon without ceasing, and we threw ourselves on the floor. In place of the "Te Deum" (all the books say it was a "Te Deum," but it was not) we sang the Magnificat. And it was de Gaulle who sang the Magnificat at the beginning alone, answered by everyone lying on the floor: "et exultavit spiritus meus." And during all this time the gunfire continued. But we sang the entire Magnificat. De Gaulle went out, and he was again fired upon as we were leaving the cathedral. The two women with me told me that they were bringing many people out on stretchers. We didn't know if they were dead or wounded. We went out not wounded, but they continued to fire upon us in the streets from the roofs.

We tried to take the rue de l'Ancienne Comédie, which was very narrow, thinking we would be safe there. But it was terrible—in all the houses they were firing and we could not take it. Then all at once, when we arrived at the store Bon Marché, the firing stopped. I think that the Resistance killed all those who were on the roofs.

The Promise Fulfilled

On 4 November 1945, the sixth anniversary of the news of Tournemire's death, as Langlais had requested, Langlais was formally appointed organist at Sainte-Clotilde. With this appointment came the
fulfillment of a spiritual and musical legacy—the Sainte-Clotilde tradition.[15] Within that tradition, until his retirement in 1988, Langlais
exercised his faith as a servant of the Church during some of its most
abundantly rich years of spiritual, liturgical, and musical growth.
On the twenty-fifth anniversary of his appointment Langlais again
paid tribute to Tournemire:

> Dear Master, for twenty-five years I have gone up to the organ
> loft that César Franck, that you yourself have made famous.
> Not a single Sunday has passed that I have not felt the awesome
> presence of these two great shadows: reason for my fervent
> admiration and my rightful humility.[16]

Langlais at the organ of Sainte-Clotilde, 1946

CHAPTER 6

Sainte-Clotilde 1945–1952

Her grand voice that swells and runs like a breeze, carries the
hymn of nature and humanity to the divine with holy vigor.
Alphonse de Lamartine

In French the general term for organ (*l'orgue*) is masculine and singular, but when it refers to the ensemble of stops, pipes, and console
of a particular organ, it becomes feminine (*les grandes orgues*) and
plural. Grammar, in this case, reflected what for Langlais and other
organists of this church was the emotional truth. His students called
him Maître Langlais, but he would laugh, saying that he always preferred that term in the feminine and often spoke of the organ at
Sainte-Clotilde as his very demanding mistress.[1] At the end of his
life Franck still spoke of "her" ("If you knew how I love her"[2]), and
Tournemire described her as "incomparable."[3] Beginning in 1945
and for the next forty-three years, Maître Langlais too remained
under her spell, almost her slave. He had known her casually while
substituting for Tournemire before the war, but now with the promise fulfilled and his appointment as titular organist at last secured,
she was at last his. Their honeymoon lasted until 1952: before his
American tours, his attention was centered only on her.

This mystical-sexual bond had a long history. The "lady" had
already been the mistress of two significant others: Franck and
Tournemire. As she herself was the servant of Christ, she led men to
Him by the offspring of their love, by the sacred music they improvised and composed through her. Each revered her and renewed
her. The particularly fine acoustics as well as the "lady" of this basilica were central to the musical tradition that grew up within it.

Sainte-Clotilde is on the Left Bank, in the government district
near the Quai d'Orsay, on the site of an earlier church. It was among

The organ at Sainte-Clotilde

The façade of Sainte-Clotilde

many Parisian churches built after the French Revolution to serve a growing affluent, educated, and upperclass congregation. The nave is unusually long and high for the size of this Gothic revival edifice; it was begun in 1846, based on architectural drawings of Franz Christian Gau (1817–1885), and completed in 1857 from the work of his successor, Théodore Ballu. In 1896 the church was designated a basilica.

This church was built with an unusual arrangement of two rear galleries: the larger for the main organ and a smaller choir loft directly below it. There was originally a harmonium without pedals in the choir loft; the bass line was supplied by a string double bass. In 1888 the choir was placed near the main altar, and a small fifteen-stop Merklin electro-pneumatic choir organ enclosed in two cases was installed near the main altar above the choir stalls.[4]

Cavaillé-Coll Organ

In 1859, two years after the completion of the church, *les grandes orgues* were installed. Although the original forty-six-stop Cavaillé-Coll organ was not as large as many, it was among the best examples of his work. It was unusual for Aristide Cavaillé-Coll to have the opportunity to build an instrument for a new building, and this may have inspired him to take special pains in its construction. In 1856 Franck had played in the erecting room of the Cavaillé-Coll work-shop an organ with an identical stop list being built for the cathedral in Carcassone. The specification duplicated that of the Cathedral of Bayonne. After the contract was signed, Franck stipulated eight additional stops: Soubasse 32, Basson 16 in the Pédale; Bourdon 16, Unda maris 8, Flûte octaviante 4, and Clairon 4 on the Positif (or Choir); and Voix céleste 8, and Clairon 4 on the Récit. He was familiar with several of these sonorities from the organ at Saint-Jean–Saint-François; even though these additional stops increased the cost of the organ by forty percent, he requested them for Sainte-Clotilde.[5]

The specifications of this organ with these additions formed the basis for many of Franck's compositions. For example, "Pastorale" and "Fantaisie" (*Six pièces*) call for the Positif Bourdon 16 with the Récit Hautbois coupled; *Grande pièce symphonique* requires the Voix céleste, and Soubasse 32 for a soft repeat of the Andante theme. Other stops, such as the Cromorne, are prominent in the same piece. Even the full Récit acts as a soft accompaniment to the solo Cromorne on the Positif. The Voix humaine and Voix céleste have an ethereal quality, different from those of other Cavaillé-Coll organs.

Franck's organ was known for the clarity of its foundations (even in the suboctave range), the purity of its flutes, and the refined brilliance of its reeds. Duruflé, who shared Langlais's style of interpreting Franck's music, would particularly remember the sound of the Récit:

> The quality of the Récit was something of a miracle. Undoubtedly several technical reasons contributed to this: the dimensions of the swell box; the responsiveness of the shutters; its location at the back of the organ case; the large sonorous space surrounding the box on all sides, giving it an extraordinary resonance; the acoustics of the church; and above all, the genius of the builder. These factors produced a miracle.[6]

Franck, Tournemire, and Langlais had in common certain religious, mystical, and liturgical practices and a veneration of Mary. Though each was imbued with a volatile, fiercely independent temperament, they admired their colleagues and tried to be modest men. They, unlike many Parisian organists for whom the mass and offices were but an excuse to perform concert music, based their music on liturgical texts. They also shared a poetic freedom of interpretation and an extraordinary skill in improvisation, both of which guided their teaching. Tournemire and Langlais each built upon the legacy of Franck and enlarged the scope of his tradition according to their own personalities.

César Franck

César Franck (1822–1890) did not set out to become the quiet leader of a movement that elevated French organ music from a period of extreme decadence to a return to the ideals of Beethoven. A keyboard prodigy, driven by his father, he emigrated with his family from Belgium to Paris. Having obtained a premier prix in fugue from the Paris Conservatory, in 1840, and a premier prix in organ from the class of Benoist, in 1841, he abandoned his pursuit of a career as a concert pianist.

Franck was connected to Beethoven through studies with Anton Reicha, a Czech friend of Beethoven who had been appointed professor of counterpoint at the Conservatory in 1818. Franck's organ compositions, with their contrapuntal integrity and frequent use of canon, show the influence of Reicha's teaching.[7]

In 1848 Franck married one of his students, Félicité Saillot Desmousseaux, whose parents were employed at the Comédie Française. Félicité's passion for opera encouraged Franck to compose for this genre, but he won little success.[8] His main interest and talent lay in orchestral and keyboard composition. After serving as organist at Notre-Dame-de-Lorette and Saint-Jean–Saint-François, he was in 1857 appointed choirmaster and organist at Sainte-Clotilde. Franck's later appointment as professor of organ at the Conservatory, in 1872, enabled him to teach many talented students, including Vierne, Tournemire, Pierné, d'Indy, Chausson, Ropartz, Bordes, Marty, Mahaut, and Boulay.

By the middle of the nineteenth century, most French organ music consisted of marches, programmatic imitations of storms, and transcriptions of piano and vocal music. The popular organist-composers were Édouard Batiste (1820–1876) at Saint-Eustache, and Louis Lefébure-Wély (1817–1869) at La Madeleine and later at Saint-Sulpice. Dufourcq described Wély as "the epitome of banality, triviality and the *style de salon*, who publishes a *scène pastorale* with storm for an inauguration of an organ which could serve as well for a midnight mass!"[9] Others, including Peter Cavallo, Auguste Bazille, Alphonse Schmitt, and Clément Loret, were brilliant improvisors, but their technique was as outstanding as their taste was poor: programmatic effects, such as thunder and bird calls, formed the basis of much of their music.

Franck brought new harmonies and extended length and richness to old forms that his colleagues generally ignored—choral (*Trois chorals*), passacaglia (Choral no. 2), prelude and fugue (*Prélude, fugue et variation*), fantasy (*Fantaisie en ut, Fantaisie en la*), andante (*Cantabile*), and pastorale (*Pastorale*)—and he developed new forms as well, such as the organ symphony (*Grande pièce symphonique*) and symphonic allegro (Final). His artistic use of counterpoint, especially canon, and his poetic melodic sense also surpassed that of his contemporaries.

During his lifetime only a small group of admirers, chiefly his students, appreciated the genius of Franck's music. The generations that followed, however, recognized its value. In our century Dufourcq described Franck's organ music as "rich in beauty and light. The hundred and fifty pages written by Franck for his instrument are far greater than the insipid, bombastic, and superficial ones that for a century had preceded them."[10] Camille Mauclair summed up Franck's contribution thus:

> Franck forms the natural link between Classicism and the polyphony to come. The direct line of descent in pure music had been broken by the descriptive Romanticism of Liszt and Berlioz, and finally by Wagner, whose deviations were marvelous, but dangerous to the destinies of their art. The intervention of Franck, which was at once traditional and innovative, set the wandering feet of a whole generation on the right track, with rare tact and without any reaction.[11]

Still Franck was a great admirer of Liszt, both as a performer and composer; he even borrowed some of his themes. Franck arranged to play a private recital for Liszt at Sainte-Clotilde on 2 February 1867. Arthur Coquard and Henri Duparc had also gone up to the organ loft to hear some of Franck's favorite pieces, including Liszt's *Prelude and Fugue on B.A.C.H.* Franck's playing greatly moved Liszt, as Coquard's letter to a friend describes:

> What a moving hour we have just spent there! He, the great pianist, we saw him join his two bony hands together on bended knee, with his eyes closed and tears streaming down his face. At the end of the variation M. César Franck was in the arms of Abbé Liszt who embraced him enthusiastically exclaiming that he was equal to the master of all, the great Sebastian Bach! In the same rush of excitement, he pulled Henri and me into his arms.[12]

Mysticism, so far removed from this concert piece of Liszt, was at the root of Franck's role as a Roman Catholic organist-composer.

The freedom in his playing and improvisations, as well as his teaching, matched his temperament and religious sensitivity. It was a freedom grounded in technical security and conservatory training under Benoist. According to Mauclair:

> This is what caused this mystic, this visionary of the golden age of music, to be not only the last master of the nineteenth century, but also the one man who could assure the free evolution of the music of the future; the evolution of music itself, which should be neither descriptive, theatrical, nor picturesque, but only psychological, moving the soul and revealing the infinite by the very song of the lyre.[13]

The basis of the Sainte-Clotilde tradition, then, is Roman Catholic mysticism, within its liturgical framework, expressed through lyricism and freedom of interpretation. Franck expressed this mysticism and his veneration of Mary in his Magnificat, published posthumously as *L'organiste, 59 pièces pour harmonium*. On his deathbed, he shared his love for this liturgical work with a Father Gardey from Sainte-Clotilde, who had come to offer him the last rites.

> Ah! that Magnificat! How I loved it! What a number of versicles I have improvised to those beautiful words! I have written down some of them—sixty-three have just been sent to the publisher, but I do want to get up to a hundred. I shall go on with them as soon as I get better—or else . . . perhaps God will let me finish them—in his eternity to come.[14]

Although liturgical, none of Franck's organ music was based on Gregorian chant. In nineteenth-century France, chant melodies, however, were known and used for improvisations and choral arrangements. Franck made his own harmonizations of several hymns and an organ accompaniment of Lambillote's office chant arrangements in 1858. Chant-based improvisation had been part of the Conservatory training since its inception, using the chant as a cantus firmus in whole notes.[15] Robert Lord further explains the liturgical background of the chant at the time of Franck.

> In France the principal mass on Sundays and for special feasts was known as the *Grande messe*. At Sainte-Clotilde, during the

time of César Franck, this mass was celebrated at 9 a.m. The congregation and the choir participated in singing the ordinary and the proper Gregorian chants for the day. Likewise, the organ provided interludes of various lengths. The conventional English term for this service prior to Vatican II was the *high mass*.[16]

Franck's students agreed that his approach to playing, improvising, and teaching displayed an exceptionally free and intuitive approach. In referring to Franck's ability to understand both his craft as well as his student, d'Indy said, "[He] excelled in his power to penetrate his pupils' thoughts and to take possession of them, while scrupulously respecting their individual aptitudes. This is why all musicians formed in his school have acquired a solid science of music, while in their works each has preserved a different and personal apsect."[17] According to Vierne, "Franck was extremely indulgent, and gave me thoughtful criticisms, which caused me to reflect."[18]

Mahaut and Marty—Franck's pupils and Langlais's teachers at the Institute—said that Franck played his works extremely freely: "And now they [the followers of Dupré] play strictly—and they are wrong."[19] As Robert Lord aptly put it: "'The Sainte-Clotilde tradition' then has provided continuity in the preservation of the proper performance style required for Franck's organ works. The key to this interpretation is a freedom and flexibility of rhythm at variance with strict rhythmic discipline fashionable in more modern times."[20]

Franck was known for his modesty, patience, and humility: unlike many other composers, he did not promote his own music. It was his students who organized concerts of his music and who were his greatest advocates. He also had what d'Indy called "the ingenuous sincerity of genius" and was intensely independent. Rather than the pursuit of worldly success, Franck considered the expression of his faith through his art to be his most important mission. In the organ loft at Sainte-Clotilde, he was far from the pettiness of those less gifted and more acclaimed. At each mass, at the consecration, he interrupted his improvisation to leave the organ bench and kneel in a corner of the gallery.[21]

Charles Tournemire

Charles Tournemire (1870–1939) was one of Franck's most gifted and esteemed pupils at the Conservatory. There, in 1891, he received a premier prix in organ. In 1898 he succeeded Gabriel Pierné as organist at Sainte-Clotilde; in 1919, like Franck, he also became a professor at the Conservatory, although not of the organ class as he had hoped, but of chamber music. Tournemire was also a brilliant improvisor and a more prolific composer than his mentor. Since he was not dependent on teaching for his livelihood as was Franck, his circle of students was much smaller.

A few weeks before he died, Franck invited Tournemire to assist him in playing the bass part of his recently composed *Trois chorals* on the piano at his home, an experience Tournemire never forgot. Langlais attached great importance to the fact that Tournemire received the tradition of interpretation of Franck's chorals directly from Franck, because Tournemire was the only person who had this experience. But the tradition of interpretation and improvisation was much more profound than a sight-reading session with a dying composer. Franck and these two disciples shared a mystical and deeply spiritual common bond that permeated their music.

Like Franck, Tournemire also expanded the concept of form as well as the mystical and modal intent in his compositions. Taking both Franck's idea of the choral and the organ symphony, he created a new form, exemplified by his *Symphonie-choral* op. 69 (1935). He was one of the first to use Biblical texts as the basis for works beyond any prescribed form, such as *Trois poèmes* op. 59 and *Sept chorals-poèmes d'orgue pour les sept paroles du Christ* op. 67.

Tournemire's fascination with the Gregorian reforms instituted by the Benedictine monks of Solesmes together with his zeal for reinstating the liturgical role of the organ, led him to embark upon a major organ work, *L'orgue mystique* ops. 56–57 (1928–1932), in the expanded form of a suite. It was originally called *L'orgue glorieux*; the later title indicates more specifically Tournemire's mystical bent. *L'orgue mystique* comprises fifty-one suites of five movements each to accompany appropriate parts of a sung mass, with Gregorian chants taken from the mass and offices of each particular Sunday and feast day. Contrary to what is frequently assumed, *L'orgue mystique* was

Charles Tournemire at Sainte-Clotilde

not composed for use at a spoken mass but for a high or solemn mass. Although it was not played during an actual mass at Sainte-Clotilde, as Tournemire's student Daniel-Lesur explains, the fifty-one offices were written to instruct the faithful in the chant.[22]

Never before had such a liturgical feat, based on chant, been attempted. The work may have grown out of Tournemire's mystical inspiration in improvising many of the liturgically appropriate chants for the mass: prelude, offertory, elevation, communion, and postlude. Particularly in the postludes, Tournemire freely paraphrased the chant in a longer, unstructured type of fantasy that has been given the name Gregorian paraphrase. He also composed smaller liturgical works for parish organists: *Petites fleurs musicales* op. 66 for manuals, which followed the plan of *L'orgue mystique* by providing five-movement suites for each of the principal feasts of the liturgical year; and *Postludes libres* op. 68, which contains fifty-one pieces based upon Magnificat antiphons.

Tournemire knew that his spiritual and mystical roots lay in the esthetics of César Franck. Although he never spoke of a Sainte-Clotilde tradition, his references to the future in his biography of César Franck suggest it: "We think of the mystical exhalation of the art of César Franck. The dangerous and disappointing reaction of these last twenty years [is to] no longer believe [in it]." This tradition was never to be a sterile duplication of the teacher; as Tournemire put it, "César Franck advised us never to imitate, but to search."[23]

Tournemire was also influenced by mystical writers of his time, including Prosper Guéranger, whose *L'année liturgique* (in fifteen volumes) he studied preparatory to *L'orgue mystique*, and Joséphin Péladan, who wrote the text for *Il poverello di Assisi* op. 73. In his preface to *L'orgue mystique*, Tournemire thanks Gajard and Letestu, Benedictine monks at Solesmes, as well as Joseph Bonnet, his friend and great interpreter, for having prompted him to write it. In the years just prior to his composition of *L'orgue mystique*, Bonnet had been a Benedictine oblate at Solesmes and had also studied Guéranger's writings.[24]

In 1933 Tournemire replaced the original console of the Cavaillé-Coll organ at Sainte-Clotilde and had it enlarged from forty-six to fifty-six stops, primarily by adding mutations and mixtures; he also moved the Cromorne (Clarinette) and the Unda maris from the

Positif to the Récit.[25] These additions made the instrument more adaptable for Tournemire's ideals of registration and for the performance of a wider range of literature.

As beautiful as the changes that Tournemire effected were, he recognized that the key action was still very difficult. He took this into account when he arranged recitals at Sainte-Clotilde for such students and friends as Daniel-Lesur, Messiaen, Langlais, and Litaize. In a letter to Noëlie Pierront one year after the organ's restoration, he wrote, "Good luck with your practice sessions at Sainte-Clotilde. The organ is in good shape, but the touch is still *terribly hard*!"[26]

Ruth Sisson explained the ambiance of Sainte-Clotilde, which these changes to the organ enhanced: "When combined with the frequent changes of textural patterns and of harmony, he created a type of musical kaleidoscope which may well be compared with the varicolored lights and shadows of his precious stained-glass windows of Sainte-Clotilde." She concludes:

> Perhaps Tournemire's most innovative contribution to symphonic writing for the organ is his apparent concept of orchestration, which takes into account both registration and scoring. Registration, which reflects the unique voicing qualities of the Cavaillé-Coll organ at Sainte-Clotilde, features the particular color of individual stops or combinations in various tessituras.[27]

Jean Langlais

Many facets of his background had prepared Langlais to embrace the Sainte-Clotilde tradition. Mysticism was the vehicle of communication from the material to the spiritual that he first learned from his grandmother. His teachers at the Institute, especially Albert Mahaut, reinforced his awareness of this tradition of mystical faith. Tournemire saw this mystical quality in him as a student, particularly in his earliest pieces, *Trois paraphrases grégoriennes* and *Poèmes évangéliques*, which he had greeted with enthusiastic acclaim. This quality informed many of Langlais's most profound works, including *Cinq méditations sur l'apocalypse* (1973); *Triptyque grégorien* (1978); *Offrande à une âme* (1979); his homage to Tournemire, *In memoriam* (1985); and *Mort et résurrection* (1990).

Langlais expressed this spiritual mysticism not only in faith and in music, but in his choice of friendships. This is not to say that he consciously sought out people who were of this persuasion, but rather that he was drawn to them. There was Jeannette, there were Mahaut and Tournemire, and there was Messiaen, well known as a Catholic mystic. In addition there were priests, Father Vigour from Rennes, Father Lefauqueur from the Oratory in Paris, and Archbishop Jules Orrière from Dol-de-Bretagne, who expressed these spiritual qualities and to whom Langlais was accordingly drawn.

Like Franck, Langlais enlarged upon existing forms and imbued them with new harmonies and style, some of which he took from the suites of the French Classical period and from Spanish and Italian models. From Tournemire he adopted the extensive use of Gregorian chant for his sacred music, both religious (*Incantation pour un jour saint*) and liturgical (*Suite médiévale* and *Hommage à Frescobaldi*).

Some aspects of the tradition that Tournemire passed to Langlais were not identical to Franck's. Franck did not use chants in his compositions; by contrast, Tournemire made heavy use of chant. Much of his music was liturgically oriented whereas Franck's was religious but not primarily liturgical. Tournemire's use of harmony was more advanced and original than Franck's, and his formal structure less clearly defined.

Langlais had the benefit of learning the tradition from Franck's students, particularly Mahaut, Marty, and Boulay at the Institute and later from Tournemire himself. Tournemire influenced him the most, however, in assimilating the rhythmic flexibility for Franck's music and his own. Langlais considered Tournemire's metronome markings inaccurate: "[He] insisted that we play very, very freely. . . . Tournemire himself was terribly free. He played the way he wanted his music to be played. . . . He said, 'Don't be so Classical—be free, because Gregorian chant is free.'"[28]

From Tournemire, Langlais learned to improvise Gregorian paraphrases, a form which became the basis for many of his improvisations and compositions. Again, there are differences: generally, Langlais's harmony is more dissonant; Tournemire often used unfamiliar chants from the propers including the offices, while Langlais almost always used chants from the ordinary—mass settings, popular hymns, and antiphons. Like Tournemire, Langlais composed a large body of liturgical music based primarily on chants from the offices and mass, designed for a specific service.

From November 1945 to November 1987, nearly his whole tenure, Langlais played the sung mass at 10:30 a.m. and the spoken mass at noon. For the sung mass, he would play an extended prelude (often a half-hour long) before the mass began as well as during the offertory, communion, and at the conclusion of the mass. For the spoken mass, he played continuously throughout, except, of course, at the homily.

All three men found inspiration for their works from the "lady" at Sainte-Clotilde, although their works are not always limited to its particular specifications. Some of their works transcended the limitations of any one organ, as did those of Vierne for the even larger instrument at Notre-Dame.

Organ Compositions 1946–1951

Langlais's organ works from this period are a clear continuation of the Sainte-Clotilde tradition. Many are among his best pieces for organ: *Fête* (1946), *Suite brève* (1947), *Suite médiévale* (1947), *Suite française* (1948), *Incantation pour un jour saint* (1949), *Four Postludes* (1950), and *Hommage à Frescobaldi* (1951). Like his predecessors, Langlais expanded older forms such as the concerto (*Fête*), French Classical suite (*Suite brève*, *Suite française*), and canzona (Épilogue from *Hommage à Frescobaldi*). The expansion was not one of length, since each piece—either as a complete work such as *Fête*, or as a movement of a suite—is relatively short, no longer than eight minutes. Instead he brought to these historic models a modern style and freer form.

Fête, for solo organ, is a brilliant concerto in rondo form; it juxtaposes tutti sections on the main division against a colorful solo combination, with softer accompaniment for the solo sections. A soft contrasting interlude on the Cornet interrupts the pattern before the closing section, which incorporates a virtuoso pedal cadenza. Both the harmony and solo passages show the influence of jazz. *Fête* has all the joyous exuberance of a holiday—one which commemorated the Liberation of Paris and Langlais's appointment as titular organist to Sainte-Clotilde.

American serviceman Clarence Barber visited Langlais at Sainte-Clotilde shortly after his appointment and offers this eyewitness account:

> Waiting at the entrance to the organ stairs, we saw a studious looking, half bald young man approach and post the musical program on the door. We introduced ourselves and our host guided us up to the tribune with such politeness and grace that it took several minutes for us to realize that he was blind. . . . Sensing the purpose of our visit, Langlais showed us the handsome console of the Cavaillé-Coll organ and pointed out the additions since Franck's time. . . . After the high mass we were invited to see the inside of the organ, and Langlais climbed around the dusty framework with an agility which put the two of us with normal vision completely to shame. The Cavaillé-Coll we saw in this brief view was of the highest order of workmanship, especially the woodwork. Like all other French organists, Langlais bemoaned the war-time shortages of repair materials and organ building facilities, for he is eager to have another manual added to the famous instrument. . . . Our host bade us farewell with a warm handclasp and something of a meditativeness and religious atmosphere of César Franck seemed to linger in our minds as we left the church after a beautiful performance by M. Langlais of the Belgian master's *Prière*.[29]

Pleased with the success of the *Neuf pièces*, Bornemann commissioned Langlais to write another shorter work, which prompted Langlais's title, *Suite brève* (1947). Comprised of four movements ("Grands jeux," "Cantilène," "Plainte," and "Dialogue sur les mixtures"), the first and last pay homage to Classical French composers, such as Clérambault, known for their suites and pieces describing the stops to be used, such as Nasard and Grands jeux. Once again, the rich colors of this special organ inspired these pieces. In the first three movements, Langlais borrows material from the orchestral work *Le diable qui n'est à personne* (1946).

The title of the first movement, "Grands jeux," indicates a broad piece employing the full reed chorus stops of the organ. Marked *maestoso*, it is to be played like a grand entrance march, reminiscent of the opening movements of the French Classical composers. A fast, spirited section follows, and the short piece ends in the regal manner of the opening.

The lyrical "Cantilène" is based on an original modal theme heard on a reed stop in the pedal and accompanied by soft chords, which reinforce the modal character of the melody. Langlais first used this theme as a baritone solo in *Le diable*. The development section plays off the melody canonically between high and low registers, simultaneously using the two melodies in the pedal. The third section uses one of Langlais's favorite stylistic devices: the melody is heard once again in the pedal, but with an added flute obbligato in the treble register, which recalls his improvisatory method.

"Plainte" is based on two notes that form a harmonic ostinato. Although it is shorter than "Chant de peine" (*Neuf pièces*), similarities in mood are evident. In "Plainte," Langlais makes his first use of the Voix humaine, no doubt inspired by the beautiful Voix humaine of his Cavaillé-Coll organ.

The last piece, "Dialogue sur les mixtures," resembles *Fête* in structure and mood. Fast, repeated chords move rapidly from the neutral key of C major to A-flat and back again, with lively echoings between the mixture combinations of all the manuals. "Mixtures" highlights Langlais's piquant sense of humor and unabashedly playful writing. He would repeat this form and mood in later compositions (for example, in *Suite baroque*'s "Grand jeu"), but never more successfully than here.

Also in 1947, Langlais composed *Suite médiévale*, an organ mass; its five movements are to be played at the same times as Tournemire's *L'orgue mystique*. Here he uses familiar chants according to the free unmetered manner introduced by the Solesmes reforms. The Prélude, marked *solennel*, opens the mass majestically, with open parallel fifths reminiscent of Medieval organum, followed shortly by the familiar "Asperges me," which was sung as the priest dispensed holy water up and down the aisle at the beginning of a sung or high mass. The Tiento, played during the offertory, is in the old Spanish form of a ricercar, an imitative forerunner of the fugue. It begins with a four-voice imitative or fughetta section for the manuals as the chant Kyrie "Fons bonitatis" is played in the pedal. Each phrase of the chant alternates with the fughetta sections, using the first imitative material occasionally in inversion. Once more,

Franck's predilection for imitation and counterpoint was echoed in his "grandchild."

The Improvisation is short and is to be played during the elevation. For this most solemn and reverent part of the mass, Langlais appropriately uses the chant "Adoramus te" in the first and third phrases. The Méditation, played during communion, is based on the familiar chants "Ubi caritas" and "Jesu, dulcis memoria." Both themes are combined with the first introductory motif in the middle of this quiet reflection. The concluding piece, Acclamations, is based on the Carolingian theme "Christus vincit" (Christ has conquered) and reflects the text's triumphant character. Like Langlais's "Hymne d'action de grâces 'Te Deum'" (*Trois paraphrases grégoriennes*) it is rhythmic and rhapsodic, with the same use of parallel fourths, strong harmonies, and rubato bravura runs. It concludes with a carillon-like pedal ostinato.

Suite française (1948), like the *Suite brève*, shows the influence both of the Cavaillé-Coll organ and of French Classical suites; Tournemire's changes to the instrument find their legacy here. The work shows Langlais's increasing independence as a composer in enlarging upon earlier forms. Like Tournemire's *Suite évocatrice*, Langlais's new work systematically borrows elements of the Classical French repertoire for a contemporary expression. Though retaining the seventeenth- and eighteenth-century practice of naming movements according to the organ registration, Langlais did not restrict himself to one key as Classical practice demanded. Also omitted was the earlier practice of using dance rhythms as a unifying device. What remains is the flavor of the Classical colors and the mood of the type of piece they represent.

The title *Suite française* is a tongue-in-cheek poke at Bach, which Langlais later enjoyed pointing out. He explained that in Bach's six *French Suites*, the opening movement is an allemande, which means "German" in the French language. In his *French Suite*, Langlais gave his fourth and pivotal movement in the form of an allemande, an old German dance form, but entitled it "Française." The suite is dedicated to Pierre Denis, a student of his and his assistant at Sainte-Clotilde.

"Prélude sur les grands jeux" is a brilliant toccata, brimming with syncopated rhythms, in one of Langlais's preferred keys, the joyous

A major. Written rapidly during the last three days of January 1948, the work is notable for the urgency of the bold opening theme, in the treble, over excited toccata figures and scales. The incessant rhythmic drive and kaleidoscopic harmonic changes are only briefly interrupted in the middle of this opening piece.

"Nasard" is a modern version of Clérambault's *Récit de nasard*, meaning a solo for this stop in the treble register. Combined with a Flûte 8, the Nasard 2-2/3 sounds an octave and a fifth above the Flûte, giving it a pleasant nasal color. The hollow open-fifth timbre of this combination is enhanced by the open fifths in the accompaniment. The plaintive modal theme flows onward in a tranquil, moderate tempo, with frequently shifting tonality.

"Contrepoint sur les jeux d'anches" (Counterpoint on the reed stops) is a dialogue in five voices between three contrasting colors, here with the two upper voices on the Hautbois on the Récit, the two lower voices on the Principal of the Grand-orgue, and the Principal 8 of the Pédale. Once again, the influence of the particular sonorities of the Sainte-Clotilde organ are evident. Langlais was obviously inspired by the richness of those stops, as he often improvised on them. The hands frequently change manuals, giving a dialogue effect between the parts. Langlais marked this movement *espressivo* and calls for a soft tone quality, as if to further draw attention to their particular beauty.

"Choral sur la voix humaine" is in variation form. The stately choral theme on the Voix humaine is repeated six times in succession, on the pitches B, E, C-sharp, D-sharp, and B, with a variety of contrapuntal devices above and below.

Langlais often remarked that nowhere else in the world could one find Flûtes as beautiful as those at Sainte-Clotilde—Flûtes that inspired the sixth movement, "Arabesque sur les flûtes," a virtuoso display of three Flûtes in dialogue, in a mood similar to some of Chopin's études, and notably impressionistic. A short, slow middle section gives both performer and listener a rest from the perpetual motion of the arabesque in triplet figures in the treble against the duple figures in the left hand. This movement resembles "Impromptu" from *Vingt-quatre pièces*.

The seventh piece, "Méditation sur les jeux de fonds," again displays all the richness of Sainte-Clotilde's foundation stops from the

32′ to 8′ range—a richness enhanced by the majestic and sustained chordal movement with double octave in the pedal.

"Trio" is the most original movement in the suite, the one movement from the suite that Messiaen played—and that with great pleasure, as Langlais often recalled. The movement consists of three trios, marked *moderato*, that alternate with three identical refrains, marked *lento*, in a curious contrast of textures: the trios are almost totally devoid of triadic harmony (a feature that Langlais would adopt more systematically after 1975); the refrains are based on parallel triads. Once more Langlais delighted in original composition, both of form and style.

"Voix céleste" is based on three contrasting themes: the first, on the string combination, is an ascending run. It is followed by an angular theme based on an ascending seventh, played on a Flûte in the treble register. The third, played entirely on the Voix céleste, combines six voices in chordal fashion with impressionistic harmonies.

"Final rhapsodique" is reminiscent of the "Rhapsodie grégorienne" (*Neuf pièces*) in its style and cyclic use of themes, although it is not based on chant themes. Here Langlais in a virtuosic rhapsody combines the themes from the first, fifth, sixth, and ninth movements. He would use this technique again in a later work (*Hommage à Rameau*).

In 1949 Langlais composed only one solo organ work, *Incantation pour un jour saint*, written rapidly between 14 and 20 February. Commissioned by Editions de la Schola Cantorum for its first volume of Easter music, it is dedicated to Rolande Falcinelli, Marcel Dupré's successor at the Paris Conservatory. The work paraphrases the musical portions of the Holy Saturday litany: the procession of the paschal candle, carried by the priest, who sings, "Lumen Christi," to which the congregation responds, "Deo gratias" (which exchange is repeated three times, at successively higher pitch levels); and the litany of the saints, to which the congregation responds "Kyrie, eleison" and "Christe, exaudi nos." Langlais accompanies each repetition of the chant with a different harmony, gradually leading to the tutti at the conclusion. It could well serve as a postlude for Holy Saturday and, with its compelling rhythm, simple style, and improvisational freshness, has remained one of the composer's most popular works.

Four Postludes, composed in 1950, shares this improvisational quality. The first piece incorporates rapid arpeggiated flourishes, similar to those that conclude *Suite médiévale*. Rapid choral changes at a fast tempo recall "Dialogue sur les mixtures" (*Suite brève*), but this time with added rhythmic values in 7/8 meter. The second piece is built on a rapid toccata figure in sixteenth notes, comprising two notes played together with the right hand alternating with a single note played in the left hand, much in the manner of his improvisations. The third postlude incorporates a toccata figure in triplets between the hands. The last movement uses an anapest (short, short, long) rhythm (Allegro energico) in the same style as the Allegro from his *Première symphonie*. The four are dedicated to Americans Walter Blodgett, Hugh Giles, Charles Walker, and Maurice John Forshaw. Forshaw was Langlais's first American student; he had fought in World War II and returned as a Fulbright scholar. Langlais would later spend time with these friends during his American tours.

In *Hommage à Frescobaldi: huit pièces pour orgue* (1951), his second organ mass, Langlais adds to the five liturgical movements three not related to the mass. The work is based on familiar chants: the Kyrie from Mass 4, "Cunctipotens genitor Deus"; the hymn "Lucis creator" for the offertory; "Homo quidam" for the elevation; "Sacris solemniis" for the communion; and "Ite missa est" from Mass 4 for the Fantaisie. The reference to Frescobaldi is in the Épilogue; in it Langlais quotes the opening theme of the canzona from Frescobaldi's *Messa della Madonna* (*Fiori musicali*).

Although each movement is short, several of them demonstrate his ideal of mysticism: to draw the listener into a state of contemplation—especially during the elevation and communion—through the suspension of time. This Langlais accomplishes by the lack of a strong rhythmic pulse and a blurring of tonic and dominant polarities. In Élévation, Langlais uses parallel harmonies in an ostinato pattern followed by long, sustained chords and a slow chromatic obbligato duet. The soft registration enhances the quiet mood.

Vocal Works 1946–1952

From 1946 to 1952 Langlais composed many vocal works, both sacred and secular: *Paroles de rechange*, "Pour Cécile," "Au pied du Calvaire," *Passe-temps de l'homme et des oiseaux*, *Trois prières*, *Trois mélodies*,

"My Heart's in the Highlands," *Hommage à Louis Braille*, and *Missa in simplicitate*. His sacred choral works included *Libera me, Domine, Cantiques, Messe solennelle, Cantate de Noël, Mass in Ancient Style*, and *Advent the Promise*. Secular choral works include *La ville d'Ys* and "*Amor.*"

In 1946 Langlais set seven poems from *Paroles*, a collection of poems by Jacques Prévert, with Prévert's permission. Langlais greatly admired the poet, who was known for expressing his nonconformist views in surrealistic poetry and films. The modal melodies and accompaniments of Langlais's art songs—similar in style and spirit to his own *Humilis* and settings by Debussy and Duparc—capture the spirit of contrasting humor and pathos in Prévert's poems. Where the text is a plaintive love song, such as "Déjeuner du matin," he uses a delicate chordal ostinato in the low register, expressing the quiet despair of a woman whose lover does not speak during the meal. Where the text expressed gladness, such as in "Pour toi, mon amour," he uses a simple two-part texture with a moving bass. In "Les belles familles," a satire of the dynasty from Louis I to Louis XVI, Langlais's setting—filled with dissonant, staccato chords and abrupt changes of key—is in perfect keeping with the humor of the text.

Langlais premiered the work at the Société Nationale de Musique. Composer Joseph Kosma, with whom Prévert had collaborated for many films, came to the performance.[30] Kosma, who was jealous of Langlais's music, prevailed upon Prévert to withdraw permission for Langlais to use his poems. Langlais then asked another poet, Edmond Lequien, to compose another text to accompany his music, which he entitled *Paroles de rechange* (Different words), but he considered them inferior to Prévert's. The new words did not fit the music as well, and Langlais was advised that after Prévert's death, either set of words might be used.

Langlais also admired Jean Cayrol, a poet who wrote the text for *Le diable qui n'est à personne*, and in 1948 set four of his poems, in *Passe-temps de l'homme et des oiseaux*. After serving as a spy for the French Resistance, Cayrol had been deported to a German concentration camp. Upon his return, he wrote these poems to protest the atrocities he had seen there, which had been so quickly forgotten in France. Cayrol's words have a genuineness not often found in language that speaks to life and death; much of his poetry is allegorical and surrealistic. These dissonant songs, although written simply like

Paroles de rechange and *Humilis*, mirror the intricate symbolism of protest suggested by birds, which represent liberty.

Some of Langlais's most lyrical, expressive writing is found in *Trois prières* (1949) for medium solo voice or unison choir with organ accompaniment. They are based on French translations of three Latin hymns: "Ave verum corpus," "Ave maris stella," and "Tantum ergo." As in *Paroles de rechange*, the vocal line and accompaniment are simple and follow the inflection of the text almost as if the words were being spoken in prayer. They are dedicated to Marie-Louise Colosier, the singer who inspired the work and gave its premiere that same year with Langlais as the accompanist. Langlais found the special timbre and richness of certain women's voices particularly seductive: Jeannette's voice had first attracted him; Jeannine Collard and Janet Walker (Charles Walker's wife) would exert a similar power over him.

Economically written and dramatically intense, *Messe solennelle* is Langlais's most significant choral work of this period, composed between 9 and 22 November 1949. The work was originally scored for SATB and two organs but was later arranged by Langlais for bass or strings. Here Langlais uses conservative choral techniques (such as fugal imitation in the Gloria and Agnus Dei), doubled vocal parts, and boldly dissonant organ accompaniment, especially in the Kyrie and Sanctus. The Gloria is based on the Gloria chant from Mass 13, "Stelliferi conditor orbis."

In 1946 Langlais composed *Cantate à Saint-Vincent*, a short choral work of poetic sensitivity, for the centenary of the École Saint-Vincent in Rennes. The choral style is similar to the mass and is largely based on the chant "Ubi caritas," which is treated fugally against a chromatic string and organ accompaniment in fifths and double thirds. It was revised and published in 1953 as *Caritas Christi*, with organ accompaniment, and dedicated to Walter Blodgett.

Radio Dramas 1946–1951

The orchestral music Langlais wrote during this period had a specific functional basis. After the war and before the rise of television, radio dramas with orchestral interludes were a popular art form in France. They were often based on religious themes, and well-known writers, composers, and actors collaborated to compose and perform them. Each production was given before a live audience and broadcast several times throughout France. Between 1946 and 1951, the French National Radio (Radiodiffusion Française) commissioned Langlais to compose incidental music for three such radio dramas: *Le diable qui n'est à personne* (The devil who belongs to nobody), *Légende de Saint Julien l'hospitalier*, and *Le soleil se lève sur Assise* (The sun rises on Assisi). This broader exposure helped to build his reputation as an orchestral composer.

The length of each drama was one hour and that of the combined musical portions, between twenty-five and forty-five minutes. Each playwright added instructions for the exact duration, mood, and dynamic range of each musical interlude.

These works mark Langlais's first use of the ondes Martenot. This exotic electronic instrument, with vast dynamic range, has a keyboard and a sliding ribbon, which permits glissandos and the sounding of indefinite pitches. Many composers experimented with the ondes Martenot during the 1930s, especially Messiaen, who wrote several pieces for it, most notably *Fête des belles eaux* for six ondes Martenot, which was performed at the 1937 Paris Exposition. By 1946 it had become a popular novelty in France, and Langlais was eager to try his hand at using it with full orchestra. Its inventor, Maurice Martenot, had invited Langlais to play the instrument and even requested that he write a quartet for it.

Langlais put his best effort into these pieces, which show considerable creativity and freedom, particularly in their extensive orchestration. Two of the scores employ full orchestra (*Diable* and *Soleil*). All three show Langlais's developed skill of orchestration and are filled with great contrasts of dramatic action and expressivity.

Le diable qui n'est à personne, based on a contemporary mystery play by Jean Cayrol, uses the ondes Martenot for the first time. Its primary function was melodic, although Langlais tried several small, one-octave glissandos in a medium register for added texture and a three-octave *fortissimo* glissando at the very end. There are twenty-seven interludes including a short overture. The work begins in the low register, with doubled low woodwinds and brass below a soft drone of strings. The orchestration in general is colorful, with many divisions in the string parts; the bass clarinet is heard frequently with the bassoons. Langlais borrows a theme from the Allegro of *Trois danses*, first for the ondes Martenot and then doubled on the flute.

One of the most haunting melodies in this work is scored for solo baritone with harp accompaniment. Strikingly mystical words in the style of Blake lend it its poetic character:

> Have mercy, dear one of the saints, with a hallowed look. / At the end of your hands the devil sleeps. / At the end of your hands the earth is hungry. / At the end of your hands the sky becomes like a body. / . . . Like a piece of bread, like a little wine, soft old fox is dead in his lair. / At the end of your hands, who will come again. / Have mercy, dear one of the saints of heaven, live with eyes closed. At the end of your hands is the army of angels who no longer hunger.

Langlais adapted this theme, with minor alterations, for his "Cantilène" from *Suite brève*, composed the following year. He also used

Le diable qui n'est à personne, no. 15, baritone solo

145

two other themes from *Diable* for movements of *Suite brève*: the first, a *forte* passage for brass (no. 20), representing heaven, as the opening of "Grands jeux," and his twice-borrowed theme from *Trois danses* a third time, as "Plainte."

Légende de Saint Julien l'hospitalier, based on a work by Gustave Flaubert, was composed in 1947. This time Langlais uses two ondes Martenot, combining them frequently with the flutes both in dialogue and with more extended glissandos for dramatic effects in a chase scene. The writing is good but produced no memorable themes. Perhaps for this reason, Langlais borrowed none of them for other works and some years later threw away his complete braille score.

Le soleil se lève sur Assise (1950), based on a mystery play by Albert Vidalie, combines the most elaborate instrumental and vocal forces of the three. Vidalie was a popular novelist and dramatist noted for his unusual plots. There are two orchestras, one large and one small, three ondes Martenot, three men's voices, and three women's voices. The play is a tableau of fourteen scenes from the life of Saint Francis of Assisi; the variety and drama of these scenes ("The Terrors of War," "The Sun of Love," "The Kiss of the Lepers") gave Langlais ample material for contrast between the small and large orchestra and the vocal forces, inspiring him to write some of his most effectively complex orchestral writing. *Soleil* ends with an extended fugue for strings that builds to a climax with a fugue for choir, with orchestral accompaniment, on the chant "Ubi caritas."

French National Radio commissioned an oratorio for radio broadcast on Christmas Day 1951. *Cantate de Noël* includes three extended movements: "Prélude," "Fuite en Egypte," and "Massacre des innocents." Scored for full orchestra, choir, and soloists, it is set to an original text by Loys Masson, an important poet. Langlais was at home in the profoundly religious text, which includes spoken narratives and sung recitative.

The prelude sets the mood of anticipation for the flight of the Holy Family into Egypt: many syncopated rising diminished fifths are followed by a march, which the divided cello section punctuates in short note values below sustained chords on the strings. "Fuite" opens with an image of the eternal Christ from two angels singing alternately in recitative, "That the child may sleep, the Cross sleep, the bloody nails fade as the child sleeps." Langlais enhances the meaning by adding an instrumental obbligato between the oboe and flute with the Marian chant "O gloriosa virginum" (O thou glorious among virgins, sublime amid the stars: Him who was thy Creator, now a tiny child, with milk thou feedest at thy breast). The march theme recurs in the last movement. This intensely dramatic work ends quietly with the "Maria mater" theme.

Langlais composed his *Premier concerto* for keyboard and orchestra in 1948 and 1949. Conceived along Classical lines, in three movements, this concerto was written for either organ or harpsichord—or both, simultaneously.

Jeannine Collard and the Gift of Healing

During the early 1950s a significant event occurred in Langlais's personal life that would mark him irrevocably. He had not been feeling well and decided to visit a healer. Singer Jeannine Collard knew a healer in Paris and urged him to accompany her. Upon arriving at the man's apartment Langlais lay down, and the healer placed his hands on him: "The man was very surprised and told me he could do nothing for me, absolutely nothing, and that I should place *my* hands on *him*. After I did this my hands became very hot. I was exhausted and had to drink a lot of liquid."[31]

He immediately set to using his gift to benefit his family, friends, students, even his concierge. He became obsessed with the power to heal. At first Jeannette supported his new interest, but eventually, concerned about his preoccupation with it, she dissuaded him from practicing it.

Like many artists, Langlais was self-centered, a quality accentuated in him by his blindness; he was happiest when conversations revolved around him. A parallel trait, which fed upon the first, was that of naiveté. Langlais frequently appeared to be removed from ordinary events and lived in a realm of fantasy, particularly regarding his relationship with women. Despite his handicap and diminutive size, he imagined that women were immediately drawn to him. He believed that the power he felt from the gift of healing ignited not only his creative forces but the women to whom he was attracted. He found women tremendously exciting—particularly artists, whom he needed to prime his compositional creativity. The women responded with equal fervor, flattered to be the source of his inspiration and desirous of participating vicariously in his creative process.

Genius often takes substance and energy from others, and Langlais found that these extramarital relationships fed his music. As the years progressed his appetite grew and with it his circle of "friends." Although completely devoted to him as an artist, Jeannette was no longer physically attracted to him. She was absorbed by their children.

It was through music that Langlais fell in love with Jeannine Collard, one of the most popular mezzo sopranos at the Opéra and the Opéra-Comique. She had graduated from the Conservatory in 1950 with a premier prix in voice; her first radio engagement was with the Orchestre Nationale de Paris late in 1951. Langlais heard the broadcast and, immediately falling in love with her rich voice, invited her to sing the mezzo solos for the radio broadcast of his *Cantate de Noël*. He wrote *Hommage à Louis Braille*, composed between 23 December and 2 January with her voice specifically in mind; she sang the premiere with Langlais accompanying her at the piano on 8 January 1952. Their relationship deepened rapidly, outlasting her brief, difficult marriage to Roger Guichaoua, a tax accountant, and continuing until Langlais's remarriage shortly after Jeannette's death, in 1979.

The period from 1945 to 1952 was one of Langlais's most prolific. That he was happy in his personal life and in his appointment at Sainte-Clotilde contributed to his productivity. His recitals throughout France increased and received favorable acclaim, and Langlais was fast becoming a renowned composer as well as a noted performer there. It was now that an opportunity to make his first transcontinental North American tour occurred. One Sunday early in 1952, the American impresario Bernard LaBerge came to Sainte-Clotilde to hear him play. During the mass he improvised and played Franck's Choral in B minor. His playing so impressed LaBerge that he offered Langlais a contract the next day. His series of concert tours in the United States and Europe were to bring him international acclaim.

American Tours 1952–1959

His presence and playing here took on interesting significance. For many of us it was the last tangible link with the
genius of the immortal César Franck.
                    Martin W. Bush, American music critic

Good Friday 1952 marked the beginning of Langlais's career as an
international artist. Under contract with the American agency Colbert LaBerge, he made the first of a series of eight extended tours of
the United States and Canada, each lasting approximately two
months.[1] These American sojourns influenced his writing and gave
him access to American publishers, who were eager to print his
music. He gave workshops at many American universities and summer workshops at Boys Town, Nebraska, where he worked in alternate years between the tours from 1959 to 1967. Throughout these
exchanges, he never lost sight of what he considered to be his primary role: that of ambassador of French culture. It was a deep joy for
Langlais to bring the French language, esthetic, and art to America,
and he likewise developed a deep appreciation for American culture, its language, people, customs, and music.

Langlais always had someone with him on tour; in 1952 and
1954, his guide was Jeannette. There are two descriptions of these
trips: Langlais's short published account and Jeannette's more personal handwritten versions.[2] In these, she refers to Langlais as Papa,
intending that the journal eventually be enjoyed by their children.
Much of her writing is a combination of Langlais's impressions,
which he dictated, her own thoughts, and their common reactions.
The point of view is sometimes difficult to determine, especially in
subjective passages.

Chapter 7

First American Tour

Jean and Jeannette left France on Friday, 11 April 1952, on the *Liberté*. In her journal, Jeannette describes her surprise at her first glimpse of the immense ship.

> Arrived in Le Havre without any stops, going directly to the dock, passing lots of construction and hangers. Finally a monstrous silhouette crowned with red smoke came into view: *La Liberté*, which we had not, unfortunately, seen in its entirety.... Once inside the ship, we looked out the porthole. The ship was monstrously large—majestic with an impressive beauty; hallways and staircases—all decorated sumptuously—where one was easily lost. It took a while to get my bearings.

Her journal reveals Langlais's first impressions as well. It is a small reminder of Langlais's keen interest in everything around him —and his reliance on her to describe what he could not see. His greatest interest, however, was always in the sounds he heard, and she comments in detail on the sound and timbre of people's voices. One entry describes their hearing the *Liberté*'s siren for the first time: "We then went out on the bridge, on the stern of the ship. We heard a terrifying blowing of the horn, which was really frightening. A huge siren—like a 32' bass, a worthy organ stop for this monster."

They spent the first day adjusting to the pitching of the ship, the sudden lack of routine, and their separation from family and friends, as Jeannette's journal entry attests:

> The vibration . . . now seemed more like that of being in a train, [but] we continued to feel the pitching. If it stays like that, I'll feel fine; but Papa is very tired and came down with a little cold. . . . This day was sad . . . with thoughts always elsewhere: regrets about leaving—no artistic distractions—the impression of solitude in the middle of a crowd. . . . We are so far and we are going so quickly farther away, that it is difficult to imagine our dear ones in their environment.

Janine was sixteen and Claude only eight. Jeannette had accompanied her husband on shorter recital trips in Europe but had never yet been away from the children for longer than a few days.

During the seven-day crossing, in the mornings, Langlais walked the decks and practiced the piano regularly. He even played for the Easter Day mass, which was celebrated by a priest from the Royal Chapel in Monaco, "who spoke in Latin with an American accent," as Jeannette wrote in her entry of 13 April. Langlais played on a harmonium of four octaves and only one fixed combination. His musical portion included Bach's Toccata in D minor and an improvisation on "Regina coeli" and "O filii." For the postlude, he improvised on the theme of Handel's Variations in G minor.

For the high mass, which was billed as having completely sacred music, Langlais played the piano in the café while the orchestra performed selections chosen by the orchestra director. These included Schubert's "Ave Maria" and Mozart's "Ave verum corpus," followed by Langlais's improvisations and ending with an orchestral rendition of Lalo's "Chants russes." Jeannette, appalled, confided her astonishment to her journal: "I laugh softly at this program which I did not have the courage to listen to." At lunch Langlais arrived, and according to Jeannette was "a little horrified" because in the Mozart, the second violins were clearly improvising their part in thirds with the fifths.

Novelties in religious observance were as interesting to them as novelties in shipboard life. Later that day, the sound of recorded bells rang out, to give those who wished it the effect of Easter. Quite an effect—bells in the middle of the ocean. In her journal, Jeannette described feeling sad, far from family and friends, by day's end: "[It] lacked the charm of Easter on land—Easter with the family. I comforted myself in remembering last Sunday, which I had spent so differently from this one, at Asnière, at the home of our friends Roger and Jeannine, with whom we had left our children the evening before and who were so very kind to us." Roger Guichaoua and Jeannine Collard were among their closest friends.

But for Langlais, the main preoccupations were always performing and composing—even on Easter Day. The following passage seems to be in his words, dictated to Jeannette: "Acclamation in progress, two and a half hours of serious study in the Café Atlantic, worked out harmony for an 'In paradisum' that I would like to finish tomorrow. We think more about the memory of those absent from us as we approach the English coast."[3]

Still Jeannette's journal would help them to recall many wonderful and surprising experiences, including a peculiar odor exuded by a certain colored algae and the time Langlais accompanied a young girl in an impromptu dance exhibition:

> Yesterday, Papa worked on a small but excellent salon piano in the tourist class. A dozen or so people were there. All at once, when Papa started the Etude in A minor by Chopin, a little girl of eleven years, a ravishing blond, dashed up to the dance floor. . . . She must have known the music—and danced gracefully [with leaps and on her toes] in the most charming Classical style. Papa then played a Mazurka in A minor, upon which the girl started to dance again with another step and other gestures. A charming moment.

Travel in America

Although other European artists frequently traveled to and around America by plane, all Langlais's early peregrinations were by steamship, train, bus, and car. He avoided flying entirely until 1964 and even then had little confidence in the safety of air travel and greatly feared vertigo. "Take Air France, take a chance," he often said. The most relaxing parts of travel during the earlier tours were the transatlantic crossings—despite the frequently turbulent weather.

The extent and pace of his travel once he arrived were brutal. On his first American tour Langlais traveled more than eight thousand miles, an average of more than two hundred miles every day, playing twenty-two concerts in forty-two days. The tour began in New Jersey and took him north to Canada, west to Nebraska, and even to Texas. Subsequent tours ranged from six weeks to two months and usually included recitals every other day. It was not unusual for him to play three or four consecutive nights of recitals.

First Impressions

In a journal entry, Jeannette captured their first view of New York from the Winslow Hotel: "From our eleventh floor, I gaze at the traffic. No bicycles, only huge cars with overly ample suspensions; three-fourths are taxis in every shade of yellow possible. We are at the front of a building with sixty floors, next to another less high, which seems to be made entirely of glass." That night she looked in amazement at the lights of Manhattan. Everything seemed enormous by comparison to what they knew in France. They were delighted to find that their room in a moderately priced hotel had a telephone and a private bath.

No sooner had they disembarked from the ship than Paul Beckley, a reporter for the *New York Herald Tribune*, requested an interview. Beckley had been given extensive publicity material about Langlais and may have also spoken with Hugh Giles, the organist of Central Presbyterian Church, where Langlais's New York debut was to take place. He began the interview, at the organ, by asking Langlais if he knew what he was sitting on. Langlais responded that he knew it was a bench, but Beckley pressed him: did he know *which* bench it was? Langlais was exasperated. Then he was told that it was the original bench from César Franck's organ at Sainte-Clotilde! This became one of Langlais's favorite stories.[4] In his article ("Blind, But He's an Organ Recitalist," *New York Herald Tribune*, 19 April 1952), Beckley more than passingly noted Jeannette's discreet help to Langlais as his collaborator and interpreter of everything he could not see; a photo that ran with the piece showed Langlais at the console of the large instrument, with Jeannette guiding his right hand to the couplers. His blindness invariably overwhelmed observers, which frustrated the independent Langlais.

Langlais's second recital took place at the Crescent Avenue Presbyterian Church in Plainfield, New Jersey. At the reception afterward, given a choice of beverages, he requested a beer, since the weather was terribly hot. The woman serving him was horrified. "Beer! My God! On a Sunday! In a church!"[5] But Langlais and Jeannette were also immediately struck by the generosity, friendliness, and spontaneity of their American hosts. The evening of their departure from New York, a performance of Langlais's *Piece in Free Form* was given at the Museum of Modern Art. The organizer of the concert told him that they were counting on his presence. Langlais explained that, unfortunately, he had to leave by train for Toronto. This gentleman then proposed that he and Jeannette take a plane to

Toronto as their guests, a generous gesture which he nonetheless declined.

For this first tour, Langlais was asked to prepare three different programs. The first, works by modern French composers (Dupré, Tournemire, Messiaen, and Langlais), was requested fifteen times. The second was more general (works by Mendelssohn, Franck, Falcinelli, Litaize, Satie, and Langlais) and was played only once. The third (Bach, Couperin, Grigny, Demessieux, Vierne, and Langlais) was played six times. Reviews thoughout the tour were glowing. Paul Hume called his playing brilliant, and Searle Wright praised his improvisations as "a truly artistic *musical individuality* literally pouring forth its personal poetry."[6]

Langlais felt an immediate rapport with his American audiences, especially while improvising, and he ended each recital with an improvisation on submitted themes. Many of his listeners thought that part of his ability to improvise was based on having perfect pitch, but this was not the case (nor did he ever develop perfect pitch). His improvisational skill was developed by years of hard work, from training by such excellent teachers as Marchal, Dupré, and Tournemire, and from an intensely creative mind. He was never afraid to experiment and to take risks, and this greatly endeared him to his audiences.

Langlais found American organs very different from the French mechanical-action organs, especially the large Aeolian and Aeolian-Skinner instruments, some with more than a hundred stops, such as those he encountered at Duke University, the Washington Cathedral, the Mormon Tabernacle, and the University of Texas at Austin. He considered their esthetic similar to the Cavaillé-Coll instruments he preferred in France, referring admiringly to their "intensely poetic sonorities," but what impressed him as much as their tone qualities was the range of mechanical accessories: the manual and general pistons and Crescendo pedals. He did encounter some organs top-heavy with mixtures and lacking in rich foundation stops ("whose reeds had so distinctive a timbre that it is difficult to use them in ensembles"); although some were finely voiced, he found it difficult to perform anything but early music on them. He did not think that Americans would easily accept pseudo-Baroque-style organs, on which even Bach's music would be difficult to perform:

America [has] many very large organ firms who maintain their tradition of building eclectic instruments. On such organs Grigny, Bach, Franck, and Messiaen, as well as Tournemire and Dupré, maintain their intrinsic richness. This esthetic does not sacrifice the builder's personal stamp nor the expression of his own genius.[7]

After three months of exhausting travel, Langlais and Jeannette returned to France aboard the *Ile-de-France*. During the crossing, Langlais composed a four-movement *Mass in Ancient Style* with masterful swiftness, between 5 and 8 June 1952. Although the mass displays many sixteenth-century counterpoint techniques, in it Langlais greatly expands the use of dissonance and melodic leaps. The Kyrie, in an untransposed Phrygian mode with no accidentals, has an even greater purity than the modes of Palestrina. *Mass in Ancient Style* is dedicated to one of his first American friends, Theodore Marier, the former director of music at Saint Paul's Roman Catholic Church in Boston, who gave its first performance with his choir of men and boys later that year. Marier, then dean of the Boston chapter of the American Guild of Organists (AGO), had invited Langlais to play at Saint Paul's during his first tour. As an editor for the Boston music publishing firm of McLaughlin & Reilly, Marier, who spoke French fluently, was instrumental in having them publish Langlais's *Four Postludes* for organ as well as this new choral work.

A week-long celebration was held that June, commemorating the centennial of the death of Louis Braille. Braille's remains were brought from his birthplace in Coupvray to the Institute, where a vigil was held. The next day his descendents, together with the Institute professors and students, formed a cortège behind the casket containing Braille's ashes and saw them placed in the Pantheon.

Amour de coeur

Langlais's passion for Jeannine Collard, which had grown during his absence from her, burst forth upon his return. Jeannine was his first great *amour de coeur*—a love which inspired some of his most poignant vocal works.[8] Jeannette understood his relationship with

Jeannine and its artistic results, and she too enjoyed Jeannine's company, although she was more than twenty years her senior.

That July the Langlais family and Jeannine Collard left for La Richardais together. Jeannine stayed in a small hotel not far from their home overlooking the Rance River. While there, the pastor of the local church heard Jeannine's richly vibrant voice and asked her to sing during the mass. So Langlais composed another Latin mass, *Missa in simplicitate*, this time inflamed by a great love, in a period of exaltation, between 18 July and 10 August 1952. The work shows great simplicity, and Collard's inspiration is apparent in the blending of the vocal line and accompaniment to display the rich timbre of her voice. The Credo, in a declamatory, operatic recitative style, was written most rapidly of all. Langlais was not able to sleep, listening to the inflection of the words and the harmonies in his mind. By the next morning the entire Credo was finished. He employed Jeannine's first name as the opening theme of the Kyrie, as he had used Jeannette's twenty-one years earlier. The final outcome of this creative symbiosis was Langlais's and Collard's joint performance of the work at the parish church of La Richardais followed by a performance later that year at a Dominican church in Paris. So sonorous was Jeannine Collard's voice that in a 1953 recording of the work, her voice drowns out the tutti of the Sainte-Clotilde organ at the end of the Credo!

Langlais's search for passions that would spur his creativity became obsessive. He placed himself outside the authority of the Church, telling those close to him that he had the authorization of a priest at Saint-François-Xavier, a sort of blanket absolution, to continue these extramarital relationships because of the great and intensely spiritual sacred works they inspired him to create. He did not receive communion regularly but only after he had been to confession. He confessed—intending to continue his current liaisons and rationalizing that perhaps he would die before the next confession. All this was completely believable and acceptable to Langlais and Jeannette—and just as completely concealed from their children, who never suspected a thing. Jeannette was his main accomplice.[9]

Jeannine Collard, c. 1962

Folkloric Suite

In October and November 1952 Langlais wrote *Folkloric Suite*, completing each movement within a two-day span. Langlais intended that three of the five movements be used in church according to the liturgical year: the first for Easter, and the second and third for Christmas. All the movements use folk tunes, proving that Langlais's knowledge of folk music extended beyond his native Brittany.[10] The influence of American organs is reflected in *Folkloric Suite*; the opening and closing movements ("Fugue sur 'O filii'" and "Rhapsodie sur deux noëls") are dedicated to American organists Claire Coci and Catharine Crozier, and even the title is in English instead of French, possibly at the request of his second American publisher, FitzSimons. For the first time the registration markings are in English and omit a French translation. In "Rhapsodie," Langlais calls for an orchestral Oboe or English horn, remembering these stops from the large Aeolian-Skinner instruments he had played on tour. He calls for a Dulciana and Chalmei as solo stops in the third movement, "Cantique" (dedicated to Roger Guichaoua, Jeannine Collard's husband). In the published version, Langlais gave some advice to American organists: "The composer asks his interpreters to use his registrations unchanged insofar as is possible."

One tour had convinced him that Americans often lacked discrimination in their registration. At one of his master classes during the 1956 tour, Langlais described the cavalier attitude of Americans toward registration:

> My second duty [is] teaching. I am called to listen to the playing of several university students. I listen to several pieces, including Bach's chorale prelude "In Thee Is Gladness." "We tried the bells in the pedal," says Miss X to me, "but I don't know if we were right." "I don't know either, dear Miss X, nor were you right to add a little bit of Tremblant in Prelude, Fugue, and Variation, nor the Hautbois with the Voix céleste for the solo in the first Choral of Franck!"[11]

Favorable Receptions

As his popularity increased, Langlais was flattered to have American publishers—McLaughlin & Reilly (Boston), FitzSimons (Chicago), H. W. Gray (New York), World Library of Sacred Music (later the Gregorian Institute of America, Chicago), and Elkan-Vogel (Philadelphia)—vying for the privilege of publishing his new works. While in New York at the beginning of his 1959 tour, he met with Mr. Gray, and recalled with pride his employer's reception, which included a hearty hope that the briefcase he was carrying was "full of manuscripts?"[12] But Langlais never aligned himself with any one publisher. He realized early on that since each publisher publicized his works separately, he would earn substantially more in royalties if more than one publisher was involved.

In 1953 Walter Blodgett, curator of musical arts at the Cleveland Museum of Art, asked Langlais to write a choral work. Langlais re-arranged his *Cantate à Saint-Vincent-de-Paul*, originally composed in 1946 for chorus and strings, in a new version for organ and choir called *Caritas Christi*. This time Langlais treats the texts "Caritas Christi urget nos" (May the love of Christ guide you) and "Evange-lisandis pauperibus" (Educate the poor) with poetic intensity. He uses the second text symbolically in a choral fugue based on the chant "Ubi caritas" (Where there is charity and love, God is there), linking love and charity to the education of the poor.

Also in 1953 his recording of Franck's *Grande pièce symphonique*, *Prière*, and *Final* for Ducretet-Thomson was given unreserved praise for its extraordinary architecture and incomparable style. Langlais was seen for the first time as among the greatest leaders of the mod-ern French school. On 25 and 26 August 1953 Langlais recorded for the same label two of Messiaen's organ pieces together with a verson of Messiaen's *O sacrum convivium* in an arrangement for one voice and organ and, with Jeannine, his own *Missa in simplicitate*. It was the first time Messiaen's music had been recorded, and this historic recording too received a favorable review.

1954 American Tour

Langlais's second tour, 3 February to 30 March 1954, included recitals in states he had not yet visited, including California and New Mexico. Once more Jeannette accompanied him. The California cli-mate, with its luxurious vegetation and exotic birds, particularly impressed them. By this time, Langlais's English had greatly im-proved, but he nevertheless often mixed the two languages in a kind of Franglais—not because he did not know the English word, but to amuse himself.

With the exception of C. P. E. Bach's Sonata no. 6 (which Lan-glais had recently edited for FitzSimons as part of the complete sonatas) and several chorale preludes and a concerto by J. S. Bach, his three programs were exclusively French, including Franck's *Final*, Tournemire's Communion from the Pentecost office of *L'orgue mystique*, Messiaen's *Les bergers*, and Saint-Saëns's Prelude and Fugue in E-flat. The last portion of each program featured Langlais's own works.

Jeannette's journal from the 1954 trip does not survive, but she later spoke enthusiastically about Americans for whom they felt a special kinship, including Hugh Giles, Janet and Charles Walker, and eminent American organist and composer Seth Bingham, who was blessed with a lively sense of humor and a French wife. There was also Richard Ross from Baltimore, a student of Joseph Bonnet, whose playing had greatly impressed them on their first tour. They had planned to spend several days with him during this tour but were shocked to learn shortly after they arrived that he had died of a heart attack at the age of thirty-nine. Langlais included Ross's *Invocation* on his programs for the 1956 tour.

The emotional highlight of the 1954 tour occurred in Boston, where Archbishop Cushing had organized a concert in the 2400-seat Symphony Hall and hired a hundred-voice choir to sing Langlais's *Messe solennelle*. Just before Langlais walked onstage to begin the recital, he received a visit from a very friendly and distinguished man smoking a cigarette. He later learned it was the archbishop. The concert was recorded for broadcast the following Good Friday.

Jeannine Collard continued to inspire Langlais: upon returning from his 1954 tour, Langlais wrote her five love songs, *Cinq mélodies*, on texts by sixteenth-century court poets Ronsard and de Baillif.

1956 American Tour

In a letter dated 1 December 1955, Jeannette advised Lilian Murtagh, LaBerge's successor as Langlais's manager, that she could no longer accompany her husband to America: "Our son needs close attention for some little while, and far from him I would not be at ease—nor would his father. Fortunately, one of our close relatives [niece Monique Legendre] will serve as his guide." Langlais could be difficult, and Jeannette may well have counted it a blessing that twelve-year-old Claude's "hazardous" growth spurt prevented her from accompanying Jean on subsequent tours.[13]

Langlais's third American tour began on 29 December 1955. He was pleased with his performance at the University of Michigan and the response of the audience—particularly that of Robert Noehren, university organist and professor of organ: "[I] played two encores, and I know that Noehren . . . considered my concert an important lesson for the students. It appears that Marchal had many accidents."[14] Langlais always looked for comparisons that would demonstrate his superiority over Marchal, and Noehren had mentioned to him Marchal's problems in performing on the same instrument on 12 November 1953.

At Philadelphia's First Presbyterian Church, where Alexander McCurdy was organist, Langlais faced one of the most complicated consoles he had ever encountered. A hundred stops were divided between two organs played separately or together from a single console, which contained separate combinations for each division. The console was located nearer the smaller division, so that when Langlais tried to play a simple dialogue by Grigny requiring a Cromorne and a Cornet, he heard the Cromorne blaring in his ears and the Cornet scarcely audible and delayed in speech. To make matters worse, the console was on an elevator and lacked stability when raised, and the bench seemed to move while he played. It took him at least fifteen concerts on different organs to rid himself of the feeling of vertigo.[15]

In Denver, at the Cathedral of the Immaculate Conception, Langlais met with a 1912 Kimball organ that lacked suitable stops for the music on his program. His description was typically candid.

> Unbelievable! Stupid Pédale: three 16s, one terrible 8, no 4; Récit: no mixture—for reeds, only an Hautbois; Grand-orgue: no mixture and strident foundations; one unusable Trompette as the only reed; Positif: one 2'—the only one on the organ; and no general pistons. The Crescendo brings on first the 16. Finally, an absurd tutti, which speaks badly.

Fortunately the tours had their amusing moments, as this journal entry by the French "ambassador of culture" shows:

> An evening of battles in the train (where I had a lower berth) . . . to get undressed in a horizontal position, to put away one's

things in so little space. That is all right, but what complicates everything is when you feel as if you have a piano under the pillow and then find it is the reverse next morning. Hopefully the night will give me strength for the new battle. . . . At six in the morning the second battle of the lower berth began, crowned by an impressive victory (put on my pants without putting my feet on the floor, thanks to the pillow raised to the thickness of a piano).

In the men's room businessmen, presumably, were speaking loudly while using electric shavers. I stood in my little corner with a one-dollar disposable razor, but I admit I did not feel inferior to my neighbors, despite my modest condition. In fact, Messieurs, it is certainly we French artists who have the joy and the responsibility of educating the tastes of your citizens, and we know by the quality of our reception here that they appreciate the gift of culture . . . and that they will make it bear fruit.

With all this, Langlais still felt compelled to compose. The journal entry of 31 January 1956 describes the conception of *Huit pièces modales*:

From ten in the morning on, I settled in peaceful solitude at the church where I played Sunday. I am writing the beginning of a suite for organ, which I want to be conceived modally. However, the initial mode chosen for each piece will be transposed as the piece goes along.

He was true to his original intent, and the eight pieces were composed by 6 June.

Langlais also writes in his journal that he had fallen in love with California and hoped to return there to teach upon his retirement from the Institute. On 9 February he dictated to his niece:

Awoke at 5:10. Between seven and eight took a walk. The marvelous poetry of the Californian morning—exotic bird calls. Near to a pond, a heron was walking, and we could hear it. . . . I love this country, although so far from mine, and I am thinking about writing down these memories and experiences in a work for orchestra.

The work that was to emerge, three years later, was *American Suite* for organ. Langlais normally acted immediately upon his inspiration; perhaps it was his wish to write a large orchestral work that delayed him for so long.

Impressions of American Culture

America struck conflicting chords within Langlais. In general, he was happiest when out of doors and walking, even in the dead of winter. The sounds of nature gave him a sense of freedom and reality that overheated indoor spaces denied him. At the end of his 1956 tour, in Washington, D.C., he met a woman from Belgium whose American husband was mentally ill. She told Langlais that in America many had lost their minds. In his naiveté, Langlais believed her:

> [This] does not surprise me with a life that is so false. [How] painful . . . to be forced to listen to a continuous stream of bad music in hotel lobbies and restaurants—and still I am happy to be spared TV. America has yet to learn the benefits of silence. They honk the car horns, the trains blast their horns midtown, with a powerful sixth chord. Ambulances blow their high-pitched sirens. And the fire trucks! On the other hand, it is impossible to hear the sound of bells or a clock soaring over the city. . . . You no longer walk. This estrangement from elemental life rhythms turns man against man . . . and the concept of comfort, which surpasses all personal effects, weakens man. Live the simple life! I prefer a stream to a bathtub and the song of a bird heard by the open window to a bad recording aired by a loudspeaker. Return to the most basic lifestyle, Messieurs Americans, and especially a more poetic one, and perhaps there will be fewer of you in padded cells.

Organ Works 1956–1959

Organ Book (1956) was written as a gift for Marchal's daughter on the occasion of her marriage to composer Giuseppe Englert. Several of the ten pieces are stylistically similar to the *Vingt-quatre pièces* and display conciseness of form and economy of thematic material. The concluding Pasticcio is an imitation of a polyphonic Italian canzona; at the end of its middle section Langlais combines the first names of the couple, Jacqueline and Giuseppe, using the braille system of musical notation, mirroring the mood and rhythm of his "Dialogue sur les mixtures" (*Suite brève*).

The British publisher Novello commissioned *Triptyque* (1956) for its Organ Music Club series. Both Melody and Trio are in repeated binary form: the thematic material is heard first in two voices, then repeated with an added voice. The Final is in A B A form, and in the middle section, the Westminster carillon theme is played in the pedals. The work struck Novello's editor as too technically demanding; their request had been for easy service music. Nonetheless, in 1957 Langlais wrote another work for Novello, *Three Characteristic Pieces*, dedicated to the memory of John Stanley, the blind eighteenth-century English organist. In the preface he states his practical intent in writing the work: "Any of the pieces can be used as voluntaries, or they may be played together as a suite for recitals. The music does not demand elaborate color, and the suggested schemes of registration may be modified to suit the smallest organ."

Miniature (1959) was commissioned by the American organist Marilyn Mason and published by H. W. Gray in 1960 as part of the Marilyn Mason Organ Series. Langlais and Mason had met several times during his tours, and on each occasion she asked that he write a piece for her. The short toccata, again in A B A form with a slow middle section, was a revision of a piece with the same title, written in 1935, that Langlais originally planned as no. 19 of the *Vingt-quatre pièces*.

Choral Works 1957–1959

La Passion (1957), commissioned by Erato, is Langlais's longest (duration 60:00) and most elaborate choral-orchestral work. Scored for choruses, full orchestra, eight soloists, and narrator, the work was given its first performance as a live radio broadcast for French National Radio on Holy Thursday, 27 March 1958. What with the difficulty of the vocal and instrumental parts, the lack of arias, and the obscure, nonscriptural text, the work received only mixed notices. Some reviewers found it monotonous; others found it extraordinarily forceful and commended Langlais for avoiding easy effects.[16] It was never recorded, except for a reel-to-reel tape made of the original broadcast. Theodore Marier translated the text into English, with the hope of having it performed in America, but to no avail.

La Passion is within the historic Passion tradition but definitely in twentieth-century style. Langlais wrote the most important solo part, Mary, for Jeannine Collard, complemented by solo parts for Jesus, Pilate, Peter, Judas, a Man, and two other women. The text by Loys Masson is heavy with symbolism: the crown of thorns, blood, the forest, the cross. Extensive tone-painting (for example, the imitation of a cock crowing at Peter's denial) permeates the work. The orchestration is expressive in its use of color: the bass clarinet and percussion are prominent in the soliloquy at Judas's betrayal; Jesus's solos are accompanied by sustained strings in the passage "Father, forgive them"; and a flute obbligato, with several tritones, provides reflective commentary. Extended spoken passages occur at dramatic moments, as at the words "Let his blood be on our children" and "Crucify." Next to that of Jesus, the part of Mary has the most developed use of symbolism. The Passion of Christ becomes that of his mother: "I am the mother, I bled so many wounds, so many times, the mother in His blood and the mother in His cross." At this point the halo of strings is transferred to accompany Mary.

Two Gregorian chants, "Ave Maria" and "Vexilla regis," bind this musical drama together. The work builds to a long crescendo, concluding with full orchestra and chorus on the text "O crux ave." Langlais loved *La Passion* and felt that he had poured his best efforts into it. He often spoke of the long hours Jeannette spent in transcribing it.[17]

Langlais wrote a second choral-orchestral work in 1957, *Le mystère du Christ*, including narrator and soloists. French National Radio commissioned three composers to write one movement each of a three-movement work based on the Christmas story. Langlais's was the second tableau. Again there is an extended solo passage for Mary. The opening theme is borrowed from *Organ Book*'s Pastoral Song; for the birth of Christ, Langlais employs a Breton folk song to symbolize the humanity of Christ. The choral parts, however, are less important than those of *La Passion*.

Cantate "En ovale, comme un jet d'eau" (1958) is written for two mixed a cappella choruses on a poem by Edmond Lequien. It was commissioned by À Coeur Joie, a French choral group directed by César Geoffray. Fifteen hundred people (four choirs of soloists and five choirs of untrained voices) sang its premiere at an international gathering near Rome in 1959. The singers, who had rehearsed two hours a day for six days, performed the work for an audience of six thousand.

Langlais was attracted by Geoffray's idealistic values and Lequien's appeal to a higher, less materialistic social order, reminiscent of Mahaut. Images of the earth, sea, and humanity in Lequien's text are opposed to images of the inhumanity of the modern age. His apocalyptic poem opens with these words: "In the shape of an oval, like a waterfall, the stonecutter hurls and succumbs. . . . The work of his hands remains in the stones, and their lively silence lights up and flashes from these men." Langlais's treatment of the poem combines melodically simple unison parts for one chorus and complex choral writing for the other. Numerous echo effects between the choirs stud the choral score, and Lequien's dramatic text is lyrically interpreted.

1959 American Tour

Langlais's 1959 tour stretched across the length and breadth of the United States. Langlais felt in full command of both the language and his abilities as a performer. He believed, perhaps naively, that he had succeeded as a cultural ambassador for France and that, at last, French art had eclipsed nineteenth- and twentieth-century German art. At the very least, he believed that Americans had come to appreciate his message. His programs continued to feature music by French composers. The first was devoted entirely to French composers (Couperin, Calvière, Vierne, and Langlais, including his own *Folkloric Suite* and *Triptyque*). The second program was varied and included his close friend Seth Bingham's *Rhythmic Trumpet*. The third program included works by Couperin, Bach, Mozart, Franck, and Langlais. Each program ended with an improvisation.

The choral traditions in Protestant churches impressed Langlais greatly:

Apparently the pastor and the organist have a prearranged understanding. A service is preceded by an organ piece. The organist gives the duration of the piece to the pastor, who respects this scrupulously. Think on that. . . . It is not rare to find . . . even seven choirs in Protestant churches. And these choirs practice under the direction of the organist. Result: a high performance level of the pieces is achieved even when the works are difficult. The organist works hard at his church, but thanks to the salary he receives he can live well.[18]

During the 1959 tour, Langlais took great pleasure in visiting Anne Larkey and her parents in California. He had met Larkey earlier, in Paris, where she had traveled to study French. They were both stopped at a busy intersection near Sainte-Clotilde; she thought Langlais seemed confused by the traffic and asked if he needed assistance. From this chance meeting grew a long and deep friendship, including many letters she wrote him in braille. He also met with Paul Henry Lang following a performance in Jacksonville, Florida. Langlais was surprised by Lang's knowledge of other blind musicians—Landino, Cabezón, and Stanley among others. It was as if he expected only someone who was blind to be aware of the contributions of these relatively obscure composers. Despite Langlais's exposure to the cultural diversity of America, his outlook remained surprisingly insular.

Sons and Daughters

Langlais's rigid outlook affected his relationships with those nearest to him, particularly his two children. Langlais clearly loved them and desired closeness with them, yet his insularity coupled with authoritarian discipline kept them at arm's length. During the 1959 tour, Langlais pressed Claude to write to him, but received only one letter, near the end. It was quite formal and focused on his progress in piano studies with his blind teacher, Gaston Régulier. It was left to Jeannette to communicate all other news of the children.

Claude traveled to America in March 1959 to accompany his father on the return voyage. He heard his last recital and, as always, was very nervous for his father during the performance. Langlais,

Jeannette, Langlais, Claude, and Janine at Claude's confirmation,
Saint-François-Xavier, 1954

battling depression and fatigue, wondered whether he had played as well as he could. As they started back to France, Claude's silence added to Langlais's low spirits. Finally, Langlais asked him what he had thought of the recital. Claude replied, "It wasn't bad." These three words lifted his mood enormously, Claude's affirmation of his playing meant so much to him.[19] Earlier on that tour, having played well in Savannah, Langlais wrote Jeannette, "Claude, even Claude would not have been unhappy with me"; and in a letter to Claude from Winter Park, Florida, Langlais wrote, "I played a Bach concert, which was recorded for the radio and which you would not be embarrassed to hear."[20]

Langlais saw the role of women in very narrow terms, as wives and mothers. His description of an American doctor's wife, whom he met during his 1959 tour, in Lansing, Michigan, is typical of his expectations: "[She] is a first-class wife who raised eight children and did everything at home herself, in addition to being the receptionist for her husband—and all this with grace and disconcerting facility. What a model for certain French wives of a lesser rank."[21] His relationship with his daughter Janine was colored by this attitude toward women. During her early years, Langlais adored her. But since the birth of Claude, his primary attention had focused on his son. In 1959 Janine married Michel Motton precipitately, after being told by Litaize that she had been adopted.

A shy, sensitive youth, Claude was very close to his mother although not to his sister. By the age of seventeen, he was very musically advanced—an accomplished pianist, a competent organist, and an excellent sight reader: he had since the age of eleven helped his mother correct errors in his father's manuscripts before they were published. He too remembered their long work on *The Passion*, and between 1954 and 1963, he was the main proofreader for Langlais's music. Claude played Messiaen's *Vingt regards* for Régulier (and more recently, he has concertized with organist Fréderick Le Droit)—but he will never forget his two organ lessons with his father.

At the first lesson, Langlais had him play Bach's short Prelude and Fugue in C major. It went well, and Claude expressed his wish to study improvisation. But his father told him that he would have to study harmony and counterpoint first. Claude then borrowed Fauré's *Traité d'harmonie* from Pierre Denis and began the exercises on his own. When he returned for the second lesson in improvisation, his father discovered parallel fifths and octaves and told him that he was not gifted. At the age of eighteen, having graduated first in his class, with highest honors, from high school, Claude was told by his father that he would have to choose between music and engineering as a career. He chose engineering, despite his wish since early youth to be a stonemason like his grandfather.[22]

American Suite

During their return voyage, on 19 March 1959, Langlais began the sketches for *American Suite*. He composed with feverish energy, as if he had subconsciously saved his creativity for one important work that would capture the essence of his American experience. All eight movements were written in their published order except for "Boys Town, Place of Peace," which was composed last, on 10 January 1960.

As in *Folkloric Suite*, the registrations were written in English, and Langlais repeated his cautionary note in the preface. Subsequent tours had not changed his conviction about Americans' capricious attitudes toward registration.

The first movement, "Big Texas," contrasts the vast grandeur of Texas with its quiet and poetic side, using two contrasting themes successively in A B A B A form. The first theme is seven measures long and consists of seven whole notes doubled in octaves and punctuated by bold harmonies on full organ like a grand entry march, recalling in mood the opening movement of *Suite brève*. The second theme, marked *più vivo*, is played on a soft Salicional and Unda maris for the ostinato octaves against a solo Bourdon for the upper part, suggesting the quietness of birds by a stream. It is dedicated to Nita Akin, a Texas organist who had impressed Langlais as very hospitable.

The second, "New York on a Sunday Morning," is a brief tone poem with unusual colors expressing the city's calm on the only day when there are fewer cars. He asked his son what he thought of certain sounds in the movement, and Claude said that they reminded him of car horns. Annoyed by this remark, Langlais was quick to have the score marked with the indication that they are the sounds of pigeons. One should hear the quiet chirping of birds, on a solo Flûte 4 and Tierce 1-3/5, alternate and combine with chimes from Saint Patrick's Cathedral. Some of the bird calls are generic but others, played on the stopped Diapason of the Positif, are identified as ubiquitous pigeons. It is dedicated to Seth Bingham.

"Californian Evocation," the third movement, was written as a remembrance of his many trips there. With imaginative use of registration, he depicts birds, the waves of the Pacific Ocean, the scent of tropical flowers, a quiet stream, and the warm sun. Although the piece is highly programmatic and rhapsodic, the general form is A B A and coda, with the first theme repeated in augmentation in the pedal at 4'. This original theme is in the untransposed Phrygian mode. In the coda, Langlais identifies the last bird call as that of a dove. He interprets the exotic sounds of California through unusual registrations beginning with a Salicional 8 and Tierce 1-3/5, Nasard 2-2/3, and Plein-jeu against a Bourdon 8, Flûtes 4 and 2.

The fourth piece, "Confirmation in Chicago," is an impression of a visit to Saint Paul's Episcopal Church in Chicago, where his former student Robert Rayfield was playing for a confirmation service. It is based on two hymns associated with the rite of confirmation, "Veni, creator spiritus" and "Lebbaeus." Langlais develops the second tune extensively, building up to full organ, and then combines the two themes in the recapitulation.

The fifth movement, "Scherzo-Cats," is also in A B A form with a quiet second section, in which a slower Più lento and Allegro alternate with fragments of the theme. The piece was originally an improvisation, the first four measures of which were based on a theme in Mixolydian mode submitted by Marchal, which Langlais played on the French National Radio. He dedicated the written version to Helen Hewitt of Denton, Texas. Hewitt had many cats whom she named after organ stops. Upon receiving word from Langlais that he had dedicated "Scherzo-Cats" to her, she wrote, "I am so grateful that in spite of the fact that Lady Quintadena died, you have immortalized my cats." Langlais then wrote a Requiem for them. Langlais enjoyed both her and her cats and spoke about them frequently.[23]

"At Buffalo Bill's Grave" recalls his visit near Denver to final resting place of one of America's great cowboys. The quiet in this high mountain spot greatly impressed him, so remote and removed from man, where eagles still patrol the skies and bears inhabit the woods. Langlais labels the theme that characterizes Buffalo Bill a "Western" folk-style tune. It is seven phrases long, pentatonic in the first two phrases and then Dorian transposed to E. Set in variation form, it may be reminiscent of the American folk songs that Kathleen Thomerson (to whom he dedicated the piece) sang to him on a long car trip from Dallas to Wichita during the 1959 tour.

The seventh movement, "Boys Town, Place of Peace," is dedicated to Monsignor Nicholas Wegner, the former director of Boys Town. Langlais played there for the first time in 1959; while he was there, the internationally famous choir boys, who had already sung both his *Messe solennelle* and *Missa in simplicitate*, asked him to play certain chants before Monsignor Francis Schmitt, their director, arrived at their rehearsal. It was in this way that "O salutaris hostia," "Ave maris stella," and the litany "Pray for us" found their way into this piece.[24] Simple sustained major chords on F, G, and A set the mood for this movement, which ends quietly and peacefully with the sound of the quail and the chimes of the chapel tolling the hour.

The last movement, "Storm in Florida," is the most virtuosic piece in the collection. It recalls Hurricane Hazel, which Langlais experienced firsthand at Rollins College, in Winter Park, where he played in late February 1959. He described his fear in a letter to Jeannette: "At 5:00 p.m. attended a party at the home of Catharine Crozier. At six we dined in the hotel. A tropical hurricane is approaching the town. For the first time in my life, thunder fills me with fear. Right now, a loudspeaker . . . plays an arrangement of Debussy's *Claire de lune*, for dancing. We are writing outside, on a veranda, amidst thunder and rain . . . many different sounds."[25] Langlais recaptures the terrifying sounds of thunder, rain, and the rise and fall of the wind by means of rapidly descending thirds and diminished fifths arranged in chromatic, ostinato figures and staccato flashes, with mixtures in the highest registers. It is programmatic music, a fantasy with striking contrasts of tonal color and tessitura that builds to a brilliant climax, with double fifths in the pedal under crashing dissonant chords.

Langlais first toured the United States and Canada when he was forty-five years old. Between 1952 and 1959, he reached the peak of his technical and musical strength. Murtagh told him that of all the artists under her management, he commanded the largest fees and was most frequently engaged. But it was his reputation as a teacher that also grew, each year drawing more and more Americans to study with him in Paris.

CHAPTER 8

New Worlds 1962–1964

He was firm but gentle, demanding but encouraging, impatient but tolerant, humorous but serious, and utterly wise. He is, of course, a genius.

Gerre Hancock, student of Langlais

Organ Study in Paris

During the late 1940s only a handful of American students studied with Langlais; but with his American tours, his published compositions, and his position at Sainte-Clotilde, his popularity as a teacher had increased. By the early 1960s he had many European, Canadian, and American pupils.

A number of his students from the United States lived at the American house in the Cité Universitaire at the southern edge of the city. Even those who were not themselves organists frequently toured Parisian churches on Sunday to hear as many musical programs as possible: Marchal at Saint-Eustache, Dupré at Saint-Sulpice, Duruflé at Saint-Étienne-du-Mont, Messiaen at La Trinité, Suzanne Chaisemartin at Saint-Augustin, Rolande Falcinelli at Sacré-Coeur, Jeanne Demessieux at La Madeleine, Norbert Dufourcq at Saint-Merry, Litaize at Saint-François-Xavier, and, of course, Langlais at Sainte-Clotilde. If the timing of the métro was perfect, it was possible to hear five organists on a Sunday morning.

Hearing these great organists before and during the mass was exciting, but a climb to the organ loft, where they could also be seen, was transporting. These organ loft visitations were a well-established custom in Paris, and most of these titular organists greeted visitors with enthusiasm, as if welcoming them into their homes. Upon entering the organ loft, the host organist usually greeted the guests by shaking hands. At Saint-Sulpice, Madame Dupré always stood at the entrance to the loft and shook hands first before presenting the visitor to M. Dupré. At Saint-Eustache, Marchal greeted the guests himself and often asked for requests for the postlude. One Sunday when the visiting became more boisterous than usual, Marchal exclaimed in a loud stage whisper, "Quiet! The organ loft is not a salon!" For most students the mass was secondary to watching and listening to these legendary Parisian musicians.

On at least one occasion, hearing Messiaen at La Trinité was initially puzzling. The door to the organ loft was locked, and the music suggested a novice substitute. The sacristan confirmed that Messiaen was indeed playing. The music during the communion sounded vaguely familiar and was extremely slow and soft, as if time were suspended. Eventually the piece became recognizable: it was Bach's *Schmücke dich*, but the distortion in tempo made it difficult to identify. Messiaen rarely played his own music at La Trinité; in a letter to Langlais shortly after his 1931 appointment, he admitted, "The wine of my dissonances has become very bitter (for those who are not used to it), and I am obliged to add much water; you will find me well behaved and Classical, alas!"[1] Years had not changed this, and Messiaen held to his mystical ideals by playing Bach in the same tempo as his *Banquet céleste*. He was, however, permitted to improvise at the afternoon's one o'clock mass, with only a handful of people in attendance.

Improvisations

Although Marchal, Langlais, and Dupré often performed major works during the prelude, it was the improvisations of these Parisian organists that held the greatest fascination to American organists. Langlais's were especially exciting and were usually based on familiar Gregorian chants from the ordinary as well as occasional proper chants from the mass. The forms of his improvisations were varied, sometimes strict and at other times very free. He was able to conclude them rapidly when he heard the clack of the wooden clapper on the rail, by which means the choirmaster alerted him to stop.

He drew fresh inspiration each time he improvised and constantly found new ways to interpret the chant. The postlude was often a brilliant toccata in A B A form, which used the full organ; he frequently introduced the theme in the pedal below rapid toccata-like figures in the manuals. During the development, he reduced the registration by removing the reeds and modulated frequently until he arrived again at the tutti, playing the entire theme in canon between the treble and bass.

His registrations often showed the colors of the organ in unusual combinations. For example, he occasionally drew a solitary Bombarde 16 on the Récit, or the Quintaton 16 with a Flûte 4 for solo lines. On tours, Langlais developed an appreciation for German organs, particularly their many mutation stops, which were less known in France. He sometimes contrasted mutation stops, such as a Nasard and Tierce without an 8 for rapid runs and arpeggiated figures in the right hand against the Récit reeds with the box closed.

For some students the study of improvisation held a special attraction. During his early years of teaching Americans, Langlais did not teach improvisation, but by the 1960s, he had a number of improvisation students. On the other hand, Marchal who had taught improvisation in earlier years, no longer taught it and recommended Langlais as a teacher of improvisation to many students. (Marchal had always said that Langlais could make stones improvise.) Before accepting a student of Marchal, Langlais was careful to be sure that Marchal had recommended the pupil; Langlais never wished to be accused of stealing a student.

Langlais taught both improvisation and repertoire at the Schola Cantorum and privately at Sainte-Clotilde, at the Institute for the Blind, and at his apartment. Lessons at the church always took place in the evening, but he was free to use the other two locations during the day. The climb to his apartment was only four flights of stairs, a little less breathtaking than those at Sainte-Clotilde.

Teaching Style

The pedagogical style of European teachers, including Langlais, was largely directive. One did not argue with a teacher nor seek to change his view; the objective was rather to absorb his interpretation as quickly as possible. This process was multifaceted. Watching Langlais play and improvise, week after week, at Sainte-Clotilde was certainly a large part of this osmosis. He taught largely by demonstration, guiding the sense of line and pulse by gently tapping the student's shoulder and singing, as he himself had been taught by his blind teachers, especially Marchal. Once a student asked Marchal why he used a certain phrasing in a Bach trio sonata. After a moment of reflection, Marchal replied, "Because it pleases me."[2]

Despite his directive style of teaching, Langlais gave many students a sense of confidence they had never known before. He overlooked occasional mistakes and permitted the student to finish the piece. Then he would work through it again in detail, instilling his interpretation in the mind of the student. His manner of teaching both blind and sighted students was the same. He maintained a verbal commentary while the student played. He was perfectly capable of working meticulously over several measures on technical questions; but at other times, he functioned as a coach. In either case, he always poured himself completely into his teaching, and his advice was always good.

His memory for music was prodigious. Even years later, he could remember every mistake a student had made and identify it. His years of training at the Institute gave him almost total recall of how a student played a piece, and he would often play back exactly a student's mistakes and even his or her imperfect attempts at improvisation. Langlais invited a number of his students to perform, often during the mass at Sainte-Clotilde and sometimes at the Association Valentin Haüy. He gave of himself without reserve, writing letters of recommendation and organizing concerts at Sainte-Clotilde, the Institute, the French National Radio, Notre-Dame, and elsewhere. He reminded his students that Alfred Cortot prepared pieces for a full year before performing them in concert. Certain students were advised to wait five years before playing a difficult piece in public.

Pupils whose technique was less sure studied nothing but Bach, and some felt frustrated at not having a chance to study Langlais's own music with this master. Langlais used Dupré's organ method and was strict about transposing the exercises up one half step. He insisted that knees be held together and sometimes would even hold them together himself. In his search for perfection, he was relentless.

Students

Langlais's first American student, Maurice John Forshaw, came to him on the recommendation of Charles Walker, then organist at the American Cathedral in Paris. Even at that time Forshaw remembered Langlais's strictness about quiet playing and quiet feet on the pedals, with no movement of the head or torso. "Every time you move your head, you make a mistake," Langlais would say.[3] Langlais, though sightless, could sense any extraneous body movement while a student played.

Many students remarked on how Langlais put them at ease during lessons: "I remember being struck by how completely natural and at ease I felt playing for him the first time."[4] Langlais had a talent for affirming the student's own feelings about the expressiveness of the music.

Both Langlais and Jeannette were especially kind to his students. Janice Beck remembered being invited to their home for dinner and to their summer home in Brittany.

> Jeannette and Jean met me at the train and took me to the small hotel close by their home. Langlais would come for me in the mornings and let me know that he was there by standing under my window (my room was on the second floor) and whistling the tune of "At Buffalo Bill's Grave" from *American Suite*. Then we would walk to his cottage, where Jeannette would have a large cup of hot chocolate for my breakfast. . . . Not often does one have the opportunity to study with a great teacher—one who is critic, mentor, and friend. Jean Langlais was such a teacher.[5]

Another student found him to be a real lifesaver in time of physical illness.

> It is a huge understatement to say that I found him to be sincerely interested in his students—as musicians and in their total well-being. For example, as I was preparing for my Schola Cantorum exams, I suffered a herniated disc in my back. . . . I was in excruciating pain; unable to walk. I was taken to the American Hospital in Paris, where the orthopedist stated that the only treatment was a spinal fusion. Langlais immediately arranged

for an appointment with his personal orthopedist, who turned out to be an internationally renowned physician. . . . His treatment for me included acupuncture. I was able to walk without pain and to continue my practicing in a couple of weeks. Since that time, I have needed X-rays of my back for various reasons, . . . in seeing the condition of that part of my spine, doctors have said that I should not be able to walk! I not only walk but I practice long hours. This would not be possible without the kind concern and direct help of our dear Maître Langlais.[6]

Most students remembered his keen sense of humor and delight at surprises. He often invited them to play during the mass at Sainte-Clotilde. On one occasion during a mass, Langlais presented a student with a composition he had written for her and which she later premiered at Sainte-Clotilde.[7] Another had vivid memories of Langlais's kindnesses, which went far beyond the expected.

Langlais invited me to assist him on his trip to New York and the Boys Town Music Conference, where he gave both master classes and concerts. Our ship passage across the Atlantic was especially memorable as it was the farewell voyage of the *Queen Mary* and was a mixture of celebration and nostalgia for the many passengers. On this trip I learned from Langlais to view things differently. Patience, trust, appreciation . . . he taught them all. In a small way, I was able to experience the needs of one who cannot see.

Mornings on ship were spent making registration notations in my music for the organ works of Bach and Langlais. I sat in amazement as Langlais discussed the complications of a fugue completely from memory. He would say, "And as the theme enters for the third time in the tenor voice, you will add an 8' reed and then when. . . ." It was a humbling experience. My admiration for this man turned to awe. . . .

When Langlais and I returned to New York, he wanted to spend the day at the Metropolitan Museum of Art. With the realization that he had no sight, this request rather startled me. I asked how I could help him enjoy the visit. He said, "Oh, you must understand, I see these masterpieces through your eyes." When we came to a Monet painting, so tranquil in shades of

blue, he said, "Ah, this one is my favorite." I asked, "How did
you know what it is?" He whispered, "I can feel from you the
beauty." Before leaving the Metropolitan, he insisted that we
stop in the museum shop to purchase a copy of that Monet
painting. While saying our last good-byes at the dock, he
handed me a package and said, "I am so grateful." It was the
copy of the Monet painting.

A few months later, a parcel arrived from France. It was a
handwritten score of a composition written and dedicated to
me "with deep appreciation." It was later published. The title
was "De profundis"—"Out of the Depths of My Heart Do I Cry
Unto Thee."[8]

A Benedictine monk also recalled Langlais's attention to detail
and a deference to this student's ecclesiastical position that was both
warmly humorous and sincere.

In all lessons with Maître one fact always remains vivid in my
mind: he missed nothing. How many times did I hear him say,
"Oh, I am sorry Father." With those words I knew immediately
I had done something wrong or displeasing to Maître. The ben-
efits which accrue from such training are inestimable. In reference to his own compositions he told me, "Americans do not
know how to play my music. They will not follow my directions." That, in itself, always taught me to be most faithful to his
text.[9]

Many students were in agreement with one who described
details of the lessons.

Sometimes Langlais sang along as I played, to help shape the
phrasing and rubato. When he wished to place emphasis on a
particular note or chord, he would more often choose to delay
it rather than prolong it. He often said, "delay" as I was approaching an appropriate place for an agogic accent.

Langlais was very encouraging and could be quite complimentary. At the same time, he did require a certain level of performance, particularly with regard to appropriate style and
interpretation. Certain wrong notes would shock him into saying "ooh-la-la." Others he would let pass. He was an inspiring

teacher, not a pedantic one. He was generally patient. Despite his blindness, he could ferret out awkward fingerings and would suggest excellent alternative solutions.[10]

Another student remembered that his "playing had to be 'quiet' (close control of the action)."[11] Some of the descriptions of his teaching were colorful.

> I always pictured Maître as a giant ear on the couch. He used his braille score for Bach. He used to start counting aloud, then would beat on the bench or beat on my shoulder as the going got tougher. Each measure had to be right before going to the next. He would sometimes play back my mistake, then play the passage correctly. The fingering had to be right—he could tell if it wasn't—either the notes were late or there was too much noise or energy expended. There were no options presented— just one way to do things. In some Franck, I asked "Which edition are you using?" He growled, "The *right* one.". . . The phrase was paramount. Pretend you're singing the phrase, breathe like a singer with the phrase. . . . He could go from being the most lovable little old man to a real dictator! . . . I have many fond memories of taking walks with him and Paf (his dog), also driving with him and Madame to their Vietnamese restaurant for lunch and his backseat driving. He never seemed handicapped.[12]

His attention to fingering was legendary. When a student was playing Bach's Triple Fugue in E-flat major for him, he began the second fugue with the fourth finger of his left hand. Langlais realized immediately which finger he had used and suggested beginning with the third finger. The student, who was already flustered, began again with his fourth finger, and Langlais roared, "You are so *stoo*pide, the third finger, begin with the *third* finger!"[13]

Nor were all the lessons of a technical nature. Langlais's faith did not go unnoticed.

> He had a deep faith. We used to talk about that a lot, and it is something that he didn't discuss with most of his pupils. . . . I mentioned to him that Simone Plé-Caussade had retired from her class at the Conservatory of Paris the year before and had entered the convent. He asked me to write to her and ask her to

pray for him every day. He stressed *every day*. It was very touching. Some years later (1978, I believe) when I was visiting him in Paris, he told me about his terrible heart attack, when he had been within inches of death. "I think that Simone Plé really prayed for me each day," he said. . . . His faith was such that he felt he should not work on Sundays, but he didn't want a day to pass without a lesson, so he got permission. I still have a letter he sent to me in Paris from Brittany telling me he would be back on such and such a date for a lesson, which was a Sunday, but not to worry, for he had permission from the priest.[14]

A former student remembered Langlais's sensitivity to linguistic needs and interpretation of his own works.

He liked to present his students with challenges, but at the same time he realized that it's essential for them to be comfortable. I suppose this is why he switched back and forth between English and French when he was talking to his students. Those who spoke French well enough were always honored by him speaking to them in French. On the other hand, when students (or guests to the organ loft) seemed uncomfortable with French, he immediately switched into English, which he enjoyed speaking. This sensitivity to the needs of others was, and is, one of his fine points as a human being. I used my period of study with him to work on as many Langlais compositions as possible, including some that I had learned previously. Through his teaching I realized that I had overromanticized some of his works and had ignored the Neoclassical elements. He soon set me straight.[15]

Not all students had positive experiences, however.

He gave me some work in harmony and counterpoint. This work was always punctuated by exasperated groans and comments about "ces Américains" who never learned harmony right. . . . Now this giant (as I saw him) was screaming at me at times, turning all his great powers of invective to goad me into doing it right. It worked. . . . My lessons were grueling and difficult. Langlais had made me a project, I think, having to undo the problems that I had developed as someone largely self-taught. I was quickly forbidden to do anything else but the six trio sonatas in a row. . . . I remember those days vividly. They were some of the most challenging of my life. What made it even harder was my hero-worship of Langlais.[16]

Another remembered his improvisation lessons as a disappointment: "There was never a hint of any harmonic plan so that one would have an idea of a tonal structure. He would occasionally improvise himself on that theme if you wanted to see what he would do to it, but it wasn't truly much help. 'Do what you wish' was the constant reply to my inquiries."[17]

A student who had hoped to gain special insights into the Franck tradition was also disappointed.

He was strict with every aspect of performance: repeated notes, unapproved-of non-legato, fingering and pedaling. Sometimes he would suggest fingering for a passage that I had played perfectly well, which I thought an odd waste of time and energy, and perhaps others that he knew from experience would work all the time. . . . I felt his "school" was primarily Dupré (absolute legato, repeated notes, etc.) but with more rhythmic elasticity thrown in. He had very definite ideas of how a piece was supposed to go, and felt I should do it *that* way. On the other hand, there were many, many instances where he allowed the student (me) to decide how to interpret a passage. In that respect he was very much a coach. It was difficult to argue with him because he was 1) so famous, 2) so much older, and 3) French. . . . I always tried to discuss a sticky point with him later, after the passage had passed and we were on to something else. That way it wouldn't seem that I was criticizing him or making him defend his point of view. . . . While I never brought up the subject of a "Franck tradition," rather trying to arrive at one naturally, I noted many times his preference of the way a modern organist would play a passage rather than the way Franck *had* to have played it. . . . He had no interest in the problems encountered on an old Cavaillé-Coll organ, obviously, because he had spent a lifetime overcoming them. Likewise, he never quoted anything any of Franck's students had said. Whether things would have occurred to him under different circumstances I could not tell, but, even a word of interpretative information from Marty or Mahaut was awaited in vain. . . . . He revealed almost nothing that I had not read previously, even telling me anecdotes that appeared in the d'Indy and Vallas Franck books, as though he had been there or, perhaps, they had told him, too.[18]

Lesson Venues

Lessons at Sainte-Clotilde had special significance. By the last of the sixty-four steps of the steep, endlessly winding circular stone staircase, students were out of breath but Langlais appeared undaunted. By evening, it was completely dark in the church, and Langlais led the way to the organ loft, down a second set of stairs. Inside the narrow organ loft, a light revealed a photograph of Tournemire on the left wall and on the right, a photograph of Franck and the shroud of Turin, reminders of the tradition that abided here.

Since Langlais had had a new console installed, in the spring of 1962, the organ had a light touch on both the pedals and manuals and was among the easiest in Paris to play. He was very proud of his additions, which he had supervised under the direction of the firm Beuchet-Debierre.[19] The second tracker console from 1933 had had a very stiff action, and the difference between the two was striking. Often during the lesson, he reminded his students of the reasoning behind his changes and the way in which they enhanced the music. One felt in his teaching his enthusiasm for these changes.

The unique blend of power, responsiveness, and lyricism in this instrument helped bring out the best in every player. He helped with the registration and, in Franck's music, added the reeds at the appropriate times. Langlais used only the stops from the original organ for Franck's music. Very often during lessons, he would explain that the breath between sections and the fermatos were too short. Given the reverberant acoustics and unique sound of the full organ at Sainte-Clotilde, his students soon learned to enjoy holding chords longer and elongating the rests while listening to the echo of the reeds slowly fade away.

The occasional lessons at Langlais's apartment were on his two-manual Schwenkedel electro-pneumatic action organ. He had ordered this instrument in 1960, using the profits from his tours to replace the old Mustel pedal harmonium. Although the organ was very small, it was more difficult to play than the large Cavaillé-Coll. The pipes were directly in front of the player, and their speech was immediate and the voicing pronounced.[20] He insisted that the nuances for Franck's music be observed painstakingly, nonetheless, which was also more difficult to do than it was at Sainte-Clotilde.

Schola Cantorum

The organ class at the Schola Cantorum had been very small under Langlais's predecessors but expanded rapidly after Langlais's appointment in 1961 upon the invitation of the new director, Jacques Chailley. Founded in 1896 by Vincent d'Indy, Charles Bordes, and Alexandre Guilmant, the Schola Cantorum became a center for the study of church music based on the best historical models, including Gregorian chant, the great masters of the Renaissance and Baroque, and modern composers, especially Franck, with whom both Bordes and d'Indy had studied. Teachers there before Langlais's tenure included Vierne, Wandowska, Daniel-Lesur, and Fleury.

In 1900, when the school moved into its present location on rue Saint-Jacques, near the Sorbonne, d'Indy became its sole musical director. The building had been a Benedictine monastery, and the chapel was converted into a concert hall that seated five hundred. The organ here was a small three-manual tracker by Cavaillé-Coll–Mutin with a very heavy touch, especially on the Récit, and by 1963 it was in poor condition.[21] After the move to rue Saint-Jacques, Bordes took over the financial and fund-raising work and established a publishing house, Editions de la Schola Cantorum, which eventually published many of Langlais's choral and organ works.

Langlais's classes at the Schola were held each Saturday afternoon from one to four. In 1963 the ten students included three Americans (Allen Hobbs, Richard Forrest Woods, and me). Although prepared pieces were played at each session in preparation for the final exam, most of the work was in improvisation.

Teaching Improvisation

Langlais had a rare gift as a teacher of improvisation. He used Gregorian chant themes exclusively for beginners. In general, all the forms based on chant could be classified as Gregorian paraphrase, in that the chant was altered and developed rather freely. The first lesson began with what he called a "contemplative prelude" that used the first phrase of one of his favorite Kyries, "Orbis factor." He explained that the form of an improvisation could be approached by thinking first about registrational colors: for example, three quiet sonorities (such as strings, Flûte 8, and Cornet with a soft pedal) could yield a double exposition of the theme. He demonstrated by alternating fragments of the theme in the right hand between the solo reed and the flute accompanied by the strings and soft pedal. He then demonstrated the second part of the prelude with a Flûte 4 in the pedal playing the theme, accompanied by ostinato chords on the Récit. This type of prelude could be complete in itself or be followed by a toccata.

The second type of prelude was the Gregorian paraphrase, similar in form to the chorale preludes of Buxtehude and Bach, which began with an introduction. Each phrase or portion of the theme was then presented in the soprano with interludes in between each one ending with a coda. The interludes were very free and usually modulatory.

The third type of prelude was in A B A form, still based on a single theme, similar to the thème libre but much simpler. The A section was the same as the contemplative prelude, but the B section developed fragments of the theme modulating to several key centers and building to a climax. The return of the A section was slightly varied from the first section, such as in the second part of the contemplative prelude, in which the theme was played in the pedal with a 4′ stop accompanied by soft chords on the Récit. This prelude and any other quiet improvisation could either end quietly or be followed by a toccata. With some students, he was strict about the length, which was to be exactly ten minutes.

Langlais's harmonic language was deeply ingrained; he appeared unaware of the mechanics of it. Likewise his teaching of harmonic style was very free and intuitive. He did not impose any particular harmonic idiom but let the student try to develop his own. Once a student stopped him during an improvisation lesson to ask what harmony he had just used; Langlais answered that he didn't know, and they could not find the same chord again. Students learned his style by listening and watching him improvise.

For a toccata, he first demonstrated many types of figures dividing the motif between the hands, at first using only two notes with each hand. He then showed how this figure could be continued by manual changes and modulating to other keys. After an introduction based on the toccata figure, the theme was first put into the pedal and then in the soprano. This was followed by a development of fragments of the theme and concluded with a recapitulation of the theme, sometimes in canon between the soprano and the pedal, accompanied by faster note values in the hands.

After a student had mastered these forms, he explained other symphonic forms, such as the scherzo and the symphonic allegro with two themes. For these forms he gave original themes. These forms were basically the same as those found in the organ symphonies of Vierne and Widor, but simplified. Students were at first intimidated and yet filled with his enthusiasm for what they could do. He always made it seem natural and easy. Langlais also taught strict forms of the scholastic fugue, ricercare, and canons. He often improvised a six-part ricercare, with double pedal lasting ten minutes.[22]

One of the French students at the Schola Cantorum had very little formal training in organ and apparently almost none in theory. Despite these weaknesses Langlais taught him to improvise. Using Gregorian chant themes exclusively, he started by demonstrating how to improvise a very simple prelude on a chant with an introduction, each phrase of the chant with an interlude between, and a coda at the end. He made the frightened student begin to play, warning him that—no matter what—he was not to stop. At first, the student wailed and protested about how terrible it sounded, but Langlais would not let him stop and continued to instruct him throughout the improvisation. They had a running dialogue as the prelude progressed. Little by little, the playing improved, and the entire class was amazed at how quickly Langlais was able to get results.

Although at the Schola Cantorum Langlais's students studied neither the harmonization of the modes nor the harmonization of

Langlais and students at the Schola Cantorum, 1966

chant melodies, Langlais did teach these privately to some students. The chant was first harmonized using triads exclusively and avoiding all 6/4 chords, dominant sevenths, and major-minor seventh chords. The leading tone diminished chords in first inversion was favored. The choice of harmony followed very closely Dupré's method.[23] Langlais's chant book was a braille copy of *Paroissen romain*, which he kept in the organ loft at Sainte-Clotilde for his improvisations.

Some years later, while giving a lesson to Naji Hakim, Langlais opined, "One should maintain great respect for the body of chant, which was composed by great composers, not the concierge." At that moment the bell sounded. It was the concierge bringing him the mail. Hakim and Langlais doubled over with laughter.[24]

Paranormal Gifts

Part of Langlais's gift as a teacher involved nonverbal communication. He imparted a sense of security and confidence, a confidence that seemed to radiate from teacher to pupil, enabling the pupil to play better. As soon as one sat down at the organ, one felt it.

Langlais claimed that he had the gift of extrasensory perception; he often knew that an event would happen before it occurred. Once at the Schola, he decided to see what would happen if he used the force of his thoughts in a negative way, and he strenuously concentrated on making a certain student unable to play. After several phrases, she stopped and asked to begin over. Things were even worse after the second start, and she stopped once more, saying that she did not think she should try again because something was wrong. The student sensed that Langlais was not open to her music and playing.

Langlais perceived himself as a Christ-figure and was compelled to use, like his Breton forebears, his gifts as a healer. He would place his hands on a patient, believing that the fluid in his hands had a healing effect. In his 1959 tour journal, he described having healed Darius Milhaud, the eminent French composer. Although he tried to keep his promise to Jeannette and neither practice this ancient craft nor speak much about it, he helped me and other students, including Naji Hakim, Marie-Louise Jaquet, and Susan Ferré, in this way.

Names in Music

Langlais in his early fifties was possessed of what should have been a satisfying domestic life, with a helpmate wife, two grown children, and a passionate mistress. Jeannine Collard was still very much present in his life and owned a house next door to them in Plaisir, their weekend home near Paris, where she took the main meal with them daily; she continued to vacation with his family in Brittany. She, Jeannette, and Langlais were a happy ménage à trois.

But Langlais's quest for passion now led him to a series of romantic liaisons with certain of his female students, relationships which were to profoundly affect his compositional techniques. In these affairs and attempted affairs, he was—as he had been—aided and abetted by Jeannette, and he continued in this way until, after Jeannette's death, he married one of his more enduring conquests. He was, in the French manner, always somewhat discreet about the physical expression of these infatuations.

He now sought to reveal, in his music, his innermost desires and thoughts as well as the names of persons, as he had Jeannine's in *Missa in simplicitate*. By using pitches to correspond to letters of the alphabet, he was able to write names and even complete sentences, in the form of a musical theme. In this system, the first eight letters of the alphabet correspond to the pitches of the scale, using a B-flat for the letter B and B-natural for the letter H. The rest of the alphabet is tied to the same pitches in the same order, thus:

A	a	i	q	y
B^b	b	j	r	z
C	c	k	s	
D	d	l	t	
E	e	m	u	
F	f	n	v	
G	g	o	w	
B	h	p	x	

Langlais was by no means the inventor of this system; many composers had used it, notably Liszt in his *Prelude and Fugue on B.A.C.H.*

Langlais used the system in *Hommage à Rameau*, begun in 1962. Revised and published by Elkan-Vogel as *Homage to Rameau*, it is a suite of six pieces, titled to form an acrostic on Rameau's name: "Remembrance," "Allegretto," "Meditation," "Evocation," "As a Fugue," "United Themes." The suite was completed in 1964, the bicentennial of the death of Jean-Philippe Rameau, with the swift composition of "United Themes" between 16 and 20 August. As suggested by its title, this last piece uses themes from the five previous movements, thus summing up the entire work. Its cyclic nature was a response to Dupré's *Symphonie-passion*, which Langlais thought had a weak ending.

In the fourth piece, "Evocation," Langlais used a name motif to build a theme, in this case a sentence—"I love you, Ann" (A, D, G, F, E, G-sharp, F, E, A, F, F)—into an expansive free fantasy.

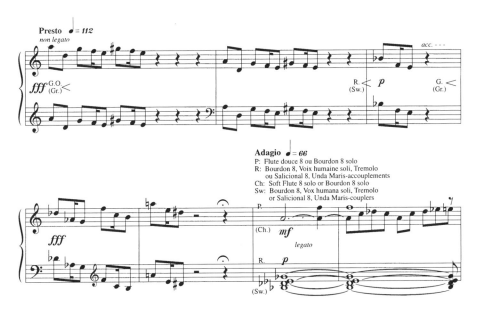

Homage to Rameau, "Evocation," mm. 1–7. © 1986 Editions Musicales Alphonse Leduc, Paris. Used by permission.

The rhythmic strength of the first part of the theme is contrasted with the lyricism of the name's setting; the middle section of the fantasy explores this lyricism in an expanded form, with the theme in the pedal at 4′ pitch below an accompanying triplet obbligato.

"Evocation" is significant because it is the first time Langlais expressed intense personal feelings in a work of such length (duration 10:47). It signals the beginning of a new period of composition. A number of works followed this departure, in even longer free forms, works that freely communicated Langlais's deepest feelings toward people and other beings he loved and lost—and his faith in response to the love and the loss. The love theme that opens "Evocation" became the basis of *Mass "God Have Mercy"* (1964), first as a prayer in the Kyrie, next as a statement of praise in the beginning of the Gloria, then as the transition between the Sanctus and Benedictus, and finally as a prayer in the Agnus Dei. And the name motif A, F, F permeated *Psaume solennel no. 3* (1964) as a kind of leitmotif, in the grand opening of the unison trombones and again at the Amen's conclusion.

The reader, I trust, will permit a personal intrusion at this point. As may have been surmised, I was the object of Langlais's declaration of love in "Evocation." In the spring of 1964, while I was studying with him, Langlais fell in love with me. He proposed, with Jeannette's acquiescence, to divorce her and marry me.

It was, of course, a very seductive experience to be the source of such profound creative energy. I was his adoring student, and as such, was most flattered by his devotion and offer of marriage. Fortunately for us both, however, I was aware of the terrible consequences to each of us that would have resulted. Had Langlais divorced Jeannette, he would have lost his position at Sainte-Clotilde, since the Church did not recognize divorce. To be cut off from this even greater source of inspiration would have devastated him. As for me, I was anticipating my marriage to Lewis Steele, who became my husband in 1965.

Though I rejected his suit, Langlais remained a close friend and collaborator. His sense of pain and loss likewise became for him an inspiration. Already inclined toward symbolic expression, he found in name motifs the opportunity to express a combination of personal and spiritual experiences in an elaborate riddle that conceals while it seems to display.

CHAPTER 9

America Revisited 1959–1969

Listening to this César Franck *redivivus* improvise, I would have given anything to descend into the mystical grotto of Langlais's tonal imagery just at the moment this fantasia reached the height.

Henry Humphreys, American music critic

Langlais felt a special attachment to Boys Town, where during the summer church music workshops of 1959, 1961, 1963, 1965, and 1967 he taught and played recitals. He also performed at Boys Town during the 1964, 1967, and 1969 tours. Not only did he enjoy the calm and peaceful atmosphere, but he felt keenly the love, discipline, and purpose of the home: to give a last chance to delinquent boys. Although Father Edward Joseph Flanagan died in 1948, his philosophy that all boys were basically good lived on in his successor, Monsignor Wegner, whom Langlais greatly admired. Langlais was impressed that the boys came to his recitals of their own accord and were friendly to him.

Father Flanagan's Boys' Home

Boys Town represented much of what Langlais found attractive in his American experience. It was quiet and reminded him of the college campuses that he loved so much. He stayed in one place for two weeks, which he would have liked to do during the tours, and was very well paid for his efforts. He walked everywhere and felt completely independent. Interesting students and faculty, many of whom, like Roger Wagner, returned each summer, contributed to the stimulating, convivial atmosphere. Although the workshops were ecumenical, he keenly felt the Catholic atmosphere of Boys

Town, especially at the rectory and chapel with Wegner and Schmitt.[1] Changes after the Second Vatican Council would put Langlais in conflict with French clergy, so he especially appreciated the spirit of these two American priests. Despite the hot climate in the summer, he always looked forward to returning.

The home is a square-mile self-contained community ten miles west of Omaha, Nebraska. Its facilities include a working farm, grade school, high school, post office, venues for Catholic, Protestant, and Jewish services, sports arena, auditorium, and group homes. By 1968 its music facilities boasted a 1261-seat hall and twenty-five air-conditioned practice, rehearsal, and conference rooms. Father Flanagan, who founded Boys Town in 1917, also organized the first choir there in the late 1930s. Shortly thereafter he appointed Francis Schmitt to the post of choirmaster with the stipulation that he build "the finest choir of boys in the country."[2]

Francis Schmitt, choirmaster from 1941 to 1975, was responsible for developing the unique Boys Town music program, which included instrumental and choral training and even several functioning string quartets. Choir boys developed a strong camaraderie and pride in their organization, both through the quality of their singing and by their common residence in choir cottages, suitably named Villa Vittoria, Palestrina Pillbox, Franck's Flats, and Chateau des Près. In addition to singing for weekly liturgies in the Dowd Memorial Chapel, the choir under Schmitt made innumerable radio and television appearances and recordings and performed around the world. The famed music program at Boys Town was the subject of a doctoral dissertation; the choir also appeared in segments of two movies, *Boys Town* and *The Men of Boys Town*.[3] The ethos of Boys Town—embodied in the image of a young boy carrying a younger crippled child on his back and captured in the slogan, "He ain't heavy, Father . . . he's m' brother"—won the hearts of Americans everywhere.

Summer Workshops

In addition to his duties as choirmaster and editor of the sacred music journal *Caecilia*, Schmitt organized and directed the church music workshops at Boys Town from 1952 to 1969. The workshops presented a microcosm of excellence in church music during this period and became a mecca for the approximately 150 church musicians of all faiths who attended. Daily courses in music history, liturgy, choir training, chant, choral literature, and organ were given. Although Boys Town was not a college, Schmitt offered through Creighton University and Saint Mary's College in Omaha both graduate and undergraduate credit for these summer workshops. Partly from this accreditation and from generous donations by participants, by Boys Town alumni, and by Schmitt, Boys Town gradually amassed a library of music and books of more than six thousand volumes.[4] During the solemn pontifical mass that closed each workshop, the Saint Caecelia Medal was awarded to leaders in church music for "recognition of outstanding contributions to the field of liturgical music." Both Langlais and Schmitt received the award in 1961.

The positive influence of these workshops was wide-ranging. Through financial backing from the archbishop of Omaha, Gerald T. Bergan, Schmitt attracted faculty with international reputations from both America and Europe: musicologists and music historians Louise Cuyler, Paul Henry Lang, and Eugene Selhorst; liturgists Alfred Bischel, Cornelius Bouman, Francis A. Brunner, Walter Buszin, George and Anna Gallos, Jozef Joris, Maurice Lasvanouz, Peter Peacock, Samuel Rosenbaum, and Richard Schuler; and Gregorian chant specialists Charles Dreisoerner and Dom Vitry.

Roger Wagner conducted the choral sessions at each workshop, preparing the participants for a concert of large sacred choral works at the end of the two-week session; works performed included Britten's *War Requiem*; Brahms's, Fauré's, and Duruflé's Requiems; Bruckner's "Te Deum"; Bloch's *Sacred Service*; and Langlais's *Psaumes solennels nos. 1–3*. Many premieres of French music were given; Tournemire's music was played frequently. Other choral leaders included George Bragg, C. Alexander Peloquin, Paul Salamonovich, and James Welch. Father Schmitt, with the assistance of Frank Synskie, led sessions in boy choir techniques, using the Boys Town choir to demonstrate.

Other organists who attended included Flor Peeters, Michael Schneider, Myron Roberts, and Everett Hilty. Often three organists appeared during the same two-week period. In 1965, when Langlais led all the organ sessions, he and Anton Heiller gave organ recitals.

In 1967 Claire Coci, Paul Manz, and Langlais played recitals. Once Father Schmitt told Langlais that both he and Coci had programmed Langlais's *Incantation*. Would Langlais like to substitute another piece? Langlais replied, "Oh no—zis way zay will know how it is to be played!"[5]

During the five summers he participated, Langlais's schedule for the two-week period would typically include eight or nine master classes, usually in the evening, one concert on the Reuter organ in the Dowd Memorial Chapel, and private lessons. His master classes in organ literature and improvisation influenced organists, particularly in the technique, registration, and interpretation of French music. He lived in the rectory across from the chapel but usually took his meals with the faculty and participants, giving everyone additional opportunities to socialize with him. At the 1967 workshop, however, Langlais dined with Paul Manz every night in the rectory, each seated at opposite ends of the long table. One night Langlais pulled out his special tool for eating, a combination knife and fork, and asked Manz what they were having for dinner and where on the plate each food was. He learned the meat was at twelve o'clock, the potatoes at four, and the peas at eight. It took him an hour to eat, but he speared every last pea. Not a single crumb was left on his plate. Manz told him that when the maid returned, she looked at Langlais and then up to heaven, as if to ask how he was able to do it.

Many Americans, including Allen Hobbs, Kathleen Thomerson, and Susan Ferré studied with Langlais at Boys Town and subsequently in Paris. Allen Hobbs, who frequently attended the workshops, described the caliber of certain summer workshop students:

> Some of them were terrible—a real penance for Jean Langlais. One day he told me he wanted to change his profession. I remember one particularly untalented pupil told him, "Oh, Mr. Langlais, you are so patient." He replied, "Yes, I have to be." Sometimes it would get on his nerves noticeably. One lady asked him (I was interpreting) if he thought she had improved. He told me to tell her, "It is very easy to improve when one is very poor."[6]

The summer workshops were not entirely restricted to academic pursuits nor were all the encounters were formal. The distances between the chapel, the auditorium, and music building gave ample time for casual discussion, and there were often light moments. During one rehearsal, Father Schmitt, in full nun's habit, sang soprano in a soprano section populated mainly by nuns, who had to work hard to keep singing. He claimed that Roger Wagner picked unmercifully on the sopranos when the tenors and basses were no better. When Langlais stopped by to listen, everyone convulsed into laughter and then included him in the joke.[7]

Langlais enjoyed the companionship of Roger Wagner very much. Before they worked together at Boys Town, a mutual professional and personal admiration had been built up between them in France, where Wagner often visited Sainte-Clotilde to hear Langlais play. Their pleasure was heightened by friendly rivalry over their romantic conquests. Langlais was overjoyed when Jeannine Collard refused a fur coat that Wagner offered her and was sure to tell everyone about the incident.

Allen Hobbs recalled Langlais's method of increasing his vocabulary during his off hours:

> He was really making efforts to speak English well, which I admired very much. By [1961] he was getting a lot of American students, especially Fulbright scholars. [Claude] too was making progress in English, but Langlais did not want to learn from his son. Instead, he made a little list of words to learn in English every day, and we would lunch together at the tourist's cafe . . . and work on his daily word list. Most of the words did not even concern music. They concerned anything which entered his mind. [8]

Claude Langlais accompanied his father to Boys Town in 1959, 1961, and 1963, and though Langlais's relationship with his son was never an easy one, both father and son appreciated these opportunities to be together. Langlais had a frustrated desire for Claude to show his admiration, but Claude found it difficult to talk to his father; Claude needed Langlais's affirmation, but Langlais could not give it. Throughout the years, however, Claude found his own ways of expressing his love for "Papa." Already a talented photographer, in March 1961 he took a series of pictures of his father at the organ at Sainte-Clotilde, which Langlais immediately used for publicity; he later built him an organ.

Claude and Jean Langlais, walking from the chapel to the music building, Boys Town, 1959

Langlais wanted Claude to see more of America. To that end, in addition to the Boys Town trip in the summer of 1961, he accepted a recital at Canadian College in Saint Catherine's, Ontario. From there they visited Niagara Falls, the first time for both. On a previous visit Langlais had had problems with the Canadian police concerning his American visa, but he overcame his worry about crossing the border because he so wanted to be a tourist with his son.[9]

Trois méditations sur la Sainte-Trinité

As Langlais and Claude were returning to France from the 1961 Boys Town workshop, they stopped in New York City, where they attended mass at Saint Patrick's Cathedral. Two of the musical selections Langlais heard there, the hymn "Saint Anne" and the Pater Noster, gave him the idea to compose a work in three movements based on the Trinity, *Trois méditations sur la Sainte-Trinité*. The hymn "Saint Anne" ("O God, Our Help in Ages Past") reminded him of Bach's Triple Fugue in E-flat major, in which three subjects are first introduced singly and then combined to symbolize the three persons of the Trinity. The piece is significant in that it is the only one in which Langlais attempts to express the triune theological concept in musical terms. He combines two God-the-Father themes for the first movement, titled "Première personne: le Père." For the second movement, "Deuxième personne: le Fils," he borrows a Breton folk song to represent the humanity of the Son, weaving it with the first two. And for the last movement, "Troisième personne: le Saint Esprit," the chant "Veni, creator spiritus," introduced by the full organ in a brilliant toccata figure, is purposefully united with all previous themes.

Essai

A significant departure for Langlais was the work *Essai*, composed on 10 and 11 November 1961. Each year the Paris Conservatory commissions a technically demanding composition, which is given to the students six weeks before the final exam; *Essai* was commissioned for the 1962 organ exam. Langlais's English translation of *Essai* ("Trial"), which he used as the subtitle, indicated that his first and only attempt at serial composition was in one sense a trial for him, as well as a trial for the technical limits of the performers. The work is dedicated to Marguerite Long, an American who studied with Langlais between 1958 and 1962. Langlais intended to tease future musicologists by this. He laughed to think of it: "They will think that Marguerite Long, the famous pianist and mistress of Fauré, was *my* organ pupil when she was almost ninety years old!"[10]

Although he had occasionally ventured into atonal writing, *Essai* was his first composition which was entirely atonal and in which he employed seven tone rows.[11] The number of tones in each row varied from eight to eleven. In the first five rows, Langlais achieved thematic and musical interest by using the first five tones as a soft, sustained chord providing an atonal background for five distinct themes. The themes are combined, treated in imitation, strict canon, augmentation, and diminution, using many contrasts in registration, tempo, and mood. The general effect of the piece is atonal, with well-defined thematic development but without a systematic use of tone rows. In the last measure Langlais uses a full twelve-tone row with the upper partials of the twelfth and nineteenth playing more softly than the sustained chord using a solo Nasard and Tierce on single notes.

Essai, last measure. © 1962 Editions Musicales Alphonse Leduc, Paris. Used by permission.

In the middle of the piece, marked *tutti*, there is a toccata motif in octaves for the hands beginning with a five-note figure above the first theme in the pedal, which Langlais suggested should be played like Messiaen's "Le verbe" (*La nativité du Seigneur*) on the full tutti.

Lilian Murtagh

Langlais's popularity in America may be credited, in part, to the careful efforts of his manager, Lilian Murtagh, who was responsible for the organ division of the Colbert LaBerge agency. Their correspondence was lively and revealed many facets of his personality—not least of which was Langlais's wish to control the agency's roster of artists. When his best friend Litaize was engaged, Langlais demanded that publicity for his own tour be sent out first so that his bookings would not diminish in number. He spoke pointedly against other artists, even to the extent of labeling them deranged.

On the other hand, much of his correspondence with Murtagh concerned arrangements for Americans to perform at Sainte-Clotilde. Langlais was eager to help those whom he felt merited it but opposed inviting those whom he believed misunderstood the French style of playing. He arranged many recitals at Sainte-Clotilde for such LaBerge artists as Claire Coci, William Whitehead, and Wilma Jensen. It was he who recommended Marie-Claire Alain to the agency and was very pleased by her subsequent success.

Many letters concerned his desire to always begin the tours in New York at Saint Thomas Church and end them at the Church of the Heavenly Rest, where his good friend Charles Walker was music director. In almost every letter Langlais included a joke for Lilian's husband, Lou. A favorite concerned Debussy and Satie: one day, Satie plays a work for Debussy; Debussy says to him, "Your music is very good but you should be more precise about the form"—so Satie titles his next work "Three pieces in the form of a pear." Several of his jokes had sexual and religious references, such as the woman who went to confession to admit she had become a prostitute. Upset, the priest asked her to repeat her confession, and then with relief he declared there was no problem, he'd misheard her the first time: he thought she had become a Protestant. Langlais's telling of these jokes illustrated his less-than-perfect command of English, which Americans found charming; one letter closed with this admonishment for "dear Lou": "Excuse my mistakes and laugh correctly."[12]

1964 American Tour

Langlais's sixth American tour came at the apex of his career as a teacher and performer. Between 4 October and 7 December 1964, he performed forty-four concerts, in venues stretching from New York to Minnesota to Florida. Though some recitals were more successful than others, every one displayed his mastery of the organ and his ability to move audiences with his music.[13]

Our round-trip transatlantic crossing was on *La France*. Langlais's shipboard routine was already fixed from previous tours, and time passed quickly in long discussions and occasional readings from the well-stocked library. (He found Victor Hugo's writing as distasteful as Brahms's music, and the volume was quickly returned.) Once in Manhattan, he delighted in staying at the Great Northern Hotel, breakfasting at the pharmacy across the street, and seeing his old friends Janet and Charles Walker and Seth Bingham and his wife. As always, Langlais took at least one meal at the Café Brittany, where he exchanged stories with the servers, all of whom were Breton.

Langlais wanted a cashmere coat like the one that Marchal had bought while on tour in America, and my job was to help him find it. He tried on one black overcoat after another, finally settling on one that was not pure cashmere. I had not realized how much the softness of the coat meant to him, nor did I understand at the time his emotional need to equal Marchal, no matter the expense. In the end the purchase was a great disappointment to him.

Langlais was a keen judge of character and personality and formed a lasting impression of a person on first contact, by listening intently to the person's voice and by the type of handshake. If the person were an organist, he wanted to know how they sat on the bench and how they moved while they played. When we were in Syracuse he met Arthur Poister. Langlais liked him on the spot but was not sure whether the feeling was mutual. At the end of the recital he was reassured; Poister came to him, shook his hand enthusiastically, complimented him on his playing, and insisted on calling him by his first name: "From now on, I shall be Arthur for you and you shall be Jean for me." Langlais took this informality as a sure sign of friendship.[14]

After the same recital Langlais introduced me to my former

teacher, David Craighead, whose playing he admired a great deal. When Craighead presented himself to Langlais in the receiving line, Langlais asked him if he recognized his guide. Craighead stared at me for a moment and then cried, "Ann!" This delighted Langlais.

Almost constantly mentally stimulated, Langlais was rarely bored; nor did he often sit quietly. Even when riding in trains and busses, his face showed intent concentration. He was thinking about music, either a piece he was to perform or an idea for a composition. Impatient, demanding, opinionated, unpredictable, earthy, anxious, bellicose—but kind: all these words described him. He took an active dislike to anyone who did not allow him to be the center of attention. Anyone who spoke only of themselves he found reprehensible, pompous, and boring. Langlais let you know what was troubling him and kept letting you know, even years after the slight had occurred. As Jeannette wrote in a letter to Lilian Murtagh dated 24 February 1969, "When he is tired, his irritability boils over to everyone."

The frequent onslaught of questions to which he was subjected while on tour especially tried his patience: "I spent a terrible day because at every meal and free moment, I was bombarded by batteries of technical, picky questions about music, organ, scale fingerings, and so forth. In spite of myself I envied our Trappist brothers and their silence."[15] Although his command of English was adequate, in private he always spoke in French, which provided him a welcome respite.

On 3 November 1964, Langlais flew from Buckhannon, West Virginia, to Tallahassee, his first plane travel in the United States. The flight was turbulent, and he panicked, wanting to know what was happening each second. In Cincinnati the printed program, which we received just as he was to start playing, was incorrect. Fortunately the console could not be seen by the audience, and I crawled around pulling the correct stops for the additional piece. (The audience suspected nothing.) At the conclusion of another recital he was presented with a key to the city in an informal ceremony: "The mayor of New Orleans told me that this city is an important cultural center. 'The proof,' he said, 'is that you are among us this evening and a little time ago the Beatles were also here.' There was general laughing!"[16]

Even though Langlais always claimed that reviews did not interest him, he was eager to hear what had been written about him the day after each recital. Critics praised his lyrical playing and clarity of line and registration, judging him a "great organist who represents a direct, unpretentious style of playing rarely offered in the United States."[17] His improvisation on "A Mighty Fortress Is Our God" was singled out for notice: "The improvisatory genius of Langlais captured . . . Luther as no other fantasia on this [hymn] ever has, or ever will. . . . Like a Boehme or Blake, Langlais 'sees' into the heart of things."[18] His playing of Bach was described as "clean, strong, yet flexible and even lyric" and his own works "the quintessence of French improvisatory art"; Langlais's independence was also noted, which compliment pleased him most: "With no aid at the console— and each organ in the world is different in its placement of controls —the sightless organist ranged through the evening's tonal palette of whisper, paean, somber simplicity, piquancy and grandeur."[19]

Each recital ended with an improvisation of a symphony in four or five movements on as many as eleven submitted themes. As Langlais put it, "This type of artistic creation was extremely interesting to the American public, which loves and demands to be taken very seriously. Bluffing and flashy showmanship are not accepted on this side of the Atlantic."[20]

It is indeed remarkable that Langlais received only one negative review during all his tours of America. The piece, written by Billy Nalle, appeared in the November 1972 issue of *The American Organist*, concerning a recital Langlais had given the previous August at the Church of the Heavenly Rest in New York:

> The evening was warm outside but far warmer inside, there being a full house and no air conditioning. Possibly Langlais was incubated in the recessed console area or tired from his summer tour or both. Whatever the reasons, the music of the evening sparkled only a few times and often it seemed as labored as it was disappointing. The charm and musicianship for which he is famous did not communicate to us and this was painful to the same degree as there was respect for a great musician. . . .
>
> [Franck's] *Pièce héroïque* suffered from unsteady rhythm at the beginning and recovered only to have us hear one section

after another having its own point of view and the piece never coming into a whole. In effect, it was a series of pieces, there being no flowing line, no cohesion, and overall it was devoid of spirit. . . . When we came to *Prière des orgues* of Erik Satie, one wished fervently that we had not. . . . "Blotter" acoustics were emphasized painfully in [*Imploration* "Pour le croyance"] with its detached phrases and chords in slashing full organ. . . .

That the drive and life of the foregoing did not carry at all into the improvisation concluding the program was a major disappointment. The dean of the New York AGO chapter, Frederick Swann, chose to submit one of the most famous and rewarding of all plainchant melodies, the "Dies irae." This made the performance all the more surprising. It came in three sections uninterrupted. The first and third lacked development and were both erratic and static; the middle movement went totally out of character. Music that expresses something like the sprightly skipping of a small child is charming in itself but nearly a shocker as the middle part *here*!

The affection in which all hold Langlais has us hoping he will return when the master and the music can spark each other.[21]

This was not a review to be ignored. Langlais wrote an angry letter to the editor reminding the reviewer that he had received a standing ovation. And in a letter to Lilian dated 2 January 1973 he wrote, "About the organ, you must have read the review of my recital at the church of Charles Walker [president of the AGO, the parent organization of the magazine]. It is a jazz-Man who wrote that. It seems questionable to me that such a man could write about a true organ and about true organ music. In any case such an article cannot change much for me, but I have difficulty with the fact that Charles could have accepted to have that appear in his magazine."

Adapting to American Organs

Langlais was in many ways the darling of American audiences, and he worked hard for that reputation, as had his teacher Marchal. A fellow American organist who was a great Francophile, having studied in Paris with Dupré, explained this phenomenon to me. He said it was Langlais's blindness in addition to brilliant and sensitive playing that endeared him to American audiences. His vulnerability before a large organ and a packed church created a kind of electricity among all participants, even before he touched the keys.

People marveled at how Langlais could manage even very large organs easily without the benefit of sight. He set as many of the piston changes as possible on general pistons, which he controlled with his feet, then arranged them in order of use according to their order in the program. It was no matter to him that they numbered eight or ten. Usually the entire recital was set on four to six general pistons, with the aid of the manual pistons for extra changes.

He always set the manual pistons in the same manner, using a gradual crescendo. The Récit pistons were arranged in the following order: Flûte 8; Voix céleste; Flûtes 8, 2; Cornet; Principal chorus or reed; Reeds. The Positif was arranged in a similar manner. The Grand-orgue was arranged successively: Flûte 8; Flûtes 8, 4; Flûtes 8, 2; Principals 8, 4, 2; Principal chorus or full great (depending on the number of pistons).

When the Crescendo pedal was well regulated, he used it judiciously, especially for *forte* sections in both the pieces and the improvisation. He particularly preferred a Crescendo pedal like that of the organ at Sainte-Clotilde, which added the pedal and manual couplers at the first stage to bring on the Grand-orgue to Pédale immediately. He also preferred that the last stage of the Crescendo pedal bring on the 16' stops but not the loudest reeds, which would be reserved for the tutti. When he was faced with an organ having neither general pistons nor usable Crescendo pedal, he somehow managed anyway.

It usually took him less than an hour to register his program. As he quickly set the registrations, his reactions to new instruments seemed as intuitive and rapid as they were to new people. He said that Messiaen would never be able to do a recital tour because it took him an hour to decide which 8' stop to use. But with Langlais, each choice was made instantly, without hesitation, and his registrations were simple yet effective.

Practice Techniques

Although the practice techniques developed over many years of patient and careful work helped him to be at ease quickly at any instrument, in some ways Langlais still suffered from not having been able to begin his piano studies before he was ten years old. Unlike some of his blind colleagues, such as Antoine Reboulot, whose technique was brilliant, he worked very hard to develop his dexterity and never stopped working on technical exercises. Each day he began with studies in double thirds and sixths, then scales in all the keys, and finally several Chopin études. His piano technique, like his organ technique, was marked by a minimum of motion and a quiet hand with a relaxed wrist.

His opinion of other organists was often influenced by their degree of technical advancement on the piano. If an organist had a poor technique, he would simply say, "He has no fingers," and he had no patience for them. An old Mason & Hamlin grand piano had been a fixture in his home since the early days of his marriage, not only for his daily practice but as the primary tool for composition. (It is now in Claude's home in Roumazières.)

His approach to learning a new piece was the method used by most blind persons. He worked a measure or short phrase at a time, first starting with the melody, then adding the bass, and finally the inner parts. He always practiced slowly, repeating the various combinations until he felt sure of them. Much of the practice was mental, however, for as soon as he heard the piece, his recall of it was extensive. This included retention of the melody, the harmony, and bass. Nothing was ever done by rote without first understanding how the parts and the harmony fit together.

He told many of his students that he had once called Messiaen lucky to be able to read a prelude and fugue by Bach, which for him would take several hours to learn. Once having learned the piece, however, Langlais would know it far better than his sighted confrères who only sight-read it.

Once he had learned a piece, the techniques he used for practicing it were quite different. He practiced portions of it and then the entire piece in a rapid tempo, often on a very soft registration. He rarely practiced on a loud registration, because it tired the ears and diminished concentration. Once when he was practicing on the softest Récit Flûte 8 with the box closed at Saint Thomas Church in New York, the sexton told him that he was the only organist he knew who could play so softly for such a long time. Langlais enjoyed telling that story to students. How he practiced depended on how well he remembered the work in question. If the practice demanded technical work, he devised all sorts of rhythms and other tricks for making the technique secure, including extensive slow practice. Once when he was particularly tired, he practiced only fifteen minutes and still played well. What was less easy for him to control was his stage fright.

He wrestled with bouts of this performer's nightmare from the beginning of his career until after his heart attack in 1973, when the doctor prescribed Valium for his nerves. Fortunately the drug did not affect his coordination, as it did for so many other musicians. During the 1964 tour the extent of his anxiety varied; sometimes it was intense before a recital and not during it; sometimes in increasingly severe degrees during a recital; and sometimes after a recital. A positive result of his stage fright was the excitement and intensely high level of performance he was able to achieve during a recital. The nervous intensity translated itself into a higher level of musical artistry.

Often an unreliable console frightened him. Even on instruments that worked well, he was anxious until he understood how the contraption functioned, especially if there were a complicated mechanism, such as was found on the 250-stop organ at Longwood Gardens in Pennsylvania, which we encountered near the end of the 1964 tour:

> I will never forget the word of fright from my guide who in seeing this formidable console, said to me, "So, it will be hard to get finished with this." She was wrong: I needed only two hours to set my pistons. Thanks to the very devoted help of this young American, I was able to save eight hours of practice because, being herself an excellent organist, Ann Labounsky knew my technique of registration very well and helped me very efficiently.[22]

Ann Labounsky and Jean Langlais, 1964

The companionship, recognition, and professional success Langlais found in America were an enormous solace to him, for at home in France the Second Vatican Council was profoundly changing the rituals of Holy Mother Church and, therefore, the most basic structure of his life.

CHAPTER 10

Vatican II Conflicts 1959–1972

The liturgists . . . tried to destroy everything that belonged to
the old Roman tradition.

Monsignor Iginio Angles,
Pontifical Institute of Sacred Music

The Catholic Church in France underwent a revolution at the hands
of the liturgists in 1959, leaving Langlais with an intense sense of
personal betrayal and isolation. In many ways, his American tours
and sojourns at Boys Town provided him with the necessary
strength to withstand these changes. The pontifical masses at Boys
Town gave him the impetus to compose some of his most significant sacred music, and the parochial character of the summer workshops added stability in turbulent times. In America, he felt the ves-
tiges of a consistency in religious practice and an admiration of his
worth as a Catholic composer that eluded him at home.

The Liturgists

Who were these liturgists who seemed bent on destroying everything that Langlais held sacred? During the Second Vatican Council
they headed a movement of priests who wished to change the language as well as the musical context of the mass. The post-Conciliar
documents were not restricted to liturgy, although that is the subject
that most affected Langlais; they reached out to every aspect of
the Roman Catholic Church and beyond, to the Catholic Church
universal, in the boldest ecumenical effort the Church had ever
attempted.

In France and elsewhere, the clergy who later became identified
as the "liturgists" had long been involved in grassroots Catholic

210

reform movements—an attempt to purify the hierarchical structure and religious expression. As early as 1900, several clerical congresses were held in Rheims and Bourges, where more than six hundred parish priests studied the Church's response to social problems caused by industrialization, urbanization, secularization, and poverty—problems that the Langlais family knew firsthand. The aim was to make local parishes more pastorally oriented by being relevant and responsive to the needs of the people.

This movement grew significantly during the five decades that followed. By 1945 it became known in France as Catholic Action, and its political and social wing in the Christian Social movement as the Abbés Democratiques. As Carlo Falconi urged, "We must belong to our own era—speak its language, respond to its aspirations, be adaptable to its methods."[1] Typical of this movement were self-sacrificing priests who lived in the urban ghettos among the destitute, sharing their poverty and misery. Such priests saw that an important way of making the Church a central part of people's lives was through the use of the vernacular in worship. Even before their requests climbed the hierarchical ladder to Rome, they experimented with the use of French in liturgical and paraliturgical services.

During the 1950s the influence of Catholic Action continued to grow through the efforts of two leading liturgists: Joseph Gelineau, a Jesuit, and Lucien Deiss, a member of the Holy Ghost order. Both took part in the Vatican II Concilium on Liturgy and stressed the importance of the congregation in singing the main liturgical chants.

Sacred music was to be chosen according to its importance in the ritual action of the community rather than as a manifestation of human culture. In effect, the more esthetically beautiful it was in its own right, as an art form, the more removed it was from the people and thus inappropriate for worship—a philosophy that ran absolutely against Langlais's ideals of church music. Their philosophy stressed the relevancy of all worship to those taking part; they believed that the term "sacred music" applied "to all music which by its inspiration, purpose and destination, or manner of use has a connection with faith."[2]

Langlais at first believed that such a conflict was not necessary because it was possible to create "esthetically beautiful sacred music" and serve the function of ritual music. Unfortunately, in the hands of lesser composers, the ideal of ritual music was often reduced to music of the lowest common denominator.

New Liturgists vs. Conservatives

By the late 1950s tension began to build between the new liturgists and the conservatives—the professional musicians, including Langlais, and other clergy who saw the new liturgists as a growing threat to the traditional liturgy and practice of church music. Their respective views were diametrically opposed. It is important to think about these categories historically rather than in current practice.

New Liturgists	Conservatives
1. Emphasis on total revision of the liturgy discarding the musical patrimony of the Church, including Gregorian chant, polyphony, and Classical music.	1. Conservation of the patrimony of Church's musical heritage.
2. Verbal emphasis: weakening of symbols. Vernacular important; Latin unimportant.	2. Nonverbal emphasis. Latin as universal language of universal Church.
3. Use of newly composed music of very simple and repetitive character.	3. Use of new compositions by professional musicians. Conservation of "art music."
4. Priest as celebrant, presider, president of the assembly, more in the Protestant role model.	4. Priest as apostle of Christ in the Holy Sacrifice of the mass.
5. No distinction between sacred and secular. Utilitarian nature of worship.	5. Distinct difference between sacred and secular.
6. Choirs less important than congregational singing.	6. Conservation of choirs.

7. External signs of piety preferred to internal signs. Action rather than contemplation.	7. Internal acts of faith must precede external. "Prayer surrounded by beauty."
8. Mass as a meal of commemoration. All parts of mass equally sacred. Informal, folksy worship. Spontaneous, human-centered meal.	8. Mass as Holy Sacrifice. Elevation of special importance. Formal worship character through centered vestments, gestures, music, and worship space.
9. Community, people-centered worship.	9. God-centered worship.
10. Subjective criteria for planning worship.	10. Objective criteria: "Only the most beautiful is pleasing to God."

For the new liturgists, God is in everything; therefore, everything is sacred. For the conservatives, the mystical and supernatural in worship are distant and distinctly holy and set apart from the ordinary. For the new liturgists, the plane of worship is horizontal, from person to person in community. For the conservatives, the plane of worship is vertical—of the faithful with God in the communion with the greater community of the saints within the universal Church.

By 1959 the liturgists had gained the upper hand, and Langlais's conflict with them began. He attended a mass in Dinard, not far from his home in Brittany, on the feast of All Saints that year. He expressed his reaction to the mass in an emotional letter to the church's pastor. "Being an organist in Paris for thirty years, I know and deplore how popular it has become to pray with a microphone, [a] distracting and unmusical device, during the mass. . . . It was impossible to find the calm necessary for meditation. Even at the elevation, the commentator lengthily explained that it was necessary to observe silence. In effect, at this grand moment of the mass, one would yearn to be spared this human intermediary in order to be elevated in the measure of his own means."[3]

Several factors contributed to his dismay: his expected experience of the transcendental was shattered particularly during the elevation; it occurred in his native Brittany, where he had hoped that this malaise had not penetrated from Paris; it was on the feast of All Saints, an especially solemn occasion; and it spelled for him a foretaste of difficulties to come. It was also symptomatic of other equally disturbing problems: the democratization of the Church and the abandonment of its artistic mission. For him there was almost a sense of conspiracy in the notion that his own country would have fallen prey to these forces. He continued in the same letter, "I hoped that my dear Brittany would resist this poorly understood popularization with all her strong vigor."

As for the artistic mission that the Church has held in nourishing the arts, he lamented that it had already departed a great distance from "that blessed time." It was clear that this negation of the arts was also an abdication of Pius X's views on the sanctity of worship. Langlais concluded: "All religious composers, of which I am one, are deeply discouraged by this movement, which is the negation of art. In my opinion nothing is beautiful enough for God. Our forebears knew this and held that to pray surrounded by beauty was central to worship, according to the holy word of Saint Pius X, who was himself a great musician. Where is his thought and what has become of his teaching?"[4]

"Prayer Surrounded by Beauty": Pius X

Although their life spans overlapped only briefly, the personal and spiritual affinity that Langlais felt for Pius X was central to Langlais's faith and his vocation of church music. Pius emphasized in his papal documents and writings the importance of the sanctity of the house of worship and the dignity, solemnity, and spiritual emphasis of public and private worship. Piety and devotion in "prayer surrounded by beauty" were the cornerstones of his teachings and refer both to the sanctity of the worship space and the spiritual attitude of the faithful in prayer. Pius X described the Church as the mother of the arts.

The more the arts are modeled on God, the supreme example of beauty from whom all natural beauty flows, the more they withdraw from the vulgar and approach the spiritual concept from which they receive their vigor and vitality. How magnificent has been the practice of making the arts the handmaids of divine worship! Thus everything worthy of God by reason of its richness, goodness, and elegance of form is offered to Him. In our special *Motu proprio* on sacred music and the restoration of the Roman chant according to the ancient tradition, we recently spoke on this subject.[5]

Pius X emphasized the importance of the education of the clergy, the sanctity of their office, and their proper conduct in seminaries. Every encyclical alludes to them, and he knew that their training was generally inadequate in the study of theology and scripture. To this end he established the Pontifical Biblical Institute and commissioned a new Latin version of the Bible, the first since Saint Jerome's translation, fifteen centuries earlier.

It was also Pius X who gave new insights into the understanding of Mary as the Mediatrix of all grace: "For who does not know that there is no surer or easier way than Mary for uniting all persons with Christ. . . . She is the safest refuge and the most trustworthy helper of all who are in danger. Under her guidance, patronage, kindness, and protection, nothing is to be feared or abandoned."[6] Pius explained this concept of grace in the duality of Mary as mother both of the physical and mystical body of Christ. As mother of the physical body of Christ, it was she who knew him best and felt most keenly his suffering on the cross. For the salvation of the world, she united her sufferings with his. As mother of the mystical body of Christ, she is also our mystical and spiritual mother and the vehicle through which God's grace is poured out to the faithful.

Marian Devotion

Langlais lived this belief in Mary as fount of grace; like his Breton roots, the Virgin Mary deeply affected his life. He often said that the words "O clemens" ("O merciful one," from his favorite Marian chant, "Salve regina") held special meaning for him: if his voice trembled at them, it was because he was praying that the mediatrix of all grace would be especially merciful to him. Because of her special relationship to Christ as his mother, she is described as our mediator and intercessor with God. As such, prayer may be addressed directly to her as if to a real person, for her real presence and existence are assured throughout eternity. Many Marian prayers and litanies, not the least of which is the Hail Mary, are very important in the prayer life of Catholics and were especially so for Langlais. Her attributes as a merciful mother and intercessor who prays for us, the sinners, "now and at the hour of our death," were very important to him.

His personal devotion to Mary was all encompassing, as it was for Jeannette. He prayed to Mary many times each day, and for him she remained very alive in his spiritual world. Her role as Mother of Mercy was particularly important. Churches and shrines in honor of Mary also had special significance for him, especially Notre-Dame, Lourdes in southern France, and the Basilica of the National Shrine of the Immaculate Conception in Washington, D.C.

Mary was the inspiration for some of his most important music. Her influence runs like an unbroken thread throughout his compositions, from "L'Annonciation" (*Poèmes évangéliques*, 1932) to *Suite "In simplicitate"* (1990).

Gregorian Chant

Pius X's role in the restoration of Gregorian chant had an important impact on the history of church music and on Langlais's faith. Gregorian chant for Pius X represented the supreme example of sacred music, which was defined as that music which possesses holiness, good form, and universality.

> These qualities are especially found in Gregorian chant. It is, therefore, the chant proper to the Roman Church and the only chant she has inherited from antiquity. Throughout the centuries she has jealously preserved it in her liturgical codices and, as is right, offered it as her own to the faithful. She commands that it alone be used in some parts of the liturgy. Finally, recent studies have restored its pristine integrity and purity. . . .
>
> Gregorian chant, therefore, which has been handed down from antiquity, must be totally restored in the sacred rites. The sacred liturgy loses none of its solemnity when only this type of music is used. Gregorian chant should especially be restored to

the people so that, as in former times, the faithful may once again more fully participate in the sacred liturgy.[7]

The rich body of Gregorian chant is the essence of sacred and mystical prayer. "Gregorian chant is the norm and measure of any kind of liturgical music because it is sung prayer."[8] Chant—as sung prayer—requires a heart of prayerful, interior reflection. Its spiritual force reaches out to the deepest core of the faith and raises it to God. It has no equal in any other sacred music or spoken prayer; not surprisingly, more than half of Langlais's compositions are based on Gregorian chant.

"To restore all things in Christ." It was especially in the mass that Langlais knew this in word and sacrament. Long before the use of the vernacular, he understood the texts, listened to the homilies, and waited to experience the presence of Christ during the elevation of the host. The mass, which he attended frequently even during the hectic pace of his recital tours, was at the center of his faith. Langlais's mysticism and his understanding of himself as a Catholic were at the core of his objection to the changes.

For this Breton Catholic, the mass was addressed above all and before all to God. Meditation was an essential part of the interior and spiritual participation of the faithful in the mass especially at the elevation of the host. His prayer would ascend with those of all the saints to Christ—the most holy one, as He became especially present in the moment of transubstantiation. At this most transcendent moment, with the communion of saints, the universal Church prepares to meet Christ. Let nothing disturb this solemn, interior "prayer surrounded by beauty." Music has the sole purpose to raise this prayer as high as it can, to meet the risen Christ.

The community of faithful—now referred to as the assembly—was for Langlais the communion of saints in the universal Church and not particularly the people sitting on either side of him. The plane of his religious experience was vertical—between him and the universal Church—and not horizontal—as a cozy feeling between him and the person sitting next to him, as his letter to Father Helbert stated. With the Second Vatican Council, it seemed to him that the sense of community took on another meaning as something the clergy organized collectively as an obstacle to prayer.

Within the next ten years, Pius X's teachings were all but forgotten. Along with them, the traditions of church music—upon which Langlais and many others had built their lives—were seriously eroded. People he knew gradually attended mass in hospitals or in clinics because the atmosphere in their churches had become unbearable. He remembered bitterly that in 1940 he had taught the little girls from La Richardais to sing the Mass 10 chant "Alme Pater" with admirable results. How far the Church had strayed in twenty years! He believed the problem was a lack of proper education for priests. It seemed to him a priest should have the necessary culture to communicate the love of beauty to his faithful, and it was the role of the seminary to impart this. In his same scathing letter to Father Helbert, he implored "that the future priests should be taught how to teach their future congregations to pray."

Father Helbert's response showed sensitivity and pastoral concern. Obviously, *he* possessed the culture to which Langlais was referring (a young, inexperienced priest had presided at the mass in question). Helbert explained that he himself had taught at the seminary in Rennes and even taught a course in homiletics, and that other problems besetting seminaries were more pressing than the musical training of its priests.[9]

It was only 1959, but Langlais knew that the patrimony of the Church was slipping away. The negation of art music and the democratization of the clergy troubled him. The long war of the next ten years, however, would make the Dinard incident seem a minor skirmish. Although the first document issued by the Council in 1963 was only difficult in its implementation and not openly opposed to conserving the patrimony of the Church, the conservatives had lost ground even before the Council.

Second Vatican Council

Langlais greatly admired Pope John XXIII and followed the sessions of the Council, beginning on 2 October 1962, with anticipation and hope. His ideals of liturgical music were reaffirmed as he recalled listening to the pope's radio address on Christmas Eve of that same year. "I listened with intense emotion to the mass celebrated by Pope John XXIII. . . . After the elevation, a Renaissance motet was performed; the pope *waited* for the conclusion, and with admirable humility began the prayers of the celebrant. How one would love to see such an atmosphere recreated in our own churches."[10]

In the early days of the Council the opposing sides struggled tremendously. According to one liturgist, during the early days of the Council, the new liturgists were active supporters of the professional musicians but argued for their own views, thereby gaining support among the bishops whom they innocently misled. For many of the musicians, the *Constitution on the Sacred Liturgy* was a mistake that resulted in tension, misunderstanding, recrimination, bitterness, and public confusion. Like other great men of vision, John XXIII was many things to many people.

Pope John XXIII publicly convened the Council in the fall of 1962 after a preparatory commission, meeting since June 1961, had worked on the preliminary documents. Unfortunately this pope, who was the guiding force behind the Council, did not live to see the reality of his vision. He died in June 1963; the *Constitution on the Sacred Liturgy* was issued on 4 December 1963.

Chapter 6 of the Constitution, devoted to sacred music, states in Article 112 that the musical tradition of the universal Church "is a treasure of inestimable value, greater even than that of any other art. Its value is calculated by its combinations of sacred words and music, and forms a necessary or integral part of the solemn liturgy." Article 116 upheld the use of Gregorian chant and polyphony. The conservatives had grounds to assume from those articles that the patrimony of the Church would be upheld, since the very nature of the liturgy demanded it. However, Article 14 from Chapter 1 states "that the faithful should be led to that full, conscious, and active participation in liturgical celebrations" and that it is their right and obligation. Article 30 states: "To promote active participation, the people should be encouraged to take part by means of acclamations, responses, psalms, antiphons, hymns, as well as by actions, gestures, and bodily attitudes. And at the proper time a reverent silence should be observed." In the practical implementation of these conflicting articles, the new liturgists eventually appeared to gain control. The destructive dispute, to which Monsignor Angles eluded in the quote that opens this chapter,[11] actually began very shortly after the *Constitution on the Sacred Liturgy*. On 25 January 1964, the Council, under the new papacy of Paul VI, sanctioned the Consilium for the implementation of the Constitution with Archbishop A. Bugnini as secretary.

The real work of the liturgists took place in the private sessions of the Consilium. In addition to the Consilium, Articles 44 and 47 of the instruction mandated establishment of regional and diocesan liturgical commissions specifying that "all initiatives directed toward the promotion of the liturgy are in mutual accord and that the different groups help one another." But that the new liturgists and conservatives should work together in mutual accord turned out to be more difficult than anyone had ever imagined. And so the battle continued.

Episcopal Commission on Sacred Music

Langlais served on the French Episcopal Commission on Sacred Music, established in 1962, along with Manuel Rosenthal, Noël Lancien, Romuald Vendello, Gaston Litaize, Monsignor P. Beilliard, and Monsignor François Picard. Monsignor Maurice Rigaud was president. In the minutes of the 18 January 1964 meeting, the new role of music was explained:

1. The vernacular would be used, requiring new compositions to be published through Editions de la Schola Cantorum. The official translation would be forthcoming within several months.

2. New liturgical music of a functional nature was needed, based on the propers rather than the ordinary of the mass. The following parts of the mass were changed: introit (processional), gradual (meditative psalm), alleluia (acclamation), and communion (psalm).

3. All these directives were to be guided by the "pastoral dimension."

Each member of the commission commented on the state of worship in his own parish. All admitted to a lack of congregational participation. Langlais reported that at Sainte-Clotilde the pastor delegated the leading of the singing to a vicar who could not be heard—and again, he charged that seminary training was insufficient. Langlais suggested that a qualified person be appointed in each parish to lead the singing.

Conflicts with Gelineau

In 1964 the Commission of Expert Musicians was established, again with Rigaud as president. The main work of this subcommittee was to furnish music for newly translated French texts of the Our Father, the preface, and the Holy Week propers. Langlais also served on the Diocesan Commission on Sacred Music, established in 1966 with Monsignor J. Delarue as president. In the course of his work on these committees, Langlais grew increasingly angry that clergy with inferior musical training were exercising control over the new music required for the liturgy. He gradually realized that the commissions were a waste of his time. The real issues, such as the texts and choices of music, were settled by the clergy. Although Picard promised the professional musicians that they would be represented in the choice of translations, it was Joseph Gelineau who was appointed to represent the musicians, and this decision came at the end of a long controversy between Langlais and Gelineau.

For Langlais this priest represented everything that had gone wrong with the Church since the new liturgists had gained control, and his letters to Gelineau give a probing view of Langlais's ideals of the education and vocation of a liturgical organist-composer. The priestly calling and its theological demands were in opposition to the demands of comprehensive musical study. In a letter to Rigaud on 3 December 1962 Langlais chided Gelineau for giving his *Douze cantiques bibliques*—composed in 1962 for the new propers for Advent—a poor review. Gelineau disliked Langlais's form, in which the congregation was to sing both the antiphon and the verse. Langlais questioned Gelineau's musical ability and reminded Rigaud in the same letter that he had never been able to get the choir at the Institute to sing Gelineau's *Responsorial Mass* because of the tessitura of the soprano part. Gelineau had no right to speak about music—he did not have the proper training. "I know in the history of music only one true musician-priest: Antonio Vivaldi," wrote Langlais. "To consecrate an entire life to the care of perfecting its artistic gift is a goal to which many of my very talented colleagues are dedicated. I am dedicated to it myself. . . . How could it be done, if in addition I had undertaken theological studies, literary studies, and all other disciplines which the Society of Jesus imposes on its priests?"

On 12 January 1963 Langlais wrote directly to Gelineau in the same vein.

> For several years already, true composers of sacred music have been replaced by people of good faith, who are the only ones to believe in their talent. . . . "Community" is the only thing upon which the present clergy organize the exercises of the faithful, which takes away from every Christian the liberty of his mysticism; you are forced to *think* at a particular moment about what they wish you to think. Many see this as an obstacle to their prayer; some find in music the possibility of experiencing the elevation.

In 1966, after hearing a speech by Gelineau on the radio, Langlais summed up his anger in a last bitter letter: "You have just spoken of the Holy Spirit; many of us are waiting for him to blow through so that he might purge the Church of the noxious dust that is presently poisoning our atmosphere."

Ideals of Liturgical Music

Father Huftier, the pastor at Sainte-Clotilde, opened a dialogue in the November 1962 issue of the *Bulletin de Sainte-Clotilde* with his article "Comment prier sur de la beauté?" He explained that although almost sixty years had elapsed since Pius X first urged "prayer surrounded by beauty," and that even though their basilica was blessed with a prestigious instrument and one of the greatest organists, the parishioners seemed to have problems with these blessings. He raised two provocative questions: 1. Does beautiful music still have a place in church? 2. If so, how can "prayer surrounded by beauty" be reconciled with the active part that the parishioners were now to take in the mass? Huftier emphasized that the mass is a dialogue, not an organ recital; he described Langlais as a liturgical organist who is at their service to help the congregation participate fully at the Sunday liturgy.

Father Huftier asked Langlais to write an article in response, concerning his personal views of the role of the organ in worship. Langlais answered that the church organist functions in a priestly capacity: "I believe that the organ has a precisely liturgical purpose, as a vehicle for prayer, in order to carry prayer beyond words, as high as possible."[12] The organist should create an appropriate atmosphere, by incorporating the chant propers and their associated Sundays and feast days. To this end, the organist should know both the Gregorian melodies and the texts of the liturgical year and be a skilled improvisor.

In the case of a low mass or organ mass, when the choir was not singing, Langlais gave in his article the following illustration for Advent: "The Grand-orgue would develop the Kyrie ["Orbis factor"] at the entrance, then the theme of the ["Rorate coeli," a familiar Advent hymn], and end on a paraphrase based on the 'Creator alme siderum' [Vesper hymn for the first Sunday in Advent]." Langlais also described having overheard a parishioner explaining to his son why Langlais had played what he played for the last Sunday after Pentecost (the twenty-third Sunday after Pentecost in 1962), the readings for which were eschatological pleas for mercy: "Bach's 'De profundis' is six parts (text of the alleluia and of the day's offertory), then he played what he had composed himself ["De profundis" from *Neuf pièces*], and to end the mass, he improvised on the same theme, but in the spirit of the Gospel [Matthew 9:18–22], which speaks about the end of the world." The remarks of the obviously cultured parishioner filled Langlais with great joy. "I did not know this parishioner, but he understood exactly my objectives as a liturgical organist."[13]

Langlais went on: "True organists consecrate their life to the study of their instruments, knowing perfectly well that they will not be able to live with their modest salaries." He admitted that they accept this reality, "but how precious it would be to them that their efforts receive something other than condescension when it isn't scorn." He concluded the article on a positive note: "Knowing that certain priests and certain parishioners of Sainte-Clotilde, beginning with our dear pastor, accord me their esteem is very precious to me." Father Huftier appreciated Langlais's position and supported him by inserting two paragraphs in the article as a prayer for the Church, hoping, among other things, that "the divine spirit will renew its wonders in our time as a new Pentecost."[14]

Several young parishioners did not agree with Langlais's views, and shortly after his article appeared he received a letter of protest.

> Permit a group of young people from the parish to give you their opinion of your article. . . . We come to the mass *for the mass*, to pray, to sing, not to listen to a concert. Enough noise! "Society" Christians—who attend Sundays, without missals, their eyes in the clouds, their legs crossed, and who would like to find an agreeable distraction in music—do not interest us. We like beautiful music and the organ in particular; but there are enough concert halls in Paris. The so-called anti-organist attempts are only the worry of true and community-oriented liturgists.[15]

The letter was signed by François Jillot and eleven others. Their views demonstrate how persuasive the new liturgists' position had become and how far removed it was from Langlais's point of view. For them, the term "community" had already taken on the "horizontal" meaning so different from Langlais's understanding of the term.

In his communication of 10 April 1965 to the Commission of Expert Musicians, Rigaud defined the Vatican position on the use of the organ in the revised liturgy, a position which might have been termed "the non-use of the organ" since there appeared to be more times during the liturgy when it was to be silent. The organ was to play both an accompanying and a solo role: as accompanist for the pieces of the congregation and choir, and as soloist before the mass, at the offertory, at the elevation, at communion, in alternation with the chants of the faithful, and after the benediction. In this same directive the bishop also explained the use of silence, which unfortunately often coincided with the places that called for the use of the organ: after the collect, at the offertory, at the elevation, and at communion. A chant was the preferred method of balancing singing with silence.

The members of the Subcommission on the Organ comprised Litaize, Langlais, Édouard Souberbielle, and Maurice Duruflé and his wife. Together they wrote their concerns to the commission president Monsignor Blanchet and asked him to meet with them on 22 June 1965 at the Catholic Institute in Paris. Blanchet listened to them sympathetically and asked them to send a copy of their concerns to the *Semaine Religieuse de Paris*, in which they were finally published on 29 January 1966. Langlais's views were central to this document and already demonstrated the anger and bitterness all felt at the impending demise of the liturgical role of the organ. They pointed out the inconsistencies of the directive, knowing full well that it had been written by those who had given little or no thought to how the organ would function in the new scheme of the liturgy.

1. "A little *before* the mass." In other words, the organist invites the faithful, arriving traditionally at 10:05 instead of 9:55, "to be put in a sacred and festive atmosphere" in vacant chairs. Not for long, since the introit is now sung as the celebrant leaves the sacristy.

2. "At the offertory, *after* the antiphonal chant, the organ *may* be played." But in the chapter on silence, it is specified that "a piece by the choir, an organ piece, silence—all can be used" during the minute that remains after the offertory chant.

3. "During the canon [elevation], a sacred moment of silence is desirable. In certain cases, this is not disturbed by a little organ music if it is discreet and well adapted." But in the chapter on silence, no hesitation is made about the role of the organ during the elevation. It is clear that the organist is invited to keep the silence.

4. "During the distribution of communion, the interludes between the sung verses may develop melodic themes." Organists may use new melodic themes. They know, from having experimented with several of them, about the vulgarities and musical platitudes they use in the name of "Liturgical Musical Renewal." For Gregorian chant is no longer possible, although Article 116 of the *Constitution on the Sacred Liturgy* states that it "maintains the first place." It is stated, "A balance between singing and silence, permits the most intimate involvement in the Eucharistic mystery."

5. Finally, at the end of the mass, after "Go in the peace of the Lord" and, as it is precisely notated, "after the recessional

song": "The organist will finally in leisure, recapitulate joyously the sense of the liturgical celebration," while the faithful head noisily toward the exits. Alas! Not for long, for the spoken mass follows immediately and he is invited to be quiet.

In conclusion, if one counts the minutes left to the organist of the Grand-orgue *during* the sung mass, which lasts usually from fifty to fifty-five minutes, nothing is left for him to do, not only to exercise in a dignified way his function, but simply even to justify his presence. In effect, the accompanying organ piece lasts not even as long as a Bach chorale, without pain of being stopped by the bell.

We are far, very far, from Article 120 of the *Constitution on the Sacred Liturgy* which "highly esteems the pipe organ". . . for we hope that in this article it is not only a question of the "sound" of the organ but also of the notes that are played on it and which we believe to have a certain importance. And if the role of the organist is so reduced to this sort of humming in the background, in this role of "hole-filling" between two verses of songs in French and to serve as accompaniment for the eventual new songs, one wonders . . . if it is now necessary to train young organists and to place them in careers that are reduced to such a farce, a career that is so long in its preparation, so costly, so laborious and difficult. One no longer even sees the necessity to maintain organ classes in our Conservatories and Schools of Music.

We are at the same time very far from the reassuring note the Commission of Expert Musicians received from the French Episcopal Commission on Sacred Music on 6 May 1964, which states: "The choir and the organs *will continue* to maintain their traditional role in liturgical celebrations."

A point that seems to us to be of equally great importance and of interest: What will become of our most beautiful instruments?

You know, Excellency, that the organs in our cathedrals as well as the instruments classified as "Monuments Historiques"—which represent an artistic richness of the highest value—are restored in large part by the care and expense of the Services des Beaux-Arts of the State and of the City of Paris. There is reason to fear that if these instruments are reduced to silence or to the simple role of accompanying songs, the officials of these services will lose interest in them, which we would perfectly understand.

We greatly hope that they will retain your benevolent attention and that, reassured by the importance that is given to the organ in Article 120 of the *Constitution on the Sacred Liturgy*, that we will continue diligently to practice our art in service to the Church, to which we remain devoted and dedicated.[16]

Rigaud's response was printed in the same issue of *Semaine Religieuse de Paris*. Arguing that his pastoral letter from the previous 10 April 1965 was directed principally to rural parishes, and that a certain latitude of their interpretation depended on the amicable cooperation between musician and pastor, which was at the base of all ecclesiastical and papal documents, he listed five main places where the organ should be used:

1. At the prelude, between three to five minutes, if the pastor eventually overcame the tardiness of members of his congregation.

2. At the offertory, a rather long piece of five minutes was possible.

3. During the elevation, in parishes with fine instruments and well-trained organists, it was possible to have soft organ music.

4. At the communion, after several verses of congregational psalmody, the organ may finish.

5. At the postlude, no length was prescribed: it depended on the beginning of the next mass.[17]

Unfortunately, this response sidestepped the issues, and the instability and confusion over how the Constitution could accommodate the two growing factions of Roman Catholic church music increased. Picard, general secretary of the Episcopal Commission on

Sacred Music, intensified the conflict by dismissing any objective distinction between the sacred and secular; the scandalous remarks he made in a certain interview (*Le Figaro*, 27 January 1966) set fire to the smoldering unrest within the Church: "Today many musical styles are found in church, from 'pop' masses 'Ye-Ye' to aleatoric masses. The task of composers consists in finding a place for themselves within this style that will correspond to the genre of sacred music. . . . If his inspiration were religious, there would be no one better to write music for the preface than Georges Brassens [a popular song composer]."[18]

This so alarmed church musicians that many signed a declaration to be read at the Fifth International Church Music Congress in Chicago, held 21–26 August 1966. This time it was Maurice Duruflé who led the revolt, in the wake of the premiere of his *Messe sur les thèmes grégoriens de la Messe 9*. It was signed by Souberbielle, Litaize, Raugel, Grunenwald, Langlais, Demessieux, and Dufourcq, among others, and quoted in many Parisian newspapers: "We are very far from Article 116 of the Constitution, which recognized that Gregorian chant as the proper chant for the liturgy, all things being equal, should occupy first place. . . . Church musicians hold to the directives of the Council and the middle road indicated by Msgr. Lallier, the bishop of Marseille, and the pastoral letter of Msgr. Rigaud."[19] The flags were raised high and the revolt was at its zenith.

It was for Jacques Chailley to codify all the issues in the declaration to present at the next International Church Music Congress. In addition to the Concilium, which worked during the councils to implement the principles of the *Constitution on the Sacred Liturgy*, Pope Paul VI organized in 1963 an international institute, Consociatio Internationalis Musicae Sacrae (CIMS) to hold international congresses on sacred music every three years. Although such congresses had been held since 1950, the Fifth International Church Music Congress in 1966 was the first function of CIMS. Monsignor Richard Schuler was in charge of this congress, which was sponsored by the Church Music Association of America, the American branch of CIMS.

According to Schuler, opposition to the congress began almost at its conception from the liturgists' camp through a rival international organization, Universa Laus, headed by Gelineau. This organization met in Lugano, Switzerland, in April 1966 for the purpose of studying chant and music in the liturgy. At first the pope encouraged this organization but shortly requested that the two organizations work side by side until they would merge.

French church musicians were conspicuous by their absence at this Congress, which fact was noted in the French newspapers. "If the great artists who are our church musicians are unable to travel to Chicago, it is probably because they are too poor to pay for the trip."[20] Only five attended the Congress, and the French press chided the auspicious presidents of the French commissions for their conspicuous absence and for their feeble excuses for not attending.

More than fifty musicians, including Langlais, had signed the declaration, leaving Chailley to defend their cause almost single-handedly. The document was sent to the Congress prior to the opening session, translated into five languages, printed, and distributed to the delegates. It was scheduled to be discussed on 24 August in the general session, along with reports from other countries; but because of time restraints, the only proposition heard was the first, from England and Wales.[21]

The document, which presented a résumé of Langlais's views and recommendations, may be summed up as follows:

1. The commissions for sacred music should be consulted more often, without any ambiguity regarding their responsibilities.

2. Both objectives of the Council—renewal and conservation of the Church's patrimony—should be pursued with equal diligence.

3. The use of Latin should be maintained along with the vernacular.

4. Choirs should be maintained, and new music of a secular nature prohibited. Gregorian chants should also be maintained. The excessive use of psalmody in the vernacular should not replace the chant and other polyphonic compositions.

5. Pastors often "consider the very quality itself of the music offered to God as an offense against Him"; on the other hand,

musicians often misunderstand a more modest role of music:
these two views must be reconciled in the spirit of mutual
respect.

6. Silent prayer and meditation are vital to the active
participation of the faithful. The proportion of words and
music in the liturgy should be balanced.

7. and 8. [These points concerned the use of the organ in the
mass, including the observation that often in a mass lasting
fifty-five minutes, the organ is used only six to eight
minutes.]

9. Future documents concerning sacred music should be
promulgated without any arbitrary discrimination. The
artistic and musical education in schools and seminaries
should be increased.

The Betrayal

On 5 March 1967, *Instruction on Music in the Liturgy* was released.
Most of the sixty-nine articles upheld the position of the conservatives that Jacques Chailley had been prepared to deliver seven
months earlier. One important change, however, proved to be a
stumbling block for their position. Articles 28 and 29 stipulated a
reordering of the sung parts of the mass into three degrees of importance. The first category included the greetings of the priest and people, the opening prayer, the Gospel acclamations ("Gloria tibi"), the
offertory prayer, the preface, the Sanctus, the final doxology, the
Our Father, and the dismissal. All the traditional parts of the sung
mass (Kyrie, Gloria, Credo, and Agnus Dei), with the exception of
the Sanctus, were relegated to the second category, along with the
prayer of the faithful. The third category continued the songs at the
entrance and commission processions, the responsorial psalm, the
song at the offertory, and the singing of the readings. The three
degrees were so arranged that the "first may be used by itself, but the
second and third, wholly or partially, may never be used without
the first." One would need a celebrant with great vocal ability to sing
all the parts given first rank, and unfortunately, the Sanctus was

usually the only part of primary importance that the congregation sang.

More than three decades later, the instruction has still not been implemented, and the wholesale destruction of the musical heritage continues unabated. The vernacular was introduced, and Latin, which was required to be continued along with it, was systematically excluded.[22]

Langlais felt betrayed. As a devout Catholic, he did not lose his faith, but he was estranged even more from many of the clergy and from the hierarchy of his Church. As a church musician he found his duties greatly curtailed. After all the shouting, for him as well as the other church musicians, there remained precious little time to improvise in the way that he had prior to the Council. As to the outcome of the conflict between the liturgists and the musicians, Monsignor Hayburn, author of a history of papal legislation, gave this answer: "Almost everyone is making music in the churches, except trained musicians."[23]

Liturgists in France, as well as those in America, promulgated new music in the popular musical idiom of the 1960s in hopes of making the liturgy more accessible to the people, but as Hayburn argued, without professional training rooted in the spiritual and artistic tradition of the Roman liturgy and its music, there could be no real composers and no new liturgical music—in Latin or the vernacular.

Duruflé, who in 1966 had predicted grave consequences for the future of church music, repeated his stance more vehemently in 1978:

> The experiments attempted during these last twelve years have often been the pretext for the introduction of unbearably vulgar songs. This new music, played with the accompaniment of guitars and drums, which was introduced into our sanctuaries for the express reason of attracting crowds, has done just the opposite. The error in calculations has turned out to be monumental. People have deserted their parishes in order to attend Sunday masses in places that have maintained the cult of beauty, the only one that counts when it comes to glorifying God. Numerous examples could be given from the Parisian churches. The most spectacular is certainly Notre-Dame, where nine or ten thousand worshippers attend the sung masses each Sunday.[24]

Two works for organ reflect the agony these conflicts provoked in Langlais. In one of his *Trois implorations* (1970), "Pour le croyance," the first phrase of the chant creed is followed by crashing tone clusters on the full organ, which represent his anguish over the clergy's lack of faith and the demise of the patrimony of the Church. This expression of bitter outrage was followed by six meditative prayers to Mary, *Offrande à Marie* (1971), who remained his guardian and source of help in time of trouble. In 1972, just before the work's premiere, in Washington at the National Shrine of the Immaculate Conception, he gave a speech that touched on the clergy's lack of spirituality and faith in the Virgin Mary. "I have written this *Offrande à Marie* as an expression of my personal faith, and within it to remind certain members of the clergy that Christ had a Mother, and that her name was Mary."[25]

The new liturgists had gained the upper hand. But unlike his colleagues Messiaen and Duruflé, Langlais did not ignore their pleas to compose for the new liturgy. With Vatican II, much of the structure on which his music was based had been destroyed; but his faith in the real Church—apart from its sometimes misguided functionaries—had been tested and survived. He continued to express his faith as one of the few professional composers to produce a large body of music in the vernacular, suitable for congregational singing.

CHAPTER 11

Congregational Music 1946–1990

Sing to the Lord a new song, his praise in the assembly of the faithful!

Psalm 149

Langlais's interest in composing congregational music began long before the reforms of the Second Vatican Council; in this sense his response as a servant of the Church was not at first to the Council but to earlier liturgical needs in France. As early as 1947, Pius XII's encyclical *Mediator Dei* established Commissions for Sacred Liturgy in every diocese to regulate all requests for exemptions from the standard use of Latin in liturgical functions. Local bishops were permitted to authorize the use of the vernacular for such services as baptism, marriage, sacraments for the sick, and funerals. Beginning around 1945, even during regular liturgies, experiments were made with or without authorization using newly composed chants in French. Langlais was himself sensitive to these needs and composed vernacular choral music during this period.

Congregational Music

Congregational music is defined as vocal music, with instrumental accompaniment and for congregational participation, that is composed for a liturgical purpose. This music differs from religious music, which has as its goals neither congregational participation nor suitability for use at a mass or service. Congregational music excludes Langlais's polyphonic masses, twenty-two other choral works, solo pieces based on a religious text but not suitable for a mass or service, and solo sacred vocal pieces such as the *Missa in simplicitate*. It includes many short antiphons for the propers of the mass, eight masses, hymns and canticles, and responses. Most are in French; the others are in Latin or English. A congregation could sing all the pieces with limited practice.

What is significant about the works in this category is that Langlais adapted his style to accommodate congregational participation without sacrificing his integrity as a composer. The decision to present them together in one chapter apart from his other music is based on several considerations, among them their importance as a genre of music; their obscurity within his total output; their relationship to his religious faith; and their consistent use of modality.

Langlais had been attracted to modality since he first heard Gregorian chants and Breton folk songs as a child. His exposure to Franck and Tournemire's essentially modal style nurtured this ffinity:

> It is said there are twelve major keys and twelve minor keys. . . .
> But in reality there are only two, one major and one minor,
> because the tones and semitones are always in the same place.
> So if you take the C major scale, you have a half step between
> three and four and seven and eight, and in each key it is the
> same. But if you take the first mode—Dorian—you have a half
> step between two and three and six and seven. And continuing
> with the next mode on E you have a half step between one and
> two and five and six. Everything is changed! And besides, there
> are neither sharps nor flats. . . . I was speaking only about the
> Classical modes, the Gregorian or Greek modes, but if you con-
> sider the modality of Messiaen, with nine tones or ten tones,
> or the pentatonic mode, which Ravel used, you see that modal-
> ity is much richer than tonality. For these reasons, I use scales
> less and less. [1]

Langlais's congregational music is here listed chronologically according to the year of composition. Most of it was composed in response to commissions and published immediately after its composition.

1946/52	*Cantiques* (in *Gloire au Seigneur*, vols. 1, 2)
1953	*Chants pour la messe*
1954	*Missa "Salve regina"*

1955	"Lauda Jerusalem Dominum"
	15 Antiphons
1956	"Accourez au passage du Seigneur"
	"Dieu, nous avons vu ta gloire"
1959	"Sacerdos et pontifex"
	"Au paradis" (in *Gloire au Seigneur*, vol. 3)
1961	*Nouveaux chants pour la messe*
	"O God, Our Father"
	"Praise to the Lord"
1962	*Douze cantiques bibliques*
1962/64	*Missa "Dona nobis pacem"*
	Psaumes solennels nos. 1–3
1963	*Propers of the Mass for Pentecost*
	Propers of the Mass in French
1964	*Mass "God Have Mercy"*
1965	*Messe "Dieu prends pitié"*
	"Chant d'entrée pour la fête de Saint-Vincent"
	Mass "On Earth Peace"
	Pater Noster (in French)
	Gospel acclamation
	Messe "Joie sur terre"
1967	*Répons pour une messe de funérailles*
1969	*Solemn Mass "Orbis factor"*
1973	*Hymn of Praise "Te Deum"*
1974	*Répons liturgiques*
1983	*Deux chants chorals*
1985	"A Morning Hymn," "The Threefold Truth"
1989	"Noël: 'Chantez, les anges'"

Between 1946 and 1959, Editions du Seuil published *Gloire au Seigneur*, three volumes of music by several composers on French texts. Langlais set two texts in volume 1, six texts in volume 2, and one text in volume 3, "Au paradis." These 6 × 4½" missals were first produced in France for congregations and small choirs of one to six voice parts. Langlais's vocal writing here is lyrical and simple, with a fairly limited vocal range.

Chants pour la messe (1953) sets the Kyrie, Gloria, Sanctus, and Agnus Dei to the newly translated French text. The setting is for one voice and organ with a very simple vocal line and accompaniment, and with a tessitura within a D octave range; throughout it is similar to his *Cinq mélodies,* composed the following year. Penciled "Donnes leurs le repos éternel" (Grant them eternal rest) in both the Agnus Dei and the Benedictus of the Sanctus indicates that *Chants pour la messe* may first have been used at a Requiem mass with a choir of girls. The harmony for each of the four movements is within the Dorian mode.

The Kyrie has two sets of words, the printed, "Seigneur ayez pitié de nous" (Lord, have mercy on us), later changed in pencil above the notes to "Seigneur prends pitié" (Lord, have mercy). Each phrase is repeated, anticipating the standard practice of having the congregation respond to the cantor or choir's initial intonation.

Chants pour la messe, Kyrie, mm. 1–6. © 1956 Editions du Levain.

Greater simplicity distinguishes this mass from his *Messe pour deux voix* (1935).

Messe pour deux voix, Kyrie, mm. 1–7

His intent had clearly changed, and by 1953 he was working to pro-vide music that a congregation could sing: music with a more limited vocal range and increased repetition. The Gloria of *Chants pour la messe* also alternates between a cantor or choir and the congrega-tion; the latter usually sings an exact repetition of the schola part.

The French translation of the Sanctus, "Saint, saint, saint," has a double meaning: "holy" and "breast." Although the two words are pronounced the same, they are spelled differently. Langlais, who disliked this French text, often joked that two were enough! Yet in *Chants pour la messe*, he managed a tone that was both majestic and simple. The Agnus Dei is eighteen measures shorter than the Kyrie; the petitions are given a singing, arch-like, repeated phrase.

Missa "Salve regina"

In 1954 *Missa "Salve regina"* brought Langlais much international acclaim. The work was the result of a request of the most difficult kind: it would involve the congregation at Notre-Dame in the singing of a new work—with only an hour's rehearsal beginning at 11:00 p.m. Father David Julien, the priest in charge of the televised mass in Paris each Sunday, commissioned Langlais only one month before the event. This midnight mass for a congregation of nine thousand people was to be televised to viewers in nine countries—one of the great highlights of Langlais's career. The instrumentation, in addition to the congregational parts, requires two choirs, two organs, three trumpets, and five trombones. It was not by coincidence that he called upon a Marian source for help to achieve this complete artistic and liturgical success: a well-known chant of Our Lady befitting her cathedral.

The mass is thematically based entirely on the more ancient of the two "Salve regina" chants in the Dorian mode. The congregational parts for the Kyrie and Gloria are taken from the "O clemens" section (B, A, B, C-sharp, D, C-sharp, B, A, B) and the Sanctus and Agnus Dei are based on the open phrase of the "Salve regina" (A, G, A, D, A, G, F, E, F, G, F, E, D).

Missa "Salve regina," Kyrie, p. 8, mm. 1–5. © 1955 Editions Jobert. Used by permission. Sole Agent U.S.A., Theodore Presser Company.

A second choir of three-part men's voices may be doubled by three-part women's voices. In all, eight brass instruments are required: a brass choir of two trumpets and two trombones doubles the organ part in most of the mass. Another brass choir with one trumpet and three trombones usually doubles the men's parts accompanied by the choir organ. The Grand-orgue, therefore, is always in a sort of antiphonal dialogue with the congregation and the men's choir.

The style is reminiscent of Dufay and Machaut, with many open fifths, triads in first inversion, and doubled leading tones; for example, in the Dorian mode of the mass, the many cadences with E, G-sharp, C-sharp lead to D, A, D in both the voice parts and the organ.

Missa "Salve regina" was first sung on Christmas Eve 1954. Langlais played the main organ and was as pleased with the participation of the congregation as he was the men's choir from the Seminary of the Holy Spirit in Chevilly-Larue, who had been prepared by Father Lucien Deiss. He described the first performance in a later interview:

> From the very first minute I was amazed. Before midnight success was a certainty. The mass began on the stroke of midnight, and I simply could not believe my ears. . . . The enthusiasm and confidence of everyone concerned proved powerful aids, and (this point is without hesitation to be called miraculous) it was carried through with a simplicity and perfection in every detail beyond all telling. . . . Its success has remained in the memories of many as a clear demonstration that it is entirely possible to bring the assembled multitude into a modern-style composition.[2]

Costallat published it the following year in two versions, one as a duplication of the first performance and the second with a single organ reduction in which the brass parts were incorporated into the organ part. The Erato recording received both the Grand Prix du Disque and the Madame René Coty prize. In honor of this event a special dinner was held, with Langlais and Jeannette the guests of honor. Pierre Petit summed up the work and the recording.

> It is a remarkable tour-de-force to have successfully recorded, more than satisfactorily, the Mass of Jean Langlais, which includes immense effects (more than six hundred people). Despite that, despite also the 32' of the organ, which is very clearly heard, nothing spoils the pleasure that one takes in discovering such a sincere work. The style of Jean Langlais never gets lost in Byzantine complications; he writes for the assembly in a language to which all can adhere but which makes none of the gross concessions that are the weakness of so many works written "for the public."[3]

Short Hymns

"Lauda Jerusalem Dominum" for SATB, organ, optional brass quartet, and congregation was written for a specific liturgical event—the solemn Palm Sunday processional after the reading of the Gospel.

The rubrics for this lengthy procession, which includes all the clergy and congregation holding palm branches, prescribed a number of hymns appropriate to honor Christ the King. The text is the first nine verses of Psalm 147, with the antiphon "Qui pacem ponit" taken from the second vespers of the feast of Christ the King. The normal antiphon is the first verse of the psalm "Lauda Jerusalem," and the first three notes of the antiphon (D, E, G) remind the congregation of the eighth psalm tone, to which this antiphon is normally sung. In Langlais's setting, it is a majestic ascending antiphon, with a marked raised fourth scale degree giving some emphasis to the high point of the phrase. This ten-measure antiphon is longer and more complicated than the *Missa "Salve regina"* people's mass parts but is repeated nine times in alternation with the choir verses; each verse has essentially the same music slightly rearranged to fit the varying prosody of the text. The raised fourth scale degree at the cadences is also reminiscent of the Medieval style of the *Missa "Salve regina."* The Gloria Patri and Amen are particularly triumphant, giving to the congregation the last measure of the Amen with two long held notes on D. The entire last section would make a striking Great Amen for today's liturgies, with the Gloria section played on the organ. As in the *Missa "Salve regina,"* Langlais recommends the additional doubling of the congregation part by two trombones, and a brass quartet for the choir parts.

"Accourez au passage du Seigneur" is a communion hymn commissioned for the Eucharistic Congress held in Rennes in July 1956. It is based on a text by Father de la Tour du Pin: "Hasten to the portal by which the Lord gives his grace! The stone to the entrance of the heart is raised: the Lord passes." Langlais captures the urgency in a simple yet compelling melody in the second mode transposed to G. The verses modulate to the relative major and are more adaptable for a choir or cantor than for congregation.

"Dieu, nous avons vu ta gloire," set to a text by Jesuit Didier Rimaud, is similar but unfortunately not as well conceived either melodically, rhythmically, or textually. As in "Accourez au passage du Seigneur," the refrain is repeated after each of the nine verses, all of which begin with "Le Seigneur" and end with "il attend." Even Langlais realized this weakness and later recommended that the refrain be sung only after certain verses. It is indeed ironic that while many of Langlais's best works are unknown, this weaker representative of his congregational music is the only one currently in print throughout the world.[4]

Some of Langlais's most useful pieces were commissioned by his nemesis, Joseph Gelineau, who had worked with Tournay and Schwab on the French translation of the psalms for the Jerusalem Bible. In 1958 Les Editions du Cerf published *265 Antiphons* to be used either with Gelineau's settings of the psalms or with Gregorian psalm tones. The psalms were arranged numerically, with several different antiphon texts set to music in the same key by several different composers. Fourteen composers set these antiphons for SATB and organ in arrangements that were equally suited for congregational singing with the support of a choir and organ or in alternation with a cantor or choir. A separate edition was available for unison choir with individual congregational cards. Langlais composed his *15 Antiphons* (1955) for this collection; they vary in length from four to thirteen measures. The type of writing required for these antiphons placed severe limitations on him: a prescribed text, length not to exceed thirteen measures, and mode. Langlais gave a solid choral intent to each antiphon, some dynamic markings, and yet stayed within his own personal style. He never failed to keep them simple and to reflect the meaning of the text: when expressing joy in the two antiphons "Criez de joie" and "Un enfant nous est né," he uses the raised fourth scale degree. Likewise the antiphon "Tu es prince" has a regal quality, whereas "J'attendais la pitié" bears a marked feeling of resignation.

"Sacerdos et pontifex" (1959) was composed for Archbishop Gerald T. Bergan on the occasion of a solemn pontifical mass held during the Seventh Annual Liturgical Music Workshop at Boys Town, where Bergan was to receive the Saint Caecelia Medal for excellence in sacred music. In honor of the occasion, Langlais composed a grand entrance song for unison choir, organ, and two trumpets. The richness of the text is carried over into the accompaniment, in the opening marked by open fifths and a heraldic triplet motif for trumpets and full organ. The people's unison part is simple and is doubled on the organ. A second verse gives the alternate text "Tu es Petrus." Langlais felt at home composing regal music for grand occasions, such as ordinations and services of dedication; the style and mood here is similar to Flor Peeters's *Intrata festiva*, and the work can be performed as an instrumental piece or played twice, first as an instrumental introduction, then repeated as written.

Before the official translation of the ordinary of the mass was codified, many different translations were in use, one example of which was the text to Langlais's *Chants pour la messe*. In 1961 he wrote an even simpler and shorter congregational mass, *Nouveaux chants pour la messe*, using texts by van Eyck based on Byzantine formulas. Each movement is only one page long, and the congregational part repeats the last phrase sung by the choir.

Nouveaux chants pour la messe, Kyrie, mm. 1–5. © 1961 Editions du Levain.

The style is similar to that of "Accourez au passage du Seigneur," and the accompaniment is again entirely modal. The tessituras are very limited, rarely exceeding an octave, yet are molded with musical sensitivity.

Omer Westendorf, the editor of World Library of Sacred Music, may have commissioned Langlais to write a new setting for the Eucharistic hymn "O God, Our Father." Composed in August 1961, it is dedicated to Westendorf but was never published, nor is there any indication that it was ever sung. Langlais satisfyingly linked words to music in a triple meter setting for unison voices or SATB; the modal accompaniment doubles the voice parts.

Langlais's "Praise to the Lord" (1961), a concertante setting of the familiar hymn "Lobet den Herren" for unison congregation or SATB, brass, and organ, demonstrates once more his love of doubling the women's voices with trumpets and the men's voices with trombones. The two-measure interludes between each stanza are effective, and the traditional harmony of the hymn is generally intact.

Douze cantiques bibliques (1962) is based on Old Testament texts taken from the office of lauds in the Breviary and paraphrased by Father Daniel Hameline. Each song has a description of the text and its liturgical application; for example, the first song, "Nous acclamons Seigneur" (We praise the Lord), is listed appropriately at the creed, offertory, thanksgiving, and for the feast of Christ the King. In the preface, Langlais explains his intent.

> [I] wished to give Christian people (children studying the cate-chism included) extremely simple melodic lines that are easy to retain and to sing. Each of the pieces in this volume can be learned by the entire assembly in a very short time. The anti-phons have been conceived in a more elaborate style, and the verse in a more meditative style. With the simple rhythmical structure identical for all the verses, the melody within a sixth, these cantiques may be sung all together by the entire assembly. It is for the "Christian people" and not for soloists that the com-poser has worked. The interpretation of these verses, very sim-ply sung by a choir, would avoid the use of a microphone: beauty would thus be gained without loss of understanding the words.

In these short congregational songs, Langlais succeeds in composing easy and singable music without sacrificing musical integrity. For example, "Un jour viendra" has a very simple antiphon and a more expressive verse. Unfortunately, these songs have not been trans-lated into English, but in France they met with considerable success.[5]

"Chant d'entrée pour la fête de Saint-Vincent" (1965) is for uni-son congregation or SATB choir. It was commissioned by Maurice Delehedde, organist at the Cathedral of Viviers. In a letter to Langlais on 17 December 1964, Delehedde sent Langlais the text for an entrance song based on Psalm 17 for the feast of Saint Vincent on 22 January 1965. The opening of his letter was very complimentary and may have encouraged him to accept this commission. "For a long time I have appreciated and used your liturgical canticles, which fortunately help us to forget the proliferation of precocious compositions of mediocre quality and often of bad taste."

On 22 December, exactly one month before the feast, Delehedde wrote again, thanking Langlais for agreeing to compose the requested piece, which was used for the feast with choir and congregation. Unfortunately, as it has not been found, no description follows, but it is significant that it was composed rapidly like the *Missa "Salve regina."*

Psaumes solennels

Between 1962 and 1964 Langlais composed three large-scale works based on Latin psalms for unison choir or congregation, SATB chorus, organ, and optional brass and timpani; all were published by Schola Cantorum. *Psaume solennel no. 1* is based on Psalm 150 ("Laudate Dominum in sanctis ejus"). It is dedicated to Roger Wagner, who gave the first performance, with Langlais's son, Claude, at the organ, during the recessional of the solemn pontifical mass at Boys Town's Thirteenth Annual Liturgical Music Workshop. *Psaume solennel no. 2* (based on Psalm 50, "Miserere mei, Deus") and *Psaume solennel no. 3* (based on Psalm 148, "Laudate Dominum de caelis") were commissioned by the Asylum Hill Congregational Church, Hartford, Connecticut. In each psalm setting the congregation sings portions of the psalm and the Gloria Patri to a psalm tone doubled by brass, organ, and choirs.

Masses

Missa "Dona nobis pacem" for unison chorus with organ accompaniment was written in 1962 and published by H. W. Gray in 1964. It was Langlais's first mass written in English. Unfortunately, there is no trace of it among his manuscripts, and it is permanently out of print.

In 1963 Langlais wrote a series of propers for Pentecost and Advent on French texts by J. Beaude. Each set contains an opening song, a gradual (meditation on the epistle), a Gospel acclamation, a communion song, and a closing song. In *Propers of the Mass for Pentecost*, published by Schola Cantorum, each proper is in the form of a very simple refrain and verses with each verse leading to the dominant, a practice very common in antiphonal music involving a congregational choir and cantor. The alleluias for Pentecost illustrate the simplicity of this music. *Propers of the Mass in French*, also published by Schola Cantorum, are in the same vein and display a wide range of singable tunes within a small vocal range, a surprise for many who have not heard this large repertoire of congregational music. They also lend themselves easily to translation.

In 1964 and 1965, a period of exceptional activity, Langlais composed four masses in direct response to the new French and English translations. All four follow the same form: antiphonal Kyrie and Gloria; recitative-like Credo; hymn-like Sanctus and Agnus Dei. It was as if through the composition of each mass, Langlais learned how to simplify his style. While refining and making the vocal line less active, he gradually added to the harmonic complexities of the accompaniments. Much of this music has a transient quality, the liturgical climate itself having become so unstable immediately after the Second Vatican Council.

Mass "God Have Mercy" (1964), published by McLaughlin & Reilly, was written for the official new English translation of the mass and dedicated to Monsignor Francis Schmitt of Boys Town. It is the best English example of the antiphonal repetition of short, simple phrases between choir and congregation. The organ accompaniment doubles the voice parts while adding mild dissonances. It was popular with the Boys Town Choir and throughout many American parishes at the same time as C. Alexander Peloquin's *Mass for Parishes* and Flor Peeters's *Confraternity Mass*, both also published by McLaughlin & Reilly. As was typical of Catholic congregational music, pew cards with only the congregational parts of these works were sold separately.

Messe "Dieu prends pitié" (for SATB, organ, and congregation) was published in 1965 by Schola Cantorum. The choir parts could also be sung in unison and are doubled in the accompaniment. The alternation between choir and congregation, with exact repetition of each phrase, makes the Kyrie easy to learn. The Gloria and Credo, with their abrupt changes of key, are more difficult. The harmony is more dissonant, but the vocal line stays diatonic.

Messe "Joie sur terre" was published in 1965 by Editions du Levain; it is similar to *Messe "Dieu prends pitié"* except that its tessitura is a fourth lower, in D minor. Again, the musical phrases are singable and have a good sense of line.

Messe "Joie sur terre," Kyrie, mm. 1–8. © 1965 Editions du Levain.

Mass "On Earth Peace" (1965) is for unison choir or congregation and organ. Published by Benzinger Brothers in 1966, it is the most monosyllabic of the four masses.

The four masses quickly went out of print, as the Catholic liturgical movement no longer stressed the need for the ordinary of the mass, and Langlais ceased to write strictly congregational masses.

In 1965 Langlais set the Pater Noster in French, essentially an eighteen-measure adaptation of the music usually sung with the Latin text. Although it appears to have been an easy task, it was difficult to arrive at a satisfactory textual underlay to the tune, and Langlais made two versions, neither of which was published. In frustration, he stated his refusal to compose for the clergy-dominated commissions:

> I am a declared enemy of artistic authoritarianism. I will not associate myself in any way with the present maneuvers of the Church, which seem to me to be based on authoritarianism. One after another, three American publishers have asked me to write three masses in English. I do not believe that they are so strictly controlled. As for me, I will write freely, I will publish my works freely, and I will not bow to the untalented censors upon whom you lean.[6]

At approximately the same time he provided a Gospel acclamation (alleluia and verse) for the choir and congregation of Sainte-Clotilde at the request of François Tricot, the choir accompanist, on the verse

"From his sanctuary, the Lord sends you his aid, and from the heights of Sion, he watches over you." The alleluia music is identical to that of *Propers of the Mass for Pentecost*.

Répons pour une messe de funérailles (1967) is for SATB, congregation, and organ accompaniment. The choir sings four verses alternating with a congregational refrain: "Pour qu'ils voient la lumière et contemplent ton visage" (So that they may see the light and come into your presence). The refrain is simplicity itself, rising on the word "lumière."

Solemn Mass "Orbis factor" (1969), for SATB, congregation, organ, and brass, was written for the tenth anniversary of the dedication of the sanctuary of the National Shrine of the Immaculate Conception, Washington, D.C., and dedicated to its musical director, Joseph Michaud. The "Orbis factor" was added to the title to indicate its chant basis and to distinguish it from *Messe solennelle*. At the premiere Langlais played the Shrine's gallery organ, and massed military choirs sang the people's part. The first performance received enthusiastic notice:

> Military pageantry, three organs, two brass choirs, several hundred choristers, and at least two acres of bishops, archbishops, and cardinals, joined with a huge congregation at the National Shrine of the Immaculate Conception last night for the first performance of the new "Solemn Mass in English" by the French composer Jean Langlais. . . . Though the fabric of his harmonies is threaded with anguish and torment, the final effect is one of nobility and grandeur.[7]

Musically the work did not succeed as well as the *Missa "Salve regina."* The Kyrie and Agnus Dei should have been accessible for a congregation to sing, since they are based on the Gregorian chant Kyrie "Orbis factor," but in general the congregational parts of *Solemn Mass "Orbis factor"* are more rhythmically and melodically complex, particularly the Gloria and Sanctus.

Later Congregational Works

Hymn of Praise "Te Deum" (1973) was commissioned and published by the Composers Forum for Catholic Worship in Sugar Creek, Missouri, using the ICEL (International Committee on English in the Liturgy) ecumenical text. Members of the forum were allowed to copy the published pieces for their choirs and congregations at no charge. Unfortunately the life of this forum was short, and the work, which is scored for SATB, organ, and congregation, with optional trumpet and timpani, did not get the broad circulation it deserved. In 1992 a Latin version was published by Pro Organo. The congregational parts are based on the "Te Deum" chant and are easy to sing; the trumpet part always doubles that of the congregation. At the end of the "Te Deum," Langlais returns to the simpler original chant for the versicles and responses for the priest and congregation, beginning with "Save your people, Lord." He ends with a rich twofold Amen using the Protestant Danish setting with a distinctly different choral setting building to a climax. The accompaniment is similar to many of Langlais's other works in this genre: broad, full harmonies with double leading tones and rapid harmonic shifts.

In 1974 Langlais accepted a request from the Federation Musique et Chant du Protestantisme Français to compose congregational responses to texts by Henri Capieu titled *Répons liturgiques*. The work was included in the ecumenical publication *Musique et Chant* (March 1974). In these pieces Langlais found particularly attractive melodies and simple yet suave accompaniments that deserve good translations and a place in standard hymnals.

Répons liturgiques, Introit, mm. 1–8. © 1974 Musique et Chant.

Langlais wrote *Deux chants chorals* in 1983. The first hymn, "Dans ma faiblesse," on a text by Father A. Ory, had singular personal meaning for Langlais:

In my weakness God has regarded me
And very soon the day inundates my eyes.
He has chosen me to live in his clarity,
his glory embraces my spirit like a fire.
He comes again in spite of my poverty
so that I hear in myself the heart of my God.
God penetrates me and searches my thoughts,
He writes my name on the hollow of his hands.
I am the temple where He wishes to dwell,
With all my being to Jesus Christ I belong
that I might experience the Resurrection,
Among mankind I will be His witness.
O wells hidden among the olive trees,
Awake in me the secret song of your waters!
Arouse pity within the heart of man,
You who the Apostle saw running on the water,
Waters of baptism which have sanctified me,
By you the Spirit will raise itself on my bones![8]

Langlais's setting for SATB and organ includes a two-measure introduction and interlude. There is a quiet affirmation of faith in each musical phrase, which rises to its cadence in a pure Phrygian mode. Of all his hymn writing, this setting is most particularly expressive. Langlais always said that he felt a special purity and pleasure in the untransposed modes with no accidentals, even in the accompaniment, and this he demonstrates here.

"A Morning Hymn" and "The Threefold Truth," both composed in 1985, were commissioned by the San Francisco chapter of the AGO for a festival service. Like the other hymns they may be sung as a solo or as a four-part hymn. These fall into rhythmic iambic patterns, which detract from the line. The texts appear to have been difficult for him to set.

The Christmas carol "Noël: 'Chantez, les anges'" (1989), on a text by Jean Rolland, begins, like many of his pieces in this genre, with the verse followed by the refrain. The melody is completely simple and happy; one of his forebears in the Noëliste school might have written it. In a number of Langlais's later vocal pieces, he returned to a simpler style, simpler even than in his first compositions.

Deux chants chorals, "Dans ma faiblesse," mm. 1–6. © 1983 Europart. Used by permission.

Langlais left a treasury, then, of practical music for congregational singing that could be translated into English and published (much of the music discussed in this chapter is either out of print or remains in manuscript). For these achievements, in 1961, he was awarded Boys Town's Saint Caecelia Medal, which bears the following inscription: "Mr. Langlais, as organist of the Basilica of Saint-Clotilde in Paris, carries on eminently the tradition of his great predecessors César Franck and Charles Tournemire. All the world is his debtor, not only for the exquisite artistry of his performances, but for his first-rank contribution to contemporary organ literature and his many compositions destined to enhance Christian worship."

CHAPTER 12

Poems of Life 1965–1972

I am obsessed with finishing the next work—a continuation
of all that came before. Maybe this one will be the ultimate
total. I can't explain my work, only feel it.

David Breeden, American sculptor

In 1965, at the age of fifty-eight, Langlais was at the pinnacle of his
success as a composer and performer. His American tours had contributed to his abiding sense of confidence, and he was made an Officer of the Palmes Académiques for his contributions as a teacher.
But in his personal life Langlais mourned our relationship, which
he had hoped would be permanent. He played three recitals at
Sainte-Clotilde on 3, 17, and 31 March 1965, and on the day of the
last recital, seeking catharsis, he wrote a few lines of verse, titled
simply "Poem," which cry out the pathos of this loss.

> There is no more sun on the earth,
> There are no more birds who sing,
> There are no more leaves on the trees,
> There are no more fragrant flowers,
> There are no more bells in the country,
> There are no more waves in the ocean,
> There is no more heaven,
> There is no more God,
> There is no more faith in my soul since I have lost my Ann.
> But there is forever the *love*, which I want never to destroy,
>   *love* given and not taken back,
> *Love that I keep for my Ann.*[1]

Not since 1939, when the Sainte-Clotilde position had been denied
him, had he suffered such an emotional bafflement. He responded to

it in the only way he knew, through a work which transcended his own pain by embracing the universality of the human condition.

His music from this seven-year period is freer in form, using not only name motifs but themes symbolic of these emotions, similar to Wagner's use of leitmotivs. Many of the works were also considerably longer than earlier ones and were based on a single generating idea stated in the title. Prior to *Poem of Life* (1965), "Evocation" (*Homage to Rameau*) had been his longest single organ work. His earlier pieces normally did not exceed five minutes. His most common practice, like that of his predecessors from the Classical French school, had been to group together a number of shorter pieces into suites, either as an organ mass, such as *Hommage à Frescobaldi* and *Suite médiévale*, or as a suite of pieces, such as *Suite brève* and *Suite française*. These short pieces from the suite or self-contained works, such as *Poèmes évangéliques*, were most frequently in A B A form with the development as the B section.

Poem of Life

Poem of Life is a musical expression of Langlais's literary "Poem," an extended free fantasy in two parts, lasting slightly longer than twenty minutes. In it Langlais evokes a broad spectrum of universal emotions; joy and anguish alternate, often with jarring rapidity. Although the two sections of the work are distinct, this division does not detract from the unity of the whole. The first section deals with the happy emotions of joy and love. The second expresses the torment of separation, loss, anger, depression, and death. The work was composed in reverse order, with the second calamitous section written very rapidly between 26 and 31 January 1965. The first section was written more slowly between 1 February and 5 April. The dedicatee of *Poem of Life*, Marie-Claire Alain, believed that the piece had something to do with Jeannine Collard; interestingly, she felt the emotion inherent in the work without understanding the exact reference.[2]

Poem is based on three principal themes, which are presented successively at the opening of the work. The first theme (mm. 1–4) is based on four descending whole tones in syncopated rhythm, symbolizing life without emotion. It serves as an introduction to the story, setting the stage for the events that are about to occur.

Poem of Life, mm. 1–12. © 1966 Elkan-Vogel, Inc. Used by permission.

At the opening, a man walks along feeling no particular emotion. In measures 5 and 6, several notes of the theme are held, as if to ask what will happen next. Then at measure 7, the second theme is announced on a Clarinette in the tenor range, the name Jean (B-flat, E, A, F-sharp), the narrator who will relate the poem of his life. The third theme, in measures 9 and 10, expresses joy and hope in an ascending synthetic minor scale with flatted fifth, sixth, and seventh scale degrees, followed in measures 11 and 12 by the name Ann (A,

F, F). The theme that in "Evocation" expressed love is used here in retrograde. The similarities with the octatonic scale are striking.

With its many thematic and stylistic similarities, *Poem of Life* may be seen as an extension of "Evocation." The themes of this second poem are then developed in a broad spectrum of contrasting emotions. For example, the embellishments surrounding the A, F, F theme in "Evocation" are further developed in *Poem* (mm. 12–16). The rhythmic ostinatos beginning in the Allegro of "Evocation," which express joy and exaltation as they accompany the opening rising motif from the third theme, are similarly treated in *Poem*. Modal and parallel harmony, especially in the accompanying chords—and by now common elements of his style—are typical of both pieces.

In *Poem*, the first section ends quietly, like a gentle love song (Andantino quasi allegro) with the joy theme in the pedal. Reminiscent of the section in "Evocation" marked *espressivo*, it is played at the same tempo and with a similar registration. Each has an expressive obbligato treble part.

Throughout this first section of *Poem*, emotions of quiet joy, exuberant happiness, and unexpected bliss ascend in an impressionistic display of color, symbolizing the various expressions of Jean's love. These love themes are interwoven by alternating use of mutation stops and solo Voix humaine, Bourdon, and Tremblant for the theme on Jean's name, which creates playful and lyrical effects. The second and third themes rise together to a high tessitura and a long held chord; a complete break follows.

The second section begins in stark contrast to the first. On a full combination without reeds, a dramatic outcry sounds in a descending scale with two augmented seconds above dissonant chords. The writing recalls the fantasy-recitative section at the end of the passacaglia variations in Franck's Choral in B minor. Langlais wanted it played in a tragic manner—free, biting, and very emotional.[3] This descending scale symbolizes the anguish of separation and its associated pain. A second descending chromatic scale follows, this time played with a soft Clairon 4 in the pedal, with sustained chromatic chords in the hands on Bourdon 16, 8, Voix humaine, Voix céleste, and Tremblant. This progression symbolizes depression and grief. A funeral knell based on a three-note ostinato in the pedal continues

Recit: -Voix celeste+Fonds 16, 8, 4, 2, +Mixtures, Anches 16, 8, 4
Pos: Fonds 8, 4, 2, Mixtures
G.O: Fonds 16, 8, 4, 2, Mixtures
Ped: Fonds 16, 8
R./G.O.
Pos./G.O.
G.P.R./Ped.

Poem of Life, p. 9, mm. 1–5. © 1966 Elkan-Vogel, Inc. Used by permission.

the same idea. At the end of the piece, it is repeated twenty-six times, representing my age at the time. The piece comes to rest with a gradual lengthening of the ostinato figure, thus ending with a fragment from the first descending scale with the softest stop on the Récit. As at the end of his earlier "De profundis" (*Neuf pièces*), *Poem* also comes to rest in a low tessitura in the key of E minor.

Langlais played the premiere of *Poem of Life* at Boys Town in August 1965 and shortly thereafter on French National Radio and at Sainte-Clotilde, all of which performances helped bring about the cathartic release he sought in writing both the poem and the music. In December 1965 he orchestrated the second section for a small orchestra of flute, oboe, clarinet, English horn, bassoon, and string quintet; this *Elegie pour dixtuor* was premiered in Rennes on 21 March 1966 by the Groupe Instrumental Musica Aeterna, directed by Odette Ramon; returning to his Breton roots was always a balm for Langlais.

Poem of Peace

By 1966 Langlais was fully distracted by another young American student, Susan Ferré. She had studied with him for several weeks in 1964, and in 1965 she traveled from Texas to Nebraska to meet him during his tour. Langlais mentioned this expression of zeal in his account of the tour: "At Boys Town, another of my students had the extraordinary courage to come forty-eight hours by bus. That is a mark of affection that warms the heart."[4]

Susan's account of her meeting with Langlais confirms what Langlais reported. "At the age of eighteen I studied with Langlais in Paris for six weeks in the summer of '64, while the Texas Christian University tour led by Emmet Smith, my teacher, moved on to other parts of Europe. I was unchaperoned, staying in a small hotel on rue Saint-Jacques, near Les Jardins de Luxembourg. He met me several times for lunch and seemed concerned for my safety. I took lessons at night at Sainte-Clotilde. The stage was then set for my Boys Town trip the following summer, and for the Fulbright years following the '67 tour."[5]

Langlais, much taken by the gentle quality of Susan's voice, and by her innocence and kindness, fell in love with her. He decided that she would be the guide for his 1967 tour. Although Susan cared for him and admired him greatly, she would not let him make more than a friendship of their relationship. He expressed his acceptance of her decision in *Poem of Peace*, composed on Good Friday, 6 April 1966. Her copy of the manuscript is inscribed "with my best affection," and the printed copy, "To my dear Susan this musical gift and my best affections. J. Langlais." In the program notes used in the recitals for his 1967 tour, he stated that the work "expresses the peace of the soul with the aid of several Gregorian themes," and indeed it is filled with quiet peace and spiritual contentment. The chants are identified in the score as "Regina pacis," "Pax Domini," and "Da pacem Domine." The name Susan, heard in whole notes (C, E, C, A, F-sharp) above a two-note ostinato accompanying figure, permeates the entire five-and-a-half-minute piece. On 10 May 1966, Langlais gave the premiere at Sainte-Clotilde; on 15 January 1967, he played the American premiere in Washington.

In a letter dated 11 May 1966, Langlais described to Susan his premiere of the work and Marchal's reaction, which was ever Langlais's barometer of quality:

I was very happy composing [*Poem of Peace*] for you and for me. After finishing it, I became very depressed, thinking this work

Poem of Peace, mm. 1–9. © 1966 Elkan-Vogel, Inc. Used by permission.

was a bad one. Then, I decided to do a Test. . . . Yesterday night, I played it at my third recital at Sainte-Clotilde. I decided to publish this Poem if I had the impression that people liked it. Marchal came to me the first and told me, "I like very, very much your Poem of Peace, which is really a beautiful work."

On 12 September 1966, he sent Susan a postcard from Holland describing another poem he had written for her, which he sent to her in braille. Clearly Langlais was still seeking to win her love. But there is a certain beauty and simplicity in his use of metaphor in this poem.

> Who am I?
> I wish to hear a new bird's song,
> to learn a new symphony,
> to kneel under a new tree,
> to know a new poem,
> to admire a new unclothed statue,

to cross a new sea to visit a new world,
to smell a new flower, which I would love to gather.
I eagerly wish what I cannot write,
what I do not deserve, for who am I?
She is my bird,
She is my symphony,
My tree, my poem,
My statue, my sea,
My flower, my world,
My sun, which I shall never see!
Who am I? I am a pipe smoker,
I am a composer,
but I am a lover needing a forgiver.

Poem of Happiness

Poem of Happiness, the third poem in the trilogy, was composed in 1966 and dedicated to Robert Noehren—although it is clearly a continuation of his thematic use of the Susan theme from *Poem of Peace* and was clearly meant for her. Langlais wrote it for Susan's senior recital at Texas Christian University; as he hoped, it was the last piece on her program.

Langlais had known Noehren in several capacities, most recently as a co-adjudicator. Langlais, Cor Kee, and Noehren had been invited to participate as judges in an improvisation competition at the Haarlem Festival in September 1965. They were given scoring sheets that included categories of musicianship—rhythm, style, and so forth. In each of the categories, the judges were instructed to rate each candidate on a scale from one to ten, with ten being the best. This Noehren and Kee dutifully did, but Langlais had a student in the competition whom he wanted to win. To this end, he changed the averages of the judge's ratings by giving nines and tens in all categories to his candidate, and by giving zeros to every other candidate, whatever their performance. This kind of manipulation was normal for Langlais, but Noehren and Kee were not pleased. Noehren was especially dismayed; he thought Langlais's student made the poorest showing overall.

Langlais and Susan Ferré at Sainte-Clotilde, 1968

Noehren recalled one in particular of his many visits to Paris in the 1960s:

> I decided to call on Jean Langlais at his apartment. . . . When he opened the door to his apartment he appeared delighted to see me, and exclaimed that he had been thinking about me and the possibility of writing an organ piece for me. After we were seated he asked me what kind of a piece I would like, what the form should take. I thought for a moment and then recalled that I could not remember he had ever written a toccata, so I suggested that he might write such a work, if it pleased him. I was leaving Paris soon after that, but told M. Langlais that I would be returning in about two weeks and would try to attend mass at the church at Sainte-Clotilde on that Sunday. When I

returned as I had planned and entered the choir loft of his church, M. Langlais presented me with the manuscript of a brilliant and exciting new work entitled *Poem of Happiness*, which he had inscribed to me.[6]

It is indeed a brilliant toccata, developing the same synthetic minor scale found in "Evocation" and *Poem of Life* to symbolize joy.

Poem of Happiness, mm. 1–5. © 1967 Elkan-Vogel, Inc. Used by permission.

Here the scale is written in a descending six-note figure in octaves, with a thirty-second note attached to five eighth notes, which creates an unexpected rhythmic kick. The scale is extended by one note with each repetition until it sounds the full octave. The motif on the name Susan follows in measure 5, this time as a rapid octave arpeggiation. It is then treated sequentially at measure 16 and throughout the bravura double octave passages, including the pedal solo passage. Contrasting with the opening material, massive declamatory chords in ascending patterns follow the arpeggiation. At the end there is a brief solitary reference to two Gregorian chant themes associated with joy: "Gaudeamus" and "Gaudete." Langlais described the piece as "an evocation of many kinds of joy: boisterous, quiet, and spiritual."[7]

As *Poem of Life* is thematically a musical extension of "Evocation," in the same manner, *Poem of Happiness* is a musical extension of *Poem of Peace*. All four use name motifs extensively as a generating force. Both "Evocation" and *Poem of Happiness* have almost identical endings, with two dissonant chords coming to rest on the same D major chord, which technique afterward became normative in his writing. "Evocation," *Poem of Life*, and *Poem of Happiness* all use the same rhythmic pattern of long, long, short, long, with the same bravura octave doublings.

Langlais again gave the premiere, this time for a most joyous occasion: the marriage of his son to the beautiful Monique Bourreau on 17 May 1969. In a letter to Lilian Murtagh, dated 5 June 1969, he wrote, "We are very busy with the marriage of Claude. The mass was very moving. One of our singer friends [Jeannine Collard] sang the *Missa in simplicitate,* and I played the organ myself. At the end Claude asked me to play my *Poem of Happiness.* That was very appropriate."

1967 American Tour

From 15 January to 12 March 1967, with Susan Ferré as his guide, Langlais made his seventh tour of the United States, playing twenty-nine recitals from coast to coast and giving frequent master classes at universities. Susan handled the details of the tour efficiently but was uneasy about her French; early in the tour she wrote to Murtagh, "All still goes well, except that my speaking in French is slow and I'm sure it frustrates him." [8] But Langlais was pleased to have her and mentioned to Murtagh that she was "gentille" and only twenty years old.

On this tour Langlais heard a performance of his *Missa "Salve regina"* and *The Canticle of the Sun* as part of his recital at the Roman Catholic cathedral in Philadelphia. Another highlight involved Joseph Michaud, who had been at Saint Bernard's Roman Catholic Church in Pittsburgh, where Langlais had played during his 1964 tour. Michaud had recently supervised the installation of two large Moeller organs at the National Shrine of the Immaculate Conception in Washington, and he invited Langlais to play for a service. Langlais was impressed by the immense size of the Shrine and its elevator, which led to the organ loft. Though he was disappointed not to give a recital here this time, he did not forget this first visit; the Shrine's extremely reverberant acoustics and two organs would provide inspiration for future works.

In Washington Langlais gave a recital instead at a Methodist church, where the organ had "many borrowed stops, borrowed twice and three times."[9] Susan's account of that recital shows how Langlais could transcend a poor instrument. "In spite of the small ten-stop organ, with too many borrowings, in poor acoustics, he played one of the most moving concerts of the tour, beginning with Mendelssohn's Sonata no. 6. It was as if the intimacy of the room, packed with people, moved him in a way that some of the larger environs couldn't. He chose real stops judiciously, not using duplications until the very end of the recital in his improvisation, and at that, only at the end. I was impressed."[10]

In California Langlais visited for the first time the politically charged atmosphere of Berkeley, where he was told "that certain young women walk around in dresses made of string."[11] Susan remembered his fascination with this manner of un-dress. "He was so intrigued by [them] that he bought one for me when we returned to Paris. He also bought me a beautiful sapphire ring in Columbus. . . . (He tried hard to win me over!)"[12]

Another first on this tour was his playing of a theater organ, at the Hammond castle in Gloucester, Massachusetts: "My recital took place in a Medieval castle built thirty years ago but on an organ which must have been from that time—it was so dilapidated."[13] John Pappenheimer wrote a review for the local newspaper there, titled "A blind organist handles hundreds of tabs, switches." It ran on 9 March 1967, accompanied by a photo of Langlais at the huge console; a portion of the text follows:

> "It is a four manual?" was the only question Langlais asked as he sat down in front of the keyboard for the first time yesterday afternoon. He began playing immediately with a rapt smile. Hundreds of pedals, tabs, stops, and switches were in front of him. Within thirty minutes Langlais was familiar with the Hammond organ: how to get different tones, how to increase its volume, how to get different couplings.

Again, Susan's account fills out Langlais's impressions of this special place, whose salt air and thick walls reminded him of Brittany: "Upon first trying the organ, he enjoyed hearing the stops such as the Fox Horn and became more and more tickled with each sound he pulled out, even though he passed up the opportunity of using some of them in the recital. He told me that the organ had three hundred stops of which forty were usable. Actually, it had 173 tabs, 14,000 pipes." [14]

After Gloucester Langlais returned to New York, where an attack of painful bursitis forced him to cancel the last of his three scheduled recitals. He did however proudly attend the New York premiere of his *Psaume solennel no. 1* at the Madison Avenue Presbyterian Church, conducted by Richard Westenburg: "Fortunately a magnificent consolation was given to me in New York. It was there that I heard a magnificent performance of my *Psaume solennel* [no. 1] for two choirs, brass, and organ. I wanted to hear the full effect of this performance, and so went to sit in one of the last pews of the church. There was no place reserved for me and I had to content myself with a simple chair placed against a door." [15] The audience was wild in its enthusiasm.

Back in France, Langlais continued to write longer and more rhapsodic as well as shorter pieces grouped into suites. *Livre oecuménique* (1968) is an example of the latter, while *Three Voluntaries* (1969) shows an expanded use of form and name motifs: Langlais dedicated the second of the voluntaries to Marie-Louise Jaquet.

Marie-Louise Jaquet

Born in 1943 to a wealthy French family, Marie-Louise Jaquet spent her early years in Casablanca, Morocco. Her family moved back to Mulhouse, in Alsace, and Marie-Louise began her organ studies at the Conservatory in Marseille. She began studying with Langlais in 1967, at first privately and then at the Schola Cantorum. She obtained the diploma for virtuosity in organ in 1967 and in improvisation in 1969, by which time she and Langlais were intensely and romantically involved.

Jeannette Langlais, as always, was entirely accepting of Langlais relationship with Marie-Louise and even encouraged it; she held the place that Marie-Louise wanted in his life, and she knew that he would never divorce her for Marie-Louise. But Marie-Louise grew increasingly envious of Jeannette, which created a strain in Langlais's marriage. The women differed in temperament, in religious and cultural backgrounds, and in personality. Jeannette was soft-spoken, refined, reserved, infinitely patient, a devout Roman Catholic, and a painter. Marie-Louise was aggressive, impatient, a devout Protestant, a competing organist, and totally unreserved.

Marie-Louise felt that Jeannette was stupid to let Langlais to speak to her the way he did; indeed she considered Jeannette her intellectual inferior in every way, and let her know this. The verbal abuse had a long history, and I myself witnessed him belittling those closest to him. Organization was not Jeannette's strong suit, and Langlais constantly berated her for this weakness. If Jeannette misplaced something, Langlais would shout and call her stupid. Jeannette accepted this behavior as part of Langlais's artistic temperament. She held her tongue.

From Marie-Louise's point of view, Jeannette lacked not only organizational skills but pride in the upkeep of the apartment, which had become run down over the years. The phlebitis in Jeannette's leg continued to slow her down, and besides, she saw no reason to spend money on the apartment when Langlais could not see the neglect. She resented Marie-Louise's high-handed tactics and the way she manipulated Langlais. As for Langlais, he enjoyed the rivalry between these two women; it was an exciting game, and he was at the center of it, just where he liked to be. He worked at keeping things agitated.

Marie-Louise was jealous of Langlais's other mistresses and often searched his music for references to them. She did not have far to look. Langlais enjoyed this sort of intrigue immensely, and it provided him with almost as much thrill as the affairs themselves. Susan Ferré and Marie-Louise were his students at the Schola Cantorum concurrently, and Marie-Louise was particularly jealous when Susan was his guide for the 1967 tour. To further perplex Marie-Louise, Langlais had Susan record a tape of conversations with him. He derived a sense of power from such games and provocations. It was clear that these affairs and their machinations were central to his identity as well as to his music. His desire to manipulate and control those around him continued throughout his life.

Three Voluntaries

In 1969 Langlais's *Three Voluntaries* were published. Each explores a different form and style within a religious context. Although they follow the spirit of earlier English models, their harmonic language and contrapuntal techniques are innovative. Together they form a triptych lasting more than thirty minutes and represent Langlais's most brilliant and technically demanding writing. Each voluntary also contains a musical reference to the person to whom it is dedicated.[16]

"Voluntary Saint-Jacques-le-majeur" is dedicated to Jacques Chailley, professor of Medieval music at the Sorbonne and former director of the Schola Cantorum. There are two Saint Jacques, the greater and the lesser. The reference to Jacques Chailley as the greater is typical of Langlais's sense of humor. Langlais maintains the Medieval flavor of the counterpoint, in its parallel fourths and fifths, and expands the style of the Prelude from the *Suite médiévale*, here at greater length. "Voluntary Saint-Jacques-le-majeur" is divided into three sections entitled Counterpoint I, Double, and Counterpoint II. In Double (the English term for variation), the entire chordal section of Counterpoint I is repeated, with the addition of an obbligato line played on a solo combination of Bourdon 8 and Nasard 2-2/3 for the right hand—a highly figured arrangement, similar to the treble passages for color stops in Stanley's voluntaries. Counterpoint II is a fast-moving dialogue for the mixture combinations of both manuals, recalling the Medieval flavor of the opening.

The opening bar of "Voluntary Sainte-Marie-Madeleine" spells the name Marie (E, A, B-flat, A, E), a reference both to Mary Magdalene and Marie-Louise, the piece's dedicatee; the second measure spells the name Louise (D, G, E, A, C, E).

Three Voluntaries, "Voluntary Sainte-Marie-Madeleine," p. 13, mm. 1–2. © 1970 H. T. FitzSimons Co. International copyright secured. All rights reserved. Used by permission.

As in the first voluntary, this work falls into three main sections, all three of which reference the dual meaning of Marie as saint and lover. The first section introduces the theme of Marie juxtaposed with a secondary erotic theme, with each note corresponding to the letters of a complete sentence in French. Immediately following the name, Langlais continues by employing notes to form a very slow sustained choral prayer of adoration to Mary; time seems to stand still here, with the length of the sustained *pianissimo* chords. The last phrase of the Cromorne theme, "je t'aime" (I love you) on the notes B, E, D, A, A, E, E, is repeated using a Bourdon in the right hand.

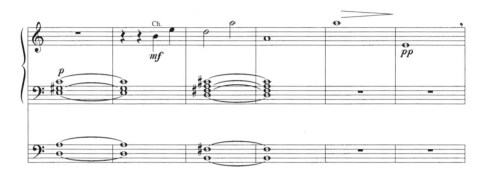

Three Voluntaries, "Voluntary Sainte-Marie-Madeleine," p. 18, mm. 15–20. © 1970 H. T. FitzSimons Co. International copyright secured. All rights reserved. Used by permission.

In the second section, Langlais forms an extended, highly erotic sentence, in praise of the woman Marie-Louise. As in *Poem of Life,* Langlais again uses a Cromorne in the tenor range for this theme, accompanying it with organum-like parallel fourths and fifths. The Final ends joyously in the form of a gigue that develops both themes from the first section in a polymodal framework. Each section is repeated using a pizzicato bass pedal. This voluntary is one of Langlais's most tightly woven works, structurally and thematically. It couples a poetic lyricism with advanced contrapuntal skill and displays the increasingly intense blending of his personal and musical identities.

"Voluntary Sainte-Trinité" also has a dual intent: to extol the sanctity of the Trinity and to express Langlais's affection and love for one of his closest friends, Olivier Messiaen, organist at La Trinité in Paris, to whom it is dedicated. It too is in three sections, also symbolic of the Trinity. The first section is long, a representation of eternity inspiring mystical contemplation, similar to both the prayer of adoration in the second voluntary and Messiaen's meditative works like *Le banquet céleste*.

In the second section, the name Olivier (G, D, A, F, A, E, B-flat) is introduced on the Clarinette, followed by the name Messiaen (E, E, C, C, A, A, E, F). Langlais again displays his fondness for using the Clarinette for name motifs, as he did in "Evocation," *Poem of Life*, and "Voluntary Sainte-Marie-Madeleine." Bird calls, so much a part of Messiaen's style, are interwoven with his name and the first name of his wife, Yvonne Loriod (A, F, G, F, F, E).

Three Voluntaries, "Voluntary Sainte-Trinité," p. 26, mm. 11–17. © 1970 H. T. FitzSimons Co. International copyright secured. All rights reserved. Used by permission.

The third section is a brilliant toccata that combines the name Yvonne in diminution in octaves on the manuals, with the name Olivier Messiaen in augmentation in the pedal. As in the second voluntary, the slow section is briefly recalled before the coda.

Langlais's use of octave doubling here is his most extensive to date. It evolved from his first sparing use in the Final from his *Première symphonie* to a more systematic one in "Storm in Florida" (*American Suite*). In *Essai*, he seems to be quoting Messiaen's use of the same device in "Le verbe" (*La Nativité*, 1936).

In his expression of gratitude for this "most original" piece, Messiaen showed again how well he understood Langlais's musical intentions, noting its fresh harmonies, its cretic (long, short, long) and bacchian (dactylic: long, short, short) rhythms, and even how the final toccata contained groups of eleven and thirteen notes, among other things:

> I was moved to see that the "Voluntary Sainte-Trinité" was dedicated to me—the printed dedication and the most exquisite handwritten one. I am most enthusiastic about this last piece, for it expresses all that I love: first, it invokes the Trinity (I have been [organist] for more than forty years in a church that carries this majestic name); and then, the Flûte 4 on the Grand-orgue rises higher and higher toward the sky, like the call of a bird. . . . I thank you, with my whole heart, for this beautiful homage. You know that I often play your music; with this sumptuous arrival, I will be able to augment my programs![17]

Friendship with Olivier Messiaen

Langlais kept every letter Messiaen ever wrote him. They total more than fifty, beginning with the first, written during the summer of 1929 when they were students at the Conservatory. Most are in longhand and many are undated, particularly the short notes. Five typewritten letters (one of them from Yvonne Loriod) express Messiaen's gratitude for receiving copies of Langlais's music.

Although Langlais's friendships with other people, such as Litaize, had cooled, these letters form a testimonial to a sixty-year friendship. Messiaen's letters often show an intimacy, closeness, and need for Langlais's approval, which is surprising in light of his international prominence as a composer. In one letter, Messiaen absolutely insists that Langlais attend a dress rehearsal of the Paris premiere of his *Quatuor pour la fin du temps*. He badly wanted to know Langlais's opinion of the work; he always counted on Langlais's frank opinion. Once, when he had played Langlais's "Les rameaux" too slowly, Langlais corrected him, and the following year he replayed it completely to Langlais's liking.

The bonds between them were forged from many common ideas. Both men were firmly rooted in the Roman Catholic faith and sought to express it through their compositions. They both held a common reverence for scripture. Each built his career on a continuing search for newness and a desire to remain independent of any school of writing. They both expanded upon earlier techniques: for example, Messiaen continued to use modes of limited transposition even in his opera, *Saint François d'Assise*. Each used symbolism frequently; Messiaen, through his birds and colors, expressed his views on contemporary reality and suffering: "God is above us, and still He comes to suffer with us."[18]

Each was influenced by mysticism, and sought to express the spiritual realm through his music. Messiaen uses static and very slow tempos, such as in the *Le banquet céleste*, the first and fourth movements of *L'Ascension*, and the end of "Le verbe" (*La Nativité*). Langlais uses these same techniques in "Meditation" (*Homage to Rameau*) and the beginning of "Voluntary Sainte-Trinité." Messiaen's music fits most definitions of mysticism, although Messiaen himself was skeptical about the term.[19] Their common heritage came directly from Tournemire, whose music—imbued as it is with a great sense of spirituality—they both greatly admired.

Langlais's students gained special insight into Messiaen's music because Langlais so deeply loved and understood it. Langlais was more concerned about showing Messiaen's music to his students than his own works.[20] He would not tolerate any negative comments about Messiaen's music. When a friend mentioned that Messiaen's new opera about Saint Francis seemed repetitive, Langlais was furious. He dismissed such a view, saying that as a Protestant, this person could not be expected to understand the opera's depth. Although Langlais never admitted that his friendship for Messiaen caused him any difficulty, he never felt equal to Messiaen as a composer and struggled to establish and maintain his own individuality as a composer.

Legion of Honor

In 1968 Langlais was made an Officer of the Legion of Honor. He was proud that it was Messiaen who gave the testimonial to his importance as a composer and personally pinned the rosette on his lapel of his jacket—even though Messiaen managed to stab him with

Messiaen and Langlais, Legion of Honor ceremony, Association
Valentin Haüy, 1968

the pin! Susan Ferré, who attended this "grand affair," gives a fascinating firsthand account:

> Before the one hundred or so guests adjourned for the most
> spectacular party, complete with petits fours and champagne—
> the good kind, which must have cost a fortune—(He always
> said he liked bad wine and good champagne!)—the assembled
> guests were treated to a memorable sonic happening, as Lan-
> glais and Messiaen improvised, four hands, at the piano. As
> themes, they used each other's names. They seemed *so* happy.
> The improvisation was brilliant, but not showy with tricks.
> Rather it was serene, strong, solid, beautifully crafted, and
> ended with a double fugue.[21]

In the summer of 1968, having seen off a last class of fifty-two
students, Langlais retired from the Institute. His recital career con-

tinued to flourish, however, along with his reputation. He made concert tours of America and continued to play in Europe. In Fribourg he played the four magnificent organs and wrote in an excited Franglais about his recitals: "C'est wonderful. I have just returned from playing in Holland and will leave in a month to be a member of an international organ jury and play six concerts before returning to play in England and again in Germany."[22]

Trois implorations

The 1969 American tour, from 5 October to 25 November, included twenty-three recitals and seven master classes. Langlais began with Colette Lequien, the wife of his friend the poet Edmond Lequien, serving as his guide, but after several concerts Lequien, exhausted by the rigorous schedule, returned to France. Marie-Louise Jaquet immediately took over in Boston.

Jaquet's influence was evident in his next work for organ, *Trois implorations*, composed during the first three months of 1970. The work was commissioned for that spring's organ exam at the Paris Conservatory, but the students were probably unaware of the hidden meaning behind his expression of joy as they struggled with this technically demanding piece. His joy at finding a love for so spiritual a young woman permeates the entire first entreaty, "Pour la joie." Her full name sounds forth on the Trompette and Clairon followed by his declaration of love, once more, in the words "je t'aime." This time there is no confusing his love for Marie-Louise with his adoration of Mary Magdalene.

In the second entreaty Langlais realized more developed freedom and lyricism of melodic line. "Pour l'indulgence" is a prayer for forgiveness, in direct contrast to the mood and timbre of the first plea. He spins out a very long melody, with long sustained chords accompanying, first on the solo Clarinette and later a solo Basson 16 and Hautbois 8. The themes are without name motifs or chant references. There is, however, an intensely personal aspect to the supplication.

The third plea, "Pour la croyance," is a statement of Langlais's difficulty in maintaining his faith following the Second Vatican Council. In his program notes for "this expressly dramatic work,"

Langlais writes, "The composer has tried to translate the state of the soul of a Christian in revolt against the current desacralizing atmosphere." The theme is the priest's intonation of the Credo common to Gregorian masses 1, 2, and 4 ("Credo in unum Deo," I believe in one God) on a solo Hautbois. The response is shockingly brutal; the full organ enters with two crashing staccato chord clusters on full organ as if to say, in Langlais's own words, "Merde, you don't believe at all!" The intonation is repeated in strict canon and then answered by several slow, but soft, mildly dissonant chords in the low register. Again the *fortissimo* chord clusters return—three of them this time. The intonation is heard once more in triple canon with the same triple chord cluster response, each time more poignant. After this first series of angry outbursts, the intonation is expanded into several other lyrical variants, the last of which uses many fast, anticipatory figures before each note. The piece ends with five staccato chord clusters, the last of which is held for two bars. This cluster contains all twelve tones of the scale, an impressive technical feat which Langlais achieved for the first time by indicating that two notes be played with each thumb.

Troisième concerto and *Sonate en trio*

Troisième concerto (1971), scored for strings and timpani, was also written in protest. In the published version, editor Thomas Daniel Schlee, who was a student of Langlais, gives an excellent analysis of the work and explains its subtitle:

> The composer's subtitle "Reaction" is derived from the formal structure and its interpretation: all sections of the Concerto are relatively free in construction, despite many thematic links; this freedom leads to a necessary contrast, the strict form of the central fugue. As a whole, the work can be regarded as a creative "Reaction" to the barely comprehensible forms that abound in contemporary music. A reversion to traditional formal schemes need not, however, produce reactionary music, as is amply demonstrated by Jean Langlais in his Third Organ Concerto.[23]

An earlier work, *Sonate en trio*, commissioned for the 1967 organ exam at the Paris Conservatory, also protests against the lack of clear musical forms. Langlais followed his rhapsodic "poems," which explored new freedom of form, with a trio sonata in a very strict form, even stricter than those written by Bach. The first section is repeated with an independent pedal line. The same procedure is followed for the second section. After a one-measure bridge, the first section is repeated in exact retrograde.

Offrande à Marie

Langlais reaffirmed his faith by composing *Offrande à Marie* (1971), a suite of six meditations for organ. Langlais establishes unity in the work by basing each movement on the litany of Loreto, chants for benediction in honor of the Blessed Virgin Mary. Each meditation is in a different form; the titles are all allusions to Mary. The first meditation, "Mater admirabilis," repeats the litany chants with its ending formula ("pray for us") throughout the length of the piece, sounding at different pitch levels, like a mantra. Variety and musical interest come from a simple organum-like accompaniment.

In "Consolatrix afflictorum" (Consoler of the afflicted), quiet sustained chords in parallel motion reintroduce the chant heard in the first meditation. They are repeated at the end of the piece. The middle section on the foundation stops is more agitated, with undulating chromatic movement and syncopated angular motives symbolizing the anguish of Christ's suffering, which Mary witnessed and consoled.

The third piece, "Regina angelorum" (Queen of the angels), is more programmatic, suggesting the flutter of angel wings around Mary. A rapidly moving melody playing in the high register on the organ on a Flûte 4 and Nasard 2-2/3 over a Salicional for sustained high-pitched chords creates this special effect. In the middle section the hymn "Virgo Dei genitrix" is heard on the Clarinette followed by the notes A, F, F (an allusion to me, Ann, to whom the movement is dedicated).

The fourth movement, "Regina pacis" (Queen of peace), is a very quiet and calm fresco, similar to his *Chant de paix*; a slow sustained progression of tone clusters alternates with their resolutions over long pedal points, and in the middle section, marked *più vivo*, the chant theme is heard. The fifth, "Mater Christi," pictures Mary as the Mother of Christ and Vine of Grace. Its first part recalls the litany here in a bitonal setting followed by the hymn "Sacris solemniis," from the feast of Corpus Christi. This hymn includes the verse "Panis angelicus," in which Christ is described as both man and our heavenly food. This duality is treated by a canon and extended in the image of Mary.

The last meditation, "Maria mater gratiae," is a joyful portrayal of Mary as the fountain of grace and clemency. The meditation displays the full tutti of the organ as the hymn "Maria mater gratiae" resounds in the pedal. The form is tripartite, with a development section based on the first phrase of the chant, on a softer registration. The dramatic flourishes of the opening are heard again in a more extended manner at the end, like a fountain of water.[24]

CHAPTER 13

Heart Attack and Aftermath
1973–1979

And the fifth angel blew his trumpet, and I saw a star fallen
from heaven to earth, and he was given the key of the shaft of
the bottomless pit.

Revelation 9:1

Langlais suffered a heart attack on Sunday, 14 January 1973. He
was taken to the hospital the next day and by Wednesday was
moved to a nursing home, where he remained for one month. He
was under the care of Alain Garderet, a cardiologist and one of his
organ students. Although the attack was not severe, and Garderet
promised Langlais he could eventually resume a normal concert
schedule, the treatment prescribed complete rest for two months.
His progress, however, was quite rapid. Less than one month later,
only days before his sixty-sixth birthday, he wrote without men-
tioning his health, only to say that he had to stay under nursing care
for two more weeks.[1]

Langlais was very eager to see his students during his period of
recuperation. Marie-Louise Jaquet, Marjorie Bruce, Marie Grandinetti, and Nathan Ensign all visited him in the hospital shortly after
the attack and found that he was reluctant to talk about his illness.
He seemed lighthearted and asked them about their studies at the
Schola with André Fleury, who substituted for him during his
absence. In addition to his students, two sisters who were nurses—
Eugénie and Geneviève Malherbe—gave him special attention. Langlais, who became very fond of them, soon thanked them by dedicating to them two pieces from *Suite baroque*.

In fact, from the original onset of pain, he feared that he was close to death, but its impact was too overwhelming for him to talk about. Marie Grandinetti had just begun her studies with him, on 1 January 1973. She reported that Garderet permitted Langlais to resume his teaching with only one student. As this first student, she felt a profound change in him between the hospital visit and her first lesson: "He seemed just to be beginning to deal with the seriousness of his health and the closeness of death. . . . I remember his wanting to talk about how sick he had been. It seemed in contrast to how he had been when Nathan Ensign and I visited him in the hospital just after the attack."[2]

Langlais's new diet was very strict, eliminating all salt and fat, and worst of all, he had to give up his pipe. With his daily medications, including aspirin to thin his blood, he became hypochondriacal. He was afraid to sleep by himself and needed someone with him at all times.

Cinq méditations sur l'apocalypse

Just prior to his heart attack, he had begun his longest and one of his most important organ works: *Cinq méditations sur l'apocalypse*, a suite of five movements based on his reading of the Revelation to John and composed in the following order: "La cinquième trompette," "Il était," "Visions prophétiques," "Oh oui, viens Seigneur Jésus," and "Celui qui a des oreilles." With four of the meditations completed, he began to think of the pieces as a whole.

Even during his recuperation at the nursing home, as he lay bedridden and often unable to sleep, he reread his braille copy of Revelation many times, pondering the mysteries of suffering, death, salvation, and eternity in their eschatological dimensions. The final meditation as published, "La cinquième trompette," leaves the listener with a sense of dreadful horror. Langlais defended this on musical rather than theological grounds. He realized that ending with the quiet prayer would be musically untenable.

Cinq méditations sur l'apocalypse represents Langlais's first extended attempt at scriptural-theological program music. It is program music, because these movements tell a story based on these visionary texts; and it is scriptural-theological, because it is derived from Langlais's most extensive use of theological concepts. Langlais had experimented with scriptural-theological music before, in "Mors et resurrectio." In *Cinq méditations*, Langlais took all the titles and their allusions directly from passages in Revelation. Listeners unfamiliar with Langlais's style, or twentieth-century music in general, but who know their scripture well, can hear the musical symbolism in these pieces.

To set the stage for the work in the first movement, "Celui qui a des oreilles" (He who has ears), he transcribed for organ his earlier setting of Psalm 123 (*Deux psaumes*, 1937), in which soprano and tenor soloists sing the psalm text "I lift my eyes to you," accompanied by a choral fugue on the syllable "ah." In the organ transcription, the chorus parts are played on the manual and the solo parts on a Clairon 4 in the pedal. It contains seven fugal entries accompanied by solos on the third psalm tone, a reference to John's vision of the seven churches.

The second movement, "Il était, il est, et il viendra" (He was, he is, and he will come), is the most theologically profound movement of the collection. Langlais seeks to express the eternal and eschatological dimensions of the apocalypse, using themes symbolizing each part of the title: Christ who was before all time with the Father, the historical Jesus, and the Second Coming. He spent much time in thought and meditation before writing.

> I wished to depict eternity, . . . a mystery since . . . our poor spirit cannot understand that something has not had a beginning. One can understand that something will not have an end, but not to have a beginning goes beyond our limits of comprehension. . . . In this piece, I wanted to be expressly austere. The melody (C, D, E, F, E) turns around four notes, to symbolize that eternity does not change.[3]

This five-section tableau reveals the theological concept of the eternity of Christ by means of a soprano pedal point on the F above high C, which is held throughout the first, third, and fifth sections. It symbolizes Christ first as one with the Father, before all time, and the same again after his short human life. To depict Christ in the present in parts two and four, Langlais chooses two chants—"Vexilla regis," the vesper hymn for the First Sunday of the Passion, and "Lauda Sion," symbolic of Christ as the living bread of life—and accompanies them with piercing dissonances; "Lauda Sion" builds to a powerful climax on the tutti. At the end of the movement, the four-note motif is repeated, this time accompanied by brief flourishes on the Quintaton 16, Flûte 4, and Tierce 1-3/5, signifying the birds in paradise. Not surprisingly, it was these birds and the special use of rhythm that Messiaen found so familiar and appealing. "I especially appreciated the second piece with its pedal point, its bacchian and dochmian rhythms and the garlands on the Quintaton 16, Flûte 4, and Tierce."[4] The bacchian rhythm is also the basis for the introduction to the "Lauda Sion" fourth section. In his program notes for the recording, Joel-Marie Fauquet writes, "The writing and mystical colors of this movement lead us to think of the most original and poetical inventions of Olivier Messiaen."[5]

The third meditation, "Visions prophétiques," is a series of programmatic images of angelic multitudes, each set apart as a separate tableau in rondo form, with dramatic changes of registration and mood. Each scene is framed by a tableau: a rapid descending arpeggiated figure, followed by two very fast dissonant chords repeated in sequence, and ending with a very long tone cluster. Significantly positioned in the work, the recurring material symbolizes either the third angel's trumpet blast and the descent of the great star (Revelation 8:10) or the shout of another angel, so loud it was likened to a lion's roar (Revelation 10:3). The dissonant chords on the tutti certainly resemble a roaring lion, and both interpretations are plausible.

After this startling opening, the first scene evokes a mood of comfort and redemption for those who have come out of great tribulation, to worship the Lamb night and day, and for whom God will "wipe away every tear from their eyes, and death shall be no more" (Revelation 21:4). After the return of the first section, the second scene shows the eternal city, where four living creatures, each full of eyes and with six wings, again sing in adoration to the lamb: "Holy, holy, holy, is the Lord God Almighty, who was and is and is to come!" (Revelation 4:8). Langlais here uses the Sanctus from the Requiem mass in the pedal accompanied by rapid obbligato lines, symbolic of angels. Again the choice of chant is symbolic, as it was in "Mors et resurrectio," to express eternal life through death. As in the first scene, a great sense of ecstasy and mysticism prevails. This mood is abruptly broken with the portrayal of an angel having one foot on land and one foot on the sea, as the angels then continue their song of holiness, singing the alleluia from the feast of John the Baptist (24 June), likewise the feast day of Jean Langlais.

The fourth movement, "Oh oui, viens, Seigneur Jésus," is a prayer expressing the certainty of Christ's imminent Second Coming; it stands in bold contrast to its neighboring movements and represents the eschatological culmination of the apocalypse. The title refers to the last two verses of the Revelation to John: "He who testifies to these things says, 'Surely I am coming soon.' Amen. Come, Lord Jesus! The grace of the Lord Jesus be with all the saints. Amen." Among the most serene of Langlais's works, it is a prayer filled with longing, especially through the rising four-note motif, heard first in the first four eighth notes and with its melodic extension on the Bourdon 8. Like incense, at the conclusion it ascends gently, higher and higher, to the end.

The fifth movement but his first musical vision, "La cinquième trompette," is the most terrifying of the five meditations. Along with "Visions prophétiques," it has the most obvious programmatic intent. Based on Revelation 9:1–11, the musical rendering of the story gives visual impact to the piece: The fifth angel blows his trumpet; a star falls from heaven to earth; he then opens a bottomless pit from which smoke erupts; then locusts appear from the smoke and torture mankind. So painful is the scourge, like five months of scorpion stings, that mankind seeks to die but cannot. We hear the trumpet with startling flourishes and staccato eruptions unlike earthly fanfare. The plague of locusts starts ominously with disjointed rapid staccato passages in the treble and develops unremittingly into a full scale toccata, which on the tutti of a large organ in a reverberant setting is formidable. In this movement, Langlais continues to exploit Greek rhythms (cretic, anapest) and their combinations.

Langlais describes his impressions of giving the premiere of *Cinq méditations* at Notre-Dame in Paris on 28 April 1974: "There were people standing and also sitting on the steps of the altar. They told me that there were more than six thousand people. I was pleased but very tired."[6] The American premiere took place four months later at the Cathedral of Saint John the Divine, where the special effects included the very large State Trumpet for the opening and real thunder from an approaching storm. At various other performances of this work, several listeners felt overwhelmed by the scriptural-musical symbolism. When Father Vigour, Langlais's close friend from Brittany, heard the piece for the first time, he said that he could not sleep the entire night and kept hearing the swarms of locusts approaching. When it was played at Saint Paul's Cathedral in Pittsburgh, a blind boy, who knew nothing about music, said that he had felt the locusts' stings.

In every period of his compositional career, Langlais's writing was influenced by major life events. The changes in his style during the 1970s are marked, in general, by a more dissonant and percussive approach. Although he had previously used added note values and Greek rhythms, in *Cinq méditations* they became an integral part of his style. Although he used chord clusters for special effects in *Imploration* "Pour le croyance," chord clusters and thirteenth and polychords became standard in the third and fifth movements of *Cinq méditations*. More importantly, this most profound scripturally based work was the only one of such length (duration 48:23) based on a single idea.

Impresario

Like his mentor Mahaut, Langlais continued to write letters of recommendation for his deserving pupils to obtain employment and recital engagements. As he had for me, he arranged recitals in Paris, particularly at Sainte-Clotilde, and elsewhere in France for Catharine Crozier, Kathleen Thomerson, Robert Lord, Marie-Louise Jaquet, Janice Beck, and John M. Palmer, among many others, including some who were not his pupils.

In May 1973 Langlais organized two recitals of his own music at Sainte-Clotilde. He even arranged for billboards publicizing the events, which were scheduled on successive weeks. Marie-Louise Jaquet, who wrote both sets of program notes, played *Incantation pour un jour saint, American Suite* (its European premiere), and "Meditation" (*Homage to Rameau*). The second program, which I performed, featured *Three Voluntaries*, "Evocation" (*Homage to Rameau*), "Dialogue sur les mixtures" (*Suite brève*), "Cantique" (*Folkloric Suite*), and two movements from *Offrande à Marie*.

Langlais, Paf, and grandson Mathieu, Plaisir 1973

Plaisir

In the aftermath of Langlais's heart attack, the doctor insisted that they go to the country, each Sunday after church, to rest for several days. By 1973 Jeannette was suffering from an ulcerated leg; she wrapped both her legs in bandages to ease the pain from her now chronic phlebitis. Therefore they went often to their weekend home, Pillbox (after the Boys Town cottages), in Plaisir, which was only a half-hour's drive from Paris.

Langlais often invited his students to visit them there, and Jeannette would fix them her famous "lapin au vin." Claude, Monique, and their three children, François-Marie, Camille, and Mathieu, lived above Jean and Jeannette on a new second floor. Claude, who had graduated first in his class as an engineer, enjoyed putting his skill to use for his family, and he built the addition and all their furniture himself. Langlais's daughter Janine lived nearby with her husband, Michel, and they frequently came to Plaisir; unfortunately, Janine was unable to have children. Jeannine Collard had a cottage next door. It was at Pillbox that the Langlaises were most relaxed and very happy with their increasingly extended family.

Claude, still quiet and shy, and Monique, soft-spoken and kind, appeared to be content with their own family and yet to remain near to his parents. Both Langlais and Jeannette felt very close to them and their grandchildren. It was for Monique that Langlais composed "Regina pacis" (*Offrande à Marie*), because, he said, she was so peaceful. But this tranquil period was to be brief. They were greatly saddened when Claude's employer moved him and his family to South America shortly thereafter to begin work on a dam in Colombia, which project lasted approximately three years.

Suite baroque and *Huit chants de Bretagne*

In the quiet of Plaisir, Langlais found a safe haven for composing. Both *Suite baroque* and *Huit chants de Bretagne* represented a kind of relaxation for Langlais after the emotional exhaustion of writing *Cinq méditations*.

Suite baroque (1973) was written at the request of Marie-Louise Jaquet for the Protestant church in Mulhouse, where she was organist. Temple Saint-Jean was replacing its organ with a replica of a Baroque Silbermann organ, and she asked Langlais to write some new pieces for this instrument. In addition, she requested that he play for the dedication on 2 December 1973. Langlais's sense of humor and parody are unmistakable in this seven-movement suite. The forms are all strictly Classical, as in *Suite française*, and the titles mimic the authentic ones of a Classical French suite; at first glance they look correct, but one, "Trémolo en taille," is a complete farce: Langlais's registration even calls for a "Trémolo royale." In the preface of the manuscript copy, Langlais requested that his registrations be followed exactly, but much to his displeasure, the publisher excluded it from the printed score. The movements are dedicated to Baroque organ enthusiasts (André Isoir, Suzanne Landale, Xavier Darasse); to former pupils (Danielle Salvignol-Nisse, Edward Harry Tibbs); and to the two nurses who cared for him during his period of recovery (sisters Eugénie and Geneviève Malherbe). The final movement, "Grand jeu," is a reworking of "Dialogue sur les mixtures" (*Suite brève*). Also in rondo form, it borrows a similar opening pattern, with rapid chordal changes, and echo effects between the manuals. At the very end, Langlais adds the familiar name motif on the notes A, F, F.

In *Huit chants de Bretagne* (1974) Langlais returned to the folk songs of his native province, using themes provided him by his Breton student Bénédicte Le Mest. Although the last movement, "Pensez à l'Éternité," is dissonant, he used modal harmony. The forms are mainly short and tripartite. In composing pieces so close to his childhood memory, he returned once again to the simplicity of his native soil. "I wanted to cleanse myself from the complex and violent style of the *Cinq méditations sur l'apocalypse*. I instinctively returned toward my Celtic origins. The result is an homage to my native country, to my compatriots. Tournemire's Gregorian harmonizations, which are very dissonant but which never destroy the melody, guided me in this work. Throughout I wished to remain simple."[7]

Several of the dedications reflect the Breton theme: one of his compatriots was the artistic director of Arion records, Ariane Segal, to whom Langlais dedicated the penultimate movement, "Aux lys avec leurs feuilles argentées" (To the fleurs-de-lis with their silvery leaves); "Noël Breton" was dedicated to Antoinette Keraudren, an organ student from Brest.

Many of his stylistic devices are reminiscent of earlier works. For example, "Noël Breton" uses the same Breton carol employed in "Rhapsodie sur deux noëls" (*Folkloric Suite*). One technique, however, is here used for the first time. To imitate the soft ringing of the Angelus bells in the third movement, Langlais writes three five-note chords in the high register and scores them for a solo Flûte 4. The effect is exactly what he intended. Although he experimented with bell sounds at the end of "Boys Town, Place of Peace," using Flûte 4 and Tierce 1-3/5, here he wrote out the harmonic overtones for the first time.

In June 1975 Langlais recorded at Sainte-Clotilde both *Huit chants de Bretagne* and the complete works of Franck for Arion. He wrote, "I did four records in four evenings. Marie-Louise did *Apocalypse* in two evenings. . . . Tomorrow I leave for St. Albans [to judge

Huits chants de Bretagne, "Angélus," p. 6, mm. 1–4. © 1975 Editions Musicales Alphonse Leduc, Paris. Used by permission.

a competition]. . . . I have not had a minute of rest. Fortunately my dog makes me go to Avenue Duquesne."[8]

Trois esquisses romanes and *Trois esquisses gothiques*

In July 1975, as they did every year, the Langlaises went to La Richardais. Even during the vacation in Brittany, however, Langlais was not idle. He had a commission from the French ministry of cultural affairs to write a work in celebration of the eight-hundredth anniversary of the Cathedral Saint-Pierre in Angoulême, a classic example of Romanesque architecture, in the south of France near Bordeaux, which housed two organs. Langlais assumed the challenge of writing for two organs for the first time and planned to compose a set of three pieces for them, *Trois esquisses romanes*. Medieval specialist Jacques Chailley provided him the themes: "Hac clara die," "Tu autem," and the Kyrie "Rex splendens" are from the tenth century, and "Jerusalem mirabilis," a martial crusade hymn, dates from 1099. Their explicit modality suited Langlais's style. *Esquisse romane no. 1* is very similar in its techniques to "Voluntary Saint-Jacques-le-majeur," which was also dedicated to Chailley.

Interesting circumstances led to the final shaping of *Esquisses*. Earlier that spring, an American organ student, Douglas Himes, had been studying with Langlais briefly in Paris, and asked him to compose a piece for his wedding at the end of November. Himes described the size of the wedding party and the approximate time needed for the procession. This request excited Langlais's imagination, and realizing that he had a commission to fulfill, he decided to compose a piece based on two sequences, "Veni, creator spiritus" and the mass for Saint Denis. Langlais wrote, "The piece for Douglas's marriage is finished. . . . This work will serve me as the final for a piece 'en style Roman' that the French State has asked me to compose."[9] As Himes later wrote, the timing of the piece, which could easily be adapted to a single organ by changing manuals, matched his directions to Langlais perfectly.[10] Robert Lord played the premiere for the wedding, on 29 November 1975.

But instead of using the piece as the concluding movement of *Trois esquisses romanes*, Langlais decided to use it as the first of three additional sketches based on Gregorian chant themes, his *Trois esquisses gothiques*. He then rethought the Romanesque themes Chailley had given him, and composed *Trois esquisses romanes* between 29 July and 14 September, beginning with Kyrie "Rex splendens." The two remaining *Esquisses gothiques* were completed rapidly between 16 and 23 October.

The word "esquisse" denotes study or beginning; hence in *Trois esquisses romanes*, Langlais was beginning to study the new effects made possible in writing for two organs, in widely separated ends of a vast reverberant church or cathedral, using organum-like techniques. He had in mind the cathedral in Angoulême, the Basilica of Saint-Denis in Paris, and the Basilica of Saint-Sernin in Toulouse.

As he reflected on his choice of themes for *Trois esquisses gothiques*, he again remembered his devotion to Mary and the Shrine of the Immaculate Conception, which had two magnificent organs. This is especially evident in the second sketch, based on two of his favorite Marian benediction themes (the hymn "Virgo Dei genitrix" and the sequence "Inviolata, integra et casta es Maria") and dedicated to Shrine organist Robert Grogan. The third piece also uses the "Salve regina." His writing for the three Marian chants is uniformly simple, quiet, and meditative—a foil for the treatment of the other themes, which use the vaulted expanses to display the resounding play of one organ against the other. Although Langlais always used reverberant acoustics to advantage in his music; their extended use is central to these pieces, and performances on single instruments in dry acoustics ruin the musical effect.

The Basilica of Saint-Sernin particularly seems to be the inspiration behind *Esquisse romane no. 2*. Kathleen Thomerson made a study of the relationship of the architecture of this church and the form of the piece:

> Langlais's visits to this partly red brick church in the south of France have given us his impressions of the barrel vaulting, sculpture carvings, small Romanesque windows topped by rounded arches, and four massive piers of the crossing. All this is set down by one who sees with his hands, his imagination and his sensitivity, the atmosphere of spaces. . . .
>
> These Sketches are not programmatic; indeed, the Basilicia is not even mentioned in the score. However, there are some definitely evocative touches in the second Esquisse: the upward sweep of the opening line; a massive chord, built one note at a time; a return to the ground via retrograde writing; then five slow chords giving the interior's aspect of five long naves; the Kyrie "Rex splendens": the same chant that pilgrims must have heard many times inside this building. These sounds form a mosaic memory.[11]

Apart from the play between two different organs, Langlais uses no completely new techniques in these pieces, except in the third *Esquisse gothique*. Here he takes the twenty-measure "Séquence pour la fête de la Dédicace," one of the many early sequences discarded in modern chant books but retained in those from Paris, and uses it as the basis for a set of ten variations, always keeping the theme in the treble. What is new here is that each variation builds toward greater dissonance and uses a different harmony from the preceding one. After the most dissonant tenth variation played on the louder first organ, the "Salve regina" chant emerges from the second organ like a ray of sun after a powerful storm. The first section is then repeated, both organs playing the last phase together. In a style similar to several of his pieces from the 1960s, two polychords resolve with a triumphant D major chord.

Mosaïque

In 1976 and 1977 Langlais compiled *Mosaïque*, three volumes of pieces, some previously published and others newly composed. He said of this collection, "Again I hope—perhaps I am wrong—to have made a big effort to vary the source of my inspiration."[12]

Pleased with the challenge of writing for two organists at two separate organs, at the request of several American and European students he turned his attention to writing for two organists at a single organ. In December 1975 Langlais composed "Double fantaisie pour deux organistes," which was the third piece in *Mosaïque, vol. 1*. Little music in this genre existed: notably a sonata by Gustav Adolf Merkel, a fantasia by Hesse, a fugue by Schubert, and duets by Wesley. Like playing a game of doubles in tennis, it took some practice with Marie-Louise Jaquet to decide which part of the pedalboard each foot should control and to orient himself to a different position on the bench. The results were worth the effort. After a lengthy introduction, the piece builds, using carillon effects and parallel motion, to a brilliant fugue, interrupted by short percussive dissonant chords on a full registration. With four hands and four feet, the effect is striking, especially in the two-octave chromatic pedal run. He had great fun learning a new technique, which was as enjoyable to watch as it was to hear.

The composition of this first "Double fantaisie" coincided with publisher H. W. Gray's decision to withdraw *American Suite* from its catalog. The decision upset Langlais greatly; he considered the work among his best. In retaliation, Langlais conceived of writing several volumes (ultimately three) for Combre, his French publisher. For the first volume of *Mosaïque*, he transcribed his motet "Ave mundi gloria" (1932), which, he said, took him only a half hour to do, changing the title to "Stèle pour Gabriel Fauré," and added two pieces from *American Suite* (this time with French titles), along with "Double fantaisie."

The second volume of *Mosaïque*, composed in 1976, contains five pieces. The first two are designed to evoke the visual images of the titles. "Gable" refers to ornamental arabesques, interwoven into the triangular pediment of the portal of the cathedral at Rheims. Dedicated to Arsène Muzerelle, organist at the cathedral, it employs extended solo passages on a colorful Tierce combination. The bells of the cathedral are suggested throughout the piece using the foundation stops.[13] Similarly, "Images" transforms the visual into the aural. The work is dedicated to Pascale Villey, a painter. Using Pascale as a name motif and a second theme from a folkloric carol, Langlais "paints" a work of contrasting dark and light images. As the work progresses, the name Pascale grows louder and more insistent, as if rendered in stronger colors.

The third piece, "Trio," is in the same form and key as that of the trio in *Triptyque* (1956). This time it is more dissonant and virtuosic, using an octatonic scale, like Messiaen's second mode, but beginning with a whole step instead of a half step (E, F-sharp, G, A, B-flat, C, C-sharp, D-sharp). The sparkling play of colors on three manuals and pedal is almost kaleidoscopic. It is a well-crafted technical tour de force, dedicated to Swiss organist Verena Lutz. Langlais explores fresh-sounding registrations with mutations and creates unusual effects with wild, unpredictable counterpoints in extreme registers.

The fourth piece, "Complainte de Pontkalleg," dedicated to Bénédicte Le Mest, could well have been the ninth of the *Huit chants de Bretagne*. The title refers to the lament of the Marquis of Pontkalleg. During the eighteenth century, Brittany experienced its greatest period of nationalism, led by the Chouannerie. One of its great leaders was the Marquis de Pontkalleg, who along with three other Breton nobles, led an unsuccessful revolt against the crown and was beheaded in Nantes. This piece is based on the Breton folk song lamenting Pontkalleg's unsuccessful uprising and untimely death. The piece is framed by a slow introduction and postlude, which encase four variations.

The boldest piece in the set is the last, "Salve regina," dedicated to his son, Claude. Langlais uses a rapidly ascending and descending scale pattern, in a brilliant, energetic display, to portray the triumphant angelic greeting, "Hail, queen, mother of mercy, our life, our sweetness, and our hope!" Drawing on the more recent of the two common tunes (the same melody he chose in "Paraphrase sur 'Salve regina'" from *Vingt-quatre pièces*), he creates a new image, this time of powerful angelic wings: rapid scale passages are followed on the tutti with polychords. This section is repeated after each of two quieter sections, which refer to Mary. The form and stylistic devices are almost identical to "Visions prophétiques" (*Cinq méditations sur l'apocalypse*): rapid staccato chords between the hands, repeated chord with anapest rhythms above, and sustained chords leading to the reprise. Once again Langlais took proven techniques and forms and crafted them into a new and different work.

The six pieces for the third volume of *Mosaïque* were composed in 1977. The title of the first, "Lumière," reflects the "impression" Langlais had of spending several hours meditating in the Cathedral of Dol-de-Bretagne.[14] It is dedicated to Colette Alain, who was organist there; her name, the principal theme of the piece, is used as an ostinato throughout. As was his habit, Langlais composed the second piece, "Parfum," at the piano. He often wrote in the morning, when he was fresh, and in the early evening before dinner. He played the main theme over and over, probing its harmonic possibilities. He recalled his simple inspiration a year later: "A student I had, Darlene Pekala, she always wore a lot of perfume, and she was very nice. And so I wanted to do something nice for her because she plays so well. So I wrote this little piece for her."[15] The name motif Darlene is the main theme of the piece. The smallest thing, even a beautiful scent, could inspire him.

The third piece, "Printemps," has another source for its inspiration. When Langlais gave a series of recitals in Denmark, in the Fredericksburg castle, he played the Compenius organ from 1610. For the improvisation at the end of the recital, he was given the "Printemps" theme, which he later worked into a set of variations dedicated to Danish organ student Kristen Kolling. The words of the theme extol the glory of spring, hence the title. His stark registrations could be adapted to that particular instrument, which had so pleased him.[16]

"Thèmes," dedicated to Charles Walker, appropriately uses the first names of Charles and his wife, Janet, as its main themes. The Janet theme is played softly on a Voix humaine combination while the Charles theme is registered for the tutti. This fourth movement is one of Langlais's most virtuosic pieces, complete with extensive pedal cadenzas and triple octaves between the hands and feet. On 30 October 1977 Langlais wrote me that "Thèmes" "includes a very important pedal part, which female organists will perhaps enjoy playing because it shows off their legs and other things of value. It is dedicated to Charles with several A, F, Fs to end."

"Pax," the fifth piece, dedicated to Jacqueline Boismoreau, uses her first name as the main theme of the piece. It is very similar in style to "Chant de paix" (*Neuf pièces*).

Langlais described the *Mosaïque* albums and his new four-footed venture to me in the same letter, with his predictable sense of humor: "These volumes [offer] a bit of everything—hence the title. There are even two pieces for two organists. They must not be too fat because they could not both sit on the same bench. . . . One could ask one of the organists to sit on the lap of the other, but I don't think that would work. (That is a joke!)"

Honorary Doctorate Degrees

In 1975 and 1976 Langlais received honorary doctorate degrees from Texas Christian University and Duquesne University. The degree from Texas Christian University was particularly exciting to Langlais because it was the first honorary doctorate he had received, and as he understood it, he and Messiaen were the only two living French composers to be so honored. His former student Emmet Smith, professor of organ at TCU, who had studied with Langlais in 1964, remained a devoted admirer and arranged the award ceremony. For the entire week of 21 February 1975, Langlais was lavished with performances of his music and assurances of his importance, as a composer, to Americans. Several of his own works were performed, including *Psaume solennel no. 3*. At one gathering, he gave full demonstration of his improvisatory prowess by playing a ricercare in two, three, four, five, and six voices on the chant Kyrie ("Fons bonitatis"); the chorale "O Sacred Head" as a fugue; and finally a scherzo on a theme submitted by a member of the audience. He also played a recital based on works by Sainte-Clotilde composers Franck, Tournemire, and Langlais, his 275th in the United States. After the recital and awarding of the doctoral robe and hood, the audience of more than thirteen hundred stood in silence. Langlais remembered this moment with great emotion. Marie-Louise Jaquet accompanied him on this trip, made exclusively to receive this honor.[17]

Even before the festivities honoring Langlais in Fort Worth took place, plans were underway to provide the same honor for him at Duquesne University. In 1976 the Duquesne University School of

Music celebrated its fiftieth anniversary and the inauguration of two new degree programs in sacred music, and Langlais had been invited to give a recital that October. David Lloyd, a Pittsburgher, who was at the time studying with Langlais, accompanied him. Several weeks before the convocation, Langlais began to worry about the state of his health and sent a telegram saying that he would not come. Panic ensued, but the next day brought another message: "I shall come definitely. Forget the other telegram. Langlais."

The sacred music convocation began with an organ concert by Langlais on the recently augmented four-manual E. M. Skinner organ in the East Liberty Presbyterian Church. The program was to open with Franck's *Final* and would include the world premiere of "Salve regina" (*Mosaïque, vol. 2*), which Langlais had composed especially for the occasion. But the worn, radiating pedalboard made him nervous, and just before he started to play, he muttered in desperation, "Eh, bien, tu verras, les fausses notes vont pleuvoir!" (Now you will see the wrong notes fall down like rain!). But he played the solos perfectly.

Each morning he taught master classes in improvisation to students who had gathered from several eastern and midwestern states. He taught strict counterpoint in a ricercare for two to six voices, duet and trio playing, the Classic fugue, canon, ornamented chorale, the scherzo, and, finally, the toccata. In the afternoons, he gave master classes on the music of Bach; the French Classical and Romantic repertoire of Franck and Tournemire; twentieth-century works of Messiaen, Duruflé, and Alain; and on the last two days, his own music. Each evening, concerts were held in the Duquesne University Chapel; many of his works were premiered in this series, including "Double fantaisie pour deux organistes" (*Mosaïque, vol. 1*). He had specified which pieces he particularly wished to have performed, among them *Troisième concerto, Psaumes solennels nos. 1–3,* and *Missa in simplicitate.* Langlais was especially moved by the audience's response to *La voix du vent;* orchestra director Bernard Goldberg led him to the front of the chapel to acknowledge the spontaneous burst of applause and shouts that followed.

The honorary doctorate was awarded during a solemn high mass, celebrated by the auxiliary bishop of the diocese of Pittsburgh. The processional was the American premiere of his *Cortège* for two organs and brass; the ordinary of the mass was *Messe solennelle*; and the congregation sang "Dieu, nous avons vu ta gloire" and *Hymn of Praise "Te Deum."* In addition, Langlais was awarded an honorary life membership in the American Guild of Organists.

The pace was grueling: never had more performances of his music been given in a single week. Langlais excused himself at a master class for being "such a bear." Soon everyone was calling him Mr. Bear, a nickname he greatly relished.[18] He oftened signed his letters "L'Ours" (The Bear) and sometimes "Saint Ours."

Life Changes

In 1976 Langlais began work on his *Deuxième symphonie* ("alla Webern"), whom Langlais had always admired for setting such a good example of brevity in his piano pieces, especially when compared to the other more long-winded German composers, such as Reger. At the opening Langlais uses themes based on the names Dieu and Marie, in a tutti passage for pedals. The shortness of each movement (all four may be performed in five minutes) precludes thematic development, but some of the techniques, such as added note values and dochmian (trochaic: long, short) rhythms, found in *Poem of Happiness* and *Cinq méditations sur l'apocalypse*, are found in abundance here.

Also in 1976, after receiving his contract for the next academic year at Schola Cantorum, Langlais compared his salary with others and came to the conclusion that he had been underpaid for years. Furious, he resigned immediately. Many of his students petitioned for him to continue; one sent a letter to his former students worldwide, in hopes that their response would cause the school to make amends. Nothing came of their efforts, and Langlais refused to return. André Fleury was appointed in his place, but the organ class decreased in size. In an interview that year, he reflected again on being a composer, "A composer is really an unfortunate sort of fellow. He is obliged to compose; he does not know why. Very often I have said, 'This is my last work; a week afterward, I am struggling with a new one.'"[19]

In 1977, at Langlais's invitation, I performed at the Association Valentin Haüy a program comprised solely of Vierne's works. Langlais gave informal introductions to each piece. He began with a long eulogy to Vierne, speaking of his last recital at Notre-Dame and his untimely death, in 1937. He also spoke of Vierne's esthetic of organ building, which he explained was "very opposed to many organ purists today who design organs with too many mixtures." At that moment, Marchal interjected from the audience, "Mais, j'avoue qu'il y a trop de trémolos!" (But I insist there are too many tremolos!). By that, Marchal meant to say that the organ revival movement was not over. The audience seemed to revel in this spontaneous repartee. Langlais and Marchal had long disagreed about organ building. Marchal was an early leader in the organ reform movement, not only in France but in Europe, and always wanted to make Romantic organs sound good for Bach; he frequently said the organ at Sainte-Clotilde needed a mixture on the Positif, and he registered Franck's music with a Neo-Baroque esthetic.

Triptyque grégorien

In spring 1978 Langlais played several recitals in Pennsylvania, Massachusetts, and New York. Kristen Kolling accompanied him on this trip. His program included Bach's Prelude in E-flat, Franck's *Prière*, Tournemire's "Offertoire pour la fête du sainte nom de Jésus" (*L'orgue mystique*), Vierne's *Carillon de Westminster*; and his own "Virgo Dei genitrix" (*Trois esquisses gothiques*), "Visions prophétiques" (*Cinq méditations sur l'apocalypse*), "Complainte de Pontkalleg" (*Mosaïque, vol. 2*), "Printemps" (*Mosaïque, vol. 3*), and *Poem of Happiness*.

In Boston, he played at Saint Paul's Roman Catholic Church, where his close friend Ted Marier was music director. At the end of the recital, he improvised on the chant "In paradisum," dedicating it to the memory of Marier's wife, Alice, who had recently died of cancer. This improvisation was the foundation for the second movement of his *Triptyque grégorien*, which he completed that summer. It was commissioned for a benefit concert for the Benedictine order in Ligugé, near Poitiers. Langlais spoke about his inspiration for the work:

> [For the "Rosa mystica"] I took the . . . theme of my "Salve regina" Mass, with the entire Gregorian chant of the "Salve

regina.". . . René Oberson [to whom the first movement is dedicated] is a Swiss organist. "In paradisum" was composed for the wife of Ted Marier. I take the chant, now without changing the rhythm, unlike Grigny and Rameau. [It is] the song which is sung as the body is taken out of the church. The chords in the beginning evoke funeral bells. The "Alleluia" is based on three alleluias: themes for life developed in different ways to symbolize the joy of the alleluia.[20]

Relationships with significant people—and the endings of those relationships—would continue to inspire Langlais's music.

CHAPTER 14

Widower, Bridegroom, Father
1979–1984

I think that you absolutely cannot remain alone.

Olivier Messiaen

Jeannette's Stroke

For years Jeannette had been in poor health. Chronic phlebitis and an increasing number of angina attacks, which worsened in 1976, had plagued her. She tired easily and could not drive, nor even walk for any distance. By 1978 she could no longer transcribe Jean's music and had ceased her cataloging of his works; Pierre Cogen and Naji Hakim took over this task. Correspondence piled up on her desk, and the apartment was in a state of disarray.

In May 1979 Jeannette suffered a stroke and was taken to a small antiquated hospital in Versailles, near Plaisir. It was a historic structure, with a miniature formal garden at its entrance; its administration had changed little since the time of the Revolution. Langlais hurried to Jeannette, who had been placed in a small ward, at the end of a dark hallway, with several other patients. The bed was old, and little else in the way of furniture graced the room.

Though she had lost her speech and the use of her left side, she communicated with her eyes, and they showed her pleasure at seeing her family. Attempts at communication between Jeannette and Jean were ironic and even tragic: she could express herself only through her eyes, which Langlais could not see; he would speak, but she could not answer. He held her hand and asked those around to describe the expression in her eyes. She had let the nurses know that she wanted pictures of Jean on the wall by her bed, and she seemed to enjoy looking at them. Jean was made aware of this.

Claude and Monique, by now returned from Colombia, came every day to visit her, and their devotion to her was apparent. Monique felt sure that Jeannette's speech would return and had already planned speech therapy exercises for her. Their positive attitude seemed to give temporary comfort to both Jeannette and Jean.

Although colleagues tried to console him with stories of the recoveries of others, Langlais was totally distracted and could think and speak only of her. He had so often taken her for granted; only now did he begin to realize how much she meant to him. He was afraid.

Progression

Despite his anxiety over Jeannette's condition, Langlais attended the premiere of his new work, *Progression*, at Sainte-Clotilde in May 1979. Afterward he approached Marchal, as he had for sixty-two years, to hear what he thought of the piece.

In *Progression*, a five-movement suite of pieces composed in the fall of 1978, Langlais felt he had succeeded in a completely original plan of composition. Harmonically, the "progression" leads from no harmonic content whatsoever in the first two movements ("Monodie" and "Duo"), through very limited harmony in the third ("Trio," with only one triad), to a rich harmonic palette in "Offering," and finally to "Fugue et continuo," accompanied by full three- and four-part chords.

The idea of limiting the number of voices to one in "Monodie" is rare. Except for Messiaen's "Subtilité des corps glorieux" (*Les corps glorieux*, 1939), organ-like music had not been restricted to a solo line since the Middle Ages, when organum (a vocal predecessor of continuo) accompanied the chant at the fourth or fifth. Langlais's use of disjoint, angular writing negates any implied harmony in its solo lines.

"Monodie" has a tonal center of E, with a synthetic scale based on the pitches E, F, G-sharp, A, B, C, D-sharp, E.

In "Duo" the scale centers around C-sharp and G, using the pitches C-sharp, D, E, F, G, A-flat, B, C-sharp. Although these scales

Progression, "Monodie," mm. 1–4. © 1978 Editions Musicales Alphonse Leduc, Paris. Used by permission.

are not used as a tone row, or in a systematic way (as Messiaen employed his modes of limited transposition), they do provide a sense of cohesion to these first two pieces without implying a harmonic background. Langlais said that his use of these synthetic scales was purely intuitive, that he was completely oblivious to them while he was composing. Many of his compositional techniques surprised him when others analyzed them for him.

"Monodie" consists of three sections: the first, a solo line for manuals; the second, a brilliant pedal solo cadenza played on full reed stops; and finally, bravura octave passages for manuals and pedal on the full organ, a solo line that makes a powerful dramatic statement.

In contrast, the scherzo-like "Duo" is a dialogue between contrasting thematic materials. In a manner similar to "Thèmes" (*Mosaïque, vol. 3*), the first theme is a musical portrait of one Simone, whom Langlais identified as an early pupil and to whom "Duo" is dedicated. Her theme opens the movement in an agitated manner (Allegro vivo). The second theme (Più lento) follows, in a slow, calm vein. Langlais described this movement as a dialogue between two people with very different personalities.

"Trio" was written upon the death of Langlais's dog, which explains both the subtitle ("Larmes," tears) and his inscription: "To the very dear friend for whom I cry, my little dog Paf." Shortly after Paf's death, Langlais wrote:

Would you please excuse me if I am brief for I am very sad and unhappy. My poor little dog has died, and the same day I gave a very important concert on the radio. On my way there, I couldn't remember my program. And people told me it was the best concert of my career. Since then I have composed four new pieces for organ, including one dedicated to my dear dog.[1]

Even several years later, when discussing this movement, he cried over the loss of this beloved pet. Although he never had a Seeing Eye dog, Paf was like one to him. Immediately after Paf's death, Marie-Louise Jaquet went to the humane society and brought him another dog, whom he named Scherzo.

In "Trio" Langlais makes a departure from the usual trio form: the voice with the name motif (Paf is immortalized in the notes B, A, F) is always heard alone at the beginning of each section. The other two parts follow, playing identical rhythms and providing a sort of grief-filled commentary. The same formula is repeated at several levels of transposition, each of which carefully avoids the use of triadic harmony. A passing minor triad is heard only twice in the entire piece. The movement ends with a long soliloquy for the Voix humaine, Tremblant, and strings, punctuated by frequent rests, through which the composer extends the notion of loss. It is the longest movement of the suite, and one in which Langlais expresses his most personal and profound emotions.

Langlais indicated that "Trio" be played "with emotion." The manuals play syncopated, angular leaps in contrary motion, giving no sense of triadic harmony. These sharp dissonances, centering around the tritone, heighten the sense of pain and grief. "When you feel that it should go faster, play faster. When you feel it slower, play more slowly. But play very freely, exactly as you feel."[2]

"Offering" has a four-part texture and—in contrast to the stark movement that precedes it—much harmonic color. The quiet, ethereal mood of the piece is created in part by the unstable tonal centers and fluctuating rhythmical patterns, reminiscent of "Lumière" (*Mosaïque, vol. 3*). Two-measure segments, with the first measure repeated, characterize "Offering," which title refers to a present, or offering, to Langlais's Scottish student Marjorie Bruce, to whom the movement is dedicated. It contains a subtle joke about the frugality of the Scots: the middle section develops the opening theme in augmentation in the tenor range while thirds played in the high register—using a Quintaton 16 and a Tierce 1-3/5—imitate the tinkle of small change falling into the collection plate.

"Fugue et continuo" is the most successful movement of the suite. Chords continue nonstop throughout the piece, so that as one hand plays the chords, the other hand or feet play the subject and answer. There are two complete expositions, several episodes, and a stretto. The subject is the only truly melodic theme in *Progression* and a foil to all that preceded it.

Progression, "Fugue et continuo," p. 22, mm. 1–6. © 1978 Editions Musicales Alphonse Leduc, Paris. Used by permission.

The first three movements of *Progression* especially illustrate an important trend of Langlais's technique: angular disjointed themes and the absence of triadic harmony. Pieces as early as "Trio" (*Suite française*, 1948) pointed in this direction. His earlier harmonic language, which remains within the post-Romantic tradition of Tournemire, Dupré, and Duruflé, returns in the last two movements, where seventh, ninth, and eleventh chords abound. The same striking eleventh chord played on the full organ near the end of "Hymne d'action de grâces 'Te Deum'" (*Trois paraphrases grégoriennes*) opens the full harmonic spectrum of "Offering."

The tritone, one of Langlais's favorite stylistic devices, acts as a unifying factor in all the pieces of *Progression*, both melodically and harmonically. Melodically, it forms the basis of the name motif in "Trio" and of the opening of "Offering." Harmonically, it is often used in conjunction with the additional clash of a minor second (a chord with a tritone F-sharp, C, and F-natural). The additional minor second is also used in chords without tritones, in which both a major and minor second sound simultaneously. Although this is the nature of eleventh chords, it is also used as a coloring device in "Fugue et continuo." The tritone even lingers in the last chord of the work.

The progression implied by the title is fully carried out in the composition. Each individual piece stands alone, yet it is in the gradual additions of line and harmonic texture that each takes its shape in relation to one another. At the same time, it is a reverse progression, from the very new to the more familiar Langlais. Even in familiar language, he continued to experiment with new forms.

Death of Jeannette

Jeannette died on 10 June 1979. Langlais had left her only fifteen minutes before; when he returned home to Plaisir, he received a telephone call from the nurse, informing him that she had just passed away of a heart attack.

Her death was a tremendous shock. Several of Langlais's close friends had worried about what would happen to him if Jeannette died: Father Flaux, the pastor of the church in Combourg; Marchal and his daughter, Jacqueline; Messiaen; and even Colette de Paris, another of Langlais's mistresses, all expressed their concerns and agreed that he could not remain alone. Prior to her death, when people asked him if he had thought about what he would do, he replied each time, adamantly, that she would recover. He could not think of life without her. Now he was faced with the loss of his faithful companion, and his major emotional as well as physical support. The reality of being completely alone terrified him. Two days after her death he wrote:

> If I have waited so long to write to you, it is because of the health of my love of a wife. Alas, since Sunday she has left us. Tomorrow, in Escalquens, her funeral will take place, after which she will rest with her parents. You can imagine how much her death is our pain, and especially mine. She was a true saint, who has left the earth, but also for all who loved her. She had no enemies. It's useless to speak to you of my state, you can imagine it. She wanted me to continue my art, I will obey her until my death. Pray for her. Thank you.[3]

Claude and Monique accompanied him to Escalquens for the funeral and burial. They had helped him in the weeks since her stroke and expected that they would care for him when she died, or at least that he would be near them. When they returned to Paris, however, Marie-Louise was waiting for him at the airport. In desperation, he asked her what would become of him; she proposed that they marry. At first he hesitated because of the difference in their ages and asked her to take time to consider it very carefully. But he knew that she would not change her mind.

Langlais spent the rest of the summer at his home in Paris with his sister, Flavie, who later related the difficulties both she and Jean experienced during this trying time:

> It wasn't very cheerful. He received many letters, and it was not always very easy to answer them. Marie-Louise came back from Corsica in August, and of course at that moment things became simpler for me. They decided to marry very soon. As for myself, I didn't see any problems, but it was still a big shock to Claude, who did not take part in the second marriage. In any case, thank God that it was arranged quickly.[4]

Marriage to Marie-Louise Jaquet

Jean and Marie-Louise were married on 24 August 1979 at Jean's parish church of Saint-François-Xavier, the same church where Messiaen had married for the second time, and by the same priest, Father Aubin. (Likely it was Aubin who had dispensed the blanket absolution, sanctioning Langlais's affairs through the years.) It was a very small ceremony, with no music, since Litaize, the church organist, was on vacation. The civil ceremony then took place at the town hall.

Less than three months had passed since Jeannette's death. Marrying may seem a casual, even callous, way for Langlais to mourn her, but the situation was complex. Jeannette had long known about his relationship with Marie-Louise, and it is a measure of her love for Jean that she accepted this liaison, as she had all the others, as a necessity for him. From a practical perspective, Jean could not live alone, and Jeannette's loyal service had accustomed him to a helpmate with musical as well as domestic abilities. Marie-Louise, for her part, had loved Langlais for years. The seemingly precipitous union was a sensible move in many ways—appearances excluded.

Only after Jeannette's death did Jean fully realize the extent of his love for and dependence on her, and his almost immediate remarriage filled him with a sense of guilt. Would people think that it had been planned? When friends and former students called to wish him well, he explained over and over, for years, why he had found it necessary to remarry so quickly. In a documentary film about his life, produced three years later, he emphasized that it was Marie-Louise who had taken pity on him, who had proposed to marry him. (Her biography claims it was Jean who proposed. It may have been a mutual decision, even one made prior to Jeannette's death.)

Messiaen's letter of 30 September 1979, offering condolences on the death of Jeannette, suggests that Langlais's letter to him had been defensive in tone. It captures the real understanding of one who knew Langlais better than many:

> Thank you for your letter and for the affection and confidence contained in it. All that you do is good. First the harsh news from you . . . I had a foreboding. I have been worried for a long

time about seeing you alone, and I thought to myself that there was something very wrong, without wanting to question you for the sake of discretion. . . . Know that I will also pray for [Jeannette] with fervor in my thoughts. The second news about you comforts me, and I approve completely, for I think that you absolutely cannot remain alone. For the sake of music and the organ, we all wish for you to remain among us for a very long time, sustained, aided, supported, as in the past. . . . Of course it is with very great joy that Yvonne and I will come to your home to make the acquaintance of your new companion.

Reactions to the news varied. When Marie-Louise announced to her boss, Pierre Barbizet, director of the Conservatory in Marseille, that she was about to marry a tradition. "Great," responded Barbizet, "you are going to marry César Franck?" She answered, "Oh no, Langlais!" When the seventy-two-year-old Langlais told his cousin from Cancale—an eighty-plus-year-old country woman—that he was going to remarry, she exclaimed over her happiness for him. "Yes," Jean replied, "but you won't be glad to know that I'm going to marry a Protestant." And Langlais expressed his reservations about their religious differences (Marie-Louise did not intend to convert) and explained to his cousin that his intended did not believe in the Virgin Mary, who was so important to them—to which his cousin replied, "Don't worry, when she arrives in heaven and sees how beautiful she is, she will have to believe in her!"[5]

The worst consequence by far of Langlais's sudden remarriage was its effect on his relationship with Claude and Monique. For them, the event was more than a shock. Jeannette, the excellent accomplice, had hidden Langlais's second life from her family too well. They had never suspected. The run-in with Marie-Louise at the airport, her proposal, and the subsequent announcement that they had already been together ten years—all this was too much to accept emotionally, and Claude's initial reaction haunted Langlais for the rest of his life. By the spring of 1980, Claude and his family had moved from Plaisir to Roumazières, near the center of France's roof tile industry, where Claude found work as a home renovation and roofing contractor. They bought a property with an old watermill, very close to the Charente River. One hears the sounds of fish jumping, birds singing, and toads croaking in the evening; it had been one of Jeannette's favorite places.

Langlais's daughter Janine, however, was very supportive of his remarriage. She had always liked Marie-Louise, and her father's happiness was her chief concern. Her husband, Michel, shared her views. They came to visit the newlyweds and helped them refurbish the apartment, which had received little attention during the last years of Jeannette's life.

Langlais's other mistresses also had difficulty with his remarriage. Jeannine Collard could not bring herself to visit the new couple. Colette de Paris did not speak to him for five years. Indeed, Marie-Louise soon found that it was one thing to be with a person for ten years, but quite another to be married to the same person. Her marriage to Jean required many adjustments. Shortly after they were married, she made it painfully clear to Jean that any further affairs would meet with her immediate departure. She had kept track of all his intimate relationships since she had first become involved with him. His particularly passionate and lengthy affair with a French student had especially angered her. (If he hadn't enjoyed talking so much, she might not have known.) She forbade him to see this student or to have any contact with her ever again.

Birth of Caroline

Soon after they were married, Jean and Marie-Louise learned that she was pregnant, and had, in fact, conceived on their wedding night. Just before the birth of their daughter, in May 1980, Langlais wrote, "In a month Caroline will probably be born. Marie-Louise is tired, and rue Duroc, the apartment, is in the throes of remodeling. I am traveling, giving many concerts in Europe." He wrote again, just after the birth: "Here, we have a turbulent life. Concerts, records, besides the birth of Caroline . . . She was born the day of Pentecost. She is fine and her mother too. . . . I must stop for I leave tomorrow for Germany and Austria."[6]

They sent Father Aubin an announcement with a note saying that they had taken to heart his homily admonishing them to be willing to have children. Langlais referred to Caroline as their gift of the Holy Spirit.

This second marriage was a Frenchman's fantasy. Langlais had fathered a child younger than his grandchildren with a woman whom people told him had the face of a Mona Lisa. Pierre Barbizet came to the hospital after the delivery and congratulated the proud father. "My friend, I was full of admiration for you before, but now all the more so." Langlais replied, "Why? It's not more difficult than playing a recital." And Barbizet provided the punch line: "Yes, provided you are able!" This story, as it concerned his virility, thrilled Langlais.

Offrande à une âme

The fall of 1979 was a period of conflicting emotions: there was the joy of having a beautiful, talented young wife, who was expecting their child; but at the same time, there was the grief, not only of losing Jeannette but also of his estrangement from his son and several close friends. In the midst of beginning a new life and coming to terms with his grief, from 8 August to 21 October, he wrote an extended work for organ, *Offrande à une âme: diptyque*, dedicated "to my very dear wife, Jeannette, called back to God, in memoriam." A long work (duration 26:00), it exceeds all others in theological, symbolic import. The inscriptions of each part explain the theological symbolism: the first ("Vers la lumière"), "Like the bird of the great mystery, one evening her soul flew away . . . toward the light"; and the second ("Dans la lumière"), "Lord, grant her eternal rest . . . in the light." "Vers la lumière" is almost an exact rendering of the Gregorian chants from the Requiem mass and burial service, with simple accompaniments, after the introduction of the bird motif, played rapidly in the high register on a Flûte 4 and Tierce 1-3/5. As it did at the end of *Poem of Life*, a funeral knell based on a descending dominant seventh chord combines with the name motif Jeannette. The funeral knell motif gradually grows into a rapid ostinato, alternating with the opening bird motif symbolic of the passage of her soul into light.

In "Dans la lumière," Langlais portrays the glorification of Jeannette's soul, using part of the braille alphabet to spell her name. The chant "Lux aeterna" grows in intensity, alternating with the second Jeannette theme in canon, symbolic of the union of her soul with its perfect ideal and with that of Jean in a burst of glory. Passing references to *Poem in Happiness* heighten this allusion. The chants "Lumen

Christi" and "In paradisum" are a further expression of the symbolism. Once again Langlais expresses the human emotion of grief along with his faith in the resurrection. His sadness over the loss of his beloved is followed by joy for her passage into heaven. The piece ends triumphantly with a brilliant toccata on the Jeannette theme, above the "In paradisum" chant.

More Death and New Life

Langlais learned early in the summer of 1980 that Marchal was suffering from prostate cancer and had not long to live. Marchal died that August, and with his death, a large part of Langlais's past also disappeared. Marchal had been his teacher, his confidant and friend, his betrayer, and his rival. Langlais would never cease to admire him, and even in death he envied Marchal's serenity. In homage he wrote:

> André Marchal kept his control to the end of his life. Did he not say to me, several days before his death, "I am not bored because of my forced rest, I relive my past, and besides, I don't find myself so badly off on this earth." His serenity then was total. . . . It is with all our heart that we address a very moving adieu. And, taking the words that Emmanuel Chabrier spoke at the tomb of César Franck, we say to you, "Maître, you have done well."[7]

Five months later, in January 1981, his close friend Father Vigour died. Langlais found it significant that this great priest and lover of music died on the feast of Saint Caecelia. Jean played for his funeral, and despite the wish of the local priest in La Richardais that there be no Gregorian chant, Langlais played the entire Gregorian Requiem. All thirty-five priests sang it.[8]

Caroline was for both Jean and Marie-Louise a new beginning. Babies always mean complications, especially to a seventy-three-year-old man in fragile health and to a young woman whose main concern was still his care. But the complications were most happy and unexpected. Such are the ways of renewal of life, from death to new birth. Both Marie-Louise and Jean viewed Caroline as a special gift. Jean wrote, "I am the only one capable of such folly, to have

Langlais, Marie-Louise, and Caroline, 1984

such a young baby. But now we must work for her, who is our marvelous sun."[9]

In 1984 Caroline was four years old and already had the personality of both her parents, as well as both of their physical attributes. She resembled Marie-Louise in many of her mannerisms, and anyone looking at Caroline could see immediately that this child was her father's daughter. They had the same shaped head and forehead and the same bodily physiognomy, even the same gait. Langlais, a devoted father, was especially good at making up animal stories that were as moving as his music. "Tell me a *long* one, one you have never told before!" she would beg, and immediately Langlais, Breton that he was, would spin an imaginative tale about rabbits or birds in a fantastical land. With Caroline on his knee, the two were like characters in a fairy tale—lost in their own world of wonder and charm. She did not appear to be completely conscious of her father's handicap, although she cautioned him about toys on the floor and asked the color of his eyes.

Caroline showed less musical aptitude than Claude had at the same age (Jean could not help making comparisons between them in her presence), but she sang perfectly on pitch, with a very well-developed sense of rhythm (something Langlais claimed was an inherited quality that cannot be taught) and sounded her French r's delightfully. Fortunately she had children her own age to play with; she was not at all bashful. She had a particular fascination for animals. A favorite request to family members and friends was this: "Draw for me *all* the animals that you know!" She was quick to remind them of any they had forgotten.

Since Claude and his family had moved away, the basement and second floor of the house in Plaisir had been rented out. By 1984 the property was rundown. Jean said that he regretted not being able to go more often to Plaisir, where he had so many happy memories and could take long walks.

Marie-Louise Langlais

Marie-Louise proved to be quite different from Jeannette, in temperament, personality, musical aptitude, and, indeed, in almost every way. Likewise, she had a different relationship to Jean. Jeannette sacrificed everything for her husband, almost to the extent of living her life through him and through his music: as his eyes, his pen, his nurturer, bookkeeper, guardian, and last but not least, his best friend in all the world, a role which evolved over their forty-eight years of married life. For Jeannette, Jean always came first before everything—herself and her needs, her children, her friends and relatives.

In many ways, Marie-Louise was the same wonderful helpmate to Jean. She served as his copyist, cook, bookkeeper, eyes, and wife. But she maintained a more modern relationship; she kept her individuality, her own autonomy as a person. She did not sacrifice everything for the marriage.

Marie-Louise's musicological interest in her husband predated their marriage by several years. Her masters thesis at the Sorbonne was titled "Jean Langlais: un indépendent," and her doctoral dissertation, "La vie et l'oeuvre de Jean Langlais" was condensed and published as *Ombre et lumière* (Combre 1995). Since 1974, she had been a professor of organ and improvisation at the Conservatory in Marseille, where she taught one of the largest organ classes in France.[10] From 1968 to 1979, she was organist on the Silbermann organ in Mulhouse, and in the early 1970s, she made several tours of the United States.

As if to define their roles, their wedding announcement read, "Jean Langlais—composer / weds / Marie-Louise Jaquet—organist." Early in their marriage, Jean refused to perform, in order for her to play.[11] He arranged for her to become co-titular organist with him and Pierre Cogen in 1979 at Sainte-Clotilde, a position she held until 1987. She traveled again to the United States for a series of recitals in the fall of 1980, after the birth of Caroline. Family demands have since curtailed the extent of her appearances.

Marie-Louise used to joke about how hectic the household was at mealtimes when Caroline was a baby. Everyone was crying to be fed at the same time: Jean, Caroline, and Scherzo. With her own wry sense of humor, she declared it was the dog who came first. (Scherzo, who was very spoiled and a constant delight to Langlais, would stand on the table and snatch the French bread, which he would then jump to the floor to eat. The crispy crusts made a mess on the rug; Marie-Louise had to run the vacuum after every meal.) That was a great change from the past and a healthy adjustment for this "bear," who was used to having everything done for him immediately. After so many years of being the center of attention, suddenly there was another creature demanding equal time—and a four-legged one, too. At that time he said that he hoped not to have any more children and that his greatest wish was for peace and tranquility.

In 1981 he accepted an honorary doctorate degree at The Catholic University of America in Washington, D.C., the same institution from which Messiaen had received his honorary doctorate. On that trip Langlais came again to Pittsburgh for a recital and gave a radio interview on WQED-FM.

Works 1979–1984

Langlais had promised Jeannette he would continue his musical art, and he kept his word. But especially with his new family, he wrote less for his own expression and more in response to commissions. He finished *Noëls avec variations* between June and September 1979; his former student Thomas Daniel Schlee of Universal Edition had commissioned it in November 1978. Karen Hastings, his pupil at the time, recalled him asking her if she wanted a slow or fast piece dedicated to her; he wove her name into the first carol, "Noël provençal." His style became even more dissonant in these pieces with much use of polytonality and modality. Although listed as variations on only three carols, the third, "Ihr Hirten, erwacht," also treats the carol "Pour l'amour de Marie."[12]

In 1979 Langlais also wrote a short piece based on several Gregorian chants, *Prélude grégorien*, which he played at his honorary doctoral ceremony at Catholic University in 1981. He also revamped five selections from *American Suite* for his *Troisième symphonie*, leaving only "Confirmation in Chicago" unpublished in a new format. He ended the year by composing a work for four equal voices (SSAA), *Corpus Christi*, commissioned by the Portsmouth Boys' Choir (England).

The early 1980s were somewhat less prolific. In 1980 Langlais wrote only two works, *Réminiscences* (a commission from a New Jersey organist for his jubilee, which used portions of *Piece in Free Form* and the fugue from *Troisième concerto*) and a significant new work for organ, *Rosace*, a commission from an AGO chapter in North Carolina. *Rosace* features a martial tune in the pedal with a typically raised fourth scale degree. The third movement, "Croquis," was written for Caroline and is based on the children's lullaby "Coucou bébé." The last movement, dedicated to Marie-Louise, was a commission of the French ministry of cultural affairs. A brilliant tour de force, its toccata figures are replaced near the end with the nursery rhyme "Au clair de la lune." Langlais explained that after the fireworks fade, the moon is once again visible, showing again his desire to create visual images with music.

In 1981 Langlais produced the short Marian vocal solo "À la Vierge Marie," which borrowed the text and theme from the fifth of his *Cinq motets*. In 1982 he composed *Pastorale et rondo*, a piece for two trumpets and organ based on "Jésus nous dit de prier" (*Huit chants de Bretagne*) and Pasticcio (*Organ Book*), and another commissioned work, *Prélude et allegro*. Pleased with the publisher Universal and the personal attention of its editor, Thomas Daniel Schlee, he gave them his *Prélude et fugue* (1927) to publish.

In 1982 two festivals featured his music: Festival de la Création Bretonne in Rennes and Organ and Harpsichord Week in Toulouse, where he presented a recital and gave master classes on the music of Franck and Tournemire. On 30 December 1982, he was awarded Commander of the Order of Arts and Letters by Jack Lang, French minister of culture. The 1983 edition of the Petit Larousse Dictionary defined him as one who had "perpetuated the tradition of Tournemire."

Pierre Lacroix, director of the August 1983 Saint-Bertrand de Comminges Festival, commissioned Langlais to write a piece for the event. Langlais obliged with *Cinq soleils*, which used both French and Gregorian themes, including Bizet's March from *L'arlésienne*, the "Ave Maria," and even the French national anthem. The writing is advanced, particularly in the first two pieces, using virtuosic organ techniques and intricate, rapid rhythmic devices, such as added notes. Equally brilliant are his *Sept études de concert pour pédale seule*. In his preface he explained what he intended by these very difficult pieces: "I have tried to unite music with virtuosity. Seven particular techniques have been developed, which constitute the pedagogical aspect of the work, but the aspect of pure music has never been neglected. And so the title . . . is justified." Many of the pieces, taken from his *Vingt-quatre pièces*, are made much more difficult by playing them with only two feet.

Huit préludes (1984), like *Progression*, expands the concept of writing a series of pieces using one to eight parts successively. Bornemann had asked for an organ method but since Langlais had already promised one to his other publisher, Combre, Bornemann published *Huit préludes* and Combre, *Méthode d'orgue* (1984), in collaboration with Marie-Louise.

The Singing Organ

In 1982 Vaclav Vytvar, a Hungarian and longtime admirer of Langlais, made a documentary film about the Langlais family entitled

The Singing Organ.[13] He caught Langlais, Caroline, and Marie-Louise on vacation in Brittany that summer and followed Langlais to the graves of his ancestors in La Fontenelle. *Psaume solennel no. 3* accompanies the dramatic opening seascapes of Brittany; "La cinquième trompette" (*Cinq méditations sur l'apocalypse*) provides background music for unfortunately incongruous Paris shots. One scene shows Langlais and Marie-Louise playing his "Double fantaisie pour deux organistes" (*Mosaïque, vol. 1*), their four feet playing the pedals. Another shows the seventy-five-year-old composer improvising nursery songs for Caroline on his house organ while she plays happily on the floor with her toys. Interspersed throughout are photographs of Langlais, and his voice is heard in several segments of the film discussing his handicap, improvisation, his role as a teacher, and his gratitude for a second life with Marie-Louise and Caroline. This documentary captured a fleeting time of happiness for the seemingly invincible Langlais. His new family had indeed given him a new beginning.

CHAPTER 15

Epilogue

I was a poor soul, and I worked hard, very hard. I want to die.

Jean Langlais

Recital, 23 May 1984

In February 1984, Langlais celebrated his seventy-seventh birthday. Bouts of ill health plagued him, and by May he struggled to ignore a pain in his neck that had become constant. On Sunday, 20 May, he found himself unable to complete a walk to Sainte-Clotilde; he returned to the apartment and called a taxi. The next day a physician diagnosed the pain as a pinched nerve coupled with a chronic arthritic condition, for which he recommended hot compresses.

Langlais continued to practice for his public recital on French National Radio, scheduled for the following Wednesday. Neither the compresses nor the injection of cortisone helped; the pain remained intense and he was legitimately nervous before the recital. He said afterward that someone had moved the bench and he therefore had great difficulty playing the first piece, Franck's *Prière*. Throughout the program, his efforts to favor his painful shoulder and neck resulted in a disconcerting play of the pistons, particularly the toe studs. But the spirit of the music was there, and he maintained masterful use of rubato and lyricism with no noticeable changes in tempos. Franck's *Final*, a foil to *Prière*, showed again Langlais's complete mastery of musical ideas; both pieces have an innate sense of grandeur, but Langlais successfully contrasted their themes. The second half of the program included Langlais's *Piece in Free Form* with string quartet. He directed the quartet from the console with great authority, and the playing and ensemble were impressive.

313

His concluding improvisation, *L'homme et son poème* (Man and his poem), lasted fifteen minutes. The title, according to the program notes, allowed the improvisor free rein to symbolize the ages of man: childhood, youth, maturity, and the continuation of life in a mysterious beyond. Langlais took the letters of "homme" as a motif for a tone poem, as well as three other themes: the French folk tune, "Fais do, do" for childhood; and "In paradisum" and "In manus tuas" for the end of life and its continuation after death. It was a free improvisation in the form of an arch, mirroring the shape of his life. After the recital, he cancelled a planned tour of Germany, which was to have included several recitals and a·recording session.

Stroke

As was their custom, Jean, Marie-Louise, and Caroline went to Brittany in June 1984 for their summer vacation. On 1 July Archbishop Jules Orrière would celebrate his last mass before retirement at the Cathedral of Dol-de-Bretagne. Langlais had a long and affectionate relationship with the cathedral; he had played many recitals there, including the dedication of the newly refurbished instrument by Beuchet-Debierre in 1979. The morning of 1 July found Langlais tired, but he was determined to participate in this important event. During the lengthy festive mass, he seemed at times confused. He played his "Hymne d'action de grâces 'Te Deum'" (*Trois paraphrases grégoriennes*) much more slowly than usual. After the homily, when the organist normally improvises briefly, Langlais played Bach's *Wachet auf*. A visitor to the loft remarked that he did not look well. Afterward, while coming down the stairs, he dropped his beret, and Marie-Louise addressed him not once but twice; there was no answer. Struck by an attack of hemiplegia on his right side, he fell into the waiting arms of the tall archbishop at the foot of the stairs.[1]

At first he was completely paralyzed on his right side and unable to speak. He was immediately transported to a hospital in nearby Saint-Malo, where he received excellent care. He was discharged after one week, and in fifteen days, he was able to walk and use his right arm and hand.

Complications

A month after his stroke, Marie-Louise described her husband's condition:

> Unfortunately Jean . . . cannot read braille; he can neither read nor write. I find that his speech is improving, even though he is depressed from finding himself in this state. He walks normally, he is not at all handicapped, although he finds that his right hand is less agile—he no longer wants to play the organ because he can't remember the pieces he wants to play; but all that should come back within several months.[2]

Never known for his patience, Langlais was frustrated by the ordeal. Not being able to express himself placed an almost intolerable strain on his ability to cope. It was Caroline who gave him courage throughout this period of recuperation. Despite her encouragement, he confided to many of his friends that he was waiting for death to come. The stroke, however, had not affected his heart and his blood pressure, which remained normal.

After six weeks, he was brought to the Clinique des Maladies du Système Nerveux, Hôpital de la Salpêtrière in Paris, where he was examined by Doctor Jean-Louis Signoret. By that time he was sufficiently recovered to be able to play a Bach chorale. A week later, he executed Franck's *Pastorale* for his doctors on his house organ. By October, he was able to return to his duties at Sainte-Clotilde. On 24 October 1984, he recorded for French television a series of improvisations based on themes by César Franck in honor of the Franck centennial. He resumed teaching in November, especially improvisation, since he relied much more on demonstrating at the organ than by verbal communication.

His stroke damaged the left temporal lobe of his brain, affecting the Wernicke area, which controls speech; a catscan indicated a lesion, which disrupted the formation of words and their pronunciation. He may have understood what was said to him but was unable to verbalize his thoughts. When his doctor asked him to speak about his illness, nonsense words and syllables came out. Short words such as "le père" he rendered "le . . . pa . . . le . . . ta . . . le frère . . . la . . .

le par . . . il y a pé." Langlais's blindness made his case so unusual that the findings were published in a French medical journal.[3]

A speech therapist, Philippe van Eeckhout, worked with him beginning in October and continued, twice a week, for the rest of his life. His speech began to return, but mostly, mysteriously, in English, and therefore, as part of the beginning speech therapy, he was no longer permitted to use the language he had labored so hard to attain. Much to everyone's chagrin, he reached a plateau after about nine months; from that time on improvements were only marginal. He was able, however, to carry on simple conversations. With the help of Marie-Louise and his speech therapist, he learned to pronounce a few proper names but required practice before saying them. He used to keep a little list of names that he used frequently in his pocket. Numbers were also impossible for him, except by counting aloud from one to add their components. He was unable to write or read braille text or type at a typewriter.

What his doctors and speech therapists found particularly surprising about his case was that the brain lesion did not affect his ability to compose and to perform. He could read and write musical notation in braille using the same signs that he was unable to use for words.[4]

Recital at Notre-Dame

Langlais's playing did not lose its ability to move the listener, as Kathleen Thomerson pointed out in her review of a recital he played at Notre-Dame on 2 March 1986, at the age of seventy-nine:

> His program opened with two works of Charles Tournemire, very powerfully and mystically played, "Eli, Eli, lamma sabach-tani" (*Sept chorals-poèmes*) and the Communion [from the Epiphany office of *L'orgue mystique*]. Langlais continued with four of his *Neuf pièces*. Here for the first time some memory lapses occurred, but always well under control, with no effect on the rhythmic pulse of the piece. Indeed, it was rather interesting to hear the spontaneous recreation of a couple of passages. The time when my blood ran cold, however, was during the second half of "Mon âme cherche": Langlais had experi-

enced difficulty remembering this part, but made a successful conclusion. I fully expected him to convert the first ending into the final cadence, thankful that he had arrived safely at the end. But no, he calmly took the repeat and played through the second half again, this time perfectly. What courage! After that, he played a thrilling, heartfelt [*Imploration* "Pour le croyance"] and concluded with an improvisation on "Salve regina" which showed much creative power and imagination.[5]

Last Recording

On 11 November 1986 Langlais made his last recording at Sainte-Clotilde, *Jean Langlais improvise à Sainte-Clotilde*, which earned the highest praise:

> What an astonishing man Jean Langlais is to deliver, at eighty years, two great improvisations on four Gregorian themes . . . what a fascinating artist who does not deny us, from his organ loft, a lesson in youth! The master recording was made in record time, only twenty-five minutes of playing, twice through. The first improvisation on two themes of the "Salve regina" . . . presents and develops its elements in six parts, in the manner of a colorist, but with a texture both dense and open, definitely very contemporary. The ideas are developed with inventiveness and freedom, imagination and movement. The second improvisation is constructed on the alleluia from the mass of the feast of the Sacred Heart and the offertory from the mass of the Holy Name of Jesus. The construction is very Classic. . . . What can you say after listening to these priviliged musical moments, except to say that they take your breath away? . . . An archival recording for every lover of the organ.[6]

Arthur Lawrence also reviewed the recording favorably: "The overall style is a continuous one, in which tonal progressions are peppered with piquant dissonances. The organ is effectively employed to show both the colorful solo stops and the various ensembles. . . . This may not be an easy record to obtain, but it will be worth the search for anyone who is an admirer of Langlais."[7]

Chapter 15

Final Decline and Last Compositions 1985–1990

The music from Langlais's final period is tinged with retrospection and introspection. His life was coming full circle, from his earliest childhood memories to the anticipation of his own death, and in his final compositions, marked by funeral bell motifs, he paid a lasting tribute to those who had inspired him: Jehan Alain, Charles Tournemire, Jeannette, Claude, and especially the Virgin Mary. Langlais's frustration and depression led to one final burst of creative energy, which both lashed out at and expressed his acceptance of his condition. After the stroke he wrote sixteen works for organ, three hymns, two choral works, and a variety of instrumental pieces, including one for four cellos. He composed nothing after December 1990.

These last works are not substantially different in style from those written prior to his stroke, although their quality is very uneven (his need to express himself perhaps compromised his analytical objectivity). Throughout this period, the pull toward chant and a very simple style becomes even stronger, exceeding even that of *Vingt-quatre pièces*. Yet each new piece is fresh.

Langlais now had to dictate his music through the piano, playing each voice separately to a copyist, who knew his ideas sufficiently well to be able to assemble the parts of the puzzle. In her dissertation, Marie-Louise thanked the seven people who, along with herself, had worked so hard to bring these pieces to light: Pierre Denis, Jean Bonfils, Pierre Cogen, Naji and Marie-Bernadette Hakim, Yves Castagnet, and Daniel Maurer.[8]

After April 1984, when he composed "Hymne du soir," almost a year passed before Langlais composed again; it took a thunderbolt to reawaken his creativity. This event occurred during Easter Week of 1985, while he attended a mass at La Richardais's parish church. He listened to the Gospel reading (Mark 5:22–43), the story of the daughter of Jairus, whom Jesus raised from the dead, and a provocative sermon that followed. Moved especially by the words, "Do not fear, only believe" and "Talitha cumi" (Little girl, I say to you, arise), he decided to compose a new collection of organ music based on the idea of resurrection; he titled this four-movement work, composed between 28 May and 10 June 1985, *Talitha koum*, the Aramaic translation of Jesus's command to the little girl. Movements one and four

("Salve regina" and "1, 7, 8") are dedicated to his doctors, Signoret and van Eeckhout, respectively; the middle movements ("Regina coeli" and "Alme Pater") are dedicated to his daughter Caroline. The last piece, an alleluia, was finished on the date of Jeannette's death; all are based on Marian themes.

"Salve regina" again suggests angels flying, as in "Regina angelorum" (*Offrande à Marie*). Like another "Salve regina" (*Mosaïque, vol. 2*), its high-pitched motifs function as bridges between simple statements of each phrase of the chant, but unlike its predecessor, this "Salve regina" uses as a united theme both chant tunes in succession. The second and third movements, "Regina coeli" and "Alme Pater" (from Mass 10, in honor of the Virgin Mary), set their respective chants in the most simple manner, mainly with parallel fifths in the accompaniment. The last movement, "1, .7, 8" (the date of his stroke), is the most original thematically The opening pedal solo is reprised backward, in retrograde, after its introduction, in the form of an arch. The alleluia is a vocalise, rising higher and higher in adoration.

In August and September 1985, in honor of Bach's tricentenary, Langlais composed *B.A.C.H.: six pièces pour orgue*. Each movement is based on the name Bach. Langlais begins with a set of variations around this motif, repeated twenty-four times in the course of forty-three measures. Nonetheless the variety of tempo, registration, and mood is sufficient to avoid a feeling of repetitiveness. One does hear bits and pieces of earlier works: the opening motif from *Poem of Life* in the second movement; "Duo" and "Trio" (*Progression*) in the third movement; and typically slow chordal settings with mild dissonances, reminiscent of many works, in the third movement.

In memoriam, composed 23 December 1985, was conceived as a tripartite rhapsody for organ in homage of Charles Tournemire and his spiritual legacy. This important work demonstrates a firm command of form, economy of thematic material, and his continued quest for mysticism through theological symbolism. Two Gregorian chants—the Kyrie "Pater cuncta" from Mass 12 and the introit "Gaudeamus omnes in Domino" from the feast of All Saints—are the basis of the first section. Free thematic material, symbolic of birds in Paradise, forms the second; and the chant "Vexilla regis," which continues the bird motifs, forms the third.

The introduction is based on the last part of the Kyrie with a motif symbolizing tears, which also serves as interlude and conclusion to the first section. Three statements of the Kyrie are followed by declamatory commentary on the full organ and syncopated ostinato of eighth-note and quarter-note rhythms. The same pattern is followed for the Christe, but with the chant in the pedal. The chant "Gaudeamus omnes in Domino" is played on the pedal with a Flûte 8. Langlais chose the chant from the feast of All Saints to symbolize Tournemire's communion with the Saints.

The second section introduces the bird motif, symbolizing eternity (as in *Cinq méditations sur l'apocalypse*) and as a symbol of the soul after death (as in *Offrande à une âme*). Staccato chords on Flûte 8, followed by bird motifs repeated on Flûtes 8, 2 and Flûte 8, symbolize the joy of the soul in Paradise.

In the third section the chant "Vexilla regis" symbolizes Christ's Passion and salvation through the cross. A reed announces the entire chant without accompaniment; bird motifs resume, and the "Vexilla regis," in canon at third, diminished fifth, and seventh, alternates with the bird motif and staccato chords. This canon symbolizes the mystical unity of his soul with his personhood and that of Christ in Paradise. A polymodal development of "Vexilla regis" in B and D dorian follows. Canons continue the symbol of Paradise, where no limits of space and hearing exist. In the conclusion, the last seven notes of chant in augmentation with the words "vitam protulit" (life procuring) symbolize Tournemire in eternal life.

In the same chant-like vein as *Talitha koum* and *B.A.C.H: six pièces pour orgue*, Langlais composed *Douze versets* for organ in the fall of 1986. Two are based on Gregorian chants: an alleluia, used by Tournemire for the feast of Corpus Christi, which Langlais often accompanied at the mass, and "Ave, regina coelorum." Each movement is set in a separate mood and registration, providing much contrast and several are marked by strong, syncopated rhythms.

Fred Bock, a longtime supporter of Langlais's music, nevertheless felt that most of his organ music was beyond the reach of amateur church organists. It was also not particularly useful for Protestant church services, because of the chant orientation. After buying out the publisher FitzSimons in 1985, Bock therefore proposed that Langlais compose six pieces based on familiar songs from Methodist,

Episcopal, and Southern Baptist hymnals.[9] The collection, *American Folk-Hymn Settings*, sold very well. Although it was not technically as easy as it appeared nor as musically satisfying, it did fill a need in this genre.

Bock then requested that he write another work, which was originally to be entitled *Elevations*, hoping that it would appeal to both Catholic and Protestant organists. It was stipulated that each of the thirty pieces be two pages in length, with minimal use of pedal, and that each segue into the next.[10] Langlais did not wish to write all thirty and proposed that Naji Hakim, his protegé and then organist at Sacré-Coeur, write fifteen of them under his guidance. Bock later changed the title to *Expressions*, to avoid a Roman Catholic connotation.[11] Langlais succeeded in fulfilling the request in his own set of fifteen pieces, in various moods. They are among his easiest, all may be played entirely without pedals, and each piece does lead into the next.

Following *Expressions*, Bock commissioned two other works: a choral piece on the text "Ubi caritas" (1986) and *Christmas Carol Hymn Settings* for organ. Composed early in 1988, several of these settings of popular Christmas carols are technically simple, and all have met with considerable success.

Even more simple than *Expressions* is *Petite suite*, which he wrote in 1985 for Caroline's exams at the Schola Cantorum in 1986 and 1987. Despite their technical ease, these four piano pieces are charming; in each, the melody is given first to the right hand and then to the left. The first two are dedicated to Caroline, and the last two to Langlais's grandson, Camille, in another attempt to reconcile with Claude and his family.

Jonathan Dimmock, then assistant organist at the Cathedral of Saint John the Divine in New York, commissioned *Trumpet Tune* in 1987. Scored for full organ and State Trumpet, it is markedly dissonant, using three-note chords, with spacing of a fourth, and syncopated rhythmic patterns. The State Trumpet is heard first in a staccato solo in the tenor and then with three-voice chords as in the opening. State Trumpet and full organ echo each other in dramatic chordal flourishes and conclude with both sounding together. Langlais clearly had not lost his ability to create a piece for a huge space and to enhance the effect of a long reverberation.

In March 1987 Langlais wrote, "Just now I am finishing a little piece for flute and organ, which was commissioned in Germany, and I have refused to write a piece for two organists. . . . I have really decided to stop composing."[12] His resolve was not to last. That summer he completed *Vitrail*, a piece for clarinet and piano, commissioned by Claude and dedicated to him; again he announced it would be his last work.[13] But in late November, in celebration of the coming Marian year, he composed *Trois antiennes à la Sainte-Vierge* for solo voice or unison choir and organ. Based on the Gregorian chants "Regina coeli," "Ave, regina coelorum," and "Salve regina," the vocal part maintains the chant themes unchanged while a prayerful sustained chordal accompaniment doubles the vocal part.

In honor of his eightieth birthday numerous festivities took place: at the Madeleine, where concerts of choral and organ music were given, in Germany, the Netherlands, Austria, and in the United States. In July 1987 the Royal College of Organists awarded him the Doctorat Honoris Causa, the fourth he received. Last but certainly not least, in November of that year the mayor of La Fontenelle organized a moving reception for him, which was headlined in the newspapers as "The return of the prodigal son."

Langlais's health continued to deteriorate, and his heart became weaker. By Christmas 1987, Marie-Louise had stepped down as co-titular organist at Sainte-Clotilde, and Langlais had requested that the pastor of Sainte-Clotilde appoint both Pierre Cogen and Jacques Taddei as titular organists of Sainte-Clotilde; Langlais maintained the post until Easter 1988, although his weakened heart had prevented his playing there since 8 November 1987.

Vitrail was given its premiere performance at the chapel in Roumazières, with Claude at the piano, in the summer of 1988. The title, bestowed by the publisher, recalls the coloristic effects between the clarinet and piano, which resemble the kaleidoscopic play of light in a stained-glass window. Langlais had been in an emotional state as he dictated *Vitrail* to Naji Hakim; he still felt the loss of Jeannette keenly and wanted to be close to Claude once again.[14] Even after nine years, Langlais's grief and guilt were the central emotions expressed in this work. The tolling of funeral bells continued to haunt him. In *Vitrail* he uses two of the tolls, the first from the bells of the church in La Fontenelle, and the second from the church in Escalquens.

The week before the premiere Langlais was hospitalized with severe chest pains. A pacemaker was installed. Claude and the clarinetist came to the apartment and made a recording of *Vitrail*, which they played for him in the hospital. Listening to the tape and being again with Claude moved him to tears.

In the summer of 1988 he composed *Contrasts*, a four-movement suite for organ. The first piece, "Glas," was written in memory of Michel Villey, a close friend and the first blind professor at Cannes. The introduction echoes the sound of a deep funeral gong; the thematic material for the piece is provided by the alleluia chant used in *Douze versets*. "Allegretto," the second piece, is a reprint of the same work from *Homage to Rameau*. The third piece is a very simple setting of the Kyrie 16 for the Sundays of Advent and Lent, similar to the Kyrie "Alme Pater" (*Talitha koum*). The most technically demanding piece is the last, "Pièce de concert," dedicated to Yves Castagnet, winner of the 1988 Chartres Competition, who suggested that Langlais compose a virtuoso piece for him. The right hand keeps a staccato ostinato pattern of descending major sevenths, over sustained chords in the left hand, followed by rapid repeated chords with double, triple, and quadruple notes in the pedal. The percussive rhythms are reminiscent of "La cinquième trompette" (*Cinq méditations sur l'apocalypse*).

Both Langlais and Litaize improvised during a festival at the Schola Cantorum in April 1989, and those in attendance felt the familiar spirit of competition between them. Langlais, of course, believed that he had brought out more possibilities from the theme than had Litaize.

A video of these sessions shows Langlais much diminished.[15] Of necessity, Marie-Louise had become his spokesperson. It was she who spoke throughout the video for her husband. Those who knew him well before the stroke recognized a shadow of the former "bear," one who at the end of his life crawled cautiously, without claws. Marie-Louise answered his mail and phone calls. Many of his old friends never knew whether he had received their letters when she was too busy to write.

Monique remembered Jean and Marie-Louise's last trip to Roumazières, when they stopped to see them on their way to Toulouse. Langlais appeared weak and talked only of his dog. Marie-Louise was totally in charge of everything and led him around as if to show him off.

Early in 1990 Langlais completed two more organ pieces, *Moonlight Scherzo* and *Mort et résurrection*, both characterized by frequent use of polymodality and tone clusters as well as repetition of short phrases.

Moonlight Scherzo, mm. 1–2. © 1990 Editions Combre, Paris. Used by permission.

Mort et résurrection, p. 2, mm. 5–7. © 1990 Editions Musicales Alphonse Leduc, Paris. Used by permission.

Moonlight Scherzo was written rapidly for the American market in February 1990. Again (as in "Feux d'artifice" from *Rosace*) Langlais quotes the French nursery song "Au clair de la lune." This time, however, the moon does not appear after the fireworks; rather, a boisterous frolic follows, with much repetition of two-measure phrase units and staccato parallel harmonies in a symmetrical form.

Mort et résurrection, Langlais's last major work and the last that he heard, was written in honor of the fiftieth anniversary of Jehan Alain's death. Here for a second time Langlais pays homage to Alain in a remarkable musical expression, depicting Alain's death and resurrection even as he anticipates his own. Marie-Louise, who was with him as he composed the work in December 1989 and early January 1990, noted her husband's "contradictory position, showing on the one hand a total serenity before his end, which he felt close, but willingly affirming before his doctors his taste for living—why not to one hundred?—which conformed to his fighter's temperament."[16]

In *Mort et résurrection* Langlais terrifyingly renders Alain's last moments, on his motorcycle, heading into enemy fire—the battery of exploding bombs and artillery blasts brought to life in the piercing repetition of brutal, percussive chord clusters and rapid flourishes like clouds of smoke. The resurrection, in contrast, symbolizes the life hereafter in its complete serenity through the use of soft, sustained chords with Alain's musical signature paraphrasing the opening motives borrowed from Alain's own works *Choral dorien* and *Deuxième fantaisie*. The chant "Regina coeli" completes the sense of eternal serenity.

Mort et résurrection may also be understood without specific reference to Jehan Alain. The piece begins as a funeral dirge, with the repeated tolling knell instilling a mood of desolation and bitterness. The funeral theme is then repeated more vehemently. Gradually the reality of death, the great unknown, builds with increasing force. Terror, chaos, and incomprehensible blackness emerge with earth-shaking force. It is like a cataclysmic rending of consciousness by the negation of life. The funeral theme recurs as if in a vast surrealistic plane, now removed from life. Chaos then returns, more and more terrifying, until the last oppressive dissonance is finally released and resurrection follows. Here the symmetrical form (A A B B C A B) gives peace, with the "Regina coeli" in the middle, as the apex.

Three short pieces—*Trois offertoires, Suite "In simplicitate,"* and "Trio"—were Langlais's last compositions. *Trois offertoires*, written in September and October 1990, returns to a more sombre and simple style based on Breton and Gregorian chant themes. The first offertory is dedicated to Jeanne Jugan, the founder of the Order of the Little Sisters of the Poor, who had recently been beatified by Pope John Paul II. The order had been founded to care for the elderly poor, and Langlais always found it appropriate that their motherhouse was located in Brittany near his home, where poverty was so much a part of his childhood. "Jesu, dulcis memoria" was one of his favorite chants and also a favorite of the mother superior of this order. It is stated very simply with no embellishments or development, as if accompanying the singing of the chant. The second offertory is very different. Dedicated to his friend Michel Marès, his general practitioner, the work appears in its opening to be an effort to put his name into the treble, while the left hand sustains a chromatic five-note tone cluster for the first six bars. Several references to *Mort et résurrection* and *Vitrail* likewise express a lament and a foreboding of his own end. He then repeats his familiar prayer to Mary, asking forgiveness in quoting the "Salve regina" theme with the funeral knell heard softly beneath it. The third offertory is dedicated to André Heulin, his cardiologist, in friendship and gratitude for his care. Here Langlais treats two of his favorite Breton themes, "Bardox dudius" (Wonderful paradise) and "Ni ho saliud" (Angelus).

Completed in November 1990, almost as a fourth offertory, *Suite "In simplicitate"* is based on the earlier, exuberant *Plein-jeu à la française* (1974), the Marian chants "Virgo Maria" and "Salve regina," and the mass "Cum jubilo." A gentle charm characterizes the last two movements, which are set very simply with uncomplicated harmonies, again as if to accompany the sung chant, alternating between treble and bass voices. They too resemble the treatment of the Kyrie "Alme Pater" from *Talitha koum*. The "Salve regina" chant reappears one last time, closing the suite peacefully with a C major chord, as if to show that all the dissonance in his life had at last been resolved.

Langlais considered this his last composition but was persuaded by his colleague Daniel-Lesur to compose one very short piece for a new pedagogical work designed to introduce young organists to contemporary music. Daniel-Lesur and Jean-Jacques Werner were the editors. "Trio," the easiest and shortest in *Collection panorama*, was composed on Christmas Day 1990, five months before Langlais's death. Langlais at last succeeded in finding a way to put the name Daniel-Lesur in the theme, with the notes A, D, F, D, A, D, E, C, D, B-flat—a final tribute to a dear friend.

During the last four months of his life, his strength ebbed and Langlais experienced a series of small strokes. He still saw friends at his apartment and kept two students. In March he resigned from his position of administrator for the Association Valentin Haüy, which he had occupied since 1943. He continued to call his blind friends on the phone and helped them as he had for over half a century. In April he and his family traveled to Brittany for Easter.

On 2 May, he made an emotional phone call to Pierre Cogen. He was crying, seeming to sense that his end was near. Langlais expressed his regrets over not having seen Cogen and begged his forgiveness for not naming Cogen the sole titular organist at Sainte-Clotilde.[17] Later that day, he and Marie-Louise attended a reception at the Schola Cantorum for the Fourth International Organ Academy.

Death

Four days later he had difficulty breathing and was taken to Necker Hospital on rue de Sèvres, near his home. Fluid continued to build in his lungs, and his condition rapidly deteriorated. At Litaize's insistence, Marie-Louise called for Father Chang, the vicar of Sainte-Clotilde, to administer last rites. Marie-Louise, who remained with her husband while Kathleen Thomerson cared for Caroline at the apartment, describes his last moments: "On the evening of 8 May the third crisis of pulmonary edema began. . . . He fought fiercely, completely conscious, for a long moment. . . . At 11:45, his hand, which I held in mine, trembled with a brief spasm and fell cold. He was dead."[18]

Robert Lord had been invited to have lunch with him that next day and called the home only to be informed of his death; it seemed to him appropriate that Langlais died on the feast of the Ascension. Claude and Monique, who had not been told of this last crisis, were shocked by the news of his death.

Langlais's body was kept for several days at Necker Hospital for viewing, as is customary in France, where embalming is not usually practiced. His coffin lay in a cold room, separated by glass from the viewing area, where friends and family paid him their last respects. A small crucifix was placed in his folded hands, and he seemed at last to rest in peace.

The funeral was held on Saturday, 11 May, in Escalquens, in a private ceremony at the little church where Jeannette had been buried. Xavier Darasse organized the music for the funeral: the choir

Terpsichore from the Conservatory in Toulouse sang the Gregorian Requiem mass and Renaissance motets; there was no organ music. He was then laid in his final resting place, next to Jeannette, in the adjoining cemetery.

On 30 May at six in the evening, a Solemn Mass was celebrated at Sainte-Clotilde in his memory. Seven clergy participated, with three organists, Jacques Taddei, Pierre Cogen, and Georges Bessonnet (on the choir organ); the Petits Chanteurs d'Antony, directed by Patrick Giraud; a brass choir from the Conservatoire National de Région de Paris; trumpeter Guy Touvron; and Pierre-Michel Bedard, choirmaster of Sainte-Clotilde. Many friends and students from Europe and the States attended as well as family members Marie-Louise Langlais, Janine Motton, Claude Langlais, Caroline Langlais, Flavie Langlais, and cousin Jacques Langlais. Portions of the Gregorian Requiem mass, the Kyrie and Agnus Dei from his *Missa "Salve regina,"* the Sanctus from his *Messe solennelle* and other works by Langlais, Franck, and Cogen were offered. The pastor of Sainte-Clotilde, Father Joseph Chonet, read the Gospel and delivered the homily, which touched on the life of the blind, scriptures on blindness, and the gift of music. Canon Jehan Revert, choirmaster at Notre-Dame, gave the address following communion, a moving tribute to his friend Langlais concerning the sense of mystery in his works and his musical witness to his faith. He repeated Langlais's description of himself: "Je suis un musicien breton de foi catholique."[19]

Afterword

In many ways too short a time has passed since Langlais's death to assess his work. Some observations may, however, be hazarded.

Langlais represents the culmination of the Sainte-Clotilde tradition—a tradition begun with César Franck and continued with Charles Tournemire. The influence of the Cavaillé-Coll organ there, the liturgical requirements of the position, and the relationship of these three principal organists of Sainte-Clotilde—first as church musicians, composers, performers, improvisors, and teachers within this special environment—created a unique school of playing and composition. Langlais's disciple and immediate successor Pierre Cogen has written a handful of pieces that show promise; but unfortunately, Cogen's tenure, which ended in 1994, was not long enough to provide promise for a greater legacy, and the present organist, Jacques Taddei, is not a composer. It is doubtful that the legacy will be reborn with Taddei's successors.

Although Langlais fiercely defended himself as an independent composer who was unaligned with any school, several arguments favor considering him the culmination of the French post-Romantic organ school, represented in the twentieth century by such composers as Widor, Vierne, Dupré, Alain, and Duruflé. Langlais was not primarily an innovator. Rather Langlais brought existing forms and styles to a new level of completeness and beauty. So an independent, then—who felt his roots deep within the Franck and Tournemire traditions of modality and harmony; who expanded the concept of the chorale and chant-oriented paraphrase; and who embraced the symphonist Dupré tradition and the colorist Vierne tradition.

Langlais may be considered the synthesis of all the influences of the twentieth century, including serial techniques; his works are among the best of the symphonic forms. The magnitude of his works for organ surpasses that of any twentieth-century French composer, but quantity is not the only factor: Langlais's music has clarity of form, thematic interest, depth of emotion, and the capacity to touch the listener profoundly and immediately by its strong harmonies, rhythm, and tightly knit structure. He was true to Paul Dukas's dictum never to repeat himself: each piece of Langlais's is fresh, no piece sounds quite like another. Because of this, it is often difficult to determine by listening to a work whether it was composed early or late in his career.

The importance of Gregorian chant to Langlais's music cannot be overstated, nor the long-range influence of chant through his music. Although he occasionally used unfamiliar chants, he preferred the canon of well-known hymns (especially Marian chants) and masses that he thought were in the hearts of the faithful. And if they weren't they may become so entirely through his music. He made chant accessible to many who never heard it in churches prior to hearing and performing his music. Likewise, the folkloric sources he tapped from Brittany and America unleashed a rich repertoire of tunes and chorales unknown to many.

Langlais's music is similar to some aspects of Medieval music in that hidden meanings and complexities are most apparent to those who study the music. The pleasure of discovering the name motifs and performing his music is sometimes greater for the performer than for the listener.

Unlike Brahms and Duruflé, Langlais could not objectively decide what to throw away—a weakness he regretted late in life. He left only a few pieces unfinished and unpublished. Instead of reworking sketches for months at a time, he usually sent them to the copyist as soon as they were finished, without a second thought, so intent was he on the creative process itself. At times a musical idea is repeated too often, making a work less cohesive. One example of a work that Langlais did successfully revise for republication is "Storm in Florida" (*American Suite*): by deleting several repetitious sections, Langlais made the work tighter and more exciting in its second appearance, as "Orage" (*Troisième symphonie*).

Above all Langlais should be recognized as a significant composer of sacred music, which distinction was no doubt the most gratifying to him. Although not a theologian, he communicated in many of his works theological truths about eternal life, the nature of the Trinity, the soul, Christ, and Mary. His canon of sacred program music in particular is a distinct contribution. Throughout his life he sought to express his Catholic faith through music, and without question he succeeded. It remains for future generations, regardless of their religious affiliation or lack of it, to discover these treasures in the choral, vocal, and instrumental areas, as well as the organ music.

He lived as he wished, with independence. Any anguish enriched his music with a pathos and emotion that touched his audiences. His tears, laughter, and joy over the surety of being greatly loved—all found their place in his music, music that continues to resonate in ever-broadening circles.

Selected Students of Jean Langlais

Langlais kept no formal list of students. Those included here were compiled from correspondence with him and with students known to me. The list is not exhaustive. In most cases those listed studied with him for a minimum of six months and a number of them at several different times. The list includes private students as well as those enrolled at the Schola Cantorum and the Institute.

Marie-Laure Alby
George Baker
Monique Becheras
Janice Milburn Beck
David Bergeron
Wayne Bradford
David Briggs
Marjorie Bruce
Philippe Charru
James Christie
Pierre Cogen
Beatrice Collins
Jeanne Rizzo Conner
Jean-Baptiste Courtois
Stanley Cox
Lynn Davis
Albert DeKlerk
Pierre Denis
Germain Desbonnet
James Dorroh
Flemming Dreissig
Marie-Bernadette Dufourcet-Hakim

Nathan Ensign
Susan Ferré
Maurice John Forshaw
Thomas Froehlich
Alain Garderet
Marie-Agnes Grall-Menet
Bo Grondbeck
Folkert Grondsma
Norberto Guinaldo
Naji Hakim
Gerre Hancock
Ruth Wood Harris
Karen Hastings
Douglas Himes
Allen Hobbs
Lucie Howells
Eileen Hunt
Audrey Bartlett Jacobsen
Marie-Louise Jaquet-Langlais
Marvel Basile Jensen
Kjell Johnsen
Elna Johnson

Roger Katz
Thomas Kelly
Antoinette Keraudren
Deborah Kim
Robert King
Steve Knight
Kristen Kolling
Edward Kooiman
Marilou Kratzenstein
Ann Labounsky
Micheline La Gache
Peter Latona
Michelle Leclerc-Barré
Bénédicte Le Mest
Jessie Jewitt Le Moullae
David Lloyd
Robert Sutherland Lord
Paul-Martin Maki
Bruno Mathieu
Daniel Maurer
Marie Grandinetti Melusky
Rosalind Mohnsen
James Nissim
John O'Donnell
Jan Overduin
André Paginel
John M. Palmer
Darlene Pekala
Patricia McAuley Phillips
William Pruitt
Robert Rayfield

Louis Robilliard
Anita Rodans
Danielle Salvignol-Nisse
Thomas Daniel Schlee
Kreis von Schulern
Robert Scoggin
Coline Serreau
Emmet Smith
Jane Parker Smith
Rollin Smith
Kenton Stillwagen
Ronald Stolk
Marguerite Thal Long
Kathleen Armstrong Thomerson
Edward Harry Tibbs
Christopher Tietze
Timothy Tikker
Peter Togni
Ian Tracey
Wim Vander Panne
John Vandertuin
Kees Van Ersel
Colin Walsh
James Welch
Richard Westenburg
Linda Lyster Whalon
Pierre Whalon
Richard Forrest Woods
Nina Wu
François Xavier
Chantal de Zeeuw

Langlais's Treatise on Teaching Blind Students

The only written document concerning Langlais's own pedagogy is his short treatise, *L'orgue, l'improvisation et la composition musicale enseignés à des élèves aveugles par un professeur aveugle* (Organ, improvisation, and musical composition taught to blind students by a blind professor). This important *mémoire* explains his views of teaching both blind and sighted students and also incorporates the teaching philosophies that he derived from other teachers at the Institute, and from his studies with Dupré and Dukas. The typed manuscript of fifty-four pages, bound in red leather, is undated and contains no musical examples. It was written as part of the application process for tenure at the National Institute for the Blind. Marcel Dupré, who was on the jury for Langlais's tenure, read and approved the work; Georges Caussade might also have read it.

The book reflects the manner in which Langlais had been taught by Marchal. In addition, it shows how Langlais taught both blind and sighted students. He makes a point of explaining that the principles are applicable to both. It marks his developing sense of organization in teaching and gives an early example of his thought process and writing style—well organized, simple, and confident. Langlais had experienced a broad range of students, and the scope of the book demonstrates this. Although they were never adopted, Langlais describes new pedagogical approaches for reading orchestral scores based on ideas from Rémy Clavers. References to d'Indy's book on composition and an anthology of early recordings of music for teaching the history of musical styles also appear.

Although Langlais's permanent tenured appointment did not occur until 1939, the presumed date of composition is around 1935. Several things support this assumption: first, Caussade died in 1936; second, the treatise contains many references to orchestration which he learned from Dukas in 1934; and third, Langlais said in 1984 that he thought it might have been written around 1935. When I read excerpts of it to him and asked him questions about its contents, he explained that Rémy Clavers had organized a system for braille study by dividing a page into four squares, in order to permit a blind student to read more than one part at a time and that Langlais enlarged upon this concept. The practical exercises are valuable, however, for sighted as well as blind students.

Langlais began these exercises for improvisation with all his students at their first organ lesson. Before this, however, each student had studied harmony for three years and piano for six years. His method for the weekly assignments also gives an insight into his own compositional process. In his introduction Langlais states that the initiation is often long and hard, especially for less gifted students. (Despite these difficulties, Langlais was proud that in all his years at the Institute, he had urged only one student to stop studying organ.)

The following excerpts are paraphrased from Langlais's original text, which was in three parts: beginning organ technique, improvisation, and composition.

Pedal Technique

Technique demands the utmost of muscular coordination, and that both sighted and non-sighted people, with equal gifts, may become artistic equals. For adapting to the pedals, one should sit in the middle of the bench, avoiding all tension and remaining natural. Place the left foot on tenor C, the right foot on tenor G. In beginning, the student should be greatly encouraged. The teacher should gently place the hand on the student's knee, for in that way the slightest muscular tension will be felt. If there is a contraction in the attack, the student is sitting too far back. Maintain contact with the pedals at all times.

To give the exactitude of touch on one note, be sure to make small and rapid gestures. The teacher is advised to adapt exercises to each student, paying attention to good preparations for each note. The exercises could be adapted in the following manner: the teacher should name a series of notes and the student play them. Then add cadences. Use black notes to find wide intervals. Use the same exercises for each foot separately.

Manual Technique

Each note value must have mathematical precision. Repeated notes should receive one half their value. The teacher is instructed to put his hand over the student's for correct hand position. Special attention is indicated in the beginning for following indicated fingerings. For manual changes, go from C on the Grand-orgue to C on the Récit and C on the Positif with the same finger. Then repeat this exercise using chords. In order to execute these exercises in the best possible way, the following guidelines should be followed:

1. One must have an aural picture of the organ console. [Location of stops and their sounds, pitches of each key.]

2. One should carefully think each gesture through before doing it.

3. One must have starting points [points de repère préamblement] well established so as to leave nothing to chance.

How to Read Gregorian Chant at the Organ

Read the melody and accompany it at the same time, using Medieval accompaniment. While the left hand reads the braille copy of the chant, the right hand plays the upper three voices and the pedal plays the bass. As for reading music in braille, the student is cautioned about the change of line, to move his hand rapidly, and not to press too hard on the raised braille points.

Registration

Do not compare the organ to an orchestra. Explain each stop and the harmonic series.

Improvisation

Results are possible even for ungifted students, provided they possess the necessary background in harmony and counterpoint and the ability to concentrate. For liturgical and concert uses in most countries, the improvisor is seen, next to the composer, as one who represents to the public the highest of musical knowledge.

Rhythm

To attain a natural flow to the rhythm, follow the rhythm of the heart beat. Play one note while breathing out and continue for several minutes. This is the tactus or first beat of each measure of four. Then breathe in on the count of three. Do this with two notes (C, D, counting 1, 2, 3, 4 with C on count 1, and D on count 3). Then try this with a metronome, accelerating the tempo. Use different meters. Then using the same one note, give a succession of different rhythms: first simple, then difficult. Then combine melodic with rhythmic elements. Rapidity of thought must be developed. Finally, a theme is added and must always be read ahead by several notes.

Melody

Practice transposing melodies, then transform a melody modulating frequently, keeping the same rhythm. The melody should then be ornamented. The student is encouraged to make up his own melodies, which is more difficult because it necessitates using the compositional process. Begin using whole notes, half notes, and quarter notes only. Give the student the key or mode and range. Begin with pentatonic modes and also Gregorian modes. Also recommended are free modes (make up your own scales), which can be transposed as you wish. Be strict about phrase lengths, begin with sixteen measures, and insist on good line. Consider various shapes of a melodic line: high to low, and low to high.

Harmony

For the development of a harmonic sense, the author recommends the study of canon, using the rhythm of two quarter notes followed by a half note in common meter; then three quarter notes followed by a dotted half note in three-quarter time; and then four quarter notes, followed by a whole note in common time.

Canons

Practice improvising canons using these notes first at the octave, then at the fifth, fourth, third, second, sixth, and seventh, in that order of difficulty. Various combinations to practice include right hand and pedal; left hand and pedal; pedal and right hand; pedal and left hand; right hand on an 8′ stop with the pedal at 4′; and left hand at 8′ with pedal at 4′. This exercise is an invaluable aid to strengthening the memory. The student should not place too much confidence in his muscles because in doing so, he could run the risk of seeing all his progress ruined in one day. After this has been mastered, the student should try canons with three voices, although this is very difficult. The teacher should play the first two parts and the student the third. The student should begin by improvising himself in order to display to the teacher his natural gifts. Although this axiom seems self-evident, it is an important one for it permits the student to play without restrictions or inhibitions.

Chords

After this, the student should play various chords with a steady pulse. For example, in common time: a tonic chord in first inversion on the second count of the first measure and on the first count of the next measure. This should be repeated at closer intervals. Various chords should be used, keeping the pulse very regular. The harmonies should be transposed according to the student's taste.

Transposition

Transposition is extremely important regardless of the student's musical tastes. The blind student, while improvising, is advised to refer back to the theme with the left hand.

Counterpoint

The exercises for the development of counterpoint follow the general format as the exercises for canon. Remember that for the teaching of the blind, one hand needs to be kept free for reading the braille copy of the theme. The themes should at first be in the same key and then modulate. At first only two voices should be used, but when that is mastered, three voices should be attempted. The registration should be 8' for the manual and 4' for the pedal. Seven possibilities for playing the cantus firmus (or melody) are listed:

1. Right hand

2. Left hand, then pedal

3. Pedal, 4'

4. Right hand, two voices in the pedal

5. Left hand, two voices in the pedal

6. Left hand, one voice in pedal

7. Right hand, then left hand, with a pedal at 2'

This entire procedure can be repeated with four parts, using double pedal with two voices in the hands and two voices in the pedal. Practice putting the cantus firmus in each one of these four voices, which is very difficult.

Dupré's book on improvision [*Cours complet d'improvisation à l'orgue*, vol. 1] is useful also for sighted students. For those with musical gifts, blindness should not be considered an obstacle to the extension of the thought process.

Composition: General Precepts

Here the importance of the eye is paramount. Sighted students have an advantage over blind students because they can see the entire page at a glance, while the blind student is reduced to a much smaller portion of what he can read at a time with his fingers. Both sighted and blind composers can become equals in dealing with the problems of creation and esthetics. Each student must develop analytical abilities. The use of recordings is helpful, and concerts are extremely important, as well as the musical examples played by the teacher.

The right hand could read above the line while the left hand reads below the line. This system for the reading of orchestral music for blind students can be expanded by dividing a page into four quadrants. The upper two quadrants were, from left to right, woodwinds and percussion; the brass and string quadrants were below the line. The student should not confuse written improvisation with a true composition.

Teaching Orchestration to Blind Students

The ear plays the most important role. Reynaldo Hahn's recordings of various orchestral instruments is recommended. With the aid of records there would be a slow and long progression. The use of recordings should include dances from the Middle Ages with odd combinations, such as flute and trombone, to the most audacious modern combinations. The following steps are useful:

1. The teacher gives one chord (C, E, G), and asks for various orchestrations such as string quartet, the real foundation of the orchestra. Then place this chord according to various clefs: F, Bass, Tenor, and Alto.

2. Woodwind combinations. For example, two flutes, two oboes. Then practice crossing instruments: C, E, G, C with flutes E, C, and oboes C, G. Clarinets sound well with bassoons. Try different combinations: flutes with clarinets; oboe with clarinet; and oboe with bassoon.

3. Instrumental combinations: woodwinds and strings; brass and two trumpets; two horns; two trumpets; four horns; then brass

and strings; brass and woodwinds. Treat percussion last. Realize the particular rhythmic quality of each percussion instrument.

According to Widor and Henri Rabaud [then director of the Conservatory], the importance of listening to live concerts is paramount. *Cours de composition musicale* by Vincent d'Indy is an important text that Paul Dukas also considered to be very important. The old set of recordings, *Anthologie sonore*, is useful.

Study of Forms

Study the following forms with great care: sonata, concerto, lied, symphony, symphonic poem, and opera. For some of the forms, Bach has furnished many rich examples. The student could take folk themes from childhood for his first efforts, being sure to keep it simple and natural. In this way, the student gradually can write according to his own personality. Count the measures in the compositions to avoid serious mistakes.

For weekly assignments, first, the teacher proposes the musical idea in a genre of funereal, tragic, programmatic, and so forth, and then gives the theme. The student chooses the harmonic and rhythmic dimensions. For the development section, work out a plan very carefully by placing only one melodic line throughout.

With the aid of special instruction, blind composers, as well as sighted ones, can explore all musical forms. It goes without saying that on the level of pure music, blindness plays no role. Its use in choreography and music for the theater can be compensated for by giving the blind composer the correct information; his imagination can furnish the rest.

In the words of Paul Dukas, "In order to write parallel fifths correctly, it is necessary to know that it is forbidden." In other words, you must know the rules in order to break them.

Chronological List of Works

The year of composition is at left. Titles preceded by an asterisk were performed by the composer. Opus numbers are from Marie-Louise Langlais, *Ombre et lumière* (Combre 1995), 341–346. Bracketed Roman numerals refer to volumes in *Jean Langlais: Complete Organ Works*, which I am recording for the Musical Heritage Society (1980–2003).

1927	*Prélude et fugue* op. 1 (organ) [XI] Universal [1 bis]
	Fugues (open score, C clefs)
1929	*Six préludes* op. 2 (organ)
	1. "Prélude"
	2. "Image"
	3. "Prière pour les morts"
	4. "Adoration des bergers"
	5. "Lamentation"
	6. "Chant héraldique"
	*"Adoration des bergers" (organ) [I] Schola Cantorum
	Prélude sur une antienne op. 3 (organ)
	*Thème libre op. 4 (organ) [IX]
1930	"Tantum ergo" op. 5 (STB, organ) Europart
1931	*Deux chansons de Clément Marot* op. 6 (mixed chorus, a cappella) Hérelle/Combre
	1. "Je suis aymé de la plus belle"
	2. "Aux damoiselles paresseuses"
1932	*Poèmes évangéliques* op. 7 (organ) [I] Hérelle/Combre
	1. "L'Annonciation"
	2. "La Nativité"
	3. "Les rameaux"

1932/42	*Cinq motets* op. 8 (two equal voices, organ) Hérelle/Combre
	1. "O salutaris hostia"
	2. "Ave mundi gloria"
	3. "Tantum ergo"
	4. "O bone Jesu"
	5. "Chant litanique"
1933/34	*Trois paraphrases grégoriennes* op. 9 (organ) [I]
	Hérelle/Combre
	1. "Mors et resurrectio"
	2. "Ave Maria, ave, maris stella"
	3. "Hymne d'action de grâces 'Te Deum'"
1933/39	*Vingt-quatre pièces* op. 10 (organ or harmonium) [IV]
	Hérelle/Combre/Masters Music
	Volume 1
	1. "Prélude modal"
	*2. "Hommage"
	3. "Arabesque"
	4. "Fugue"
	5. "Paraphrase sur 'Salve regina'"
	*6. "Noël avec variations"
	*7. "Choral varié"
	8. "Ricercare"
	9. "Scherzetto"
	10. "Toccata"
	*11. "Prière pour les morts"
	*12. "Hommage à Fr. Landino"
	Volume 2
	13. "Homo quidam"
	14. "Allegro"
	*15. "Prière"
	*16. "Choral orné"
	*17. "Pour une sainte de légende"
	18. "Fantaisie sur un thème norvégien"
	19. "Prélude et fuguette"
	20. "Fuguette"
	21. "Fantaisie"
	22. "Chant élégiaque"
	23. "Point d'orgue"
	24. "Impromptu"
1934	*Suite pour piano à quatre mains* (manuscript lost; extant copy has only several measures)
	La voix du vent op. 11 (chorus, orchestra, soprano soloist)
	L'essai sur l'évangile de Noël op. 12a (orchestra, organ)
	Hymne d'action de grâces "Te Deum" op. 12b (orchestra, organ)

"Une dentelle s'abolit" op. 13 (piano, soprano)

Suite bretonne op. 14 (piano four-hands)

Suite brève op. 15 (flute, violin, viola)

1. "Prélude blanc"
2. "Guirlandes"
3. "Fuguette"
4. "Gigue"

1935 *Cloches de deuil* op. 16 (strings, woodwinds)

1. "Lent et triste"
2. "Menuet"

*Humilis op. 17 (voice, piano)

1. "Le ciel est translucide"
2. "Je t'aime"
3. "J'étais empêché par ces bruits"
4. "Je pleure, je ne peux plus parler"
5. "Mon amour est-il"
6. "Ayant renoncé aux yeux"

*Pièce en forme libre op. 18 (string quartet, organ) H. W. Gray/Belwin Mills as *Piece in Free Form*/Combre as *Pièce en forme libre*

Adagio, Maestoso energico, Adagio

Adagio op. 18 bis (piano transcription of final Adagio from *Piece in Free Form*)

Messe pour deux voix op. 19 (two voices, organ or harmonium)

1936/38 *Suite concertante* op. 20 (cello, orchestra)

Adagio sostenuto, Introduction et vivace, Adagio (final Adagio from *Piece in Free Form*), Allegro appassionato

Symphonie concertante op. 21 (piano, orchestra; reworking of the cello part from *Suite concertante*) Carus

Adagio sostenuto, Introduction et vivace

Quatre mélodies op. 22 (voice, piano)

*1. "Epitaphe" (text by Gauthier-Ferrières)
*2. "L'arbre" (text by André Romane)
3. "Le rien de tout" (text by H. Pouplain)
*4. "La concièrge" (text by F. LeGuével)

Mouvement perpétuel op. 23 (piano) Combre

Nocturne-danse op. 24 (chorus)

1937 *Légende de Saint-Nicolas* op. 25 (organ) [III]

Ligne op. 26 (cello) Combre

Deux psaumes op. 27 (mixed chorus, soprano and tenor soloists, accompaniment, ad libitum)

1. Psalm 123
2. Psalm 58

Thème, variations et final op. 28 (brass, strings, organ)
Choral médiéval op. 29 (three trumpets, three trombones, organ)
Pièce symphonique op. 29 bis (brass, strings, organ)
1. "Pièce en forme libre"
2. "Toccata" (*Vingt-quatre pièces*; brass, organ; not written)
3. "Thème, variations et final" (brass, strings, organ; used in opus 122)

1938   *Prélude et fugue* op. 30 (piano)
Suite armoricaine op. 31 (piano) Clavier/Lissett
1. "Épitaphe pour les marins qui n'ont pas eu de tombe"
2. "Le vieux pêcheur au large"
3. "Danse bretonne"
4. "Coquillage solitaire"
5. "Conciliabule chez les mouettes"
"Parfums" op. 32 (voice, piano; text by Michel Poissenot)
Suite bretonne op. 33 (string orchestra; arrangement of opus 31, first movement)

1940   "Tantum ergo" op. 34 (eight mixed voices, organ) Schola Cantorum
Quatre mélodies op. 35 (soprano, piano; text by Clément Marot)
1. "Frère Lubin"
2. "À une damoyselle malade" (manuscript lost)
3. "Huitain" (manuscript lost)
4. "À une damoyselle" (manuscript lost)

1941/42   "O salutaris hostia" op. 36 (two voices, organ)
Première symphonie op. 37 (organ) [X] Hérelle/Combre/Masters Music
Allegro, Eglogue, Choral, Final

1942   *Deux pièces* (flute, piano) Combre
1. "Histoire vraie pour une Môn" op. 38
2. "Rondel dans le style médiéval" op. 39

1942/43   *Neuf pièces* op. 40 (organ) [I] Bornemann/Leduc
1. "Chant de peine"
2. "Chant de joie"
3. "Chant de paix"
4. "Chant héroïque"
5. "Dans une douce joie"
6. "De profundis"
7. "Mon âme cherche"
8. "Prélude sur une antienne"
9. "Rhapsodie grégorienne"

1943   *Mystère du Vendredi-Saint* op. 41 Costallat/Combre

1. "O crux ave" (mixed chorus, orchestra, organ)
2. "Miserere mei, Deus (Déploration)" (mixed chorus, organ)

Deux offertoires op. 42 (organ) [III] Durand

Suite concertante op. 43 (violin, cello) Combre

1. "Danse rustique"
2. "Cantilène"
3. "Chasse et danse"
4. Final

"Pie Jesu" op. 44 (voice, organ)

"Ave Maria" (voice, organ, violin, cello)

Trois motets op. 45 (voice, orchestra, bells; alternate version for voice, organ)

1. "O salutaris hostia"
2. "Salve regina"
3. "Oremus pro pontifice" (also arranged for two treble voices, piano, organ)

1944   *Trois danses* op. 46 (woodwinds, piano, percussion) Carus

Allegro, Andante, Allegro vivo

Suite pour claveçin op. 47

Allegro, Choral orné, Fuguette, Fantaisie

1946   *Paroles de rechange* op. 48 (voice, piano; text by Jacques Prévert with substitute text by Edmond Lequien)

1. "Déjeuner du matin" ("Inventaire")
2. "Chanson" ("Chanson")
3. "Pour toi, mon amour" ("Enfantillages")
4. "Le jardin" ("Une rose")
5. "Sables mouvants"
6. "Paris at Night" ("Emerveillement")
7. "Quartier libre" ("Poisson d'Avril")
8. "Conversation" ("Existentialism")
9. "Les belles familles" ("Emploi du temps")
10. "La batteuse"

Cantate à Saint-Vincent-de-Paul op. 49 (chorus, strings)

Le diable qui n'est à personne op. 50 (orchestra, ondes Martenot, baritone solo; incidental music for a radio play by Jean Cayrol)

*Fête op. 51 (organ) [VIII] H. W. Gray/Belwin Mills

"Pour Cécile" op. 52 (voice, piano; text and music by Jean Langlais)

1946/52   **Cantiques* op. 63 (one to three voices, organ) Ed. du Seuil in *Gloire au Seigneur*, vols. 1, 2

Volume 1

"Amis, nous partons" (text by Paul-Louis Bernard)

"Seigneur Jésus, ne sois pas rebute" (text by Paul-Louis
    Bernard)
Volume 2
"L'étable au bord du talus" (text by Jean-Claude Renard)
"Il y a eut des couronnes" (text by Jean Cayrol)
"Gloire à toi, Marie" (text by Louis Aragon and Bernard
    Geoffroy)
"Je suis pauvre, je suis nu" (text by Jean Cayrol)
"Comme cherche le soir" (text by Louis Aragon)
"Heureux celui" (text by Luc Estang)

1947   *Cantate en l'honneur de Saint-Louis-Marie-de-Montfort* op. 53
    (organ, three women's voices, three trumpets, ad
    libitum)
*Suite brève op. 54 (organ) [I] Bornemann/Leduc
1. "Grands jeux"
2. "Cantilène"
3. "Plainte"
4. "Dialogue sur les mixtures"
La ville d'Ys op. 55a (chorus) Combre
"La ville d'Ys" op. 55b (voice, piano)
*Suite médiévale op. 56 (organ) [II] Rouart,
    Lerolle/Salabert/Masters Music
Prélude, Tiento, Improvisation, Méditation, Acclamations
"Au pied du Calvaire" op. 57 (solo voice, piano or organ;
    text by Henri Lafragette)
Légende de Saint Julien l'hospitalier op. 58 (orchestra, two
    ondes Martenot; incidental music for a radio play by
    Gustave Flaubert)

1948   **Suite française* op. 59 (organ) [II]
    Bornemann/Leduc/Masters Music
1. "Prélude sur les grands jeux"
2. "Nasard"
3. "Contrepoint sur les jeux d'anches"
4. "Française"
5. "Choral sur la voix humaine"
6. "Arabesque sur les flûtes"
7. "Méditation sur les jeux de fonds"
8. "Trio"
9. "Voix céleste"
10. "Final rhapsodique"
*Passe-temps de l'homme et des oiseaux op. 60 (voice, piano;
    text by Jean Cayrol)
1. "J'ai chanté"
2. "À bas la feuille"

3. "Oiseaux fatigués de m'entendre"
4. "Il y a des hommes"
Premier concerto op. 61 (organ or harpsichord, strings)
    Universal
Allegro, Andante, Final
Libera me, Domine op. 62 (three voices, organ) Procure du
    Clergé

1949   *Incantation pour un jour saint* op. 64 (organ) [I] Schola
    Cantorum
Trois prières op. 65 (voice or unison chorus, organ)
    Bornemann/Leduc
1. "Ave verum corpus" (French text)
2. "Ave maris stella" (French text)
3. "Tantum ergo" (French and Latin texts)
Trois mélodies op. 66 (voice, piano; text by Alain Messiaen)
Messe solennelle op. 67 (mixed chorus, two organs) Schola
    Cantorum (versions with one organ and string
    orchestra, or brass)
Kyrie, Sanctus, Agnus Dei

1950   *Le soleil se lève sur Assise* op. 68 (large orchestra, small
    orchestra, three ondes Martenot, three women's voices,
    three men's voices; incidental music for a radio play by
    Albert Vidalie)
Four Postludes op. 69 (organ) [IX] McLaughlin &
    Reilly/Summy-Birchard

1951   *Hommage à Frescobaldi* op. 70 (organ) [VII]
    Bornemann/Leduc
Prélude au Kyrie, Offertoire, Élévation, Communion,
    Fantaisie, Antienne, Thème et variations, Épilogue
*"My Heart's in the Highlands" op. 71 (soprano, piano; text
    by Robert Burns)
Deux pièces op. 72 (violin, piano) Ed. Noël Ronde
Cantate de Noël op. 73 (oratorio for flute, oboe, two clarinets,
    bassoon, trumpet, two horns, percussion, piano, celesta,
    harp, choruses, soloists; text by Loys Masson)
1. "Prélude"
2. "Fuite en Egypte"
3. "Massacre des innocents"
Hommage à Louis Braille op. 74 (voice, piano; text by F.
    LeGuével)
1. "Coupvray 'Petit bourg calme'"
2. "Serve bone et fidelis 'C'est que, tandis que jeune'"

1952   *Mass in Ancient Style* op. 75 (mixed chorus, organ)
    McLaughlin & Reilly/Combre as *Messe en style ancient*

Missa in simplicitate op. 76 (voice, organ) Schola Cantorum
(version with strings and English version)
Folkloric Suite op. 77 (organ) [III] FitzSimons
1. "Fugue sur 'O filii'"
2. "Légende de Saint-Nicolas" (see opus 25)
3. "Cantique"
4. "Canzona"
5. "Rhapsodie sur deux noëls"
"Amor" op. 78 (voice, piano; text by Tristan Corbière, not
transcribed)
Advent the Promise op. 79 (mixed chorus) Augsburg

1953   *Caritas Christi* op. 80 (mixed chorus, organ or orchestra)
Schola Cantorum (published version of opus 49)
Chants pour la messe op. 81 (one voice and organ or
harmonium; French text) Ed. du Levain with Credo as
Messe "Joie sur terre"
Kyrie, Gloria, Sanctus, Agnus Dei

1954   "Saint-Clément" op. 82 (voice, piano or organ; text by Alain
Messiaen)
*"Dominica in palmis" ("In die Palmarium") op. 83 (organ)
[X] Schola Cantorum/*The American Organist*
Trois chansons populaires bretonnes op. 84 (women's voices)
Lemoine
1. "Dessus les sables"
2. "Lamentation"
3. "Le lin"
Missa "Salve regina" op. 85 (chorus of three equal voices,
unison chorus, congregation, two organs, five
trombones, three trumpets, ad libitum) Costallat, Jobert
Kyrie, Gloria, Sanctus, Agnus Dei
Cinq mélodies op. 86 (voice, piano; text by Pierre de Ronsard
and Jean-Antoine de Baillif) Combre as *Cinq chants
d'amour*
1. "À Françine"
2. "Je veux mourir"
3. "Marie qui voudrait"
4. "Demandes-tu, chère Marie"
5. "Marie, levez-vous"

1955   *"Lauda Jerusalem Dominum" op. 87 (mixed chorus,
congregation, organ, two trumpets, four trombones, ad
libitum) Combre
15 Antiphons op. 88 (mixed chorus, organ) Ed. du Cerf in *265
Antiphons*
1. Psalm 25 ("J'aime le Seigneur")

2. Psalm 26 ("Une chose")
3. Psalm 44 ("Salut, O sainte mère)
4. Psalm 68 ("J'attendais la pitié")
5. Psalm 79 ("Peuple de Sion")
6. Psalm 80 ("Criez de joie")
7. Psalm 85 ("Prends pitié")
8. Psalm 96 ("Dieu regne")
9. Psalm 97 ("Un enfant nous est né")
10. Psalm 102 ("Le Seigneur est tendress")
11. Psalm 109 ("Tu es prince")
12. Psalm 112 ("De la poussière")
13. Psalm 117 ("Voici le jour")
14. Psalm 131 ("Je mettrai sur le trône")
15. Psalm 137 ("Je chanterai le Seigneur")

1956   *Prélude, fugue et chaconne* op. 89 (mixed chorus; not
             transcribed)
        Huit pièces modales op. 90 (organ) [VII] Combre
        Organ Book op. 91 (organ) [III] Elkan-Vogel
        Prelude, Pastoral Song, Chorale in E minor, Flutes, Musette,
             Chorale in F major, Scherzando, Andantino,
             Epithalamium, Pasticcio
        "Accourez au passage du Seigneur" op. 92 (congregation,
             organ; text by Patrice de la Tour du Pin) Schola
             Cantorum as *Cantique eucharistique*
        *"Dieu, nous avons vu ta gloire" op. 93 (mixed chorus,
             congregation, organ; text by Didier Rimaud) Combre/in
             English as "God, Your Glory in Christ We Have Seen" in
             New Catholic Hymnal and *More Hymns and Spiritual Songs*
             (Episcopal)
        *Six Sonatas (by C. P. E. Bach, organ) FitzSimons (two
             volumes, edited by Langlais with added pedal parts,
             registration, and a foreword on their performance)
        Prélude au Kyrie ("Orbis factor") op. 94 (organ) [II] Die
             Praestant as *Prélude à la messe "Orbis factor"*
        Triptyque op. 95 (organ) [II] Novello
        Melody, Trio, Final

1957   *Three Characteristic Pieces* op. 96 (organ) [II] Novello as
             Hommage à John Stanley
        Pastoral-Prelude, Interlude, Bells
        Office pour la Sainte Famille op. 97 (organ) [XII]
             Christophorus Verlag/Pro Organo
        Prelude, Offertory, Communion, Postlude
        Office pour la fête de la Sainte-Trinité op. 98 (organ) [VI]
             Christophorus Verlag/Pro Organo

La Passion op. 99 (choruses, orchestra, eight soloists, narrator; text by Loys Masson) Costallat

Le mystère du Christ op. 100 (choruses, orchestra, soloists, narrator)

1958 "Regina coeli" op. 101 (two equal voices, organ) World Library of Sacred Music/Pro Organo

Cantate "En ovale, comme un jet d'eau" op. 102 (two mixed choruses, a cappella; text by Edmond Lequien) Presses d'Ille de France

Psaume 150 op. 103 (TTB, organ) McLaughlin & Reilly as "Praise the Lord in His Sanctuary")

Motet "Venite et audite" op. 104 (four mixed voices, a cappella) Schola Cantorum

Missa "Misericordias Domini" op. 105 (STB or SAB chorus, organ; Latin text) Gregorian Institute of America/Carus

1959 *Mass 16* op. 106 (organ) World Library of Sacred Music

Deo gratias op. 107 (organ; from *Organ Postludes Mass 16*) [XII]

Miniature op. 108 (organ) [XI] H. W. Gray/Belwin Mills

"Sacerdos et pontifex" op. 109 (congregation or unison chorus, two trumpets ad libitum, organ) World Library of Sacred Music/Pro Organo

Trois noëls op. 110 (mixed chorus, a cappella)

"Entre le boeuf"

"Guillaume, Antoine, Pierre" (Noël provençal)

"Michaud veillait"

American Suite op. 111 (organ) [X] H. W. Gray/Belwin Mills

1. "Big Texas"
2. "New York on a Sunday Morning"
3. "Californian Evocation"
4. "Confirmation in Chicago"
5. "Scherzo-Cats"
6. "At Buffalo Bill's Grave"
7. "Boys Town, Place of Peace"
8. "Storm in Florida"

"L'errante" op. 112 (voice, piano; text by Minou Drouet)

"Au paradis" (voice, organ) Ed. du Seuil in *Gloire au Seigneur*, vol. 3

1960 *Rhapsodie savoyarde* op. 113 (organ)

Deux petites pièces dans le style médiéval op. 114 (organ) [V] Schola Cantorum

Verset du 8ème mode op. 115 (organ) [XII]. See opus 130, nos. 11 and 12

Sept noëls populaires (*Noëls populaires anciens*) op. 116 (mixed chorus, organ or piano) Combre

1. "Nous étions trois bergerettes"
2. "À la venue de Noël"
3. "Entre le boeuf et l'âne gris"
4. "Allons bergers, allons tous"
5. "Joseph est bien marié"
6. "C'était à l'heure de minuit"
7. "Boutons nos habits les plus biaux"

Neuf chansons folkloriques françaises op. 117 (unison chorus, piano; recorded as *Neuf chansons populaires*) Combre

1. "Où allez-vous, la belle?"
2. "La nuit passée"
3. "Rossignol du bois sauvage"
4. "La-haut, dessus ces côtes"
5. "J'ai pris la clef de mon jardin"
6. "C'était P'tit Jean r'venant du bois"
7. "Si tu parles encore"
8. "Quand le marin revient de guerre"
9. "Tout près du Pont-Scorff"

Motet pour un temps de pénitence (*Propre pour le mercredi des cendres*) (Propers for Ash Wednesday) op. 118 (mixed chorus, a cappella)

Introit ("Misereris omnium, Domine"), Gradual ("Miserere mei, Deus"), Tract ("Domine, non secundum"), Communion ("Qui meditabitur in lege Domini")

1961   *Nouveaux chants pour la messe* op. 119 (voice, organ; French text by van Eyck) Ed. du Levain

Kyrie (Trisagion byzantin), Gloria (Doxologie byzantine), Sanctus, Agnus Dei (la fraction du Pain)

Sonnerie (Intrada) op. 120 (eight brass instruments, four trumpets, four trombones)

Europa op. 121 (three equal men's voices; text by Edmond Lequien)

Deuxième concerto op. 122 (organ, strings) Universal
Thème, Variations, Interlude, Final

"Ave maris stella" op. 123 (three equal voices)

"O God, Our Father" op. 124 (mixed chorus, organ)

*"Praise to the Lord" (Psalm 150) op. 125 (mixed chorus, three men's voices, brass, organ, or unison chorus, congregation, organ) McLaughlin & Reilly

Deux chansons populaires de Haute-Bretagne op. 126 (six mixed voices, SSATTB) Combre

1. "La fille entêtée"
2. "L'amoureux de Thomine"

À la claire fontaine op. 127 (SSATBB chorus) Combre
*Essai op. 128 (organ) [XI] Bornemann/Leduc

1962   **Trois méditations sur la Sainte-Trinité* op. 129 (organ) [III]
    Philippo/Combre
  1. "Première personne: le Père"
  2. "Deuxième personne: le Fils"
  3. "Troisième personne: le Saint Esprit"
Douze petite pièces op. 130 (organ or harmonium; includes
    opus 114) [V] Schola Cantorum/Masters Music
Offertoire pour l'office de Sainte-Claire op. 131 (three equal
    voices)
Douze cantiques bibliques op. 132 (mixed chorus or
    congregation, organ; French text paraphrased by Daniel
    Hameline) Fleurus
  1. David ("Nous acclamons Seigneur")
  2. Isaïe ("Chantez les hauts faits de Dieu")
  3. Tobie ("Béni soit Dieu")
  4. Ezechias ("Ni la mort, ni la vie")
  5. Judith ("Seigneur, Maître de la vie")
  6. Anne ("De riche qu'il était")
  7. Jérémie: "Tu nous as comblés"
  8. Isaïe ("Un jour viendra")
  9. Moïse ("C'est Toi, Seigneur")
  10. Moïse ("Dieu de bien veillance")
  11. Universalist ("À votre église sainte")
  12. Habacuc ("Qui sera contra nous")
Missa "Dona nobis pacem" op. 133 (unison voices, organ;
    English-Anglican text) H. W. Gray/Belwin Mills
Kyrie, Gloria, Sanctus, Agnus Dei
Homage to Rameau. See opus 134
Hommage à Rameau op. 134 (organ)
Ouverture, Chant pastoral, Invocation, Interlude, Fugue
*MacKenzie ("chanson de marin") op. 135 (voice, piano with
    SATB refrain; text by Daniel Hameline)
*Psaume solennel no. 1 (Psalm 150) op. 136 (mixed chorus,
    unison chorus or congregation, organ, two trumpets,
    two trombones, four timpanies, ad libitum; Latin text)
    Schola Cantorum

1963   *Prelude on "Coronation"* op. 137 (organ) [XII] Oxford
Propers of the Mass for Pentecost op. 138 (congregation, cantor,
    unison chorus, organ; text by J. Beaude) Schola
    Cantorum as *Chants pour la Pentecôte*
Entrance ("Ouvrons nos coeurs à l'Esprit"), Gradual
    ("Alleluia, source jaillisante"), Gospel acclamation

("Alleluia, qui m'aime garde"), Communion ("Esprit du
Christ"), Closing song ("Esprit le monde espèrt")

Deux mélodies sur des poèmes de M. J. Durry op. 139 (voice,
piano)

1. "Mon ombre"
2. "Soleils de sable 'Le géant'"

Homage to Rameau (revised version) [VII] Elkan-Vogel

1. "Remembrance"
2. "Allegretto"
3. "Meditation"
4. "Evocation"
5. "As a Fugue"
6. "United Themes"

Psaume solennel no. 2 (Psalm 50) op. 140 (mixed chorus,
unison chorus or congregation, organ, two trumpets,
two trombones, four timpanies, ad libitum; Latin text)
Schola Cantorum

Propers of the Mass in French op. 141 (cantor, unison chorus,
congregation, organ; text by J. Beaude) Schola
Cantorum as *Chants pour les 3 premiers dimanches de
l'Avent*

First Sunday in Advent

Entrance ("Le Seigneur est délivrance"), Gradual ("Arrache-
nous à notre nuit"), Gospel acclamation ("Alleluia,
malgré nos frayeurs"), Communion ("Viens Seigneur,
Tu es l'aurore"), Closing song ("Seigneur notre
lumière")

Second Sunday in Advent

Entrance ("Peuple de Dieu"), Gradual ("Dieu d'espérance,
comble nos coeurs"), Gospel acclamation ("Alleluia, les
morts ont reçu"), Communion ("Viens nourrir les
pauvres"), Closing song ("Nous te cherchons Seigneur
qui viens")

Third Sunday in Advent

Entrance ("Que la joie regne"), Gradual ("L'amour de
Dieu"), Gospel acclamation ("Alleluia, une voix crie"),
Communion ("Notre coeur garde courage"), Closing
song ("L'aurore est certaine")

1964   *Psaume solennel no. 3* (Psalm 148) op. 142 (mixed chorus,
unison chorus or congregation, organ, two trumpets,
two trombones, four timpanies, ad libitum; Latin text)
Schola Cantorum

Mass "God Have Mercy" op. 143 (unison voices, congregation,
organ; English text) McLaughlin & Reilly

Kyrie, Gloria, Credo, Sanctus, Agnus Dei

1965 *Messe "Dieu prends pitié"* op. 144 (mixed chorus, congregation, organ; French text) Schola Cantorum

Kyrie, Gloria, Credo, Sanctus, Agnus Dei

"Chant d'entrée pour la fête de Saint-Vincent" op. 145 (mixed chorus or unison congregation, organ)

Poem of Life op. 146 (organ) [V] Elkan-Vogel

Mass "On Earth Peace" op. 147 (unison chorus or congregation, organ; English text) Benzinger Bros.

Kyrie, Gloria, Credo, Sanctus, Agnus Dei

The Canticle of the Sun op. 148 (three equal voices, organ or piano, quintet or string orchestra; English text) Elkan-Vogel in version with piano or organ accompaniment

Elegie pour dixtuor op. 149 (flute, oboe, clarinet, horn, bassoon, quintet of strings; transcription of second section of *Poem of Life*)

Pater Noster op. 150 (voice; French text)

Gospel acclamation (mixed chorus, congregation, organ)

Messe "Joie sur terre" op. 151 (mixed chorus, congregation, organ) Ed. du Levain as *Messe brève*, a revision of *Chants pour la messe*

1966 *Poem of Peace* op. 152 (organ) [V] Elkan-Vogel

Poem of Happiness op. 153 (organ) [V] Elkan-Vogel

1967 *Carillons pour cloches* op. 154 (thirty-seven or fifty-three handbells) H. W. Gray/Belwin Mills

Sonate en trio op. 155 (organ) [XII] Bornemann/Leduc

Allegro, Andante, Final

Répons pour une messe de funérailles op. 156 (mixed chorus, congregation, organ; French text) Ed. du Levain

"Venez, saints du ciels" (three voices)

"Jusqu'en paradis" (three voices)

"Je crois que mon sauveur" (one voice)

"Toi qui as brisé" (three voices)

1968 *Livre oecuménique* op. 157 (organ) [VIII] Bornemann/Leduc

*1. "Sacris solemniis"

2. "Du fond de ma détresse, je crie vers Toi"

3. "Verbum supernum"

4. "Notre Dieu est une puissante forteresse"

*5. "Ave maris stella"

6. "Mon âme exalte le Seigneur"

7. Pater Noster

8. "Notre Père qui est aux cieux"

*9. Kyrie ("Orbis factor")

*10. Kyrie ("Dieu, Père Éternel")

*11. Gloria ("Orbis factor")
*12. "Gloire à Dieu, au plus haut des cieux"
*Deux pièces op. 158 (organ) [XII] Eulenburg/Pro Organo
1. "Prélude dans le style ancien"
*2. "Adoration"
Psaume 122 ("des montées") op. 159 (mixed chorus, organ; French text)

1969 Solemn Mass "Orbis factor" op. 160 (mixed chorus, congregation, organ, brass, ad libitum; English text) Elkan-Vogel/Anglo-American Music Publishers
Festival Alleluia op. 161 (mixed chorus, organ) Elkan-Vogel
Cortège op. 162 (two organs, eight brass, timpani)
Three Voluntaries op. 163 (organ) [V] FitzSimons
1. "Voluntary Saint-Jacques-le-majeur"
2. "Voluntary Sainte-Marie-Madeleine"
3. "Voluntary Sainte-Trinité"

1970 Le Prince de la Paix op. 164 (mixed chorus, organ)
"Le people qui marchait"
*Trois implorations op. 165 (organ) [XI] Bornemann/Leduc
1. "Pour la joie"
2. "Pour l'indulgence"
3. "Pour la croyance"

1971 Troisième concerto ("Réaction") op. 166 (organ, strings, timpani) Universal
Cinq chorals op. 167 (organ; commissioned for an anthology of German hymns) [XI] Barenreiter/Pro Organo
1. "Was uns die Erde Gutes spendet"
2. "Nun singt ein neues Lied dem Herren"
3. "Wie lieblich schön, Herr Zebaoth"
4. "Gesegnet uns, Herr, die Gaben dein"
5. "Wir wollen singn ein Lobgesang"
Pièce op. 168 (trumpet, oboe or flute, organ or piano) Combre
*Offrande à Marie op. 169 (organ) [V] Combre
1. "Mater admirabilis"
2. "Consolatrix afflictorum"
3. "Regina angelorum"
4. "Regina pacis"
5. "Mater Christi"
6. "Maria mater gratiae"

1972 *Supplication op. 170 (organ) [II] Stichting Int., Orgel Haarlem/Combre
Sept chorals op. 171 (trumpet, oboe, or flute with accompaniment of organ, piano, or harpsichord) Combre

1. "Aus tiefer Not"
2. "Ein feste Burg"
*3. "Vater unser"
4. "Christe, du Lamm Gottes"
5. "In dulci jubilo"
6. "Jesu, meine freude"
Petit prélude sur deux thèmes grégoriens op. 172 (organ) [XII]

1973   *Hymn of Praise "Te Deum"* op. 173 (mixed chorus,
      congregation, organ, trumpet, timpani, ad libitum;
      English text) Composers Forum/Pro Organo in Latin
Trois oraisons op. 174 (voice or unison chorus, organ, flute)
      U.C.P./Combre
1. "Salve regina"
2. "Iam sol recedit igneus"
3. "Jesu, dulcis memoria"
Cinq méditations sur l'apocalypse op. 175 (organ) [IX]
      Bornemann/Leduc
1. "Celui qui a des oreilles"
2. "Il était, il est, et il viendra"
3. "Visions prophétiques"
4. "Oh oui, viens, Seigneur Jésus"
5. "La cinquième trompette"
Suite baroque op. 176 (organ) [III] Combre
1. "Plein-jeu"
2. "Trémolo en taille"
3. "Dialogue"
4. "Flûtes"
5. "Dialogue entre le hautbois, le bourdon, et le nasard"
6. "Voix humaine"
7. "Grand jeu"

1974   *Répons liturgiques* op. 177 (congregation, organ; text by Henri
      Capieu)
Prelude (organ), Psalm 43, Introit ("Au nom de nos
      détresses"), Hymn of praise ("Que toute créature"),
      Gloria ("O Père, Père de Jésus Christ"), Communion ("Il
      est bon et joyeux"), Responses to the preface ("Accorde
      nous Seigneur"), Benediction ("Notre Père et notre
      Dieu")
Plein-jeu à la française op. 178 (organ) [IX] Musique
      Sacrée
Diptyque op. 179 (piano, organ) Combre
Allegro, Mouvement perpetuel (arrangement of opus 23)
Cinq pièces op. 180 (flute or violin, piano or harpsichord;
      arrangement of opus 86) Combre

Huit chants de Bretagne op. 181 (organ) [I] Bornemann/Leduc
*1. "Le paradis"
*2. "Disons le chapelet"
*3. "Angélus"
*4. "Noël Breton"
5. "Jésus, mon sauveur béni"
*6. "Jésus nous dit de prier"
*7. "Aux lys avec leurs feuilles argentées"
*8. "Pensez à l'Éternité"
*"Vocalise" op. 182 (voice, organ or piano) U.C.P.

1975   *Celebration* op. 183 (organ) [XII]
*"Hommage à Louis Braille" op. 184 (voice, piano; text by
     Jean Langlais)
"Ton nom sonne comme un carillon de France"
Quatre préludes op. 185 (organ) [XII] Klavarskribo, The
     Netherlands
Andante, Moderato, Allegro, Allegro
Trois esquisses romanes op. 186 (one or two organs) [VIII]
1. "Hac clara die," "Tu autem"
2. Kyrie "Rex splendens"
3. "Jerusalem mirabilis"
Trois esquisses gothiques op. 187 (one or two organs) [VIII]
     Bornemann/Leduc
1. "Veni, creator spiritus"
2. "Virgo Dei genitrix"
3. "Séquence pour la fête de la Dédicace 'Salve regina'"
Gloire à toi, Marie op. 188 (mixed chorus) Procure Romande
     de Musique Sacrée

1976   *Six petites pièces* op. 189 (organ) [XII] Lissett in *Allen Hobbs
     Organ Method*
Mosaïque, vol. 1 op. 190 (organ) Combre
1. "Stèle pour Gabriel Fauré" (from opus 8)
*2. "Sur la tombe de Buffalo Bill" (from opus 111)
*3. "Double fantaisie pour deux organistes"
*4. "Boys Town, lieu de paix" (from opus 111)
Mosaïque, vol. 2 op. 191 (organ) [IX] Combre
1. "Gable"
2. "Images"
3. "Trio"
*4. "Complainte de Pontkalleg"
*5. "Salve regina"
Sonatine pour trompette op. 192 (trumpet, piano, harpsichord,
     or organ) Combre
Allegro, Andantino, Mouvement perpetuel

"Cantique en l'honneur d'Anne de Bretagne" op. 193
    (voice, organ; text by Yves Cosson)
Psaume 117 ("Laudate Dominum omnes gentes") op. 194
    (mixed chorus, three trumpets, organ; Latin text)
    FitzSimons as *Psalm 117* ("Praise the Lord")
Deuxième symphonie ("alla Webern") op. 195 (organ) [X]
    Combre
    Prélude, Lude, Interlude, Postlude

1977 *Mosaïque, vol. 3* op. 196 (organ) [X] Combre
    1. "Lumière"
    2. "Parfum"
    3. "Printemps"
    *4. "Thèmes"
    *5. "Pax"
    *6. "Deuxième fantaisie pour deux organistes" op. 197
    "Ave maris stella" (organ)
Psaume 111 ("Beatus vir") op. 198 (mixed chorus, organ;
    Latin text)

1978 *Triptyque grégorien* op. 199 (organ) [II] Universal
    1. "Rosa mystica"
    *2. "In paradisum"
    3. "Alleluia"
Progression op. 200 (organ) [III] Bornemann/Leduc
    *1. "Monodie"
    2. "Duo"
    *3. "Trio" ("Larmes")
    4. "Offering"
    5. "Fugue et continuo"
Three Short Anthems op. 201 Hinshaw Music
    1. "Grace to You" (mixed chorus, a cappella)
    2. "Beloved, Let Us Love" (one voice, organ)
    3. "At the Name of Jesus" (mixed chorus, organ)
La prière pour les marins op. 202 (chorus)

1979 Mass *"Grant Us Thy Peace"* op. 203 (mixed chorus, organ;
    English text) Basil Ramsey, London
    Kyrie, Gloria, Sanctus, Agnus Dei
Noëls avec variations op. 204 (organ) [IV] Universal
    1. "Noël provençal"
    2. "Il est né le divin enfant"
    3. "Ihr Hirten, erwacht," "Pour l'amour de Marie"
Prélude grégorien op. 205 (organ) [XI] Universal
Offrande à une âme: diptyque op. 206 (organ) [II]
    Bornemann/Leduc
    1. "Vers la lumière"

2. "Dans la lumière"

Troisième symphonie op. 207 (organ; republished movements
from opus 111) [X] Universal
1. Introduction ("Big Texas")
2. Cantabile ("Californian Evocation")
3. Intermezzo ("Scherzo-Cats")
4. "Un dimanche matin à New York"
5. "Orage" ("Storm in Florida")

Corpus Christi op. 208 (SSAA chorus, organ, Latin text)
U.C.P./Combre
Introit ("Cibavit"), Gradual ("Oculi"), Alleluia ("Caro mea"),
Offertory ("Sacerdotes"), Communion
("Quotiescumque"), "Panis angelicus"

Four Chorale Preludes and Choral Harmonizations op. 209
(organ) [XI] Breitkopf & Härtel
1. "Lob preiset all zu dieser Zeit" (mixed chorus, organ
accompaniment for unison voice)
2. "Erfreue dich, Himmel" (mixed chorus, organ
accompaniment for unison voice)
3. "Freu dich, du Himmels Konigin" (harmonization)
4. "Pange lingua" (harmonizations 1 and 2)

1980   *Réminiscences* op. 210 (strings, two trumpets, two oboes, or
two flutes, timpani, harpsichord or organ)
Allegro, Adagio, Allegro, Adagio, Allegro, Allegro vivo

Rosace op. 211 (organ) [XII] Combre
1. "Pour une célébration"
2. "Introduction et marche"
3. "Croquis"
4. "Feux d'artifice"

1981   *Chant des bergers* op. 212 (organ) [II] Universal (reprint of
"Adoration des bergers" from opus 2)
Prière des mages (deleted section from *Troisième concerto*)
"À la Vierge Marie" op. 213 (voice, organ or piano; text and
music by Jean Langlais)

1982   *Pastorale et rondo* op. 214 (two trumpets, organ) Elkan-Vogel
Prélude et allegro op. 215 (organ) [XI] Universal
"Alleluia-Amen" op. 216 (voice or unison chorus, organ;
arrangement of opus 8)

1983   *Deux chants chorals* op. 217 (mixed chorus, organ) Europart
1. "Dans ma faiblesse"
2. "L'aube se lèvera"
Cinq soleils op. 218 (organ) [XII] Combre
1. "Soleil du matin"
2. "Soleil du midi"

3. "Soleil du soir"

*4. "Soleil des étoiles"

*5. "Soleil de France"

Sept études de concert pour pédale seule op. 219 [XI] Universal

1. "Chromatique"

2. "Contrepoint 1"

3. "Alternances"

4. "Contrepoint 2"

5. "Staccato"

6. "Trilles"

7. "Alleluia"

Deux pièces brèves op. 220 (organ) [V] Combre

Petite rhapsodie op. 221 (flute, piano) Gerard Billaudot

1984   *Huit préludes* op. 222 (organ) [VI] LeDuc

1. "Une voix"

2. "Duo"

3. "Trio"

4. "Quatre voix"

5. "Cinq voix"

6. "Six voix"

7. "Sept voix"

8. "Double fantaisie pour deux organistes"

Méthode d'orgue (pedal studies, with Marie-Louise Jaquet-
    Langlais; includes arrangement of opus 10, no. 7, for
    pedals) Combre

Miniature II op. 223 (organ) [XII] Combre

"Hymne du soir" op. 224 (mixed chorus)

1985   *Talitha koum* ("Résurrection") op. 225 (organ) [VI] Combre

1. "Salve regina"

2. "Regina coeli"

3. "Alme Pater"

4. "1, 7, 8"

Trois pièces faciles op. 226 (organ) [XII] Pro Organo

Libre, Récitatif, Allegro

"A Morning Hymn" op. 227 (mixed or unison chorus,
    organ)

"The Threefold Truth" op. 228 (mixed or unison chorus,
    organ)

B.A.C.H.: six pièces pour orgue op. 229 [XI] Bornemann/Leduc

American Folk-Hymn Settings op. 230 (organ) [VI] FitzSimons

1. "Amazing Grace"

2. "Battle Hymn of the Republic"

3. "How Firm a Foundation"

4. "On Jordan's Stormy Banks I Stand"

5. "There Is a Fountain Filled with Blood"
6. "When I Can Read My Title Clear"
In memoriam op. 231 (organ) [VIII] Combre
Petite suite op. 232 (piano) Combre
1. "Danse bretonne"
2. "Il est né, le divin enfant"
3. "Ah! vous dirai-je Maman"
4. "J'ai du bon tabac"

1986   *Ubi caritas* op. 233 (chorus, organ) FitzSimons
Neuf pièces pour trompette et orgue op. 234 Combre
Douze versets op. 235 (organ) [VI] LeDuc
Expressions op. 236 (organ) [VI] FitzSimons
Fantasy on Two Old Scottish Themes op. 237 [XI]
    (commissioned by the Edinburgh Festival) Novello
Three Pieces (organ) [VII] (from opus 134) LeDuc
1. "Ostinato" ("United Themes")
2. "Méditation"
3. "Evocation"

1987   *Trumpet Tune* op. 238 (organ, State Trumpet) [IX]
    FitzSimons
Mouvement pour flûte et orgue op. 239 Pro Organo
Noël breton op. 240 (piano)
Vitrail op. 241 (clarinet, piano) Combre
Trois antiennes à la Sainte-Vierge op. 242 (voice or unison
    chorus, organ) Pro Organo
1. "Regina coeli"
2. "Ave, regina coelorum"
3. "Salve regina"

1988   *Christmas Carol Hymn Settings* op. 243 (organ) [VI] FitzSimons
1. "O Come, All Ye Faithful"
2. "Angels We Have Heard on High"
3. "Silent Night, Holy Night"
4. "In dulci jubilo"
5. "Joy to the World"
6. "He Is Born"
Contrasts op. 244 (organ) [XII] Combre
1. "Glas"
2. "Allegretto" (*Hommage à Rameau*)
3. Kyrie
4. "Pièce de concert"
Deux cantiques bretons op. 245 (voice, piano or organ)
1. "Cantique de l'Ile de Sein, en l'honneur de Saint
    Gwenole, patron de l'ile"
2. "D'ar Vartoloded ar Guilvinec" ("Les marins du Guilvinec")

1989	"Noël: 'Chantez, les anges'" op. 246 (voice, piano or organ; text by Jean Rolland)
	Séquences (Pièce) op. 247 (flute) Combre
	Études op. 248 (one, two, or four unaccompanied cellos) J. M. Fuzeau
	Ceremony op. 249 (six trumpets, four trombones, two tubas)
1990	*Mort et résurrection* op. 250 (organ) [VIII] Leduc
	Virgo Maria (organ) [XII]
	Moonlight Scherzo op. 251 (organ) [XII] Combre
	Trois offertoires op. 252 (organ) [IX] Combre
	Three Fugue Subjects (in Allen Hobb's *The Fugue*) Lissett
	Suite "In simplicitate" op. 253 (organ) [IX] Europart
	1. "Plein-jeu à la française"
	2. "Virgo Maria"
	3. "Cum jubilo"
	"Trio" op. 254 (organ) [XII] Billaudot in *Collection panorama* (ed. Daniel-Lesur and Jean-Jacques Werner)

Notes

Chapter 1

1. *Bretagne* (Paris: Pneu Michelin, 1992), 28.
2. Christian Querré, *Mystères et légendes de Bretagne* (Rennes: Editions Ouest France, 1995), 39.
3. Marie-France Motrot, *Bretagne insolite au début du siècle* (Saint-Malo: Editions "L'Ancre de Marine," 1992), 7, 62.
4. Jack E. Reece, *The Bretons Against France: Ethnic Minority Nationalism in Twentieth-Century Brittany* (Chapel Hill: University of North Carolina Press, 1977), ix.
5. Querré, *Mystères et légendes de Bretagne*, 87.
6. Reece, *Bretons Against France*, ix.
7. Jean Langlais to the author, 31 December 1977. In these taped interviews, all conducted in Paris, Langlais normally spoke in French, although at times lapsed into English. Whatever the language, his speech often had a run-on, jerkily narrative quality, and always a sense of excitement, which flavor I have tried to retain.
8. A copy of the marriage certificate is filed in the town hall at La Fontenelle.
9. Kathleen Thomerson, *Jean Langlais: A Biobibliography* (New York: Greenwood Press, 1988), 20. The quarry is no longer in operation, nor do any Langlais relatives remain in La Fontenelle.
10. Langlais, 31 December 1977.
11. Flavie Langlais to the author, Rennes, 18 September 1997.
12. Ibid.
13. Ibid.
14. Langlais, 31 December 1977.
15. Interview in Denver, 1956, as reported by Allen Hobbs.
16. Langlais, 31 December 1977.
17. Flavie Langlais, 18 September 1997.
18. Ibid.
19. Langlais, 31 December 1977.
20. Ibid.
21. Jean Langlais, "Quelques souvenirs d'un organiste d'église," *L'Orgue* 137 (January–March 1971): 5.

22. Ibid.
23. Langlais, 31 December 1977. He always used the English word "complexes" for psychological problems.
24. Jean Langlais to the author, 13 February 1978.

Chapter 2

1. Edgard Guilbeau, *Histoire de l'Institution Nationale des Jeunes Aveugles* (Paris: Belin Frères, 1907), 18–19. Guilbeau (1850–1930) established the Valentin Haüy Museum, with books and artifacts of the braille system.
2. Ibid., 53.
3. Ibid.
4. M. Louis Ciccone, "L'Association Valentin Haüy: cent ans au service des aveugles," *Le Valentin Haüy* 3 (1989): 4–7.
5. The name was changed to Institut Nationale des Jeunes Aveugles after World War I to emphasize its educational orientation.
6. Jean Langlais to the author, 2 January 1977.
7. Antoine Reboulot (b. 1914), who attended the Institute seven years after Langlais entered, remembers how annoyed young Jean was by his tapping him on the wrist to tease him. Antoine Reboulot to the author, Pittsburgh, Pennsylvania, 15 February 1990.
8. Gaston Litaize to the author, Paris, 20 May 1984.
9. Langlais, Litaize, Reboulot, and Marchal all remembered this sensational event.
10. Langlais, 2 January 1977.
11. Ibid.
12. Émile Trépard, "À la mémoire d'Albert Mahaut," *Le Louis Braille* (June 1943).
13. Albert Mahaut, *Le Chrétien: l'homme d'action* (Paris: Perrin, 1915). The print edition is unavailable; Jacqueline Englert-Marchal graciously sent a copy of the four-volume braille version from the library of the Institute, which Antoine Reboulot read to me 12–16 February 1990.
14. Quoted in Marie-Louise Jaquet, "Jean Langlais, un indépendent: essai sur son oeuvre d'orgue," *L'Orgue* 144 bis (1972): 5.
15. The Institute was responsible for a long tradition of important French organists and composers, including Gabriel Gauthier (1809–1853), Louis Lebel (1831–1888), Adolphe Marty (1865–1942), Albert Mahaut (1867–1943), Joséphine Boulay (1869–1925), Louis Vierne (1870–1937), Maurice Blazy (1873–1933), Augustin Barié (1884–1915), André Marchal (1894–1980), and Gaston Litaize (1909–1992).
16. Jean Langlais to the author, 18 May 1979.
17. Jean Langlais, "Hommage à André Marchal," *L'Orgue* 1 (1981): 57.
18. Langlais, 2 January 1977.
19. Flavie Langlais, letter to the author, 26 March 1990, and interview with the author, Rennes, 19 September 1997. The sibling rivalry that Flavie felt, even after so many years, is amusing to note.
20. Langlais, "Quelques souvenirs," 4–6.
21. Built by Cavaillé-Coll in 1884, this chapel organ was restored with tubular action by Puget (1910); restored by Convers (1926); restored by Beuchet-Debierre (1949); and restored adding a new console and electric action and

sixteen divisional and general pistons by Danion-Gonzalez (1961). The last restoration, which increased the stops from thirty-four to sixty, was supervised by Marchal, much to Langlais's disapproval. See Pierre Denis, "Les aveugles et l'école d'orgue française," *L'Orgue* 83 (April–September 1957): 20; François Sabatier, "Les classes d'orgue en France," *L'Orgue* 39 (1988): 40.

1961 alterations are marked with asterisk

Grand-orgue (extended to 61 notes*)

Bourdon 16	Quinte 2-2/3
Principal 8	Dessus de cornet V*
Diapason 8	Plein-jeu VI*
Flûte harmonique 8	Cymbale IV*
Bourdon 8	Bombarde 16
Prestant 4	Trompette 8
Flûte douce 4	Clairon 4
Doublette 2	

Récit

Quintaton 16*	Sesquialtera II*
Principal 8*	Plein-jeu IV
Flûte 8	Cymbale IV*
Cor de nuit 8*	Bombarde 16*
Salicional 8	Trompette 8
Unda maris	Clairon 4
Voix céleste*	Basson-hautbois 8
Principal 4*	Clarinette 8*
Flûte 4	Voix humaine 8*
Flûte 2*	Tremblant*

Positif (enclosed: deleted*)

Montre 8* (Diapason 8)	Septième 1-1/7*
Bourdon 8*	Piccolo 1*
Prestant 4	Plein-jeu IV
Flûte 4	Cymbale III
Doublette 2	Ranquette 16*
Nasard 2-2/3	Cromorne 8*
Tierce 1-3/5	Chalumeau IV* (Voix humaine)
Larigot 1-1/3*	

Pédale (extended to 32 notes*)

Soubasse 32*	Tierce 1-3/5*
Flûte 16	Plein-jeu IV*
Soubasse 16*	Bombarde 16
Bourdon 16 (G.O.*)	Trompette 8
Principal 8*	Clairon 4
Flûte 8	Bombarde 16 (Récit Bombarde 16*)
Bourdon 8*	Trompette 8 (Récit Bombarde 16*)
Flûte 4*	Clairon 4 (Récit Bombarde 16*)
Flûte 2*	

In addition to that instrument there were two other smaller organs, with tracker action, for the boys and the girls. The organ in the boys' quarters was built by Cavaillé-Coll (c. 1860); completely restored by Beuchet (1932); and revoiced by Costa (1956).

Grand-orgue
  Principal 8
  Flûte harmonique 8
  Bourdon 8
  Prestant 4
  Flûte douce 4
Récit (enclosed)
  Flûte 8
  Gambe 8
  Voix céleste
  Flûte 4
Pédale (enclosed)
  Bourdon 16
  Flûte 8

  Nasard 2-2/3
  Doublette 2
  Tierce 1-3/5
  Plein-jeu IV

  Doublette 2
  Cymbale III
  Trompette 8
  Basson-hautbois 8

  Flûte 4
  Trompette 8

The organ in the girls' quarters was built by Cavaillé-Coll (c. 1885) and restored by Beuchet (1953).

Grand-orgue
  Bourdon 16
  Principal 8
  Flûte harmonique 8
  Prestant 4
Récit (enclosed)
  Cor de nuit 8
  Gambe 8
  Voix céleste
  Flûte 4
Pédale (enclosed with Grand-orgue)
  Soubasse 16
  Flûte 8
  Flûte 4

  Flûte douce 4
  Doublette 2
  Plein-jeu IV

  Nasard 2-2/3
  Quart de nasard 2
  Tierce 1-3/5
  Hautbois 8

  Basson 8
  Soprano 4

22. Jean Langlais to the author, 31 May 1984.
23. At the end of each trimester all the professors decided which students would receive this honor, basing their judgment on the students' grades and good conduct. Those with gold braids sat at a table of honor; the one with three, called the doyen, sat at the head of the table and acted as student representative to the administration. Antoine Reboulot to the author, Pittsburgh, Pennsylvania, 16 February 1990.

Chapter 3

1. Langlais, 13 February 1978.
2. Quoted in H. C. Robbins Landon, *Beethoven* (Macmillan: New York, 1970): 205.
3. Sabatier, "Les classes d'orgue en France," 3–4. Three professors have taught

organ since 1997: Michel Bouvard (interpretation), Olivier Latry (improvisation), and Loic Maillé (early music and figured bass).

4. Most themes from Dupré's treatise *Théme libre, exercices préparatoires à l'improvisation libre* (LeDuc: Paris, 1937) contain some chromaticism. This last free improvisation, the thème libre, had been taught at Conservatory since the time of Franck and was codified by Dupré. Based on a single theme, the thème libre includes elements of both a sonata-allegro and an andante, the exposition of which includes four phrases in the main key, two of which are slightly modified and heard in the relative and subdominant; a bridge based on a motif from the theme; a development; and a recapitulation.

5. Three blind organists entered the Conservatory from the Institute and received premier prix in organ and improvisation from the class of Eugène Gigout: Marchal (1913), Cécile Joseph (1915), and Gustave Noël (1917). Marie-Louise Jaquet, "L'école française des organistes aveugles: depuis la fin du 18ème siècle," *Jeunesse et Orgue* 27 (1976): 10.

6. Langlais, 13 February 1978. He then played it through for me in its entirety, with his harmonization on the piano.

7. Archives, Fondation Marcel Dupré–Rolande Falcinelli, 15 rue Georges Moreau, 7613 Froidment, Belgium.

8. Langlais, 13 February 1978.

9. René Ségalen, from *Jean Langlais et Gaston Litaize,* an unpublished, undated typescript in the collection of the author. René Ségalen often rode the bus from rue de Sèvres to near the Conservatory with Langlais and Litaize and became good friends with them. He often entertained them in his home, and Langlais taught piano to one of his sons. His memoire, which tells of their escapades at the Institute, is inscribed: "For my old friend, Jean Langlais . . . in remembrance of our youth and with all my brotherly affection. René Ségalen."

10. Litaize recalled no such prejudice, either from the director or from Dupré. He suggested any tension might have had as its root Dupré's jealousy of Marchal. Litaize, 20 May 1984.

11. Langlais, 13 February 1978.

12. Robert S. Lord, "The Sainte-Clotilde traditions—Franck, Tournemire, and Langlais: conversations and commentary with Jean Langlais," *The Diapason* 66 (March 1975): 3.

13. This and all subsequent recollections in this chapter, Langlais, 13 February 1978.

14. Several articles have stated incorrectly that Langlais received first prize in counterpoint and fugue.

15. J. C., "Deux concerts d'orgue," *Courrier artistique* [Toulouse, France] (August 1930); Norbert Dufourcq, "Chroniques et notes," *La Revue Musicale* 116 (June 1931): 58–59.

16. Tournemire addressed Langlais in the familiar form; he used the formal form of address with other students.

Chapter 4

1. In other words, a composer should vary his style. This quote from his composition teacher influenced Langlais profoundly.

2. This and all subsequent recollections in this chapter (unless otherwise noted), Langlais, 13 February 1978.

3. Raymond Barrillon, "La poétesse americaine Ellen Keller est à Paris," *Parisien Liberé*, 16 November 1946.

4. J. C., "Deux concerts d'orgue."

5. Jean Langlais to the author, 15 May 1979. In 1930–31 Tournemire had only three other pupils: Daniel-Lesur, Maurice Duruflé, and Henriette Roget. At other times his pupils included Noëlie Pierront, André Fleury, Gaston Litaize, Joseph Ermend-Bonnal, Joseph Bonnet, Pierre Moreau, and André Bourquin; see Allen Hobbs, "L'enseignement de la technique d'orgue de Charles Tournemire," *L'Orgue* 1 (1989): 54.

6. Pierre Denis, "Concours des Amis de l'Orgue," *L'Orgue* 201 (Soixante Années au Service de l'Orgue, 1927–1987): 58. The members of the jury included Bonnet, Bret, Gallon, Jacob, La Prèsle, Lecotart, Marchal, Sergent, Tournemire, and Vierne.

7. Langlais, 15 May 1979. (He repeated the story in Hobbs, "L'enseignement de la technique," 14.)

8. Ibid.

9. Pierre Denis, "Souvenirs," *L'Orgue* 201 (Soixante Années au Service de l'Orgue, 1927–1987): 44.

10. Gustave Bret, "Musique: le Concours des Amis de l'Orgue," *Intransigeant*, 25 July 1931.

11. Olivier Messiaen, undated letter to Jean Langlais. Messiaen's letters to Langlais were often undated.

12. Olivier Messiaen, undated letter to Jean Langlais.

13. Robert S. Lord, "The Suite Médiévale: Jean Langlais and the 'Tournemire' Tradition," in *Hommage à Langlais*, ed. Marilyn Mason (Ann Arbor: The University of Michigan School of Music, 1996), 34.

14. Marcel Dupré to Hérelle, 8 July 1932: "My excellent pupil, Mr. Jean Langlais, has asked me to write a letter of recommendation for his three [*Poèmes évangéliques*]. . . . These pieces are poetic and written in a new style which is charming, brilliant without being difficult, and I believe them destined for success."

15. Pierre Denis, letter to the author, 19 September 1990; Jo M. K. Sandwick, letter to Jean Langlais, 9 July 1939: "My father gave me another theme which was sung to children long ago: (Norwegian Theme in G minor)." Chronological listing of premiere performances of *Vingt-quatre pièces* prior to 1940: no. 9, 29 January 1935; no. 5, 21 May 1935; no. 6, 9 February 1936; no. 2, 26 May 1936; no. 7, 26 May 1936; no. 13, 23 June 1936; no. 12, 28 January 1937; no. 11, 11 March 1937.

16. The newspaper *Ouest-France*, "Au Conservatoire de Paris," 25 June 1934, states, "The jury of musical composition from the Paris Conservatory has just announced its prizes for 1934. The second has been attributed to M. Jean Langlais, who has obtained this recompense the first year with two pieces for organ and orchestra." Other sources offer conflicting information: first prize 1932 (Darasse in *The New Grove Dictionary of Music and Musicians*); second prize 1935, according to Thomerson's biobibliography.

17. A. M. Caylot, "Concerts du Conservatoire," *L'Art Musical* (Paris), 9 December

1938; H. P. "Concerts musique/deuxième concert du Conservatoire," *Nancy Spectacle*, 10 December 1938.
18. Jean Langlais, "Paul Dukas n'est plus," 1935.
19. Jean Langlais to the author, 8 May 1984.
20. Translations by Sandy Sterner.
21. Pierre Whalon, letter to the author, 11 May 1990.
22. Jean Langlais, "Charles Tournemire," *Bulletin de Sainte-Clotilde* (1949).

Chapter 5

1. Pierre Lataillade of the municipal archives in Bordeaux relayed the following information on 23 April 1987: "Charles Tournemire, coroner's report, Mayor's office, Arcachon no. 206: 4 November 1939, 5:00 p.m., we witness the death approximately twenty-four hours ago, of Charles Arnaud Tournemire, living in Paris (Seine) rue Milne Edwards, born in Bordeaux (Gironde) 22 January 1870, composer of music, Officer of the Legion of Honor, son of Dominique-François Tournemire and Marguerite Renard, parents deceased. Husband of Alice Espir. The body was found in the territory of our Commune." Mayor's office, Ville d'Arcachon: "The archives of the Ville d'Arcachon contain no documents relative to the death of Charles Tournemire." The local press is silent, and all correspondence between the county and municipal police seems to have disappeared. There is no trace in either the Gironde departmental archives nor in the Arcachon municipal archives.
2. Allen Hobbs, letter to the author, 28 January 1990. Hobbs interviewed both Madame Tournemire and Jean Langlais.
3. Langlais, "Charles Tournemire."
4. Hobbs, 28 January 1990.
5. Charles Tournemire, undated [c. 1935] letter to Jean Langlais.
6. Langlais, 15 May 1979.
7. André Marchal to the author, Paris, 23 May 1979.
8. Olivier Messiaen, letter to Jean Langlais, 3 April 1940.
9. Samuel Osgood, *The Fall of France, 1940: Causes and Responsibilities* (Boston: D. C. Heath & Company, 1965), vii.
10. This and all subsequent recollections in this chapter, Langlais, 13 February 1978.
11. Pierre Cressard, "L'artiste doit être un apôtre," *Ouest-Éclair*, 15 May 1941.
12. Norbert Dufourcq, *La musique d'orgue française*, 2d ed. (Paris: Librairie Floury, 1949), 231.
13. Robert Bernard, *Les Nouveaux Temps* (Paris), 25–26 June 1943.
14. Quoted in Marie-Louise Langlais, "La vie et l'oeuvre de Jean Langlais" (Ph.D. diss., University of Paris, 1992), 141.
15. Robert S. Lord, "The Sainte-Clotilde tradition: toward a definition," *The American Organist* (February 1982): 38.
16. Langlais, "Tournemire."

Chapter 6

1. Jean Langlais, conversations with the author, 1962–1964. Before his last American recital, he said, "Organ music is like ladies, each one is different." Don

Knorr, "Organist reunited with former pupil," *The Observer Dispatch*, Utica, New York, 1 October 1981.

2. Quoted in Charles Tournemire, *César Franck* (Paris: Delagrave, 1931), 74.

3. Ibid., 52. Upon his return to Paris in June 1915, Tournemire wrote thus to Alice Lesur, one of his composition students: "It was with a uniquely true joy that I have found again my faithful companion (I am speaking of my organ at Sainte-Clotilde) yesterday! How I love this mysterious friend, always mine . . . She takes me as I am and we love each other." Quoted in Daniel-Lesur, "Une tribune d'orgue franco-belge," *Bulletin de la Classe des Beaux-Arts* 65 (1984): 264.

4. Pierre Cogen (titular organist of Sainte-Clotilde, 1976–1994), letter to the author, 9 September 1990. For more history on the Sainte-Clotilde choir organ, see Rollin Smith, *Playing the Organ Works of César Franck* (Pendragon Press: New York, 1997), 43–46.

5. Fenner Douglas, *Cavaillé-Coll and the Musicians: A Documented Account of His First Thirty Years in Organ Building*, vol. 1 (Raleigh, N.C.: At the Sunbury, 1980), 113, 114.

Pédale (27 notes)

1. Soubasse 32	3. Basse 8
2. Contrebasse 16	4. Octave 4

Jeux de combinaison

5. Bombarde 16	7. Clairon 4
6. Basson 16	

Récit (54 notes)

1. Flûte harmonique 8	6. Voix humaine
2. Viole de gambe 8	7. Flûte octaviante 4
3. Bourdon 8	8. Octavin 2
4. Voix céleste 8	9. Trompette 8
5. Basson-hautbois 8	10. Clairon 4

Positif (54 notes)

1. Bourdon 16	8. Flûte octaviante
2. Montre 8	9. Quinte 2-2/3
3. Gambe 8	10. Doublette 2
4. Flûte harmonique	11. Plein-jeu
5. Bourdon 8	12. Trompette
6. Unda maris 8	13. Cromorne (Clarinette)
7. Prestant 4	14. Clairon 4

Pédales de combinaison

1. Tirasse I	7. Anches I
2. Tirasse II	8. Anches II
3. Tirasse III	9. Anches III
4. Octaves graves I	10. Accouplement II/I
5. Octaves graves II	11. Accouplement III/II
6. Octaves graves III/II	

Grand-orgue (54 notes)

1. Montre 16	5. Flûte harmonique 8
2. Bourdon 16	6. Bourdon 8
3. Montre 8	7. Prestant 4
4. Viole de gambe 8	

Jeux de combinaison

8. Octave 4	12. Bombarde 16
9. Quinte 2-2/3	13. Trompette 8
10. Doublette 2	14. Clairon 4
11. Fourniture VI	

In the original specification there was no separate Tirasse III. The Récit to Pédale coupler was available only through the Jeux de combinaison and by coupling through the Positif and Grand-orgue to the pedal.

6. Maurice Duruflé, "Mes souvenirs sur Tournemire et Vierne," *L'Orgue* 162 (April–June 1977): 4, 18.

7. Maurice Emmanuel, *César Franck* (Paris: Henri Laurens, 1930), 22–27.

8. Laurence Davies, *César Franck and His Circle* (London: Barrie & Jenkins, 1970), 82.

9. Dufourcq, *La musique d'orgue française*, 128.

10. Ibid., 145.

11. Quoted in Vincent d'Indy, *César Franck*, trans. Rosa Newmarch (New York: Dover, 1965), 21.

12. Quoted in Léon Vallas, *La véritable histoire de César Franck* (Paris: Flammarion, 1955), 158.

13. Quoted in d'Indy, *César Franck*, 21.

14. Ibid., 177–178. Tournemire also quotes this passage in his biography of Franck.

15. Examples of Franck's harmonizations of the Agnus Dei from Mass 4, "Victimae paschali laudes" and "Adoro te devote," show the very slow rhythm of the chant with a chord of each note of the chant in completely tonal rather than modal settings. Nothing suggests Franck used chant themes for his improvisations (Smith, *Playing the Works*, 18, 216). His registrations for improvisation are documented in Lawrence Archbold and William J. Peterson, *French Organ Music from the Revolution to Franck and Widor* (Rochester, New York: University of Rochester Press, 1995), 103–117.

16. Lord, "Suite Médiévale," 34. In an interview with the author, 19 June 1998, Lord clarified that the choir sang abbreviated versions of the propers and that the choir and congregation alternated in the Kyrie and Credo. Practices varied; occasionally the organ replaced the choir.

17. d'Indy, *César Franck*, 234–235.

18. Louis Vierne, "Mes souvenirs," in *Cahiers et mémoires de l'orgue*, vol. 3 (Paris: Les Amis de L'Orgue, 1970), 16.

19. Jean Langlais to the author, 21 May 1984.

20. Lord, "Sainte-Clotilde tradition," 39.

21. d'Indy, *César Franck*, 69.

22. Daniel-Lesur to the author, Puteaux, 11 June 1994. According to Daniel-Lesur, the parishioners at Sainte-Clotilde sang three masses: Mass 8 (Mass of the Angels), Mass 11 (Orbis factor), Mass 4 (Fons bonitatis) as well as some Marian hymns. Possibly Langlais also wished to instruct the faithful in the riches of the chant repertoire.

23. Tournemire, *César Franck*, 13, 63.

24. Joseph Bonnet, "Nécrologie," *L'Orgue* 43 (April–June 1947), 60.

25. Program, Inauguration du Grand Orgue de la Basilique Sainte-Clotilde de Paris,

30 June 1933. The ten additional stops were Récit: Quintaton 16, Nasard 2-2/3, Tierce 1-3/5, Plein-jeu IV; Positif: Tierce 1-3/5, Piccolo 1; Grand-orgue: Cornet; and Pédale: Bourdon 16, Flûte 4, Quinte 5-1/3. The new console was extended from fifty-four to sixty-one notes in the manuals and from twenty-seven to thirty-two notes in the pedal. Tournemire's changes were carried out under the direction of Beuchet-Debierre, director of the Cavaillé-Coll firm.

On 21 November 1933 Tournemire wrote to Daniel-Lesur specifying additional changes (Daniel-Lesur, "Une tribune d'orgue franco-belge," 269): "The Gambe of the Récit was incomplete: the bottom octave was borrowed from a foundation 8' stop: a fault; it should be known that the original organ, although splendid, was not perfect. . . . I had the Récit to Pédale coupler added . . . the soft Flûte 4 on the Grand-orgue replaces a 'terrible whistle,' and the 4' of the Positif, very much softened." Madame Tournemire gave the original console to Flor Peeters at the end of World War II. It was transported to Belgium by American troops stationed in Paris. Hugh Giles acquired the bench from Peeters, and it eventually made its way to New York City's Central Presbyterian Church. Its present location is unknown to me.

26. Charles Tournemire to Noëlie Pierront, 11 April 1934. Quoted in "Correspondance de Charles Tournemire à Noëlie Pierront," *L'Orgue* 43 (1989): 92.
27. Ruth Sisson, "The Symphonic Organ Works of Charles Arnould Tournemire" (Ph.D. diss., Florida State University, 1984), 142, 371.
28. Langlais, 21 May 1984.
29. Clarence H. Barber, "Jean Langlais and the Ste. Clotilde organ visited by American," *The Diapason* 37 (August 1946): 8. The fourth manual was not added during Langlais's tenure.
30. Joseph Kosma (1905–1969) was trained at the Budapest Academy of Music and studied privately with Hanns Eisler in Berlin. He composed many film scores and popular songs, the most famous of which is "Autumn Leaves."
31. Jean Langlais, telephone conversation with author, 3 June 1990.

Chapter 7

1. 1952 (11 April–18 May), 1954 (3 February–30 March), 1956 (29 December–8 March), 1959 (1 January–18 March), 1962 (26 January–2 April), 1964 (4 October–7 December), 1967 (15 January–12 March), and 1969 (5 October–25 November). He returned five more times, for less extended tours, in 1972 (19 August–10 September), 1975 (14–21 February), 1976 (14–27 October), 1978 (20 April–6 May), and 1981 (18 September–2 October). In his tour journals, Langlais also counted his trips to summer sessions at Boys Town, in 1959, 1961, 1963, 1965, and 1967, as Voyages Artistiques, which may account for his counting his trip in 1975 as his fifteenth. In total he played more than three hundred recitals in America.
2. Jean Langlais, "Mon voyage en Amérique," *Musique et Liturgie* 30 (November–December 1952): 10–11. Jeannette's account of their first trip, written in French on nineteen pages of graph paper in a 5 × 8" notebook, ends on Friday, 18 April 1952, the day after their arrival in New York City. Langlais's published account continues after hers finishes but does not list the cities. The guides for Langlais's tours were Jeannette Langlais (1952, 1954), Monique Legendre

Notes

(1956), Christianne Chivot (1959), Marie Villey (1962), Ann Labounsky (1964), Susan Ferré (1967), Colette Lequien and Marie-Louise Jaquet-Langlais (1969, 1972, 1975), David Lloyd (1976), Kristen Kolling (1978), and Marie-Louise Jaquet-Langlais (1981). Boys Town guides were Claude Langlais (1961, 1963), Ann Labounsky (1965), and Marvel Basile Jensen (1967).

3. "In paradisum" was the last piece in a three-volume collection, *Cantiques dans Gloire au Seigneur* on a text by Bernard Geoffroy published later that year. "The memory of those absent" is a reference to his drowned Breton cousin.

4. Langlais, "Mon voyage en Amérique," 10.

5. Ibid.

6. Paul Hume, *The Washington Post*, 29 May 1952, 35; Searle Wright, "Langlais makes American debut," *Choral and Organ Guide* 5 (June 1952): 20–21.

7. Langlais, "Mon voyage en Amérique," 10–11. Langlais believed that mechanical-action organs should be superseded by the modern direct electric action. On the other hand, organists who were more interested in the type of action than the music were an anathema to Langlais, and he used the following argument against their views: if organists and organ builders looked only backward at the time of Frescobaldi, the organ would never have evolved into a modern instrument but would have regressed to a hydraulis.

8. Jeannine Collard, telephone conversation with the author, 21 July 1990. She permitted me to describe their relationship as an *amour de coeur*, which phrase denotes a much deeper relationship than the term "mistress."

9. Claude Langlais to the author, Roumazières, July 1996. Confirmed by Susan Ferré to the author, Denver, Colorado, 8 July 1998.

10. The first movement is based on a melody from *Airs sur les hymnes sacrez, odes et noëls* (1623); the second on a French folk song from Lorraine describing Saint Nicholas's rescue of three poor boys from a malicious butcher; the third on an Angelus from Brittany; the fourth (dedicated to French student Jean-Marie Georgeot) on a theme from the Battle of Pavia, in Italy, where the Spanish wounded and captured Francis I in 1525 (it was incorporated into the chorale "Durch Adams Fall," which Langlais knew from Bach's *Orgelbüchlein*); and the fifth on two carols, "Joseph sommeillait encore," a somber Breton melody and French text found in *Nouveau recueil des plus beaux Noëls*, Poitiers (1824), and the joyous "Lève-toi vite, Barthélemy," from the south of France, *Anthologie des chansons occitaine*.

11. Jean Langlais's 1956 journal of his "tournée aux USA." His niece and guide Monique Legendre took down ninety-three handwritten pages of dictation in French in a 4×6" spiral notebook.

12. Langlais, 2 January 1977.

13. Most of the Langlaises' correspondence with Lilian Murtagh between 1951 and 1975 is housed in the Organ Library at Boston University's School of Theology.

14. This and all subsequent recollections in this chapter (unless otherwise noted), Jean Langlais's 1956 journal.

15. Jean Langlais, "Mon troisième voyage en Amérique," *Musique et Liturgie* 53 (September–October 1956).

16. Clarendon [pseud. Bernard Gavoty], "La Passion par Jean Langlais," *Le Figaro*, 29 March 1958; Eric Sarnette, "Premières auditions," *Le Figaro*, 29 March 1958, and *Musique et Radio* 570 (November 1958): 40.

17. The great expenditure of time and effort in copying parts discouraged Langlais from writing for large orchestral and choral forces. In her biography, Marie-Louise Langlais cites the number of pages written in various categories of music (organ, sacred vocal, orchestral, chamber music, and secular vocal music) over the course of his life, demonstratingly convincingly the decline in Langlais's orchestral writing after 1960; see Marie-Louise Langlais, "La vie et l'oeuvre de Jean Langlais," 338.

18. "Mon quatrième voyage artistique aux États-Unis," *Musique et Liturgie* 70, 71 (July–October 1959): 47. Langlais's journal of his 1959 tour, fifty-seven typed pages in $5 \times 8^{1}/_{2}''$

stapled notebook, was dictated in French to his guide, Christianne Chivot. Jeannette created the typescript, adding letters she had received from him.

19. Jean Langlais to the author, 9 May 1984.
20. Jean Langlais's 1959 journal.
21. Ibid.
22. Claude Langlais, July 1996.
23. Ferré, 8 July 1998.
24. Francis Schmitt to the author, Boys Town, Nebraska, 18 December 1988.
25. Jean Langlais's 1959 journal.

Chapter 8

1. Olivier Messiaen, letter to Jean Langlais, 30 September 1931.
2. Duruflé shared this teaching style. Donald Wilkins, a student of his at Fontainebleau just after World War II, once returned to class with the piece they had worked on at the previous lesson, in order to test his understanding of Duruflé's indications. Duruflé, visibly embarrassed, exclaimed, "But I told you all I knew about that piece last week!" Donald Wilkins, undated [1996] letter to the author.
3. Thomas Davis, letter to the author, 27 August 1990. Davis was a pupil of Forshaw, who died 19 August 1983.
4. Timothy Tikker, letter to the author, 12 June 1989.
5. Janice Beck, letter to the author, 5 July 1989.
6. Audrey Bartlett Jacobsen, letter to the author, 14 July 1998.
7. Beatrice Collins, letter to the author, 11 April 1997.
8. Marvel Basile Jensen, letter to the author, 17 July 1998.
9. John M. Palmer, undated [1989] letter to the author.
10. Karen Hastings, undated [1989] letter to the author.
11. Colin Walsh, undated [1997] letter to the author.
12. Linda Lyster Whalon, undated [1989] letter to the author.
13. Ferré, 8 July 1998. This story was also related to me by the student, who wished to remain nameless!
14. Allen Hobbs, letter to the author, 10 May 1989.
15. Marilou Kratzenstein, letter to the author, 18 June 1989.
16. Pierre Whalon, letter to the author, 31 August 1989.
17. Norberto Guinaldo, letter to the author, 25 July 1989.
18. Rollin Smith, undated [1996] letter to the author. Smith relayed another funny story that he received in a letter from Lew Williams on 22 July 1998. Although

the student in question is unknown, it fits well with Langlais's personality:

> I am reminded of a story recounted to me by a pupil of Jean Langlais back in the mid-70s. Seems that Langlais had a student at the time who came in for a lesson bearing one of the Bach Trio Sonatas. The student's performance was all tap-dance staccato. When Langlais inquired why the student was playing the piece in such a way, the withering reply came back that "Well, I don't want it to sound like Dupré." Langlais paused a moment and quietly replied, "When you play as well as Marcel Dupré did, then you may say that . . . and not before!"

19. Jean Langlais's additions to the Sainte-Clotilde organ: Récit: Italian Prestant 4, Clairon 2; Positif: Larigot 1-1/3; Pédale: Prestant 4, Doublette 2. His deletions: Récit: none; Positif: Gambe; Pédale: Quinte 5-1/3, suboctave couplers. New electro-pneumatic console with Récit pedal, Crescendo pedal, six general pistons, six manual pistons for each division, general tutti, and appel anches for each division. (He said that the organ at the Mormon Tabernacle in Salt Lake City influenced him to add the Clairon 2 on the Récit.)

20. The organ case and connected console include a Principal chorus on the Grand-orgue and mutations and a reed on the Récit. Normally Langlais practiced using only the Bourdon 8 on the Grand-orgue. Vaclav Vytvar filmed and recorded Langlais playing this organ for *The Singing Organ* (Canada: Cantus Productions Ltd., 1983).

21. Vincent d'Indy, *La Schola Cantorum: son histoire depuis sa fondation jus qu'en 1925* (Paris: Librarie Blond & Gay: 1927), 284. Cavaillé-Coll–Mutin organ, Schola Cantorum (1902), thirty stops, C-g.

Grand-orgue

Bourdon 16	Bourdon 8
Montre 8	Prestant 4
Flûte harmonique 8	Trompette 8
Salicional 8	

Positif

Cor de nuit 8	Nasard 2-2/3
Dulciana 8	Quart de nasard 2
Flûte creuse 8	Tierce 1-3/5
Flûte douce 4	Cromorne 8

Récit

Flûte traversière 8	Plein-jeu IV
Viole de gambe 8	Basson 16
Voix céleste 8	Basson-hautbois 8
Flûte octaviante 4	Clairon 4

Pédale

Contrebasse 16	Flûte 8
Soubasse 16	Violoncelle 8
Basse 8	Bombarde 16

Tirasse: Grand-orgue, Positif, Récit

22. For a detailed account of all these forms with slight variations, see Jan Overduin, "Jean Langlais As a Teacher," in *Hommage à Langlais*, 19–30.

23. Marcel Dupré, *Manuel d'accompagnement du plain-chant grégorien* (Paris: LeDuc, 1937).

24. Naji Hakim to the author, Pittsburgh, Pennsylvania, 24 October 1989.

Chapter 9

1. According to Francis P. Schmitt, "Boys Will Be Boys: A Memoir of Boys Town" (an unpublished typescript dated 4 January 1983), Boys Town was "Catholic in inspiration, foundation, development and atmosphere."

2. Fulton Oursler and Will Oursler, *Father Flanagan of Boys Town* (Garden City: Doubleday, 1959), 214.

3. Mildred Ann McDonald, "Music at Boys Town, 1917–1970" (Ph.D. diss., University of Colorado, 1972). *Boys Town*, with Spencer Tracy as Father Flanagan and Mickey Rooney as an orphan boy, popularized the history of Boys Town and included a segment on the choir. The second film continued the theme.

4. In 1989 Duquesne University acquired this collection, which contains much choral music of Langlais that is now out of print.

5. Schmitt, 18 December 1988.

6. Allen Hobbs, letter to the author, 13 June 1989. Langlais was opinionated and blunt about just about everything; a Des Moines newspaper, publicizing his first session in 1959, ran a piece on his views regarding electronic organs—which may be summed up as "no pipes, no organ."

7. Schmitt, 18 December 1988.

8. Hobbs, 10 May 1989.

9. Jean Langlais, letter to Lilian Murtagh, 26 March 1961.

10. Langlais, 21 May 1984.

11. Langlais included a brief description of the work in the program notes for his 1964 tour: "The first work of J. Langlais in an atonal style, which explains its title."

12. Jean Langlais, letters to Lilian Murtagh, 1 February 1969; 16 November 1969; 3 March 1966.

13. Jeannette did not keep a journal for the 1964 tour as she had previously done, since their children were grown. I served as his guide, however, and thus report as an eyewitness.

14. Jean Langlais, "Un organiste français aux États-Unis," *Musique et Liturgie* 103 (July–September 1965): 13. In correspondence to Jeannette, he mentioned when he changed to a first name basis with Lilian Murtagh and Catharine Crozier.

15. Ibid.

16. Ibid.

17. Marie van Patten, "French organist Langlais is outstanding in recital," *Evening Bulletin* (Philadelphia), 7 October 1964.

18. Henry S. Humphreys, "Fabulous improvisateur," *Cincinnati Enquirer*, 2 November 1964.

19. Paul St. George, "Music," *The Pilot* (Boston), 17 October 1964.

20. Langlais, "Mon voyage en Amérique," 13.

21. Billy Nalle, "Langlais in New York," *The American Organist* (November 1972), 18, 19, 43.

22. Langlais, "Un organiste français aux États-Unis," 14. He was frustrated in his attempt to control the four expression pedals until I located the control "All Swells to Swell."

Chapter 10

1. Carlo Falconi, *The Popes in the Twentieth Century* (Boston: Little, Brown, 1967), 60.
2. Joseph Gelineau, *Voices and Instruments in Christian Worship*, trans. Clifford Howell (Collegeville, Minn.: Liturgical Press, 1964), 59. See also Gelineau, "Les rôles dans l'assemblée qui chant," parts 1–6, *Église qui chant* (1958–1959).
3. Jean Langlais, letter to Maurice Helbert, pastor of the parish of Dinard, 14 November 1959.
4. Ibid. Pius X used the phrase "prayer surrounded by beauty" in an interview with a French journalist c. 1903. It was widely quoted throughout France thereafter, and Langlais used the phrase repeatedly in his correspondence with Joseph Gelineau and in his own writings.
5. Papal encyclical *Incunda sane*, 12 March 1904, the thirteenth centenary of Pope Saint Gregory the Great.
6. Papal encyclical *Ad diem illum*, 2 February 1904, the jubilee of the definition of the Immaculate Conception.
7. Papal encyclical *Inter plurimas pastoralis*, 22 November 1903, *Motu proprio* on the restoration of sacred music.
8. Johannes Overath, "Sancta, Sancte," in *Crux et cithera*, ed. Robert A. Skeris (Altolling: 1983), 270.
9. In the minutes to the 18 January 1964 meeting of the French Episcopal Commission on Sacred Music, Langlais charged, "The seminary in Rennes did something, but it has not been followed."
10. Jean Langlais, letter to Joseph Gelineau, 12 January 1963.
11. Monsignor Iginio Angles, letter to Monsignor Richard J. Schuler, 31 March 1967. Angles, president of the Pontifical Institute of Sacred Music in Rome, was present at the Vatican II Councils and active in formulating *Instruction on Music in the Liturgy* (1967).
12. Jean Langlais, "Qu'en pense notre organiste?" *Bulletin de Sainte-Clotilde* (February 1963).
13. Ibid.
14. Ibid. These paragraphs were not in Langlais's typescript for the article.
15. François Jillot et al., undated [1963] letter to Jean Langlais.
16. Jean Langlais et al., "Musique sacrée," *Semaine Religieuse de Paris*, 29 January 1966, 133–135.
17. Maurice Rigaud, *Semaine Religieuse de Paris*, 29 January 1966, 137.
18. Quoted in Edith Delamare, "Saint Ambroise contre Saint Grégoire," *Le Figaro*, 27 January 1966.
19. "Aspects de la France," *Le Figaro*, 18 August 1966.
20. Ibid.
21. Richard Schuler, letter to the author, 12 June 1987.
22. For a detailed explanation of this history, see "Church music since Vatican II," *Sacred Music* 103 (spring 1976).

23. Robert F. Hayburn, *Papal Legislation on Sacred Music* (Collegeville, Minn.: Liturgical Press, 1979), 407–408.

24. *Sacred Music* 106 (summer 1979), 25. Quoted from the French review *Una Voce* 83 (November–December 1978).

25. Jean Langlais's journal of his "14ème voyage aux USA," 1972.

Chapter 11

1. Langlais, 8 May 1984. He went on to discuss Franck's Choral no. 3: "Consider the choral portion itself. If I take only the melody, it is completely modal—E, A, G, E, A, D, C, B, A. Even when he transposes it, he keeps the same modality. Even at the end, with the full organ, the same principle applies."

2. Quoted in Robert Stephan Hines, ed., *The Composer's Point of View: Essays on Twentieth-Century Choral Music by Those Who Wrote It*, trans. Madeleine M. Smith (University of Oklahoma Press: 1963), 190–191.

3. Pierre Petit, "Les disques/Jean Langlais/Missa 'Salve regina,'" *Conservatoire* (May 1955).

4. *New Catholic Hymnal* (London: Faber Music Ltd., 1971); *More Hymns and Spiritual Songs* (New York: Walton Music, 1972); *The Australian Hymn Book* (Sydney: Wm. Collins, 1977); *Cantate Domino* (London: Oxford University Press, 1980); *The Church Hymnary* (London: Oxford University Press, 1973), and others.

5. Six of them ("À votre église sainte"; "Béni soit Dieu"; "Chantez les hauts faits de Dieu"; "Ni la mort, ni la vie"; "Nous acclamons, Seigneur"; "Un jour viendra") were recorded in 1963 by Les Petits Chanteurs de Saint-Laurent, Zurfluh, director: *Six cantiques bibliques à l'usage des paroisses*, Disques Pastorale et Musique, PM 17038 LD.

6. Jean Langlais, letter to Father Jacques Cellier, Centre National de Pastorale Liturgique, 9 April 1966.

7. Lawrence Sears, "New Langlais mass filled with grandeur," *The Evening Star* (Washington, D.C.), 11 November 1969.

8. Translation by Sandy Sterner.

Chapter 12

1. This poem, written in French, was the only verse I received from Langlais; I destroyed the many love letters he sent me prior to 31 March 1965.

2. Marie-Louise Langlais believed the ending of the work referred to Jehan Alain's death; see *Ombre et lumière* (Paris: Combre, 1995), 241–242.

3. In May 1977, as I prepared to perform this work in recital at Sainte-Clotilde, Langlais urged "même plus tragique" (with an even greater sense of tragedy) at the repeat of the Allegro (m. 28).

4. Quoted in Sue Regan, "Sacred music 'week' honors Jean Langlais," *The Duquesne Duke*, October 1976. The interview was conducted in English.

5. Ferré, 8 July 1998.

6. Robert Noehren, letter to the author, May 1990.

7. Jean Langlais, program notes for 1967 American recital tour.

8. Susan Ferré, letter to Lilian Murtagh, 23 January 1967. Jean Langlais–Lilian Murtagh Correspondence, Boston University.

9. Jean Langlais, "Mon septième voyage aux États-Unis," *Le Louis Braille* 119 (September–October 1967): 3.

10. Ferré, 8 July 1998.

11. Langlais, "Mon septième voyage aux États-Unis."

12. Ferré, 8 July 1998.

13. Jean Langlais, "Mon septième voyage aux États-Unis."

14. Ferré, 8 July 1998.

15. Langlais, "Mon septième voyage aux États-Unis."

16. For a full account, see Ann Labounsky, liner notes, *Jean Langlais: Complete Organ Works*, vol. 4 (January 1985), Musical Heritage Society, MHS 932018A.

17. Olivier Messiaen, letter to Jean Langlais, 20 February 1971.

18. Quoted in Almut Rössler, *Contributions to the Spiritual World of Olivier Messiaen* (Duisburg: Gilles & Francke, 1986), 52.

19. Ibid., 89. Said Messiaen to Rössler in 1979, "I deeply distrust this word."

20. Marguerite Thal Long, letter to the author, 15 June 1989.

21. Ferré, 8 July 1998.

22. Jean Langlais, letter to the author, 31 July 1968.

23. Thomas Daniel Schlee, ed., *Troisième concerto: Réaction*, miniature score, Philharmonia Partituren, no. 504 (Universal Edition, 1980).

24. Labounsky, liner notes, *Jean Langlais: Complete Organ Works*, vol. 4.

Chapter 13

1. Jeannette Langlais, letter to the author, 19 January 1973; Jean Langlais, letter to the author, 9 February 1973.

2. Marie Grandinetti, letter to the author, 31 May 1989.

3. Langlais, 13 February 1978.

4. Olivier Messiaen, letter to Jean Langlais, 7 April 1974. A proud Langlais insisted that this letter be reproduced in the recording's liner notes.

5. Joel-Marie Fauquet, liner notes, Jean Langlais, *Cinq méditations sur l'apocalypse* (1976), Marie-Louise Jaquet aux Grands Orgues Cavaillé-Coll de Sainte-Clotilde, recorded under the supervision of the composer, Arion, ARN 38312.

6. Jean Langlais, letter to the author, 5 May 1974.

7. Jean Langlais, liner notes, *Huit chants de Bretagne*, performed by the composer, Arion, ARN 3631. For an analysis of each piece, see Ann Labounsky, liner notes, *Jean Langlais: Complete Organ Works*, vol. 1 (1980), Musical Heritage Society, MHS 4129.

8. Jean Langlais, letter to the author, 21 June 1975. He added that often when he walked his dog there he would kneel and pray for me, remembering his happy times at Duquesne University, where he taught on several occasions.

9. Jean Langlais, letter to the author, 26 July 1975.

10. Douglas D. Himes, "A new wedding processional of Jean Langlais," *The Diapason* 69 (January 1978): 1, 16.

11. Kathleen Thomerson, "Jean Langlais: An eightieth birthday tribute," *The Diapason* 78 (February 1987): 8–9.

12. Langlais, 13 February 1978.

13. Marie-Louise Jaquet, "Les oeuvres récentes pour orgue de Jean Langlais (1973–1977)," *Jeunesse et Orgue* 35, 36 (1978): 8.

Chapter 15

14. Ibid.
15. Langlais, 13 February 1978.
16. Jaquet, "Les oeuvres récentes."
17. Marie-Louise Jaquet, "Hommage des États-Unis au compositeur Jean Langlais, 21 February 1975," *Le Louis Braille* 165 (May–June 1975): 1–2.
18. Ann Labounsky and Robert S. Lord, "Langlais Honored at Duquesne Convocation," *The American Organist* (March 1977): 35–36.
19. Michael Redmont, "Music in Jersey: Langlais plays up 'tradition,'" *The Star-Ledger* (Madison, New Jersey), 28 October 1976.
20. Jean Langlais to the author, 13 May 1979.

Chapter 14

1. Jean Langlais, letter to the author, 29 October 1978.
2. Jean Langlais to the author, 24 May 1979.
3. Jean Langlais, letter to the author, 12 June 1979.
4. Flavie Langlais, letter to the author, 26 March 1989.
5. Langlais, 24 May 1984.
6. Jean Langlais, letters to the author, 8 May 1980; 27 May 1980.
7. Langlais, "Hommage à André Marchal," 57.
8. Langlais, 24 May 1984.
9. Jean Langlais, letter to the author, 14 June 1983.
10. Sabatier, "Les classes d'orgue en France." Other important organ classes were those of Marie-Claire Alain at Rueil-Malmaison, Gaston Litaize at Saint-Maur, and Marie-Thérèse Jehan at Saint-Nazaire. Marie-Louise Langlais has made a number of recordings, including Langlais's *Cinq méditations sur l'apocalypse* at Sainte-Clotilde. Since 1985 she has been on the faculty of the Schola Cantorum, where she has organized a series of International Organ Academies. She has taught organ and improvisation at the Conservatoire National de Région in Paris since 1988.
11. Elna Johnson, letter to the author, 3 October 1979.
12. "Noël provençal" is based on the carol "Nous sommes en voie," text from a 1674 manuscript, melody, "Dureau la Durée." The second, "Il est né le divin enfant," is a nineteenth-century text with a melody from the time of Louis XV, "La tête bizarde." The text for the third, "Ihr Hirten, erwacht," is given with a different setting in *Deutsche Volkslieder mit ihren Original-Weisen* (Georg Olms Verlag, 1969); text for "Noël pour l'amour de Marie" is from Lyon 1506, and its melody is given in Marcel Rouher's *450 Noëls* (1910) as a twelfth-century tune.
13. Vaclav Vytvar, *The Singing Organ* (*Die singende orgel*; *L'orgue chantant*), 1983 documentary film. A 26-minute videocassette is available from Cantus Productions Ltd., 156 Woburn Ave., Toronto, Ontario, M5M 1K7, Canada.

Chapter 15

1. Jules Orrière, letter to the author, 23 May 1987.
2. Marie-Louise Jaquet-Langlais, letter to the author, 16 July 1984.
3. J.-L. Signoret et al., "Aphasie sans amusie chez un organiste aveugle," *Revue de Neurologie* (1987): 172–181.

Notes

4. Only one other example of this type of brain damage has been documented: that of Russian composer Shebalin, director of the Moscow Conservatory, who after a stroke in 1953 continued to compose until his death in 1959. Doctors have since suggested that words and music are formed in separate hemispheres of the brain.

5. Thomerson, "An eightieth birthday tribute," 9.

6. Jean Galard, "Disques," *L'Orgue* 200 (October–December 1987): 26–27.

7. Arthur Lawrence, review, *The American Organist* (May 1987): 39.

8. Marie-Louise Langlais, "La vie et l'oeuvre de Jean Langlais," 357.

9. Langlais knew three of the ten tunes Bock sent him: "How Firm a Foundation," "Battle Hymn of the Republic," and "Amazing Grace." Contrary to what Bock reports in the preface to the collection, Langlais vehemently denied ever hearing Joan Baez sing "Amazing Grace" at Notre-Dame.

10. Fred Bock, letter to the author, 24 March 1987.

11. Fred Bock, telephone conversation with the author, 2 August 1989. *Six American Folk-Hymn Settings* and *Expressions* sold over three thousand copies each in their first two years of sales—a marked success compared to *Three Voluntaries*, which had sold only several hundred copies since Bock acquired FitzSimons. Bock died in July 1998 at age fifty-nine.

12. Jean Langlais, letter to the author, 24 March 1987.

13. B. M. Guillemaud, "Le devoir de vacances de Jean Langlais sur les flots de la musique," *Ouest-France*, 19 August 1987.

14. Naji Hakim to the author, Pittsburgh, Pennsylvania, 23 October 1989.

15. Jean Langlais and Marie-Louise Langlais, *Lectures and Performances at the Schola Cantorum*, 1989 videotape. Available from Pender's Music Company, 314 S. Elm, Denton, Texas 76201. Includes footage of Langlais performing, in his own home, Franck's *Pièce héroïque* and demonstrating fingering and pedaling in Franck's *Final* and a typical improvisation lesson with Tournemire.

16. Marie-Louise Langlais, *Ombre et lumière*, 302.

17. Pierre Cogen to the author, Paris, 9 May 1996. Cogen was appointed co-titular organist with Langlais in 1976.

18. Marie-Louise Langlais, *Ombre et lumière*, 305.

19. "I am a Catholic musician from Brittany." Kathleen Thomerson, "*Messe solennelle* for Jean Langlais," *The American Organist* (September 1991): 33.

Selected Bibliography

Barber, Clarence H. 1946. "Jean Langlais and the Ste. Clotilde organ visited by American." *The Diapason* 37 (August).

Denis, Pierre. 1961. "L'oeuvre d'orgue de Jean Langlais." *L'Orgue* 100 (October–December).

Jaquet, Marie-Louise. 1972. "Jean Langlais, un indépendent: essai sur son oeuvre d'orgue." *L'Orgue* 144 bis.

———. 1975. "Hommage des États-Unis au compositeur Jean Langlais, 21 February 1975." *Le Louis Braille* 165 (May–June).

———. 1978. "Les oeuvres récentes pour orgue de Jean Langlais (1973–1977)." *Jeunesse et Orgue* 35, 36.

Langlais, Jean. 1952. "Mon voyage en Amérique." *Musique et Liturgie* 30 (November–December).

———. 1956. "Mon troisième voyage en Amérique." *Musique et Liturgie* 53 (September–October).

———. 1959. "Mon quatrième voyage artistique aux États-Unis." *Musique et Liturgie* 70, 71 (July–October).

———. 1963. "Mon septième [*sic*] voyage aux États-Unis." *Musique et Liturgie* 91 (January–February).

———. 1963. "Qu'en pense notre organiste?" *Bulletin de Sainte-Clotilde* (February).

———. 1965. "Un organiste français aux États-Unis." *Musique et Liturgie* 103 (July–September 1965).

———. 1967. "Mon septième voyage aux États-Unis." *Le Louis Braille* 119 (September–October).

———. 1971. "Quelques souvenirs d'un organiste d'église." *L'Orgue* 137 (January–March).

———. 1981. "Hommage à André Marchal." *L'Orgue* 1.

Langlais, Jean, and Marie-Louise Langlais. 1989. *Lectures and Performances at the Schola Cantorum*. Denton, Tex.: Pender's Music Company. Videotape.

Selected Bibliography

Langlais, Marie-Louise. 1992. "La vie et l'oeuvre de Jean Langlais." Ph.D. diss., University of Paris.

———. 1995. *Ombre et lumière*. Paris: Combre.

Labounsky, Ann. 1980–2000. Liner notes to *Jean Langlais: Complete Organ Works*. 12 vols. Musical Heritage Society.

Lord, Robert S. 1975. "The Sainte-Clotilde traditions—Franck, Tournemire and Langlais: conversations and commentary with Jean Langlais." *The Diapason* 66 (March).

———. 1982. "The Sainte-Clotilde tradition: toward a definition." *The American Organist* (February).

Mason, Marilyn, ed. 1996. *Hommage à Langlais*. Ann Arbor: The University of Michigan School of Music.

Monahan, Matthew. 1976. "Musician-composer gets honorary degree." *The Duquesne Duke*, 21 October.

Thomerson, Kathleen. 1987. "Jean Langlais: an eightieth birthday tribute." *The Diapason* 78 (February).

———. 1988. *Jean Langlais: A Biobibliography*. New York: Greenwood Press.

———. 1991. "*Messe solennelle* for Jean Langlais." *The American Organist* (September).

Vytvar, Vaclav. 1983. *The Singing Organ* (*Die singende orgel; L'orgue chantant*). Toronto: Cantus Productions Ltd. Documentary film.

Wright, Searle. 1952. "Langlais makes American debut." *Choral and Organ Guide* 5 (June).

Index

Index

Index

Index